# PRACTICAL ANALYSIS AND DESIGN FOR CLIENT/SERVER AND GUI SYSTEMS

Selected Titles from the
**YOURDON PRESS COMPUTING SERIES**
Ed Yourdon, *Advisor*

# PRACTICAL ANALYSIS AND DESIGN FOR CLIENT/SERVER AND GUI SYSTEMS

## DAVID A. RUBLE

To join a Prentice Hall PTR Internet
mailing list, point to:
http://www.prenhall.com/mail_lists

Yourdon Press
Prentice Hall Building
Upper Saddle River, NJ 07458

**Library of Congress Cataloging-in-Publication Data**
Ruble, David A.
     Practical analysis and design for client/server and GUI systems /
David A. Ruble.
        p.   cm. -- (Yourdon Press computing series)
     Includes bibliographical references and index.
     ISBN 0-13-521758-X (cloth : alk. paper)
     1. Client/Server computing.   2. Graphical user interfaces
(Computer systems)   I. Title.   II. Series.
QA76.9.C55R82   1997
004'.36--dc21                      97-9895
                                       CIP

Editorial/production supervision: *Patti Guerrieri*
Cover design director: *Jerry Votta*
Cover designer: *David A. Ruble*
Manufacturing manager: *Alexis R. Heydt*
Marketing manager: *Dan Rush*
Acquisitions editor: *Paul W. Becker*
Editorial assistant: *Maureen Diana*

©1997 by David A. Ruble

Published by Prentice Hall PTR
Prentice-Hall, Inc.
Upper Saddle River, NJ 07458

The publisher offers discounts on this book when ordered in bulk quantities.
For more information, contact: Corporate Sales Department, Phone: 800-382-3419;
Fax: 201-236-7141; E-mail: corpsales@prenhall.com; or write: Prentice Hall PTR,
Corp. Sales Dept., One Lake Street, Upper Saddle River, NJ 07458.

Printed in the United States of America
10 9 8 7 6 5

**ISBN 0-13-521758-X**

Prentice-Hall International (UK) Limited, *London*
Prentice-Hall of Australia Pty. Limited, *Sydney*
Prentice-Hall Canada Inc., *Toronto*
Prentice-Hall Hispanoamericana, S.A., *Mexico*
Prentice-Hall of India Private Limited, *New Delhi*
Prentice-Hall of Japan, Inc., *Tokyo*
Prentice-Hall Asia Pte. Ltd., *Singapore*
Editora Prentice-Hall do Brasil, Ltda., *Rio de Janeiro*

*To my wife, Mary*

# CONTENTS

## CHAPTER 9    RELATIONAL DATABASE DESIGN . . . . . . . .    241

## CHAPTER 12   INTERNAL COMPONENT DESIGN ........ 343

# FOREWORD

The computer industry is fond of organizing its history into various "epochs" or "generations." Everyone is familiar with the notion of generations of hardware, even if it consists only of "286," "386," "486," and "Pentium." Similarly, almost everyone in the software field has suffered through many sermons about the differences between first-generation, second-generation, third-generation, and fourth-generation programming languages.

When it comes to "architectures," the common tendency today is to divide the world into mainframe systems, client/server systems, and Internet/intranet systems. There is a generational aspect to this, also: mainframes are old-fashioned, client/server is "mainstream," or state-of-the-art; and anything associated with the Internet is new, exciting, risky, and potentially dangerous.

There are several other aspects of the computing field to which generational labels could be attached, and there's one that is particularly relevant for a good understanding of David Ruble's new book, *Practical Analysis and Design for Client/Server and GUI Systems*: the generations of METHODOLOGIES. In the "old days," when systems were developed in assembly language on primitive mainframes, the simplistic (though somewhat unrealistic) assumption was that developers had no methodology at all. Then, from the mid-1970s through the late 1980s, developers tended to focus on structured analysis/design (SA/SD) techniques, combined with a sequential "waterfall" lifecycle approach to development.

By the late 1980s and early 1990s, the transition from mainframes to client/server architectures coincided with a transition from waterfall lifecycle approaches to RAD/ prototyping/spiral lifecycle approaches. Along with that, the emphasis on graphical user interfaces (GUIs) initiated a transition from structured methods to object-oriented (OO) methods, though it's interesting to note that as this book is being published in mid-1997, OO is still used far less commonly than SA/SD. On the other hand, it's interesting to note that the new generation of software developers (those who are typically in their mid-20s today) often reject SA/SD for the same reason they reject mainframe computers and COBOL: as far as they're concerned, it's hopelessly obsolete. It's also interesting to note that in many cases the rationale for such a rejection is that SA/SD *requires* a waterfall approach; and since the waterfall approach is obsolete, they assume that SA/SD is, too.

David Ruble shows that this is not the case at all. Systems developed for the current "mainstream" form of architectures—the client/server and GUI combination—can indeed be developed with a robust structured analysis/design approach. And all of this can be done with an intelligent, common sense *iterative* approach to building the system. And while the newer generation of OO methodologies may believe that they are the ones who invented "events" (often referred to as "use cases"), Ruble shows us that an event-based model makes eminently good sense for client/server systems, and that it can be used quite nicely with a structured methods approach. This is not an entirely revolutionary concept. Steve McMenamin and John Palmer articulated the notion of an event-based approach to structured analysis in 1984 (*Essential Systems Analysis*, Prentice-Hall/Yourdon Press, 1984), but their discussion didn't have the opportunity to illustrate the ideas within the modern context of client/server and GUI-based systems.

In short, what you'll find in Dave Ruble's book is an excellent mixture of the "old" and the "new." There's a brief overview of object-oriented methods, but the primary emphasis is on using robust, mature structured analysis/design methods, with an intelligent spiral/iterative lifecycle, to build today's client/server, GUI-based systems. It may not be brimming with the latest buzzwords and references to Java that you'll find in the industry trade magazines, but this is exactly the kind of systems development approach that most of today's application developers need. Follow the guidelines, methods, and techniques described in Ruble's straightforward, easy-to-read style, and you're almost certain to succeed.


Ed Yourdon
New York City
March 1997

# PREFACE

Client/server technology has dramatically changed the way we design and build information systems. In most businesses, the glory days of the single mainframe processor are gone. The one big box has been replaced or augmented by an integrated network of personal computers, communication networks, file servers and database servers. The popularity of the graphical user interface (GUI) has placed ever-increasing demands on information technology professionals to create applications that are complex, yet intuitive and easy to use. Client/server systems knit together sectors of the business organization into a broad computing fabric that reaches far beyond the boundaries of traditional mainframe systems.

This book offers a practical guide to the core competencies required for analysis and design of today's client/server business information systems. In it, you will find analysis and design techniques which have been employed with success on many large-scale projects. Today's information environment is one of rapidly expanding complexity. Successful client/server project teams must master the design and creation of the graphical user interface, manage and maintain systems using object-oriented programming constructs, design databases capable of serving the needs of multiple business sites, and link geographically-distributed users together, both inside and outside of the enterprise. As if that isn't enough, the ever-expanding scope of today's information systems requires an even more savvy analytical understanding of the business and a well-coordinated partnership with the users and business management teams than in the past.

## WHAT IS *PRACTICAL* ANALYSIS AND DESIGN FOR CLIENT/SERVER AND GUI SYSTEMS?

The reason I call this "*Practical* Analysis and Design" is because I am an analyst and designer, myself. I don't want to wade through an academic dissertation offering mathematical proof for some hypothetical methodology, and I figure that you don't have the time either. We've got deadlines to meet. So I've included the key analytical techniques and design concepts that I have used to get client/server projects delivered in a timely and sensible manner.

These techniques can be employed using a variety of project-management philosophies, ranging from traditional waterfall to iterative spiral approaches. Some activities presented herein have definite predecessor–successor relationships while others can be conducted concurrently. This is simply the stuff that needs to be done to ensure adequate understanding of the business problem and provide reliable, traceable design specs to build and test a system.

As for the last part of the book's title, "for Client/Server and GUI Systems," this book assumes your new systems will include at least one, perhaps many computers fulfilling the role of "server," that your terminals or "clients" are likely to be personal computers with some type of graphical user interface, and that your database will probably be of the relational variety. The amount of object-orientation in your system will vary tremendously, depending on the capabilities of your target development languages. While the analysis and design techniques in this book are not limited to this environment, they are exceptionally well suited to this scenario.

## WHAT'S THIS BOOK ABOUT?

If this book weighed 100 pounds, about 60 pounds of it would be analysis and 40 pounds would be design. The analysis section starts with a chapter on project charters, which marks the beginning of the analytical process even though this activity is commonly referred to as the "planning" phase of a project. The activities of analyzing the business need are covered in the subsequent five chapters on context modeling, event modeling, information modeling, interface prototyping and resolving business issues. Then the book moves on to system design. The design chapters show how to consume the models created during the analysis phase for making architectural decisions, designing the database, and creating the interface and internal componentry.

## THAT'S A LOT OF STUFF! WHAT ISN'T IN THIS BOOK?

This book is about writing specifications for systems, *not* about writing code at the line level. There are plenty of programming and technical issues which are well beyond the scope of this work. Computer hardware is something that this book definitely *not* about. I won't be telling you how to wire up your network or which plug goes in which socket. I do not endeavor to endorse (or deride) any particular brand or type of hardware, language or development tool, and I can't possibly tell you whether to use version 1.342A versus version 2.417B. That kind of advice would be out of date before the ink was dry from the press.

## WHO NEEDS TO KNOW ALL OF THIS?

Developers, managers, business analysts, programmers . . . a lot of people need to know this stuff. Within these pages are the core competencies that form the foundation of successful software engineering. These techniques have evolved over the last three decades, along with the capabilities of the available technology and the maturity of our industry. Whether you are a traditional mainframe developer, an experienced client/server veteran with many projects under your belt, or a mouse-slinging "PC cowboy" riding the range of the GUI desktop frontier, you should be able to find something useful in this book.

Today's information technology professional is becoming more and more specialized. Like the medical field, there is simply too much to learn to know it all. You can carve out a specialized career niche by picking just one or two techniques from this book and getting really good at them. Other readers may opt for a more generalized approach by mastering many of the techniques along with a variety of programming languages and technical skills.

## HOW THIS BOOK IS ORGANIZED

The first chapter reveals the secret for a successful client/server project. It takes the right people, sensible management, and a sound methodology. (Having a big sack of money doesn't hurt, either.) I discuss the skills required of a good analyst and the skills to look for in a designer. I offer my thoughts on the waterfall versus spiral methodology debate, and then move on to describe the key characteristics to look for in a good methodology. The chapter closes with a brief overview of the techniques covered in the rest of the book.

Chapters 2 through 7 detail the deliverables of planning and analysis. In Chapter 2, *The Project Charter*, I initiate the analytical process with a technique called the project decision-making framework, which is used to help the business members determine the true objectives of their new system. Chapter 3 covers *The Context Model*, a venerable yet important technique for exploring and defining system scope and external interfaces. *The Event Model* is the subject of Chapter 4. The event model defines the system's observable behavior in business terms, and documents the business policy and rules which comprise the process requirements. It is a crucial model which guides the development of the event-driven graphical user interface. *The Information Model*, covered in Chapter 5, creates an organizational map of the data that the system is required to remember. This is a vital technique for sound relational database design and object modeling. Chapter 6 shifts from building models to consuming models. *The Interface Prototype* is our first foray into design. Prototyping can be used to validate models, design the interface, or even elicit requirements. Chapter 7 rounds out the analysis section with some suggestions on resolving business issues.

Chapters 8 through 12 address the design of a client/server system and graphical user interface. Chapter 8, on *The Architecture Model*, shows how to use the essential models from analysis to determine the most desirable (or least offensive), technical architecture for your system. Chapter 9 covers the basics of transforming an information model into a *Relational Database Design*. Chapter 10 introduces key *Graphical User Interface Concepts*. The written *External Interface Design* specification is the subject of Chapter 11. A written specification is a vital management tool for partitioning the development work among multiple programmers, and for devising adequate test plans. Chapter 12 is the final technical chapter, covering *Internal Component Design*, with an emphasis on object-oriented concepts.

In the final chapter, I present *Dave's Top Ten Myths of Client/Server Development*. This chapter is intended to help separate the fact from the fiction surrounding client/server development. Following the formal chapters, I have included a comprehensive case study which gives you an opportunity to exercise the techniques covered in this book for a fictitious business, rife with many of the same types of problems and issues that you find in real companies.

The philosophy of this book is simple. Building solid software applications requires rigor and discipline. No amount of arm-waving and fad-of-the-year hoopla can eradicate the need for getting into the gory details of the business problem. Techniques for analysis and design need to be sufficiently robust and expressive to articulate the business need and devise a solution, yet they must be practical enough to be practiced with everyday tools in a format that allows analysts and designers to work closely with their users.

By using the techniques in this book, you can build reliable systems which realize the goal of client/server, to exploit the power of micro, mini and mainframe computers by allocating them to their most propitious use. By doing this in an organized and rational manner, you will avoid the anarchy which is unleashed in less disciplined shops, and your efforts will yield information systems that are flexible enough to meet your business' needs while maintaining safe custody of the corporate data asset.

Questions or comments regarding this book can be addressed to the author at
**www.ocgworld.com**

## AUTHOR'S NOTE

Several conventions employed in this book are worthy of explanation.

The English language lacks a word to express "he or she" in the singular. "They" denotes plural, and "he/she" is awkward. In the interest of readability, I have used the words he and him instead of he/she and him/her. You may take any instance of the word he or him in this book to describe either a male or female person, with the notable exception of my reference to General Eisenhower in Chapter 3, and various methodologists named throughout.

In information modeling, the term *entity* is formally differentiated from the term entity type. The entity type is the classification of the person, place, thing or abstract idea, and the entity is a member or instance of the classification. *Customer* represents the entity type. *Bob's grocery store* represents an entity. This distinction is not always made in the vernacular of common speech among practitioners. In the interest of smooth sentence flow I will use the word entity at times in this book to mean either entity or entity type. The context of the sentence should make it clear what I mean. This disclaimer also applies to my use of the words *attribute* versus *attribute type*, and *relationship* versus *relationship type*.

The distinction is more clear in object-oriented design where we have entirely different words to distinguish between a *class* and an *object*. Objects are the instances that exist at runtime (e.g., *Bob*). Classes are the templates from which the objects are wrought (e.g., *Customer*). Since class can have different meanings in our language, I will sometimes use the term *object class* instead of simply class to make it clear that I am referring to an object-oriented construct.

# ACKNOWLEDGMENTS

Writing this book would not have possible had it not been for the ideas, concepts and ingenuity of several colleagues who have profoundly influenced my thinking through the years. Most notably, I extend my sincere thanks to Meilir Page-Jones, who has long been a voice of reason in this industry. I also owe a debt of gratitude to Gary Konkel, who first introduced me to the project decision-making framework and has taught me so much about the art and science of analysis.

I would next like to recognize those outstanding developers, managers, visionaries and project team members with whom I have had the distinct pleasure of working; Jeff Brock (who produced the GUI windows for the screen-shots in this book), Rick Story, Tom Mehrer, Chris Emerson, Bill Metro, Pennie Dembry, Tom Looy, Ray Craft, Howard Woodard, Steve Weiss and my coprincipals at *Olympic Consulting Group*, Bill McNaughton and Bob Burlingame. I would also be remiss if I didn't thank the many users of my systems, the good, the bad and the ugly (systems, not users), as well as my many seminar students who never fail to teach me something new.

To the fine people at Prentice Hall—Paul Becker, Patti Guerrieri, Dan Rush, Carolyn Gauntt, Ronnie Bucci, and the many others behind the scenes who reviewed, copy edited and assembled this work—thank you for your tremendous skill and patience. I also wish to thank Gerry Pasternack and Rex Hogan who reviewed my completed manuscript, Amjad Umar, Ed Yourdon, Meilir Page-Jones, Gary Konkel and Bill McNaughton who provided important feedback along the way, and many others who took the time to read various chapters as they developed; Bob Burlingame, Gary Schuldt, Rita Litchfield, Lan Ma, Allison Brazil, Skip Carter, Lori Pry, Scott Walker, Tom Mehrer, Jeff Brock and a special thanks to Dave Duranceau who miraculously recovered Chapter 5 from the evil clutches of a general protection fault.

Finally, a special thanks for the unwavering support of my wife Mary, who endured the trials of a stay-home husband while raising a toddler. And for Alix, Daddy will always treasure all of the little interruptions . . . really!

# CHAPTER
# 1

# WHAT IS ANALYSIS AND DESIGN?

## INTRODUCTION

Welcome to Chapter 1. In this introductory chapter, I take a look at the purpose of analysis and design as well as the characteristics of a good analyst and good designer. Laying the groundwork for the chapters which follow, I review the trend toward specialization in our industry, discuss the waterfall versus spiral methodology debate, and suggest some criteria for what makes a methodology a "good" one. Finally, I give an overview of the techniques which comprise the rest of this book, namely the activities and deliverables for the analysis and design of client/server systems with graphical user interfaces.

## THE PURPOSE OF ANALYSIS AND DESIGN

Analysis is the process of determining *what* needs to be done before deciding *how* it should be done. Design is the process of determining which of many possible solutions best accomplishes what needs to be done, while respecting the project's budgetary and technological constraints. Design chooses a specific *how* to apply to the *what*. Analysis is the act of discovery. Design is the art of compromise.

Traditionally, analysis efforts have a dubious track record in software development. Just about everyone knows of a project which spent untold months (or sometimes years) drawing acres of bubbles, arrows, boxes and lines, only to abandon them to a sorry bookshelf and start coding in a panic. You might even know of a project that skipped any pretense of analysis altogether and commenced coding on the first day.

Building software is analogous to building a house. Very few people in their right mind would purchase a plot of land, hire fifteen carpenters and turn them all loose in the field with a pile of lumber, a crate of nails, and say "build me a house." (The carpenters won't be too worried because they've all built houses before, so if issues over details such as the required number of rooms or floors crop up, they're sure to be able to resolve them among themselves.)

The cost of such a folly might range around one or two hundred thousand dollars and would yield a strange structure indeed. It's quite probable that the owner wouldn't be entirely pleased with the result, and possible that the home would be completely uninhabitable.

As silly as the story of our architecturally-challenged homeowner seems, it pales in comparison to the millions of dollars lost each year on software projects that fail to deliver what the users need, or collapse completely without delivering anything. Just as it would be foolish to blame the carpenters for failing to produce a decent house under these circumstances, it is rarely the case that a software development project fails due to lack of technical prowess on the part of the programming staff. Most projects that fail do so because of lack of sound project management and failure to analyze the business need and failure to design a solution prior to construction of the product.

One could say that the purpose of analysis and design is, at worst, to keep your project from going down in flames, or at best, to fully articulate the business need based on an understanding of its current problems, and to derive a solution which best meets the need and fits within the budgetary, resource and time constraints set by the business. A residential architect determines the homeowner's desires, tastes, particular problems, needs and budget then explores design solutions to verify and validate the requirements prior to building it. The software analyst defines the nature of the business problem and the software designer explores the various solutions, making informed decisions to arrive at a product that will satisfy the users.[1]

---

[1]   Analyst and Designer are roles. They can be the same person, separate persons, or entire teams of people, depending on the size of the project and skill set of the staff.

This boils down to a pretty simple concept: *"Find out what the business requires to be done before you start figuring out how to do it."*

The complicating factor is that businesses are not simple and their intrinsic problems are compounded by people with differing opinions of how to solve them (or whether to solve them at all), and the whole mess is topped off with an absolute labyrinth of pathological legacy systems.[2]

## THE SKILLS OF AN ANALYST

The role of the analyst is to go forth and find out what problems exist in the business and determine what those in charge of the business desire to have happen. This is a radically different role and set of responsibilities from, say, a programmer, whose job is to write reliable code. It stands to reason then, that the skills required of the analyst are different than those required of the programmer.

I am torn between the terms "business analyst" and "software analyst" because successful analysts are a mixture of both. As an analyst, you need to be acutely aware of how a business *makes money*. As we'll see in Chapter 2, business information systems exist to contribute to the bottom line. On the other hand, the object of the game is to build *software*. For this reason, the analyst cannot be completely oblivious to the basic principles of automation. The analyst needs to be profoundly aware of what is possible, feasible and practical when it comes to business computing.

Overall, the analyst is an *investigator*. Analysis is the process of discovery. The analyst must be comfortable in the role of archeologist, unearthing untold gems of data from the twisted wreckage of a legacy system's flat files or deciphering the hieroglyphics of a long-dead programmer's ancient algorithms. Many times, the analyst becomes a sociologist, forced to venture out and live among the tribe to learn their customs and dialect, and to separate their mythology from reality.

Superb communication skills are of the utmost importance. Analysis is not a "heads down" activity. In the analysis phase of a project, you will be spending a great deal of your time coaxing information out of potential users of the system, reorganizing what you learn and presenting it back to them for their validation. You may be called upon to play *diplomat*, resolving conflicts and brokering solutions between warring factions of the business, or to spend time in the role of *camp counselor*, assuaging users' fear of change.

Some information technology (IT) shops subscribe to the belief that if a person spends two years incarcerated in their cubicle maintaining COBOL code, they become magically endowed with the above-mentioned skill-set and ascend to a higher order of existence; "programmer-analyst." Sadly, this is not true. Like so many other skills in life, a good analyst is created through dedicated practice and an original aptitude for the job. Analysts need

---

[2] *Legacy systems* are those which already exist in the company, including the systems you may be replacing. They have usually been developed some time ago with older technology.

"Don't worry. They say this is a documented part of their ISO process."

the proper training and an environment where they can hone their talents through repetition of the analytical techniques.

Many talented programmers become excellent analysts; however, programming is not a prerequisite for the job of analyst. The skill sets and aptitude required to do either are widely disparate, and may not always arrive in the same person. In many IT shops, the promotion to "programmer/analyst" involves little or no change in the amount of programming required in the job, and very little time is spent actually conducting analysis. In these situations, "analyst" is a title that is indicative of salary level only.

The reality is that no software development effort of any appreciable size can get along without the skills of good managers, analysts, and technologists. A well staffed IT shop will endeavor to attract and to cultivate all three skills sets within the organization and reward each group according to their expertise.

Some shops have shown success turning system users into analysts, although this usually requires some degree of training in the details of automation. Many colleges and universities are now offering degrees in business with a concentration in information technology, or augmenting their computer science curriculum with courses in accounting, marketing, manufacturing and general business. This is precisely the type of educational foundation which forms a solid basis for a career as an analyst.

## THE SKILLS OF A DESIGNER

The designer is a slightly different animal than the analyst. While the focus of the analyst is mainly business-oriented, with a strong grounding in technology, the focus of the designer is mainly on technology, with a strong grounding in business.

Design is all about making trade-offs. The designer is faced with the daunting task of mapping the business requirements articulated in the analysis document to the available technology. The analyst enjoys the luxury of assuming perfect technology. They document the user's requirements as if all processors were infinitely fast and all data instantly available. The designer, however, must make the users' whimsy and fantasy run on the sorry collection of boxes made available by the IT department.

The designer drafts the blueprint from which the system will be constructed, making him part engineer, part craftsman. A good designer is creative, resourceful, and savvy at evaluating choices between less than perfect solutions. The skills of a designer are much closer to the skills of a programmer. In fact, most designers are culled from the ranks of the programming population. Although programming is not always a prerequisite to becoming a good designer, you must have a firm grasp of the capabilities of the target environment in order to craft systems which take advantage of its strong suits and avoid its more anomalous proclivities.

"Don't use the rotate function in version 12. It makes flames shoot out of the A: drive."

## WHAT IS NEEDED FOR A SUCCESSFUL CLIENT/SERVER PROJECT?

The secret to successful development in today's multi-platform client/server environment is really no secret at all. It takes the right *people*, sensible *management*, and a sound *methodology*. Of course, it doesn't hurt to have a big sack of money handy as well; but since this book is conveniently not about *funding* client/server projects, let's get back to the subject of "the right people."

## The Right People

### The Era of the Generalist

On occasion, when I find myself before an audience of programmers or project managers, I like to pose the question, "When was the last time in this industry that you felt that you *knew everything*?" The younger programmers look at me like I've gone mad, but some of the more seasoned participants have been known to lapse into a brief reverie after which I hear dates uttered wistfully and reverently; "1967," "1974," "June of 1979."

By the mid to late 1970s, the prototypical mainframe shop was pretty much under control from a technological standpoint.[3] The languages employed to move data in and out of files, put little green characters on terminal screens or process vast quantities of data were fairly well established. If a project needed more help, a manager could pick up the phone and have an additional platoon of qualified bit warriors sent over from the local stable of programmers. It was typical by the early 1980s to see a resume that boasted over twenty years of programming experience in a given language. If you had hardware problems, you could call your shop's designated vendor and they'd send a team of blue-suited technicians winging your way on the next flight.

The workings of the mainframe were well understood, and a superb generalist could mount tapes, lay out files, write program logic and manipulate screens. While there were some areas of specialty emerging in the industry, the vast majority of data processing workers did a little of everything. With a largely homogenous resource pool, a project manager could almost get away with throwing enough people at any given problem, secure in the belief that they'd figure it out and get it done.

Everyone could go home at night knowing that the corporate store of all knowledge was safe and secure in the mainframe. Especially comforting to data processing managers of the era was the knowledge that they were the only game in town. Their staffs were competent, highly interchangeable, and the users had nowhere else to go.

All sense of control ended with the advent of the personal computer (PC). The first personal computers started to appear in the back offices of many businesses in the early 1980s. Many mainframe shops failed to recognize the importance of these wimpy little machines and regarded them in the same genre as pocket calculators, typewriters and

---

[3]   Whether it was under control from a *methodological* standpoint is entirely another issue.

adding machines. The users saw the PC as their savior, freeing them from the evil clutches of the dreaded and inflexible mainframe and its white-coated attendants in the air-conditioned glass room.

Before long, any user with a respectable petty cash allowance could amble down to the corner store and purchase a PC and box of floppy disks. A new species of techies appeared on the planet who weren't entirely programmers in the traditional sense, yet they were being hired by users in droves to write spreadsheet macros, build little desktop databases, and hook up laser printers. The result in many shops was chaos and anarchy. The mainframe was no longer considered to be the vast ocean of information that it once was. Instead, the repository of corporate knowledge was scattered on the hard drives and floppy disks of the PCs throughout the enterprise like so many tidal pools.

The PC explosion forced the status quo to recognize the power of packaged software and end-user computing in the business community. By the mid-to-late 1980s, IT shops were scrambling to make sense of what hit them and construct a strategy to get the corporate information flow back under control. About the same time, reliable network technology began to emerge which enabled personal computers to be hooked together into work groups and to access the mainframe and shared file servers. Client/server technology had entered the mainstream of business computing.

## The Trend Toward Specialization

Those IT managers who were huddled in the bomb shelter during the technology boom of the 1980s emerged to a completely foreign landscape in the 1990s. A robust IT department is no longer composed of iterations of the same skill set. Much like the medical profession, the body of knowledge required to keep up with the technology explosion has become so large that *specialization* is becoming a must. A development team needs skills in business analysis, event modeling, information modeling, interface design, database design, user representation, business issue resolution, database administration, object class library management, network communications, host systems hardware and operations, personal computer hardware and operations, graphical user interface programming, object-oriented programming, SQL expertise, traditional programming, electronic data interchange, project management, test planning and execution, user training, help administration, software release management, version control and so on. (My apologies if I've left out your favorite skill.)

This is not to say that the generalist has gone the way of the iceman. A stellar development team is almost always held together by a few general practitioners who know enough about each specialty to help orchestrate the technical effort. I also don't wish to imply that you need to hire a different body for every skill. Most people come through the door with sufficient expertise in several areas; however, it is highly improbable to expect a person to achieve competency in all or even a majority of the skills listed. The complexity of today's development tools, coupled with the overwhelming reach of automation into every facet of the business enterprise demands a level of expertise in each area far beyond what is reasonable to expect from one individual.

The key to assembling a successful team isn't just to hire the requisite number of smart people and throw them at the problem. Rather, it is to build a matrix of skills needed throughout the duration of the project, and to determine which skills are needed at what time. Then the project manager can go shopping for a core team to provide project continuity, and augment the team with specialists who may serve an abbreviated tour of duty, providing critical skills only when needed (Figure 1–1).

| Skill level rating:<br>0 = no experience<br>1 = book or classroom trained<br>2 = practiced on one project<br>3 = proficient practitioner<br>4 = master, mentor | Bob | Cecile | Jeanne | Kathy | Michael | Yvonne | Brian | Mary | Annette | Elsie |
|---|---|---|---|---|---|---|---|---|---|---|
| Business analysis | 0 | 4 | 0 | 3 | 0 | 1 | 0 | 1 | 2 | 0 |
| Event modeling | 0 | 4 | 0 | 0 | 0 | 0 | 0 | 0 | 3 | 0 |
| Information modeling | 0 | 4 | 0 | 3 | 0 | 0 | 1 | 1 | 2 | 0 |
| External Interface design | 0 | 4 | 0 | 0 | 1 | 0 | 2 | 1 | 0 | 0 |
| Database design | 0 | 4 | 0 | 3 | 1 | 0 | 1 | 1 | 3 | 0 |
| **Internal or OO design** | 0 | 2 | 0 | 0 | 1 | 0 | 1 | 0 | 4 | 0 |
| Target GUI tool programming | 3 | 3 | 0 | 0 | 1 | 0 | 2 | 0 | 0 | 0 |
| SQL programming | 3 | 3 | 0 | 4 | 1 | 0 | 2 | 0 | 3 | 0 |
| Target language programming | 1 | 1 | 0 | 0 | 1 | 0 | 1 | 0 | 4 | 0 |
| Electronic data interchange | 0 | 0 | 0 | 0 | 1 | 0 | 0 | 4 | 0 | 0 |
| Database administration | 3 | 0 | 0 | 4 | 0 | 0 | 0 | 0 | 0 | 0 |
| Class library management | 0 | 0 | 0 | 0 | 0 | 0 | 0 | 0 | 2 | 0 |
| Network communications | 2 | 0 | 0 | 0 | 0 | 0 | 2 | 0 | 2 | 0 |
| Server operations | 2 | 0 | 0 | 0 | 0 | 4 | 0 | 4 | 0 | 0 |
| Client operations | 3 | 0 | 0 | 0 | 0 | 0 | 2 | 1 | 0 | 0 |
| Version control | 3 | 0 | 0 | 0 | 0 | 0 | 1 | 2 | 0 | 0 |
| Project management | 0 | 0 | 0 | 0 | 0 | 3 | 0 | 0 | 0 | 0 |
| User representation | 0 | 0 | 4 | 0 | 0 | 0 | 0 | 0 | 0 | 0 |
| Business issue resolution | 0 | 0 | 4 | 0 | 0 | 1 | 0 | 0 | 0 | 0 |
| Testing | 3 | 3 | 0 | 0 | 1 | 1 | 1 | 0 | 2 | 4 |
| User training | 0 | 4 | 0 | 0 | 0 | 0 | 0 | 0 | 0 | 4 |
| Help administration | 0 | 0 | 0 | 0 | 0 | 0 | 0 | 0 | 0 | 4 |

**Figure 1–1.** A sample skills matrix

The sheer complexity of today's client/server environment forces us to recognize that we can't rely entirely on generalists. We need people who are highly skilled in areas that have steep and long learning curves. Specialties are cultivated by repeated experience. Allowing an individual to engage in the same types of tasks over and over is the best way to build skills. This assertion challenges many traditional IT organizational structures where groups of programmers build a system for a particular part of the business, and then stay there and maintain it until either the system or the programmers retire or die of old age. Instead, IT shops need to concentrate on specific skill building by letting people move around from project to project so they can surpass mere competence and rise to the level of expertise that today's business systems demand.

## Sound Project Management

The project manager's job is to plan and assign the work, measure progress on a continuous basis, and adjust the plan based on his measurements. This is an impossible task unless you have some plan against which to gauge progress.

This book details a series of techniques for conducting analysis and design of client/server systems and graphical user interface applications. A **technique** is a repeatable, structured method for achieving a specific task. Examples of techniques in this book include event modeling, information modeling, and window navigation diagramming. A software engineering **methodology** is the orderly arrangement of techniques into a systematic approach to the construction or acquisition of information systems.

While the individual analysts, designers and developers are responsible for mastering and executing the techniques, the project manager serves as the guiding force for ordering tasks into a coherent methodology to meet the project's objectives. The manager of a software development project is very much like the general contractor of a construction project. The construction manager makes sure that concrete crews, framers, roofers, plumbers, electricians and wallboard crews arrive on the project on the appropriate date, and he coordinates their efforts with each other. In the same fashion, the software development manager has to juggle the agendas and timetables of the network and hardware crew, the business analysts, interface designers, communications specialists, programmers, testers and trainers. The bigger the project, the more likely these will be individual teams of people, not just different roles played by the same people.

## Sound Methodology

### Of Spirals and Waterfalls

Methodologies come in many shapes and sizes. Much ado has been made about the advantages of a "spiral methodology" versus the "waterfall methodology." Other entries in the field of methodological metaphors include pyramids, whirlpools, vortices and something that resembles overlapping camel humps. Their philosophies range anywhere from a Draconian cookbook approach to "evolutionary programming," which is the latest fancy euphemism for hacking.

### The Waterfall Approach

The traditional waterfall has a certain logic to it. You do a plan for your project, then you conduct your analysis of the problem domain. When victory is declared on analysis, the design commences, and once the design is completed, construction begins. The outputs from one stage are the inputs to the next, hence the metaphor of the "waterfall" (Figure 1–2).

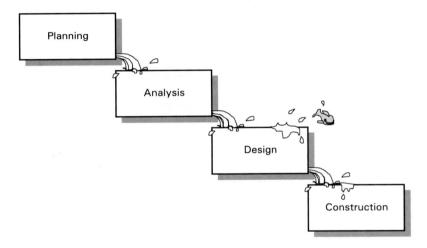

**Figure 1–2.** A waterfall methodology

The waterfall has an orderly appeal that makes it an especially convenient model for *teaching* software engineering techniques. In fact, you will note that this very book is laid out in a similar manner, with the charter chapter preceding the analysis chapters, and the design chapters following thereafter. However, the organization for *learning* a series of techniques does not always equate to the organization for *employing* a series of techniques in our rather chaotic and ambiguous real world. While few would argue that planning should occur before detailed analysis, and that analysis is a logical precursor to design and construction, it would be foolish to insist that a large-scale development project complete *all* of its analysis before conducting an iota of design, or that it should design *all* of the system before constructing of any part of it.

Software engineering instructors have long cautioned that while their courses were presented in a waterfall approach, real projects were executed in phases, with many tasks occurring concurrently and with a moderate degree of iteration as you learn things downstream that cause you to revisit upstream tasks. My theory is that many project managers were out of the room, on the phone during this particular speech. Thus, the history of software engineering is dotted with monumental failures that were more the result of poor management of the techniques rather than due to inadequacies of the techniques themselves.

Incremental phased development and some degree of iteration has always been a key practice in the successful implementation of any of the so-called waterfall methodologies (Figure 1–3). Good project managers have been doing this for years. The waterfall methodologies really suffer from an unfortunate metaphor. Water, being a victim of gravity, tends not to gallop back up hill for another ride over the falls. Likewise, people tend to treat forays back into analysis or design as a retreat rather than a step forward.

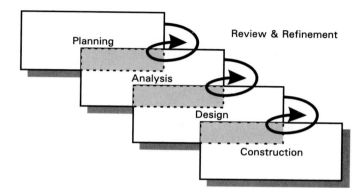

**Figure 1–3.** A waterfall with iteration built in

### Phased Implementation

It is a sensible practice to phase large projects (Figure 1–4). One of the primary reasons is that the learning that accrues while taking a piece of the project through the whole life cycle provides valuable expertise that speeds the development of the subsequent phases. Another benefit is the early delivery of some portion of the system that can be used by the business.[4]

Many project failures which have been chalked up to the waterfall really were the result of failure to employ sound modeling techniques in a sensibly phased implementation plan. The term "analysis paralysis" was coined to describe projects which found themselves entangled in a hopelessly large problem domain with no foreseeable conclusion to the mammoth modeling effort. Such projects were usually terminated by frustrated sponsors, convinced that the IT department had become professional students, studying the problem rather than doing something about it; or worse, the business needs had changed so drastically in the ensuing eons since the project started that the resulting system would be obsolete before it was installed.

---

[4]  This is traditionally known as the "18 month rule." Any project failing to deliver *something* within 18 months is likely to be canceled. Unfortunately, the 18 month window of expectation is shrinking in today's fast-paced business environment.

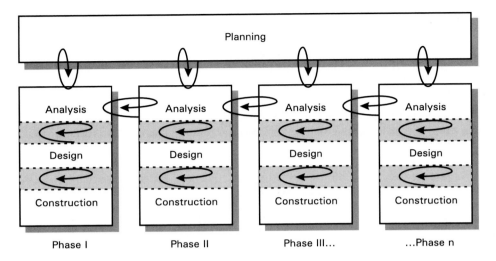

**Figure 1–4.** A phased waterfall approach

### *The Spiral Approach*

In contrast, the spiral development model (Figure 1–5) has phasing and iteration built right into the metaphor. The spiral model originally was developed at the Pentagon as a method to control runaway costs on massive weapons and defense system development projects. The idea was to break the projects into shorter phases of analysis, design, development and evaluation. After each phase, the viability of the work completed would be evaluated, along with a refined estimate for the next phases. This budgeting technique provided crucial feasibility checks for projects which were often researching entirely new technology. A decision would be made at the evaluation phase whether to continue with another iteration.

The idea of the spiral has mutated slightly to adapt to the peculiar sensibilities of the software industry. Instead of focusing on controlling the budget, the spiral has been employed as a method for early delivery of code in a methodology which has become popular under the term RAD, which stands for "Rapid Application Development."

RAD couples the spiral approach with a strategy of dividing a large project into "time boxes" (Figure 1–6). A time box is a defined set of functionality that is promised to be delivered to the users within a fixed time frame, say, 90 days. Within the time box, a modicum of analysis is done, a brief design, and then, using high-powered development tools, a working prototype is constructed. The prototype is reviewed by the users and modifications are requested. The cycle of coding and refining the prototype is repeated three times, spiraling through re-analysis, re-design, coding and evaluation. At the end of the time box, the resulting application is installed.

In practice, RAD suffers no less spectacular misapplication than the waterfall. Many managers and programmers see the spiral model as three iterations of "coding stuff." RAD's primary lure is early code, and in many shops, the production of code is viewed as the only tangible measure that meaningful activity has occurred. This leads to a "three strikes and it's out" mentality where any semblance of analysis and design is quickly abandoned, resulting in rickety systems which perform dubiously in the maintenance phase of their lives.

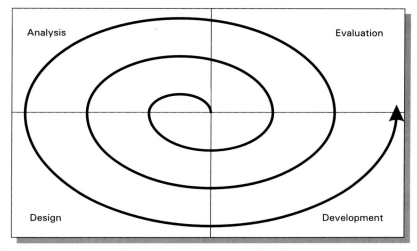

**Figure 1–5.** A spiral methodology

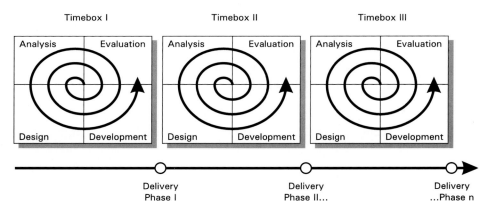

**Figure 1–6.** Three spiral iterations within time boxes

RAD's strong points are intensive user involvement, early prototyping, and phased implementation. Its weak points include a bias toward early coding which shifts many analysis and design tasks into the hands of the programmer, hence a dependency on superb generalists. It relies on programmers who are masters of their respective development tools and programming environments and at the same time are adept at interface design and business analysis and are skillful communicators. The overwhelming focus on the time box makes it difficult to engineer reusable components for the long term, and when the due date approaches, the first thing to go is the documentation. Instead of managing against a tangible specification, the manager finds himself armed with nothing but a bullwhip and a stop watch. The primary measure of progress becomes the number of revisions made to the code.

I recently encountered a client who had been sent to a seminar to investigate spiral development. While there, he learned about RAD techniques and how software is incrementally improved with each iteration through the spiral. He returned to work on Monday, beaming with enlightenment and announced to the project team, "The quality of a software system is proportional to the number of versions you throw away." To me, this sounded vaguely like the chorus from an industry that has all but given up trying to build it right the first time. His budget-rattling conclusion reminded me of the story of Odius and Tedius, two temple builders in ancient Rome.

> Odius was a Roman project manager stationed near Salisbury, England in the 3rd century AD, who is credited with declaring, "The quality of a temple is proportional to the number of temples you throw away." After ordering the construction and subsequent demolition of at least three versions of the town's temple, he was brutally murdered in an uprising by his Briton conscripts. As it turned out, the locals had saved the Emperor the cost of a public execution, since Odius had woefully overspent his capital budget and had nothing to show for it except three piles of rubble.
>
> Odius was succeeded by his cousin, Tedius, who employed a strict waterfall approach to temple building. After three years of analyzing and balancing the needs of the priests, gods and worshipers, Tedius had produced rolls and rolls of models and diagrams but a temple had still failed to materialize on the Salisbury plain. Tedius was simultaneously dispatched from the project and the planet for failure to deliver.

The waterfall and the spiral approaches both have good points. Unfortunately, they both suffer from shocking abuses in the real world. I believe that the key to project success lies somewhere between these two extremes. The fact is, a superb manager will be able to make either a waterfall or a spiral approach work. If handed a waterfall to work with, he will break the project into multiple phases and may introduce some manner of controlled iterations. If given a spiral, he will continue to employ sound "waterfall" techniques through each phase and iteration to create more discrete units with which the project can be effectively managed.[5]

By assembling the right people with the appropriate skills, employing sensible management of phased deliverables, and using a sound development methodology, a

---

[5]  A poor project manager is likely to make a mess of either approach.

project can enjoy the benefits of a rich foundation of models without sinking into the quagmire of analysis paralysis or without hacking out inadequate solutions in a clicking and coding frenzy.

## WHAT MAKES A METHODOLOGY "GOOD"?

A good methodology arms practitioners with a tool kit of reliable, repeatable techniques that are particularly well suited to the problems they are trying to solve. The techniques in the modeler's quiver should allow him to assemble the proper balance and mix of techniques for the problem at hand. Not all business problems are created equal. Some are rich in data but have very little processing requirements. Others are event-rich, with almost no process but entail large amounts of data, and so on. A balanced methodology includes techniques which give the analysts and designers full coverage of all of the aspects that they *might* need to model, but allows them to skew their modeling emphasis to match the bias of the business problem.

Any good analysis or design methodology should have five basic traits. It should:

1. Encourage the intended activity,
2. Be complete,
3. Be verifiable for correctness,
4. Produce deliverables against which progress can be measured,
5. Be easily consumable in the subsequent phase.

Let's examine these traits of good analysis and design methodologies, starting with how they apply to good design practices.

### Characteristics of Good Design Methodologies

Design is the act of deciding how the system shall be constructed to meet the users' requirements. Good design methodologies share the following characteristics:

1. Good design should encourage decision-making by helping to evaluate choices. Design is all about trade-offs. As we will see, later in the book, there is no perfect solution in the client/server environment. For each essential business requirement, there will be many possible ways to achieve it. A design technique should allow the designer to evaluate their decision against other possibilities. For example, using the analysis event model coupled with a database design schema, the designer can simulate the volume of reads and writes to the database for any given business event (e.g., *Customer places order*). This allows the team to evaluate the feasibility and projected performance of a given database table layout and data distribution scheme prior to building it.

2. The design needs to be complete, in that it covers each major aspect of the software that needs to be built. This will cause you to have several different kinds of models in the design documentation. Much like the architectural blueprints for the foundation, framing, electrical and plumbing systems of a house, the software design blueprint includes a model for the database layout, window and report layout, window navigation, specifications for any other electronic interfaces, and static and dynamic models of the internal componentry. Each model is specialized to depict a particular aspect of the system. You will find that models are particularly adept at articulating those aspects for which the modeling technique was intended, but fail miserably when you attempt to stretch the model beyond its original purpose. No model can depict all facets of the entire working system. That would be the system itself.

3. The design should be verifiable prior to construction. One of the primary purposes of design is to review and discuss the solution before charging ahead and coding it. Part of the verification process is traceability. With a good design specification, you should be able to demonstrate that the requirements of the project will be met, as well as distinguish between various versions of the design at any point in time.

   The design documentation has two distinct audiences. The externally visible portions of the design (window layouts, reports, navigation diagrams, menu and button specifications) need to be reviewed by the user community. This means that a large portion of the external design should be written in a non-technical manner. The internal specifications for what happens behind the scenes is another matter. The audience for internal specifications is limited to the IT community that must build, test and maintain the system. The internal specification should be written directly for this audience.

4. A good design methodology creates distinct deliverables which are measurable. One of the most formidable tasks of any project is estimating when it will be done. In order to make an estimate, the project manager must take measurements. Taking measurements involves counting things that need to be done and applying some sort of metric against them to estimate how long it will take to do them. The metric, of course, comes from having counted these things in the past and having measured how long it took to do them before (or from stealing someone else's metric). Therefore, a design methodology must render up countable components as early as possible. "How many tables do we have? How many windows will be required for the interface? How many reports are required? What is the number of objects we need to design and construct?"

   As soon as the manager can get a hold of solid deliverables to count, he can start refining estimates on the requisite effort and skills sets needed to accomplish the task. As the project progresses, he then has intermediate deliverables against which progress can be gauged. "How many windows have been designed? How many are left to be designed? What is the team's productivity rate? What is the average time it is taking us to code and test a window and its background functions? What does that do to our original estimate?"

5. Last, but not least, the design should be easily consumed in the final product. It should express the usage and structure of the system in a form very close to the intended result. This point may seem obvious, but I have seen projects which attempted to use design techniques which were entirely inappropriate for the target language in which the system was to be coded. You wouldn't want your home architect to render a blueprint that was so esoteric that you had no idea what manner of house would arise on your lot. The motto of the designer is: *map the technique to the target.* If your system is to operate over a relational database, then choose techniques which are particularly well-suited to relational database design. If your system will employ an object-oriented language, then you should be using object-oriented design techniques for those parts of the system which will require objects to accomplish their tasks. If your system will include more traditional components, such as structured functions on the client or batch routines on the server, then more traditional structured design techniques are in order for those parts of the system.

Many of today's client/server business systems have all of the afore mentioned language paradigms, attempting valiantly to live in harmony. If this is true for your system, then your design document will include a variety of design techniques, ranging from relational, object-oriented to traditional, each mapped to their respective target portions of the system.

## Characteristics of Good Analysis Methodologies

Analysis is the act of understanding and documenting the user's needs. Understanding comes from asking questions and writing down the answers, examining the answers and asking more questions. An analyst who asks no questions is conducting questionable analysis, indeed. An analyst who writes nothing down has done no analysis at all, rather he is on a journey of self-improvement by expanding his personal knowledge of the business. Failing to document your analytical discoveries sabotages all five of the benefits of successful analysis. The result is neither analytical, complete, verifiable, measurable or consumable. Assuming then that good analysis *is* written down, a successful analysis methodology will exhibit the following characteristics:

1. An analysis technique should encourage the act of discovery by providing a framework in which the analyst can write down what they know and evaluate what they have yet to learn. This includes having a rich set of heuristics to guide the analysis. For instance, the analysis technique of information modeling dictates that the analyst discover the business policy for all four points of cardinality on each relationship.[6] The model gives you a place to record this information and the result is visually apparent on the entity-relationship diagram for review.

---

[6] The concepts of information modeling are covered in Chapter 5.

2.  The analysis methodology should be complete in that it adequately covers each aspect of the business problem. As we will see later in this book, business systems have data they must remember, processing rules, and definable behavior. The analysis methodology needs to be sufficiently rich to model all three viewpoints. Because no model can serve all masters adequately, we will need to employ a suite of specialized, interlocking models which allow us to rotate our perspective to each facet of the problem domain.

3.  The results of the analysis needs to be verifiable. The analysis phase also has a dual audience. The users are the primary audience for blessing the documents as an accurate representation of their needs. Most software engineering models fail to live up to this requirement. Your average user isn't going to point out an inaccurate relationship cardinality on an information model any more than they are going to challenge your employment of multiple inheritance on an object-oriented class diagram. Instead of subjecting users to the technical models, a good analytical technique will be easily convertible into something with which the users are more familiar, such as a prototype of window layouts.

    It is imperative that the users understand what the analyst has discovered. Analysis should not be conducted in the dark dungeons of the IT department with the resulting epic tome mailed out to users for their signature. Instead, users need to be personally involved with the project from the beginning, and as much as possible, joint application requirement sessions (JAR), periodic analysis reviews and inspections should be conducted by the analyst with groups of users present. An adept analyst will stop at nothing to make sure the users are on the same wavelength as the project team. I call this the "interpretive dance" portion of the project, where you may find yourself engaging in wild gesticulations, pasting clip art over the top of an entity-relationship diagram, or inviting users to fill real data into your window layouts on an overhead project with colored pens.

    The other audience for the analysis document, is of course, the project team itself. The quality of the analysis will impact the quality of the design. The analysis techniques need to be precise and unambiguous such that a designer can devise a solution without having to retread through the entire analysis process.

4.  The analysis methodology must also create measurable units for the project manager. At the start of the analysis stage, the size and scope of the project may still be a bit fuzzy. The business wants to know when their software will be delivered, and the project manager still doesn't know the size of the problem. The early analysis models can go a long way toward serving up things for the manager to count. These early counts are used to extrapolate the effort required for the rest of the project. The manager should be asking, "How many entities are involved? Does our system create, read, update or delete all of those entities? How many significant business events is the system chartered

to recognize? Do those events entail simple table updates or do they require significant processing? How long does it take us to analyze problems of this size? Given the number of entities we expect to maintain, how many windows will we need to design?"

5. This brings us to the final topic of consumability. Nobody in this industry would argue that an analysis methodology should encourage analysis, be complete, verifiable and measurable. The extent to which it should be easily convertible into a design, and therefore, might be biased towards a particular type of design, has provided the catalyst for many heated and contentious conference debates.

Conventional wisdom has long held that analysis should be an articulation of the problem's essence, completely free from any particular solution, hence the term *essential analysis*. People have found, in practice, that some analysis techniques are predisposed to being more easily convertible into a particular design than others. As a practical matter, if you are confronted with a set of competing analysis methodologies, each replete with techniques which encourage good analysis; have balanced coverage of data, process and behavior; are equally verifiable; and produce measurable results, then the tie breaker over which one to use will likely come down to consumability.

In my own career, I have not yet found an analysis modeling technique that is completely without some technical bias. Structured analysis,[7] and its emphasis on data flow diagramming is very process-oriented. It is fairly easy to convert a set of data flow diagrams into a structure chart for a 3GL system. That is fine for building process-oriented systems. It is not so easy to convert a set of data flow diagrams into an object-oriented design. The technique is also quite cumbersome for designing graphical user interfaces.

In a very similar manner, object-oriented analysis (OOA),[8] enjoys a much higher convertibility factor if the target is a full-blown object-oriented system. If the target is not an object-oriented system, or perhaps a mixed-paradigm system (e.g., relational, 4GL and some objects), then object-oriented analysis will have a lower convertibility factor and can actually make the designer's life more difficult. OOA is simply another way to organize the same essential information that must be articulated for any successful analysis effort. The OOA organization may be well suited to object-oriented projects, only because it is more directly consumable in object-oriented design, *not* because it enjoys any superiority as analytical technique or is any way more complete, verifiable, or measurable.

---

[7] De Marco, 1979.

[8] Booch, 1994, Jacobsen et al., 1992, Rumbaugh et al., 1991.

The ability to easily convert an analysis model into a design walks a fine line between articulating the problem and mandating a solution. The shape of the analysis models can profoundly influence the shape of the design. A particular analysis methodology could *dictate* a particular type of design, in that to choose any other style of design would entail a re-write of the analysis document. In this instance, the analysis actually *prohibits* the devising of an alternative design paradigm. The danger of this situation is that the analyst may make premature design decisions in the name of analysis, closing off options that can be safely deferred until a time when better information exists on which to base a decision. A common example arises in object-oriented analysis models when the analyst attempts to allocate a particularly vexing method to its single best home, only to find that the process could live in a variety of classes, each solution with its respective pros and cons.[9] This type of trade-off is indicative of a design decision, not an analysis discovery.

On the other hand, a particular analysis methodology might *encourage* or *allow for* a variety of designs by providing enough analysis material that is easily assembled in different ways. It is likely that if an analysis methodology encourages certain types of design, it may *discourage* others (e.g., an information model may encourage a relational design, but discourage the use of, say, 3-dimensional array technology).

Finally, an analysis technique could be entirely neutral as to the various design options which might be employed. The conversion into one paradigm versus another would be done with equal ease or equal difficulty.

For this book, I have chosen a set of analysis techniques, specifically, context modeling, event modeling, information modeling and interface prototyping, which I believe are appropriate for the vast majority of today's client/server business systems, and stand up well to the five criteria for a good methodology. Each model has a firm historical grounding in software engineering, and a long successful track record in the industry. They have been proven to encourage good analysis, and cover the gamut of process, data and system behavior. The inclusion of the interface prototype goes a long way toward making the results of the analysis verifiable by the user community. The models also produce discrete units which can be counted and measured, such as entities, events, windows, and reports. These units have been around long enough to have amassed a modest base of metrics within the industry.

So, where do the techniques in this book stand on the issue of consumability? The activities of analysis, detailed in the following chapters, were selected with consumption in mind. As one who has spent roughly equal time designing systems as I have analyzing them, the ability to transition easily from analysis to design is very important to me.

---

[9]   Object-oriented techniques are covered in Chapter 12.

The technological premise of this book is that your target business system is most likely to include a relational database, a graphical user interface, and a variety of programming languages which may range from object-oriented, to object-based, to SQL-based, to traditional 3GLs, with the industry trending more and more toward object-oriented constructs. The analysis models will need to convert handily into designs for this environment. I have included techniques which fall into the category of encouraging and allowing for the likely target design, without absolutely mandating a particular design paradigm or prohibiting others.

I have chosen the information model as the primary data model because of its excellent track record for creating well-normalized relational database designs. It is a technique which has been very popular and successful, and as a result, the discipline enjoys a wide field of expert practitioners. The information model shows quite clearly what needs to be remembered in the system, without cluttering the view with procedural elements that current relational database management systems are not capable of handling.

The event model is included because it is particularly well suited to organizing the analysis specification in such a manner that it lends itself well to designing the event-driven graphical user interface, a task which will consume a great deal of project time. The event dictionary provides the framework for the system's internal process specification. Taken together with the information model, these two models contain the raw materials needed to declare a class structure for an object-oriented system, design structure charts for traditional system components, or design stored procedures for the database server.

The context model is included as a time-honored technique for determining and depicting project scope. It is mainly a planning tool that helps clarify the area of study and determine what lies inside and outside of your span of control.

## OVERVIEW OF THE TECHNIQUES IN THIS BOOK

Let's get on with the important task of previewing what lies ahead between here and the index.

I shall use the pyramid as the primary geometric metaphor to organize the activities of system development (Figure 1–7). There isn't tremendous significance attached to the pyramid per se. I could just as easily use a square, circle or a set of amorphous clouds, but I find the pyramid representation convenient for a number of reasons.

The pyramid never lets you forget that the code you build is simply the foundation of a structure which is chartered to reach a set of business objectives. At the top of the pyramid is the project charter. This includes the goal of the project and its supporting objectives. These are the reasons that the project exists in the first place. Beneath the charter are all of the activities, roughly arranged in a descending fashion, that need to occur between the identification of the project's business objectives, and the deployment of the ones and zeros at the bottom of the pyramid that constitute the resulting software.

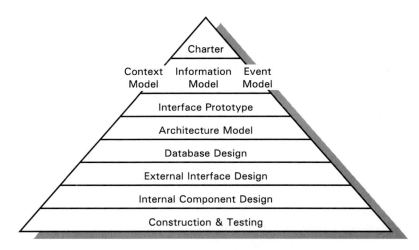

**Figure 1–7.** The software development pyramid

If you think of time traveling roughly north to south, the pyramid graphically depicts your ever-expanding base of knowledge about a subject as you descend from the lofty reaches of analysis, down through design, and then start grubbing around in the code. Project managers, business sponsors, and the more cynical among us may prefer to picture the pyramid as the ever-widening expenditure of money as time marches on.

The structure of the pyramid metaphor is not intended in any way to mandate a waterfall or a spiral approach to get from the top to the bottom. Rather, it shows how the final code and intermediate analysis and design products support the business charter. Whether you phase your project, or develop it in one grand sweep, will depend on the size of the project and the demands of your business.

Let's start at the top and work our way down.

Every project needs a **charter** (Figure 1–8). The charter contains the marching orders from the business that articulate the end goal and objectives of the project. The charter is a planning tool that is developed by the IT group, in concert with the business. It is vital for defining and controlling scope. Without a charter, the analyst has no clear direction or priorities for what to analyze, and has no idea when to stop. You will find the project charter covered in Chapter 2.

You may find it curious to see the next three models aligned on the same level of the pyramid. The context model, event model and information model are so interdependent that it is impossible to finish one without having a good handle on the others. I call them the "big three" because together they form the bulk of the system requirements.

The **context model** (Figure 1–9) defines the system's boundaries and shows how it is situated within the business environment. This is a venerable old modeling technique which hails from the days of structured analysis. It is particularly handy in today's client/server world to explore the impact of moving the automation boundary in the business. Context modeling is covered in Chapter 3.

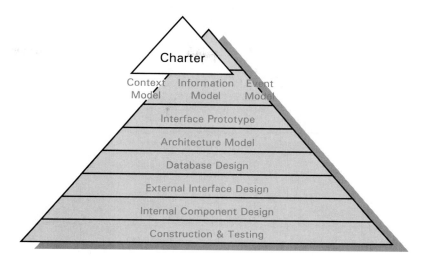

**Figure 1–8.** The project charter

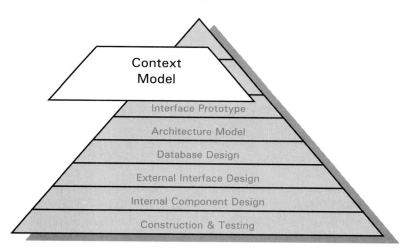

**Figure 1–9.** The context model

The **event model** (Figure 1–10) defines the system's behavior by showing how the system is expected to respond for each business event in the charter. Not only does the event model map inputs to outputs, it includes the processing specification for each event that provides crucial detail for the internal design of the system's functions, methods and procedures. Event modeling is a vital analytical technique for discovering and documenting business rules. Because graphical user interfaces are, by definition, "event driven," the event model provides the framework and rationale for the design of the user interface. Chapter 4 in this book is dedicated to event modeling.

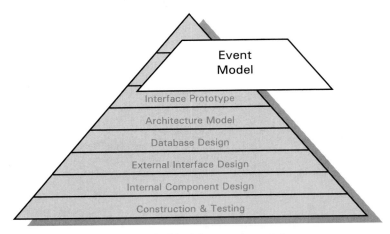

**Figure 1–10.** The event model

The final model of the "big three" is perhaps the most crucial of all. The **informa-tion model** (Figure 1–11) contains the static map of the data that the system is required to remember. It profoundly influences the database design and impacts virtually every aspect of the system. The modeling techniques include entity-relationship diagramming, attribute definition and state-transition diagramming. Information models also respect no project boundaries. Much of the data you will be modeling for your system will also make an appearance in other systems within your organization (and perhaps outside of it too). For this reason, it is imperative that information modeling efforts have some enterprise-wide coordination. Information modeling should always be conducted with a strong sense of context, bound by a scope of business events. Otherwise, you can model data forever or until you run out of time or money. Information modeling is the topic of Chapter 5.

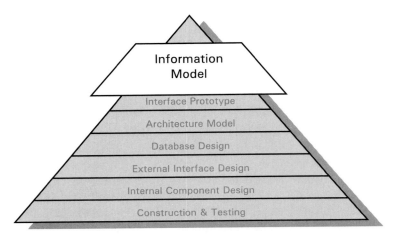

**Figure 1–11.** The information model

The **interface prototype** (Figure 1–12) lies just below the "big three" models. I am a strong advocate of early prototyping, especially those of the quick and easy variety. The prototype puts a face on the abstract models by sketching out what the windows and reports could look like in the new system. Although prototyping is begun early in the analysis phase, it is the first foray into system design. In practice, I have found it virtually impossible to finish the "big three" without verifying the requirements with some level of interface prototype. On some projects, I have used prototyping even earlier to drive out business event requirements and the information model. You may find yourself bouncing back and forth between the "big three" and the prototype several times until you and your users are convinced that you understand their needs. A robust system may have many different kinds of prototype. The key to successful prototyping is to first identify the learning objective, and then to choose the most cost-effective method of prototyping for reaching that particular objective. Prototyping is the subject of Chapter 6.

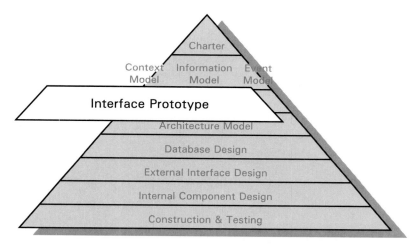

**Figure 1–12.** The interface prototype

Chapter 7 takes a brief pause from modeling to discuss the important topic of resolving business issues. One of the most insidious project-killers of client/server endeavors is the hidden cost of re-engineering the business. Client/server often brings standardization and automation to frontiers of the business that were heretofore the domain of the spreadsheet, word processor, yellow sticky-note and scribbled cocktail napkin. As an analyst, you may find yourself in the unfortunate position of discovering gaping holes in the target company's business practices or policies with absolutely no authority to resolve them. Chapter 7 lays out an issue resolution process that can be used to remove these project roadblocks.

We return to our pyramid in Chapter 8 with **architecture modeling**. Architecture modeling is the process of mapping the business requirements articulated in the analysis models onto a variety of hardware configurations, and choosing the most appropriate, or the least offensive. For this task, the analysis models need to be supplemented with some statistics, such as transaction volumes, event rates, record sizes and user expectations for response time and data currency. There is no "right" answer in architecture modeling. Every business and every target programming environment comes with its own peculiar warts and wrinkles. The key to successful architecture modeling is to be able to use the models to evaluate the design trade-offs and relative performance of different geographic distribution schemes, as well as the distribution among hardware tiers within the same business site.

While many of the analysis and design activities can be easily partitioned and phased, much of the overall client/server architecture for the whole project is likely to be decided prior to the design of the first phase. In practice, it is also unlikely that the hardware will be chosen after all of the analysis is conducted. The architectural track often runs parallel with the analysis effort. In some projects, you may not be able to choose the most appropriate hardware at all; instead you may be forced to squeeze your software into the ramshackle collection of boxes already in residence in the computer room. Architecture modeling (Figure 1–13) takes up this late position on the pyramid because this is the last point to which you can safely defer architectural choices, and it is also the point at which you are armed with the best information on which to base those decisions.

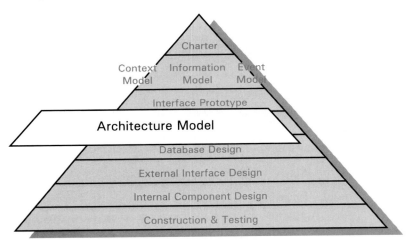

**Figure 1–13.** The architecture model

The **database design** (Figure 1–14) transforms the information model into a physical database schema. Whether you design all of your database at once or in phases, may depend on whether you phase your project. Like many of the subjects in this book, a full discussion on the art of database design could fill an entire volume. The purpose of Chapter 9 is to show how the information model transforms into a first-cut relational database design, and to discuss the various options at your disposal for optimizing performance.

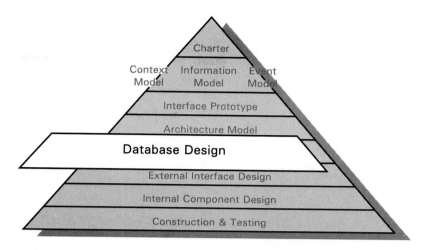

**Figure 1–14.** The database design

Chapters 10 and 11 cover the design of the graphical user interface. Chapter 10 starts with a discussion of what makes a "good" GUI. Many of the concepts represent a significant shift from the green screen world of the mainframe. The last part of Chapter 10 introduces the concept of window cohesion. I have applied Larry Constantine's[10] measure of module cohesion from structured design, and adapted it as a rating of the impact on usability and maintainability of combining multiple business events on the same window.

**External interface design** (Figure 1–15) is covered in Chapter 11. This includes window navigation diagramming, an important and cost-effective technique for determining window type, navigation and defining the user's appropriate unit of work. The external interface design refines the analysis prototype into a formal design specification from which the interface can be coded. A written specification is crucial for the testing of a GUI and for downstream user training and documentation. I have conducted GUI development many times both with a written specification and without. I need no further convincing that the written external design specification is vital to the construction, testing and implementation of the project.

The **internal component design** (Figure 1–16) of the system includes models which map directly to paradigm of the target coding language. If the system includes object-oriented code, then the internal design will include both class models and dynamic object-communication models for that part of the system. If the system includes more traditional functions and database procedures, then you will find yourself drawing structure charts and writing specs for stored procedures. Chapter 12 shows how the models of analysis are consumed in the activities of internal design.

---

[10] Yourdon, Constantine, 1979.

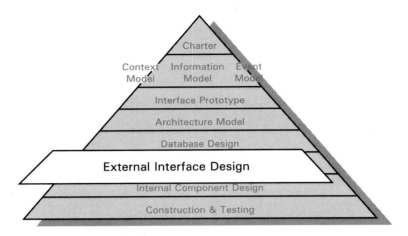

**Figure 1–15.** The external interface design

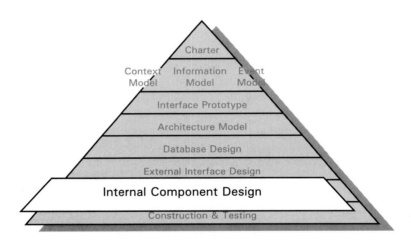

**Figure 1–16.** The internal component design

At the bottom of the pyramid is the construction phase, which includes coding, testing and deployment. While coding and testing are not the primary topics of this book, I include a discussion at the end of Chapter 11 on the challenges of testing a graphical user interface, and how the analysis and design specification can be used to create test scripts and scenarios.

The book concludes with Chapter 13 which includes some issues for managers. The client/server revolution has spawned a number of myths and exaggerated claims. In this closing chapter, I chime in with my two-cents-worth, debunking **ten myths of client/server development**.

## SUMMARY

Analysis is a voyage of discovery in which the participants determine a business system's data, process and behavioral requirements. Design is the act of deciding how to implement a system that meets those needs. We are experiencing a trend toward specialization in our industry which is driven by the ever-expanding universe of knowledge required to conduct software development. The skills needed to be a good analyst are not necessarily the same skills needed to be a good programmer. Project managers are increasingly finding themselves managing teams of specialists rather than the groups of generalists that tended to be employed on traditional development projects.

While the individual project member is a competent practitioner of his respective techniques, a project manager's job is much like the general contractor, coordinating the activities of the specialists into a sensible methodology. Methodologies come in many forms. Both the traditional waterfall approaches and spiral models have many good points, but both suffer from abuses in practice. A sensible manager will phase large projects and build a degree of iteration into the project plan. While I have chosen the pyramid in this book to represent the organization of the models, their dependencies and the project's expanding level of commitment over time, it does not imply a waterfall, nor does it endorse radical iteration.

Imagine your development team deposited by helicopter on the top of a pyramid in Egypt. You would not be compelled to descend directly to the bottom, but instead you may explore the terrain of various levels, sometimes retreating back up in your eventual journey to the bottom. However, there is a logical progression of activities in software development. Like our imaginary hike down the pyramid, it would be risky to jump from the top level to the bottom in one step. Leaping from charter directly to code carries with it similar risk. It is up to the project manager to decide whether it is appropriate to lead his troops en masse in a direct descent from top to bottom, or to divide and conquer the pyramid with multiple journeys and iterative side trips to ensure complete coverage of the terrain.

Any good methodology should encourage the intended activity by providing a framework in which to record knowledge. The techniques employed should be complete, in that they cover all aspects of the problem and solution domain. The models created should be verifiable for correctness by their intended audience. This audience can be both technical and non-technical. The methodology must produce units against which progress can be measured, forming a basis for estimating level of effort. Finally, the deliverables must lend themselves to being easily consumed in the subsequent phases of the project.

The models and activities of the analysis phase include project charters, context modeling, event modeling, information modeling, interface prototyping and business issue resolution. The design activities produce an architectural model, database design, external interface design and internal component design which form the blueprint for constructing and testing the system.

# CHAPTER
# 2

Charter

Context Model | Information Model | Event Model

Interface Prototype

Architecture Model

Database Design

External Interface Design

Internal Component Design

Construction & Testing

# THE PROJECT CHARTER

## INTRODUCTION

A successful project begins with a good plan. In Chapter 2, I cover the project chartering process and introduce a valuable technique called the project decision-making framework. This technique is particularly useful for leading the business members through the steps of understanding their current problems and recognizing new opportunities that have gone previously unexploited. Those problems and opportunities then form the basis for articulating the objectives of the project in clear, measurable terms. Rather than simply accepting a list of "requirements" at face value, this technique helps the business people and the IT professionals come to consensus on what business problems the new system is really supposed to solve. The charter gets everybody aligned and pointed in the same direction. It states the project's reason for existence for all to see, and clearly prioritizes the project's objectives. The objectives stated in the charter become part of the evaluation criteria that can be used to choose between various solution options all throughout the project. The first solution option, as we will see near the end of the chapter, is whether to even proceed with the project in the first place.

## THE PURPOSE OF THE CHARTER

The charter states the goals and objectives of the project. More important, it provides a set of measurements which let you know when you have achieved your objectives. It also states who does what, for both the IT department and the users. The charter is a contract, and like a contractual agreement, it takes two parties to complete the transaction. There are significant roles and responsibilities on both sides.

Most builders wouldn't dream of building a house without a contract. These days, the neighborhood baby sitter might even ask you to sign a contract before watching over your little darlings. Likewise, it makes no sense at all to embark on building large-scale information systems without any semblance of a contract with the business.

## WHO DOES THE CHARTER?

The chartering process is a cooperative effort between IT and the business. It is the responsibility of the IT organization to provide technical, analytical, and procedural assistance and to lead the business through the process of producing a charter. IT acts as a facilitator to lead the business through the various solutions which could help the business meet its goals.

It is the responsibility of the business to commit the people and the time to articulate the business' goals, objectives and evaluation criteria, and to materially participate in the decisions made. The information systems people are usually not the policy-makers in an organization. This is why it is critical for members of the business to articulate their goals and objectives clearly so IT can provide the appropriate technical support.

Unfortunately, for many organizations, the goals and objectives are not clearly stated, or worse, not even written down. In these cases, the IT department must extend their responsibility further to help the business communicate, and sometimes discover, their needs. If the information systems people don't step in to fill the void in the planning phase, the project may be doomed from the start. This constitutes a large leap "out of bounds" for many technical people. In addition to delivering systems, we have a responsibility to educate business leaders as to their role in the planning and development process.

## HOW ACCURATE MUST THE CHARTER BE?

The charter is the project's strategic plan and marching orders. The chartering process determines the feasibility of proceeding with a project, and what direction and pace the effort should take. In addition to stating the objectives of the project, the charter details the estimated cost of pursuing those objectives. The quality of the charter is crucial to the success of the project which follows.

The accuracy of the project time and resource estimates made in the charter are directly proportional to the amount of effort put into them. The more up-front modeling done for the charter (covered in the following four chapters), the better the estimates. This is not to say that your typical chartering effort will require a full-blown analysis. The amount of modeling and research that you put into a charter is determined by how detailed a project time and cost estimate you must submit. In more cynical terms, the quality of the estimate in the charter is determined by how broad an estimate the business will let you get away with. A very small and innocuous project has little downside of being off the mark, and therefore requires very little in the way of a formal charter. A large and high-profile project, however, should include careful planning. Whether your project is small, medium or large, it is advisable to go through the chartering steps outlined in this chapter. It is the need for accuracy, or perhaps the risk of inaccuracy, that will determine how rapidly you proceed through this phase.

Many of you may have found yourselves trapped in a meeting where your business sponsors demanded a gold-plated, engraved, one-hundred-percent-accurate cost estimate for a project on the very day that they saw fit to reveal their requirements. (Even though they reserved the right to change the requirements at any point in time without affecting the due date or budget.) While common, this situation is largely due to ignorance, inexperience or wishful thinking on the part of the user. (I have found the occasional executive who believes it profitable to play such games, and usually this type of individual is steering the firm down a risky and treacherous course on many fronts due to his recklessness.)

It is not in your best interest to roll over and blurt out a number under duress. An estimate is only one-hundred percent accurate on the *last* day of the project. On the *first* day of the project, an estimate is usually not worth the oxygen it took to utter it. What you need is a way to pull yourself quickly up the accuracy scale from zero percent to a level you and the business can live with. The chartering process is designed to rapidly increase your understanding of the problem, and therefore, allow you to increase the accuracy of your estimates for a solution *as early in the project as possible.*

I have found that by involving the business members intimately in the creation of the charter, their sense of ownership in the project and its estimates is greatly increased, as is their appreciation of the challenge of producing meaningful cost, time and resource projections with limited information.

A good charter is never cast entirely in stone. It is periodically revisited as the project progresses to check and to revise the estimates. Managing a project against a well-crafted charter is also the best way I know of to assess the impact of scope changes that occur along the way. When the business members help you create the charter, they are more likely to understand how mid-stream changes in requirements can affect the time and budget required to finish the system.

## BEWARE OF SLOPPY CHARTERS

Many project disasters can be traced back to a sloppy or missing charter. A spectacular example occurred once at Frieda's French Fry Factory.[1] The factory floor manufacturing systems were run via a motley collection of ancient batch applications. The system was written about fifteen to twenty years ago in a mix of COBOL and Assembly Language. The users were beginning to wonder aloud why their children were using a PC at the local pre-school to identify stellar constellations, while at work they were still typing mnemonics on a blank screen.[2]

Fenwick Prescott, the chief information officer, moved quickly to convene a project team, nominate an acronym, and get started with the important work of requirements analysis. Unfortunately, he didn't bother to produce a charter which stated the project's objectives and scope. A team of analysts descended on the business, producing reams of diagrams, bubbles and arrows, and boxes and lines. Within months the scope of the analysis had spread from the production systems into sales, order entry, invoicing, accounting, human resources and payroll. Each user and business manager added their own personal laundry list of requirements to the project, creating monumental scope creep. The project manager had nothing to manage against, because the original expectation had never been written down and agreed upon.

After eighteen months, it was clear that the project team was lost in the wilderness. The initial euphoria had long since worn off and open animosity and acrimony had broken out between the business and the IT department. Convinced that the IT department was incapable of producing anything, the CEO negotiated a secret deal to outsource the company's information management, and summarily fired the entire IT staff, including a beleaguered and bewildered Mr. Prescott.

The lesson to be learned is that the charter establishes a contractual obligation between IT and the business. It is important to state each party's expectation and responsibilities explicitly. If it is not written down, the unstated expectations may come back to

---

[1]   The names have been changed to protect the guilty.

[2]   This is a mundane, but powerful example of how the PC has changed user expectations of what constitutes an acceptable interface. Many workers are simply refusing to use the old technology, and companies are finding it increasingly difficult to lure new college graduates into jobs that involve using character-based systems.

bite you. In today's global information marketplace, a technical or political project failure can result in the wholesale elimination of the IT department.

## THE PROJECT DECISION-MAKING FRAMEWORK

Any sensible development life cycle includes a planning or feasibility stage. I like the term "project charter" because the word *charter* connotes "reason for being." The project decision-making framework is a technique for bringing people together to reach consensus on the goal, objectives, and evaluation criteria for a project. This common vision is then used as the basis for making choices throughout the project's existence.

Figure 2–1 shows a diagram of the project decision-making framework. At the very top of the pyramid is the project's goal. The goal is a summary statement which lets everyone know what the project is attempting to achieve. Supporting the goal, in the next layer, are a variety of objectives. Objectives are like mini-goals. Each objective contributes to the goal in some way. When all of the objectives are met, the goal has been reached.

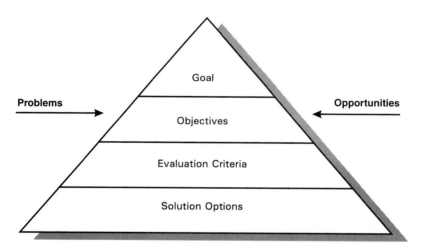

**Figure 2–1.** The project decision-making framework

Underneath the objectives is a layer called the evaluation criteria. This layer contains the measurements that you will need to determine whether an objective has been met. The bottom-most strata of the decision-making framework represents the various solution options that are possible. Solution options are all of the various paths that could be taken to reach the goal. The solution options are evaluated against the objectives by using the evaluation criteria to determine which solution best meets the project's objectives.

The remainder of this chapter will focus on how to use the decision-making framework to create a charter for your project. This is not an exercise that is done by a manager, hidden away in a dark corner. The project decision-making framework is a technique which requires open participation from users, technical staff, and managers who represent all of the stake-holders in the new system. The most successful project charters are the result of careful planning and execution of a series of consensus-building sessions in which a facilitator leads the group through the process of building the framework.

For many projects, some degree of additional modeling, such as context, event and information modeling, will also be required before reasonable estimates can be made of the project's scope and size. These modeling topics will be covered in subsequent chapters.

## The Goal Statement

I am reminded of a ride I once took to the city dump with my next-door neighbor. He was a retired engineer who worked on the booster rocket for the Apollo program. I remember asking him, "How did a team of thousands of individuals from all over the country land a man on the moon in the 1960s and today it's a struggle to deliver a decent order entry system?"

His answer was quite simple. "We all knew the goal. Every person involved on the Apollo project had no doubt about its mission. We had to land a man on the moon before the end of the decade, and return him safely to the earth." (I'm convinced that the astronaut's union inserted the "return" clause in version 1.2 of the goal statement.)

The Apollo program's goal was clear. It was short and to the point. It was unambiguous because it used simple language that everyone could understand. The best thing about it was that it was measurable. You knew what constituted success, namely, get someone to the moon and back safely before December 31, 1969. Another key factor was that many people believed that it was achievable. Aside from the explicit goal, there was also an implicit goal on the Apollo project which wasn't officially stated. Can you remember what it was?[3]

Every information systems project has a goal. The complicating factor is that business systems are not simple. People have differing viewpoints on what a project is all about. A charter is needed to bring the goal of the project into focus. The goal needs to be *clear*, *unambiguous*, *concise*, and *measurable*. Everybody needs to agree on what it is, and know when it has been achieved.

But how to come up with the goal? I have found it very difficult to start by writing one simple goal statement that sums up an entire project. A better way to tease out the goal is to determine the entire list of individual objectives that must be achieved for the project to be deemed a success. Objectives are determined by uncovering all of the problems with the current way of doing business, and brainstorming unexploited opportunities. After the list of objectives has been ratified by the group, it can be distilled into a summarized goal statement that represents the whole of the project's objectives.

---

[3]   The implicit goal was to "beat the Russians to the moon." This unstated goal probably served to motivate the project far more than the official stated goal.

I'll come back to the goal statement after we've discussed problems, opportunities and objectives.

## Problems and Opportunities are the Basis for Objectives

When you first gather a group of system users, business managers and technical staff together to discuss a new information system, it is inevitable that people will start out by telling you everything that's wrong with the old one. In fact, little or no discussion is likely to take place about a new vision for the future until everyone has had a chance to vent their frustration with the current way of doing business.

This is an important human dynamic to recognize, and as an analyst, you can take advantage of it. The venting process is critical. You need to give your users the opportunity to vent, in a controlled environment, early in the planning phase. If they don't get their issues out in the open, they are likely to grumble and cause trouble for the entire duration of your project.

For the best results, a cross-section of users and managers should join the project team members for a session that can last anywhere from several days to a week. A facilitator plays the role of leading the discussion and asking the questions, being careful not to interject his own personal opinion. It is often worth it to pay for a professional consultant to provide the third-party neutrality that is required for this role. All of the proceedings are recorded, either electronically or manually. It is of paramount importance that when a user tells you a problem, they see you write it down.

### Problems

The beginning of the analytical process begins by asking people what is wrong with their current environment. Typically, people start out slowly, not wanting to offend or draw attention to themselves, but quickly the gloves come off and the group erupts into a litany of sins visited upon them by the current system. Each of these statements is recorded on a list of *problems*. The point of the exercise is to discover as many problems as possible, but not to attempt to solve them at this point.

A new information system is a *solution*. In order to design the proper solution, you must understand the problem you are trying to solve. Problems may range from the show-stopper variety (such as, "The old system produces spurious results and can no longer be relied upon for accurate data."), to the mundane (such as, "The line printer reports are hard to read.").

A problem exists any time someone is dissatisfied with the behavior or capabilities of their existing information systems, and can express to you what they think appropriate behavior or capability should be. For example, if an order entry clerk complains that the system is too slow, then what is an acceptable response time? In the 1982 best seller, *The One Minute Manager*, Drs. Kenneth Blanchard and Spencer Johnson gave a wonderful definition of a problem in behavioral terms.

*"A problem exists if there is a difference between what is* actually *happening and what you* desire *to be happening." And they add: "If you can't tell me what you'd like to be happening, you don't have a problem yet. You're just complaining."*[4]

By stating each complaint as a problem, you leave the door open to many different solution options.

### The Difference between Problems and Opportunities

In addition to problems with the current systems, organization and procedures, there may be unexploited opportunities available to the business that are yet untapped. The difference between problems and opportunities is subtle. A problem exists when something isn't working and you want to fix it. With an opportunity, nothing is necessarily broken. An opportunity arises when you can leverage new technology, products or services that didn't exist before or hadn't been considered.

Opportunities are often inspired by new technology. For instance, a participant may come up with the idea to give the sales people laptop or hand-held computers so they can write up orders electronically while they're on the road. We have to be careful not to state a technological solution in our opportunity statement. There may be many ways to exploit the opportunity, both technological and non-technological. A good opportunity statement for our example is, "Eliminate redundant entry of data by moving data capture closer to the source."

## Objectives

While many project plans traditionally start and stop with an exhaustive list of requirements, the purpose of determining the objectives is to get to the reasons behind the requirements. For example, a common requirement that I have seen is, "the system shall interface with a laser printer." After searching for the underlying objective, you may find that the real problem is that your customers can't read their invoices because they are printed on multi-part pink paper with pale purple impact-printer type. The "requirement" was someone's proposed solution to the problem. The true objective of the requirement might be to "reduce errors in payment and increase customer satisfaction by clearly communicating the charges due from the customer on each invoice." When you've stated the issue in this manner, it opens the door for a variety of solution options, ranging from changing the color of paper in the impact printer to invoicing your customers electronically.

An objective is a statement which, when realized, removes a problem or exploits an opportunity. Objectives are like "mini goals." They should also be *clear*, *concise* and *measurable*. Each objective supports one piece of the goal (Figure 2–2). If you reach all of your objectives, you have reached the total goal.

---

4    Blanchard and Johnson, 1982.

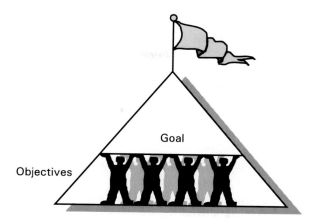

**Figure 2–2.** Many objectives can support the goal

Each problem and opportunity is turned into an objective statement by applying a simple concept called *IR AC IS*, (pronounced 'ear-ack-iss). This is an old IBM® term. It's an acronym which stands for *Increase Revenue, Avoid Costs, Improve Service* to our customers. We need to remember that businesses exist to make money and have happy customers.[5] The reason business information systems exist is to help the company in this mission.

Using *IR AC IS*, it is fairly easy to convert a problem or opportunity into an objective which states whether the business will realize a gain in revenue, lower cost, or improved service to customers when the objective is met. Many of your objectives may fall into more than one category. By determining whether we intend to increase revenue, avoid costs or improve service, this exercise sets us up for finding a way to ultimately *measure* the objective. The objective statements also tend to move the chartering participants away from overtly stating technical solutions, and forces them to consider the business reasons for their proposals.

Let's take a problem identified by a marketing group at a security check printing firm that supplies checks to banks and other financial institutions. When patrons open new accounts at the bank, they are shown a dazzling array of personal checks that can be theirs for a small fee. Many of these checks are products created by the check printing firm especially for that bank.

The check printer's sales force was supposed to be the primary customer contact for all aspects of the relationship. The marketing department's product development

---

5   Cynics may argue that some government agencies exist to lose money and irritate customers, but their underlying business mission *should* be the same.

group was having a problem. The problem was that the sales people in the field had incomplete and inconsistent methods for collecting vital information about new customers and the new products that these banks required. This forced the product development group to establish separate contacts with the customers to clarify their needs, causing delays in the specification for new products.

> **Problem:** Sales people provide incomplete information about new customers and new product requirements to the product development group.

How can we turn this into an objective? Start by making the negative problem a positive statement.

> Sales people need to provide complete information about new customers and new product requirements to the product development group.

Next, we need to apply IR AC IS. As an analyst, you ask, "By addressing this problem, are we likely to increase revenue, avoid costs or improve service to our customers?" Let's brainstorm some possibilities:

> **Increase Revenue:** There is no apparent correlation between getting complete customer and product information and getting more customers or more sales from existing customers.

> **Avoid Costs:** Getting complete customer information will definitely lower the cost per new product to process the information through the product development group because they won't have to call customers back so many times for clarification.

> **Improve Service:** It will also improve service to the customer. When customers are bothered less, it lowers their actual cost of doing business with the company.

> Now we can restate the objective, using the proper IR AC IS terms.

> **Objective:** Avoid cost of calling customer for clarification by having sales people provide complete new product information. This will also improve service to our customers by reducing the number of times they are contacted.

## Measuring Objectives — The *X-Factor*

We're not finished with our objective yet. This objective is clear and concise, but how do we measure it? This is where many project charters fall apart. They get to this stage and declare victory, but the real work is just beginning. We need to find what I call the elusive *x-factor*. The *x-factor* puts a number to the increase in revenue, the decrease in costs and the improvement in service for every objective which is possible to measure. If we never state the *x-factor*, how will we ever know if the project was a success?

Getting back to the check printing firm, this particular company had no idea how much time was actually being spent by the product development group contacting customers for clarification. Therefore, they didn't even know if they had a problem! There is an old business adage that says, "*You cannot improve that which you do not measure.*" If you only perceive that you have a problem, you really can't proceed to make any rational decisions about fixing it until you know its relative importance, and have some idea of the degree to which you can address it.

The process of creating a project charter often uncovers the need to take some baseline measurements in the organization. It is important that these measurements be taken. When you discover an objective that is lacking any measurement as to the degree of the problem, the following steps will allow you to record the deficiency and move on with your group meeting.

1. Establish with the group how they could measure the objective. Hard measurements can be taken in terms of dollars or time. Some objectives may require soft measurements such as "customer satisfaction." Objectives designed to improve service to customers may be difficult to measure. One technique is to try to measure the customer's cost of doing business with you, in either time, dollars or effort expended. Try to get as many hard measurements as you can in your charter. It will help you establish the benefit side for any cost-benefit analysis that may be performed on your various solution options.

2. Insert an *x-factor* into the objective statement, showing where a measurement is needed. The existence of the variable makes is it clear to any reader that the objective statement is incomplete until a value is supplied.

> **Objective, (with x-factors inserted):** Avoid cost of calling customer for clarification (*by $ x*) by having sales people provide complete new product information. This will also improve service to our customer by reducing the number of times they are contacted by (*y number of calls*).

3. Assign specific people to establish baseline measurements to evaluate the extent of the problem. In the example, they could measure the number of calls and the duration of each call. They could also classify the calls by what information was being requested. An average labor cost for the department will also have to be established.

4. Schedule a time to reconvene the group, after the measurements are taken, to review the measurements and evaluate the degree to which they want to address the problem.

You must be very careful if your charter includes an objective which promises a reduction in labor costs. The implication is that your project intends to reduce head count. Do not make this statement in your charter unless you intend to deliver that result. Quite often labor savings doesn't reduce head count, instead it shifts workers from clerical activity to more advantageous tasks. This doesn't eliminate the cost of the worker from the company, but hopefully makes them more productive. Make sure your charter makes it clear which result your project intends to deliver. The charter should clearly state the criteria by which you will be judged when the project is over.

Another common trap to avoid is what I call the "motherhood and apple pie" objectives. These are broad sweeping statements such as, "The new system will avoid costs by eliminating all errors in the production cycle." Everybody can agree that this is a good thing, but it is entirely unachievable. This kind of statement leaves a project wide open for failure. The project can be lambasted as a disaster when the first error occurs in production after the new system's installation.

It doesn't take any research to write a "motherhood and apple pie" objective. Instead, you should be asking, "What is the error rate in the current production cycle, and what is the root cause of those errors?" "To what extent can a new or improved information system reasonably be expected to lower the rate of these errors?" "What other creative solutions might be employed to reduce errors in production?"

The *x-factors* that are put into the project charter will be used to justify the project's existence, and will ultimately be used to rate its success when delivered. Think of them as your test cases and take the time to measure and negotiate reasonable expectations with the business.

## Coming Back to the Goal Statement . . .

After you have compiled an exhaustive list of objectives with your group, and determined the method for measuring each objective, it is time to return to the goal statement. If you have a rough draft goal statement for the project, review and amend it in light of your objectives and see if it still summarizes the project. If you deferred the goal statement until after the objectives were complete, now is the time to distill the objective statements into a short summary which can serve as the project's ultimate goal.

A good technique for analyzing and summarizing objectives is to group them into categories. List all of the objectives which increase revenue, followed by those which avoid costs, and finally those which improve service to customers. Some objectives may fall into two or even all three categories.

### Prioritizing Objectives

All objectives are not created equal. The chartering team needs to determine which objectives are more important than others. For this exercise, you will need to have your *x-factors* filled in. The team will need a strong indication as to which problems are the most severe, and which objectives will contribute the most to the company's well being.

This type of analysis often requires some direction from upper management as well. The strategic direction of the business can also skew the weighting of the objective list.

Good goal statements are like good objective statements. They need to be:

**clear and unambiguous,** (use short, common, understandable words),

**concise,** (one sentence to three sentences should suffice),

and **measurable,** (include measurements from your most critical objectives).

Let us return to our check printing firm example for a moment. Prior to going through the decision-making framework, they drafted an initial goal statement. On the morning of the first day of the sessions, the users and their management were perfectly happy with the following goal:

*"The goal of the project is to deliver to the marketing department a computer system for collecting and disseminating new product information."*

They had stated a solution instead of a goal. After following the steps outlined in this chapter, they rewrote their goal statement as follows:

*"Our goal is to reduce the time it takes for the marketing department to validate and complete the specifications for a new product from five days to two days, from the time of receipt of complete information from the sales office to the delivery of accurate, approved specifications to the plants."*

It is clear, unambiguous, concise and measurable. In fact, when this particular group finished with the project decision-making framework, they settled on a solution which didn't even involve a new computer system. It turned out that through a combination of sales training and new forms design, they were able to achieve their objective without re-writing a single automated system!

When your objectives are sorted and weighted in terms of their relative importance, then you are ready to finalize the project goal statement and move on to the next tier of the decision-making framework.

## Evaluation Criteria

The next layer of the project decision-making framework is the evaluation criteria. The evaluation criteria establishes how you will measure any given solution against the objectives.

Your *x-factor* measurements in your objectives will already provide you with many of your evaluation criteria. For example, if an objective is to "avoid cost of $1,400 per month by eliminating paper transfer of documents between warehouse and plant," then the evaluation criteria is to measure to what degree any proposed solution option meets the $1,400 per month reduction target.

### Convert Your Objectives into Evaluation Criteria

To establish a list of evaluation criteria, start by listing the measurable or tangible objectives. Establish how you will rate any solution against the measurement. Must the objective be entirely met, or can solutions be accepted that meet the objective target to some lesser degree? For the objectives that cannot be easily measured, you also need to determine the evaluation criteria. Discuss within the group how you might attempt to rate a solution against each intangible objective.

When you finish this step, you should have an evaluation criteria established for each objective. Your evaluation criteria should carry a weighting that corresponds to the objectives' relative importance.

### Extend Your List with Standard Cost-Evaluation Criteria

Any evaluation of proposed courses of action should involve some cost/benefit determination. Until now, we have focused on the benefits of improving the business. The objective list gives us a measurement of those benefits. The evaluation criteria also needs to weigh the cost of any given solution.

Costs come in many flavors. The following list includes several cost categories that should be part of any evaluation for an information system. You may have a more detailed list of costs in your organization.

Optimal cost to procure (build or buy)

Optimal cost to implement

Optimal cost to maintain over time

Avoids undue technical risk

Acceptable time to deliver

Feasible with available people and expertise

Add these costs-related items to your list of evaluation criteria. Your team needs to agree on how important these items are in relation to the others on the list. For instance, does *time to deliver* outweigh all others? Will a solution be rejected if the *cost to implement* outweighs the benefit measured by the objectives?

Some companies demand that each project be independently cost-justified. Experience has shown that the first client/server project is several times more expensive than if it were developed using mainframe technology. This makes it very difficult to justify on the basis of one project alone.

So, if the learning curve and technological complexity of this environment is so expensive up front, then why switch? I can't answer that question for you directly. I can offer these observations, however. The move to client/server technology is often driven by powerful, yet mundane forces in the business workplace. The personal computer has clearly won the war for the users' hearts. The sheer multitude of PC packaged software that can be exploited is mind-boggling.

Usually, client/server has to be justified on a far more strategic level, such as re-engineering the business to move data capture and manipulation out of the glass room and out to the frontiers of the organization where people have direct contact with customers, vendors and the product.

Since the first project is going to get hit with an inordinate amount of learning, modeling and technological infrastructure, it makes sense to start small and work up to the big systems, rather than with a big-bang approach. The real benefits occur on the second, third and fourth projects, when, by reusing the people, models, methodology and technology, systems can be developed in a far more productive time frame.

### Additional Evaluation Criteria for Information Systems

In addition to the evaluation criteria related to the benefits of the project's objectives and the costs associated with a solution, there are considerations which are universally applicable to information systems that should be on your list. This is often called the "*-ility*" list because so many of the quality vectors on the list end in "-ility."

Usability

Reliability

Maintainability

Extensibility

Flexibility

Security

Efficiency

Currency of information

Immediacy of response

Ability to communicate with other systems

The items on this list need to be carefully considered. Experiments by Gerald Weinberg[6] have shown that if a programmer is told or perceives that one of these items is more important than others, they will vary the degree to which they meet the others. Many of these quality vectors are in conflict with one another. For instance, a programmer who strives for immediacy of response may not write a program which is easy to maintain or flexible.

Compounding this issue is the fact that the primary quality vector for the application may vary dramatically across the system. The on-line customer service system may require sub-second response time, but the users may tolerate much slower performance in the month-end inventory balance application.

---

6   Weinberg, 1971

Try to avoid sweeping statements in your charter such as "the new system must be user-friendly." Instead, develop a list of measurements of system quality and have the group rate the importance of each item for *each major subject area or sub-system within your scope* (Figure 2–3).

| Qualtiy vector rating:<br>0 = not applicable<br>1 = low<br>2 = medium<br>3 = high | Order entry | Invoicing | Customer service | Ad hoc reporting | Sales forecasting | Production allocation |
|---|---|---|---|---|---|---|
| Ease of training | 2 | 2 | 2 | 3 | 3 | 1 |
| Rapid reponse time | 3 | 2 | 3 | 1 | 1 | 1 |
| Flexibility | 1 | 1 | 2 | 3 | 3 | 2 |
| Conservation of keystrokes | 3 | 3 | 3 | 1 | 1 | 2 |
| User customization | 0 | 0 | 0 | 2 | 3 | 0 |
| Currency of information | 3 | 3 | 3 | 2 | 1 | 3 |

**Figure 2–3.** Quality vector ratings by subject area

You may have noticed, that so far, we haven't talked about hardware. All of the evaluation criteria to this point can be applied to non-automated systems as well as automated solutions. It is important not to bias the evaluation criteria toward purely technical solutions. For instance, if your shop has selected a standard database management system, the underlying quality vector may be to achieve *maintainability and extensibility, ability to communicate with other systems* and *optimal cost to procure and maintain over time.* Standardized development software also *avoids undue technical risk* and is *feasible with available people and expertise* within the department.

When you have compiled your list of evaluation criteria, you should have the following:

A weighted list of criteria which measure the benefit of achieving the tangible and the intangible objectives.

A list of cost, time and risk criteria which measure the resources required to implement any given solution, and agreement over the constraints on the project. The cost criteria also should be weighted for their relative importance.

A matrix of quality vectors for each major sub-system within your scope, which provides technical direction for the user's expectations of the system's performance and behavior.

When finished, each item on the evaluation criteria list should be assigned a weighting which reflects its criticality. Armed with this information, the group is ready to brainstorm various options and will be able to reach consensus on a rational course of action.

## Solution Options

There are many points during a project when you will be confronted with choices. The planning stage is just one of them. Any decision involves trade-offs, and the decision-making framework helps bring focus back to the original objectives of the project so people can make choices rationally. Later in the project, many decisions will have to be made involving the architecture of the hardware and the distribution of process and data across the network. Having a solid charter, and a model of the business as described in the next few chapters will help you understand the engineering trade-offs and make well-informed choices. Without the foundation of the charter, these critical issues are often solved by management fiat, or by "he who shouts the loudest or longest."

Solution options should be brainstormed with your chartering group. Brainstorming rules dictate that any suggestion must be written down, and all evaluation is deferred until the group has finished adding solution options to the list. A good facilitator will guide the group through brainstorming a variety of technical solutions, running the gamut from very high-tech to low-tech implementations. The group should also be encouraged to see if the problem could be solved without a purely technical solution. Sometimes changing the way the business operates and leaving the technology alone is a good fit.

Whatever solution options end up on your list, the first option should always be "status quo." Always measure the cost/benefit of doing something against the baseline of doing nothing at all. Sometimes "status quo" ends up being the best solution.

Let's return to our example of the check printing firm's product development group. Their goal statement was as follows:

> *"Our goal is to reduce the time it takes for the marketing department to validate and complete the specifications for a new product from five days to two days, from the time of receipt of complete information from the sales office to the delivery of accurate, approved specifications to the plants."*

After they developed their objectives and evaluation criteria, they began brainstorming solution options.

### Marketing Department's Solution Options

1. Status quo
2. Hire more people
3. Replace the paper files and filing cabinets with a PC-based on-line database

4. Redesign the paper forms used by the sales people

5. Redesign the work-flow so marketing keys information directly into plant systems

6. Better training of the sales staff

7. Capture data electronically at the source (e.g.: give the sales people laptops), and download data directly to production systems.

8. Combination of #4 (new forms) and #6 (better training)

After an exhaustive list of solution options has been created, it's time to measure which option or options are the best fit to the evaluation criteria. A matrix can be created (Figure 2–4) which lists all of the evaluation criteria and their associated weightings down the left side. Across the top, the solution options are arrayed, with "status quo" in the first column.

| Evaluation criteria | Weighting | Status Quo | Solution option 1 | Solution option 2 | Solution option 3 | Solution option 4 | Solution option 5 |
|---|---|---|---|---|---|---|---|
| **Measure of fit to objectives** | | | | | | | |
| Objective 1 | % | | | | | | |
| Objective 2 | % | | | | | | |
| Objective 3 | % | | | | | | |
| Objective 4 | % | | | | | | |
| Objective 5 | % | | | | | | |
| Objective 6 | % | | | | | | |
| **Assessement of cost / risk** | | | | | | | |
| Cost to procure | % | | | | | | |
| Cost to deploy | % | | | | | | |
| Cost to maintain | % | | | | | | |
| Risk assessment | % | | | | | | |
| Time to deliver | % | | | | | | |
| Feasibility | % | | | | | | |
| **Summary of quality vectors fit** | | | | | | | |
| Quality vectors rating | % | | | | | | |

**Figure 2–4.** Sample evaluation form

I like to list the objective-based evaluation criteria first, followed by the cost-based criteria, then followed by the quality vector criteria. The group can first focus on scoring the benefits as determined by the objective-based criteria. Any scoring system will work as long as it is consistently applied. For example, you can use a rating from zero to five. If a solution option completely satisfies an evaluation criteria, you put a five in the cell where they intersect. If it fails to address the evaluation criteria at all, you write in a zero. If it meets the criteria somewhat, the group will have to determine a suitable score which reflects the degree to which the option fits the criteria. When you're finished, you can weight the scores based on the weighting of the evaluation criteria, and add them up.

### *Estimating Cost*

For cost-based criteria, it is best to use the estimated monetary costs, time costs and resource costs. Since this book's primary focus is on software engineering and not project management, I do not propose to cover cost estimating in great detail. It would take up an entire volume to do it justice. However, within the context of business system analysis, let me offer these observations.

To estimate the cost of any given solution, you will need to have a good idea of the size of the problem. The best way I know to determine the size of a business problem is to do some preliminary analysis. The larger the project, the more important it is to begin modeling the "big three," the context, event and information models, in the planning phases.

Estimating cost begins with finding things you can count. The context model will declare the system boundary and show the interfaces required. Your context model may expose electronic data interfaces or complex integration with existing systems as well as on-line and reporting components. The event model will provide you with a list of all of the major business events to which the system is chartered to respond. This list is crucial to determining the desired functionality of the system. The information model, perhaps, is the most important indicator of system complexity. By determining how many entities are involved in the business problem, the size of the solution can be measured against the cost of similar business systems.

Once you have an idea of the system's size, as expressed by your models, there are a variety of ways to determine the cost of construction or purchase of such a system. Just about anything you can count can be assigned a metric to determine the total effort required to create that object. You can count entities, number of reports, function points, number of windows and so on.

For GUI applications that will concentrate heavily on the creation of the interface and underlying database, I have successfully estimated project size based on number of windows. The number of windows in the interface is particularly relevant to GUI business applications because that's where most of the development effort is expended. The object-oriented structure of a GUI program makes "lines of code" estimating particularly irrelevant.

An estimated number of windows can be extrapolated from the entity count and event list. If you accept that a good GUI application which is responsible for the creation, inquiry, update and deletion of an entity will at minimum need a window to select from multiple instances of the entity, and a window to update a single instance of the entity, then a ball-park estimate for number of windows in a system is "number of entities times two." Other factors that can increase the number of windows are unusual events which are beyond the pale of simple create, read, update and delete functions.

The next step is to beg, borrow or steal some metrics from a similar type of client/server-GUI project. You can divide total effort for analysis, design, coding and testing by the number of windows yielded in the final application to get a "per window" metric.

If your shop has some metrics for software development, you're way ahead of the game. If it doesn't, you can call around to your local user groups, consultants and professional associations to borrow some metrics from other companies.

After you have costed out each of the solution options, you can evaluate them as to their relative delivery cost, maintenance cost, time to delivery and relative risk. The last criteria to apply are the quality vector ratings. Remember that criteria such as *rapid response time* may be applied unevenly across the application, so when evaluating solution options, you must be conscious of for which portions of the system the quality vector is intended.

When the evaluation is finished, your group should be able to agree on a course of action. Sometimes a group will choose a less optimal solution simply because it is expedient. Other times, the more expensive solution will be chosen for long-term strategic reasons. Whatever solution is chosen, the important thing is that the business and the IT organization have arrived at a consensus together. Everyone knows why the project exists, and has a vision of what it should be upon completion.

## THE WRITTEN CHARTER AS A CONTRACT

The majority of this chapter illustrates the process that people go through to reach consensus on the goals and objectives of an undertaking. I feel strongly that understanding the process is more important than the actual structure of the written document that the process yields. I would be remiss in my duties if I didn't tell you how to write it all down, so here's a suggested format for a project charter document. Your actual format may vary depending on corporate standards, however, the content should include the following:

> **The goal.** A written charter should clearly state the goal of the project on the front page.
>
> **The objectives.** Immediately following the goal statement, the project's individual objectives should be listed in clear, concise, measurable terms. The objectives should also be ranked according to their relative importance so every reader is aware of the primary versus secondary objectives.

**The recommended course of action.** The next section should state the recommended solution or next steps. (Some companies will insist on an entire project plan, others may commit only to proceed with business analysis and reconvene another chartering session to determine the optimal design solution.) Included with the overview of the chosen solution, you also should include a review of the evaluation process so the reader understands how the group settled upon the stated direction and which options were rejected.

**Solution scope.** The solution option should include a statement of scope. The scope tells the reader how much of the business is included within the boundary of the project. For this section, you will often need to venture into the next few chapters and produce a conceptual-level context model, event list and entity-relationship diagram. The context model and event list are very good at defining scope. I also find it advisable to include an explicit statement of what is out of scope. This is far safer than implying that a part of the business is out of scope simply by omission.

**Project plan.** Prior to proceeding with analysis, many companies will insist on a project plan. This includes a detailed statement of the methodology to be employed, usually stated in terms of a work breakdown structure. Staffing, budget and schedule can be determined only after the project size has been estimated by doing some modeling.

**Roles and responsibilities.** The roles of both IT and the business need to be spelled out in the charter. Both parties need to execute their responsibilities for the project to be successful. To ensure that the business holds up its end of the bargain, I am very explicit in my charters as to which people are needed and for how long. Go ahead and name names. Also include the names of the project sponsor, business steering committee and issue resolution team.

**Critical success factors.** Any preconditions to success that are out of the control of the project manager must be stated up front. I always reiterate the names of the business people and time commitment required in this section. If acquisition and installation of any new technology is required, it is best to state that the success of the software development is dependent on the successful installation and testing of the hardware.

**Signatures.** Just like any other contract, the charter must be ratified by both parties. IT management and the project sponsor must sign on the dotted line. The most successful projects are those which get business commitment at the highest levels of the organization.

By the time the charter is completed, the analytical process is already well underway. The next chapters will focus on the details of models needed for sound analysis of business information systems.

## SUMMARY

To state it simply, the charter is the *why*, analysis is the *what*, design is the *how*. The charter lays out the justification and objectives for the project. It spells out who the players are and states everyone's roles and responsibilities. It tells the analysts where to start and tells them when they're finished.

The analyst can turn to the project charter and ask, "what are the most important objectives?" That's where you focus your efforts. If your project runs out of time and money, you want to make sure that the most important objectives have been met.

The project charter is the beginning of the analytical process. The project decision-making framework is technique for determining the goals and objectives of a project. Picture the goal as a flag planted on the top of the pyramid. There are many ways to reach the goal. All subsequent activity on the project should be focused to achieve it.

Individual objectives are derived from problem and opportunity statements. An effective way to discover problems is to collect the interested parties together in a room and let them vent about their current situation. The problems and new opportunities can then be converted into objective statements which should be clear, concise and measurable. Since all objectives are not created equal, each objective needs to be weighted in terms of its relative importance.

When attempting to measure objectives, determine if achieving the objective is likely to increase revenue, avoid costs or improve service to your customers. Perhaps the most important task in defining objectives is the search for the elusive *x-factor*. The *x-factor* is the variable that you place in your objective statement to indicate how much of an increase in revenue, reduction of cost or improvement of service is desired. It takes some additional research, but each *x-factor* should be replaced with meaningful, achievable numbers. These become the measurements by which your project will ultimately be judged.

After the objectives are established, they can be quickly converted into a set of evaluation criteria to use for considering solution options. The evaluation criteria should also include cost factors such as time, cost to procure, cost to maintain and a recognition of potential risks. Additional evaluation criteria which measure system quality should be stated for those parts of the system to which they are relevant. Once this framework is established, the project has a rational basis on which to evaluate choices. Solution options are brainstormed and evaluated against the criteria. Once the group has reached a consensus on a course of action, a project plan can be drawn up.

The result of the chartering process should be written down. This document is not meant to be cast in stone for all time. The charter is continually negotiable. If the users demand additional functionality which was not included in the original project charter, then IT now has a basis for negotiation for either more time or resources. (You will find yourself in an even better position if you had specifically excluded the functionality in your statement of scope.)

The importance of a good project charter should not be underestimated. If you readily accept that the quality of a good piece of code can be attributed largely to the quality of its design, then you should be willing to accept that the quality of the design can be traced to a great extent to the quality of the preceding analysis. It is by no means a stretch of the imagination then to state that the quality of any analysis effort is due to the clarity and completeness of its charter.

The charter tells the analyst why they are analyzing the business in the first place. It states which areas of the project are most important and limits the scope to those areas of the business which need to be modeled in order to meet the project's objectives.

## EXERCISES

1. *Old Mother Hubbard's Cupboard* is an old-fashioned family grocery store that has been in business for fifty years in the same street corner building. Mother Hubbard recently retired, leaving the business to her son, Hubble Hubbard. Hubble is considering replacing the old key-punch cash register with a laser-scanning bar-code reader. Using concepts from the project decision-making framework, what should Hubble Hubbard consider before proceeding with the project?

2. Most information systems are designed to **Avoid Costs** and/or **Improve Service**. Systems which are intended to **Increase Revenue** are more rare. What are the two main ways in which a company can increase revenue?

3. Imagine that you are brought on to a project with at least 24 objectives on the list. You are asked to write a concise goal statement. How might you go about it?

4. Name three benefits of doing a project charter.

## ANSWERS

1. Hubble should ask himself what problem he is attempting to solve with scanners. Bar-code scanners are a solution option. Hubble needs to work back up the decision-making framework and state the original problem. For instance, scanners can be used to speed the check-out process. Hubble could examine whether speed of check-out is a problem at his store. It may be that his customer volume is low enough that nobody ever has to wait in line very long. Perhaps Aunt Edna, who runs the cash register, can ring up items by hand just as accurately and rapidly as a scanner. He may also find that Edna also doubles as the town gossip, and most of the neighborhood relies on her for keeping them informed of any newsworthy events — a service that could be seriously impaired by faster check-out. Scanners can also be employed to help track inventory. If Hubble has

an inventory-tracking problem, then he should first state the true nature of that problem and determine to what level he wants to improve his inventory management. Then he should re-examine whether scanners are the most cost-effective solution. Perhaps he should hire cousin Nelson to count the stock after school instead.

2. Revenue is increased by either increasing volume, or increasing price. An information system that affords the business the capability of doing either might contribute to an increase in revenue. It is far more common for business information systems to allow the business to reduce costs, and therefore increase profit margin. Improvement in service to customers is far harder to measure, but can often be thought of as reducing the customer's cost of doing business with your company.

3. The goal statement is a high-level reflection of the most important project objectives. Its purpose is to remind everyone about the project's intended outcome. The long list of objective statements needs to be prioritized by the business members to determine which objectives are more important than others. The objectives should include a measurement (the *x-factor*) which quantifies the desired increase in revenue, reduction in cost, or improvement in service. With the benefits of meeting the objectives quantified, the business can then prioritize the list based on potential payback and/or immediacy of need. Then the goal statement can be written as a summary of the most important objectives of the project.

4. (1) The project charter delineates the roles and responsibilities of both parties, the business and the information technology staff, to the project. It makes it clear that, to obtain the desired benefits of meeting the project's objectives, it will take effort and cooperation on both sides. (2) The charter also prioritizes objectives so that the analysts and designers of the system know which are the most important. That way, they can start analyzing and designing the most critical parts of the system before the money or the allotted time runs out. (3) The charter also provides a means against which subsequent scope changes or requests for additional functionality can be measured and managed. Projects rarely have their requirements "frozen" for the duration of development. When changes occur, the project manager can assess the new or altered objectives against his original or updated cost assumptions and inform the business members of the impact of their new requests.

# CHAPTER

## 3

Context
Model

Interface Prototype

Architecture Model

Database Design

External Interface Design

Internal Component Design

Construction & Testing

# THE CONTEXT MODEL

## INTRODUCTION

This chapter introduces the first of the "big three" analysis models, the context model. While I devote the next three chapters individually to context modeling, event modeling and information modeling, on a real project they are created together, iteratively and often in phases. The veracity of each model depends on the integrity of the other two. The context model defines the scope of your new system. As a diagram (Figure 3–1), it looks deceptively simple. It contains one circle which depicts the entire proposed system as one big process. The boxes around the edges show the people, organizations, customers and other systems which will have to communicate with your new system. The input and output arrows show the flow of data as it stimulates your system into action, and as it leaves your system in the form of a response to the world at large. You can draw a context diagram simply by tracing around your coffee cup. The hard part starts when you begin to name and define the things on your diagram and find that pinning down the exact scope of your project can be a difficult task. The context diagram looks so simple that many projects skip this important step to rush on to the "fun stuff," only to find themselves lost in the analysis wilderness with ill-defined project boundaries. "Scope creep" can be a monumental problem on many real-world projects. The act of creating a good context model lends clarity and focus to the project's boundaries and responsibilities which can go a long way toward helping you control and measure the impact of scope changes as the project proceeds. In this chapter, I will cover data flow diagramming notation, the concepts of expanded and reduced scope, and show you how the context model fits in with the other models.

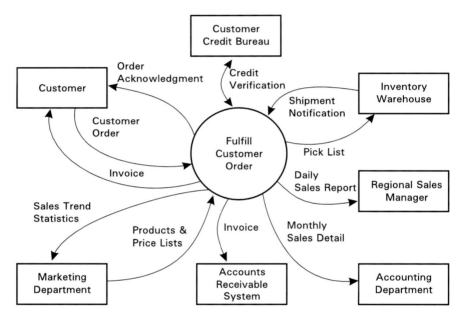

**Figure 3–1.** A context diagram example

## THE PURPOSE OF THE CONTEXT MODEL

General Dwight D. Eisenhower once said, "It's not the plan that matters, it's the *planning*." He was, of course, referring to the Allies' D-Day invasion of Europe in World War II. What appeared deceptively simple on paper had taken years and years of planning and preparation.

The context diagram also looks deceptively simple on paper. It has only one bubble in the center which represents "the system." Classic data flow diagram notation is used to show all of the stimulus flows into the system and their response flows back to the outside world. Agents which are external to the system are shown as boxes. They represent the originators of the stimulus flow and/or the destination of the response flows.

To borrow a concept from General Eisenhower, "It's not the resulting context diagram that matters, as much as the act of doing it." Now, before the rabid defenders of process modeling start lighting torches and coming for me in the night, shouting "blasphemy," allow me to explain.

It is of paramount importance that the project members understand, define and communicate the *scope* of the area of study as early as possible. The act of creating a context model will help you toward that end. Later, we'll see that scope is a relative concept. It is quite likely that the project will have several context diagrams before it is delivered.

The context diagram is less useful downstream in the project when it comes to creating relational database or graphical user interfaces. The information model and event model have far more value in terms of consumption, but beware of skipping the context step! Those other models must work within a specific scope to be effective. The act of creating a context model provides such a boundary.

I call the context, event and information models the "big three." The context represents the whole of the process model. When embarking on a new project, the context may consist of a business area which is a new candidate for automation, or one or more legacy systems that are being expanded, integrated, re-hosted, or completely rebuilt. The event model defines the system's behavior by detailing the appropriate stimulus, activity and response for each business event. The information model contains the static map of data required to carry out the policy for each event. Together, they define the shape of the business through three interdependent views; process, behavior and data.

## DATA FLOW DIAGRAMMING NOTATION

The context model uses classic data flow diagramming notation (Figure 3–2). Data flow diagrams (DFDs) were first introduced in 1979 by Tom DeMarco in his book *Structured Analysis and System Specification*.[1] Data flow diagrams are models which depict the path that data takes through an organization, unbiased by any specific implementation.

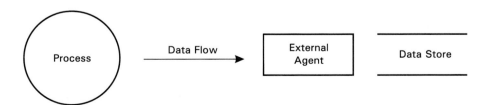

**Figure 3–2.** Data flow diagramming notation

---

[1]  DeMarco, 1979

The primary strength of the DFD notation is that is treats a process as a *black box*. The term *black box* comes from the world of electrical engineering. A black box represents any system with known inputs and outputs, but with the internal mechanism hidden from the user. (This is not the infamous black box from airliner disasters; however, after surveying the wreckage of numerous software projects, I've come to wish I had one.)

A television set is a wonderful example of a black box. The user of the television need not know how it does its magic. In fact, most of us are completely ignorant of the inner workings of our electronic friend. We do know how to use it. As television viewers, we are familiar with the inputs and outputs. What's even more important, the *behavior* of the television is well understood. I know that if I click "4" on the remote control, the program will switch to whatever is currently being broadcast on channel 4. (I also know that if I do this repeatedly, my wife will wrestle me to the ground and take the clicker away from me.)

To the users of business software, the computer application is also a black box. Our users don't care how we get their data onto their screen, or whether their invoices are being created on the client, server or any tier in between. For them, the inner workings of the system remains an enigma. It is useful to begin by taking the user's perspective because it is ultimately a black box that you will deliver.

The notation for the context diagram is very simple. I'll cover the formal definitions as briefly as possible, and then get on to explaining why this seemingly innocuous diagram is so useful for client/server development projects.

There are four primary notations for the context diagram; the circle or ellipse used to represent process, the data flow arrow, a rectangle to depict external agents, and a set of parallel lines to show stored data.

## Processes

Conventional data flow diagramming rules insist that a process be named with a strong action verb, followed by the object to which the action applies. Lower level processes, those which carry out one functionally cohesive activity, are fairly easy to name.

Create customer invoice

Accrue unpaid wages

Ship finished product

Determine vehicle speed

For most business systems, the process bubble on a context diagram is such a potpourri of various activities that coming up with a good name can be arduous. Before you give up and slap the project acronym on your bubble, try to come up with a good verb–object name that describes the entire system. You will find it to be a challenging but clarifying experience that will help you understand what your system is all about.

Try brainstorming several names for your context bubble, being careful to nominate fine, upstanding verbs and relevant object names. Then define the process in a simple, short paragraph of clear text. Include in your definition a brief overview of all of the processes contained within your context scope. You may also want to specifically exclude neighboring process which are not within your area of study. After you are satisfied with the definition of the process, re-examine the names you have nominated and see if one fits, or if a better one becomes apparent.

There are a few rules and assumptions regarding processes. The *law of transformation* states that a process actually transforms the data in some way.[2] The output must be different than the input. Figure 3–3 shows a data flow diagram fragment which violates the law of transformation. The customer order appears to be both input and output of the validation process.

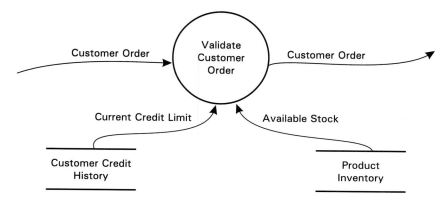

**Figure 3–3.** Inputs and outputs appear to be identical

The apparent violation is really due to sloppy naming. The process, *Validate customer order* has a customer order as input, reads some static approval limits from a data store, and sends out either an invalid customer order or a valid customer order. When we correct the data flow names, we can see that the data has truly been transformed (Figure 3–4).

The *law of conservation* insists that a process bubble's output must be derivable from its input, and furthermore, it should only be given enough information to do its job.[3] Process bubbles are not in the business of forwarding superfluous data on to some other process which will actually use it. In other words, "starve your bubbles." This technique allows you to remove all of the "nonsense" paths that data may follow as it meanders through the current system.

---

[2]   Page-Jones, 1987

[3]   Page-Jones, 1987

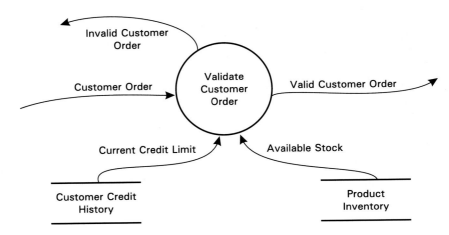

**Figure 3–4.** Corrected data flow names

The purpose of imposing these rules is so the diagram can be used to analyze how data is amended, validated, converted, calculated and consumed within an organization, without regard to any physical constraints of location, speed or storage capacity.

## External Agents

Each party in the environment around the system, that interacts with the system, is shown as a rectangle on the context diagram. I hesitate to give a name for this symbol, because, for some unknown reason it is subject to extreme prejudice of fashion. In the late 1970s, anything sending information into the system was known as a *source* of data. Any party receiving information from the system was known as a *sink*. Apparently, the term *sink* didn't sit well with the industry, because in the 1980s it was quickly changed to *terminator*. You might imagine that this conjured up images of bionic programmers annihilating their way through cyberspace, so both terms were quickly abandoned in favor of *external entities*. This lasted only a few short years until the 1990s where hem lines were shorter, men wore flowered ties and these boxes became *external agents*. It was about this time that I gave up trying to be trendy. I've stuck with the name, external agents, but if you really want to be hip, you can call them *actors*, although by the time you read this, they'll probably be referred to as *business-oriented inter-activity objects*.

External agents are outside of the context's area of study. For this reason, we never show flows between any two external agents. Only data flowing into or out of the system is displayed on the context diagram. External agents are named with a noun. They can represent specific departments or user groups within your business, customers, vendors, shippers, or even other information systems. Each external agent on your model requires a name and a definition.

### Do's and Don'ts of Naming External Agents

I am often asked "are people inside the system or outside the system?" It's a perfectly legitimate question. Even though people go home at night, the activities they carry out at work may exist inside our area of study as processes. Some of their roles may be outside our area of study, and show up as external agents. For instance, in a medical system, a doctor may perform an appendectomy, and also update the patient's records. It is unlikely that you'll be asked to automate the process *Perform appendectomy*, but *Update patient medical history* is a good candidate.

It is inadvisable to put the actual name of a person as an external agent. At Samson Demolition, Inc. (Figure 3–5), everybody in the company may know that Delilah enters customer payments into the receivables portion of the system, but Delilah is not a proper name of an external agent. You could get a very strange diagram indeed, if you discover that Delilah also processes employee medical claims and enters benefit data into the human resources module.

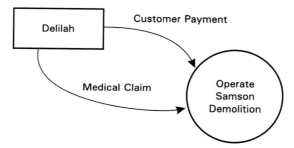

**Figure 3–5.** Don't use a person's name for the external agent

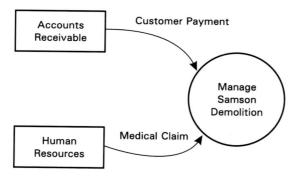

**Figure 3–6.** Instead, use the person's role or function name for external agents

Whenever dealing with people or departments, try to determine the *role* they are playing in any given event (Figure 3–6). As we will see, later in the chapter, it may even be preferable to expand the scope of the context model all the way out to ultimate initiators of the information (Figure 3–7).

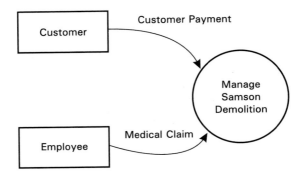

**Figure 3–7.** Initiators of the data as external agents

I'll have a lot more to say about external agents in the section on expanded versus reduced scope. Choosing an external agent can be very complicated and can have important ramifications in the client/server world.

## Data Flows

I like to picture data flows as being made up of individual data attributes, grouped together in packets of information on a conveyor belt. Each time a packet is delivered into the system, the system is required to react in a predictable manner. That reaction may include issuing a response which is likewise a packet of information composed of individual data attributes.

On the context diagram, data flows fall neatly into two categories, stimulus and response. The stimulus flows are the "innies," and the response flows are the "outies." There is no convention that insists that flows travel left to right on a data flow diagram; however, in the western world, people tend to perceive them in this manner. Because of the vast number of flows that are usually represented on a context diagram, it is unlikely that all data will travel neatly in an easterly direction.

The definition of a data flow is critical. It is ironic that the strongest aspect of data flow diagramming is exactly where the technique often falls apart in practice. You must always remember that data flows are made up of *data*. I'm not trying to be glib about this. If the data flows are made up of data, then in which model is data defined? (If you answered *"the data model,"* you win. It's a trick question, since our industry has cleverly changed the name of the data model to the information model.)

Ultimately, you can derive an information model (covered in detail in Chapter 5), by attributing all of the data elements on the input and output flows of your context model to entities on your information model. Furthermore, we'll see in Chapter 4 that the stimulus and response data flows on the context model exist solely to carry out specific business events. Therefore, it is highly unlikely that you'll be able to sit down and draw the perfect context model without getting a good start on the event model and information model at the same time.

The reason that data flow naming and definition becomes so complicated is because data attributes can be grouped together in a fairly arbitrary manner by the modeler for graphical convenience. To illustrate this point, I've drawn the same logical idea several different ways.

In Figure 3–8, a single flow, named *New customer order*, comes into the system from the customer. In Figure 3–9, we have essentially the same information entering the system, but it is shown as two flows, *Customer dossier*, and *New order*.

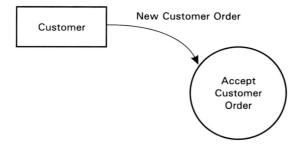

**Figure 3–8.** *New customer order* shown as one data flow

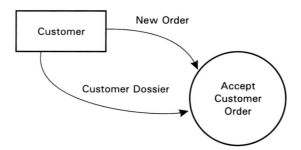

**Figure 3–9.** *New customer order* shown as two data flows

If we peel the top off of our context bubble to see where these flows are going, we find that the customer dossier portion of the data has been routed to the process *Update customer dossier*, and the order information has been routed to *create new order*. To comply with the law of conservation, Figure 3–10 uses a data flow *splitter* or *junction* to separate the flow into two flows so only requisite information is routed to each process. Figure 3–11 already has the flows separated, so they can flow directly into their respective processes.

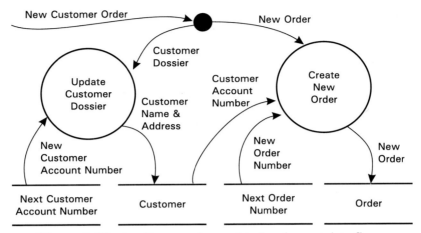

**Figure 3–10.** A splitter can be used to break apart data flows

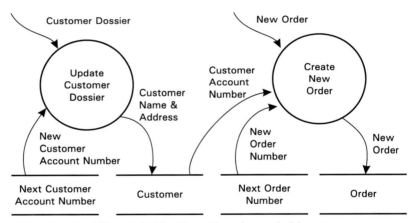

**Figure 3–11.** No splitter is needed here

Either choice is valid. It may seem that keeping the flows separate is clearer, but don't be fooled by the simplicity of this example. On real systems, the data flows become so complex that many of them will have to be bundled together on high-level diagrams to achieve any sense of readability.

Looking at the data definition of our two versions in this example, we see that the data elements contained on these flows are absolutely identical. Figure 3–12 uses a fragment of the information model to define the data and their relationships depicted on *New customer order*. Figure 3–13 shows that the same fragment of the information model has been split into two smaller pieces to define the flows *Customer dossier* and *New order*.

New Customer Order:

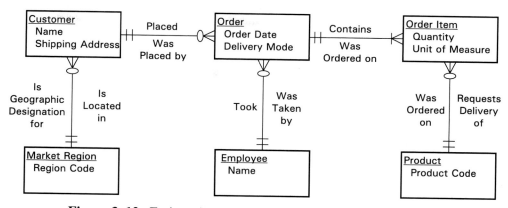

**Figure 3–12.** Entity relationship diagram of *New customer order*

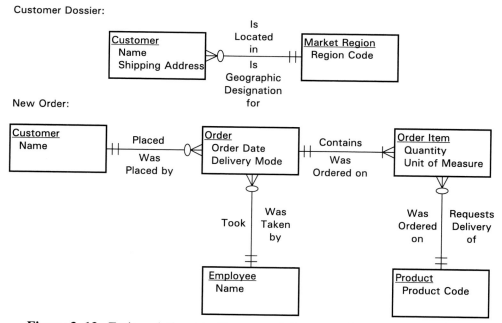

**Figure 3–13.** Entity relationship diagrams of *Customer dossier* and *New order*

No matter how we bundle data flows graphically, it is the data definition which is the most important. You may already have surmised that bundled data flows can defined simply by giving the name of the component data flows which make up the bundle. At some point, however, you *must* define each data flow in terms of the data elements it is carrying. The best way to do this is by using the information model.

## Material Flow

As an information analyst, you will spend most of your time modeling data. There may be some occasion, especially when dealing with manufacturing systems, that you will be confronted with understanding the flow of *material*. Material flows show the actual movement of physical material through a process, while data flows show the movement of data through a process.

When dealing with information systems that track data about material, it is often useful to do a material flow diagram to help you develop the context diagram for the information system. Figure 3–14 shows a material flow diagram for an automated manufacturing process which fills jars with baby food, caps the jars and applies the appropriate labels.

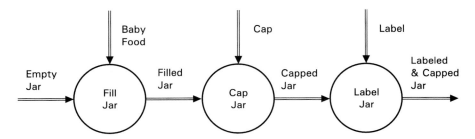

**Figure 3–14.** A material flow diagram

For manufacturing systems, several machines may be employed to handle the material. Any given machine may be capable of providing data to the information system which tracks and controls the automated process. By creating a material flow diagram (Figure 3–15), you can verify your knowledge of the process and establish a basis for communication with your users (who may know nothing about computers, but they've been making baby food for twenty-five years).

By converting the material process bubbles into external agents, we now can establish an automation boundary for an information system, and understand its relationship to the material which it tracks and controls (Figure 3–16).

## Data Stores

Data stores are places in the system where data is remembered when it is not being used. They are shown as parallel lines. In the real world, these can represent databases, filing cabinets, computer memory, or even human memory. Since the dawn of time, it has been decreed, "thou shalt not place data stores on a context diagram." The conventional wisdom is that data stores depict data at rest inside the context boundary.

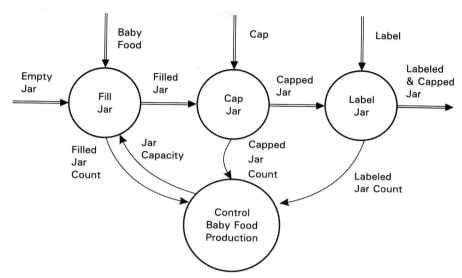

**Figure 3–15.** The data flow may track or control the material flow

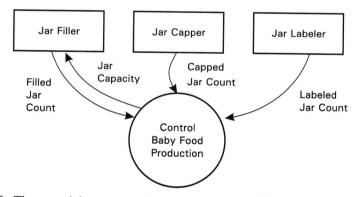

**Figure 3–16.** The material processors become external agents for the information system

There is one instance where I don't mind putting data stores on a context diagram. That is the case of *passive* data stores. If the data flowing into the system is being consumed from a data store over which your system has no control (your system has read access only), then I think it's just fine to show it as a data store. Likewise, you could show it as an external agent. If your system ever updates that data store, then it becomes an *active* data store and you are compelled to move that portion of the data store inside your context boundary (Figure 3–17).

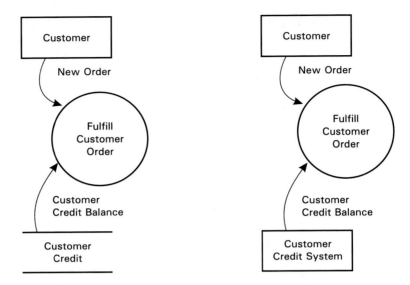

**Figure 3–17.** Two acceptable notations for passive data stores

## NAMING AND DEFINITIONS

You've been given a bubble, a handful of arrows, some boxes and the occasional set of parallel lines. Your task is to describe, on one page, an overwhelmingly complex business system. This is why it is so important that you choose descriptive, meaningful names, otherwise, the diagram can't tell you much. Even if your naming is superb, every person who reads it will form a slightly different opinion about what you are trying to convey. You will need clear textual definitions for every object on the diagram.

Beware of falling into the lazy-name trap. The worst name you can put on a process bubble (aside from no name at all), is *Process data.* We already know it processes data. That's what a bubble does. Similarly, it is inadvisable to put the words *Data* or *Information* on a data flow. You will have squandered valuable real estate and told the reader nothing.

Graphical diagrams alone do not constitute an analysis specification. Nothing replaces clear, concise text. The diagrams provide a structure and organization for the text, but in no way do they negate the need for explanation and definition. The best analysts I have ever had the pleasure to work with all had one thing in common, they excelled at writing.

## TECHNIQUES FOR CREATING THE CONTEXT MODEL

Context diagramming is a lot harder than it looks. It is unlikely that you are going to absolutely nail down the scope of your system by drawing one bubble on a blank page, surround it with boxes and start connecting them with arrows (Figure 3–18). Rather than draw one bubble, I like to draw a "flattened" data flow diagram of the business subject area (Figure 3–19). It's like taking the lid off of the context bubble and exposing the major processes inside. Additionally, I also include neighboring processes that may or may not be within my scope. I find it very useful to make an events list based on my charter (see Chapter 4 for a detailed discussion of event modeling), and let my events list guide me by tracing each major group of events through the business.

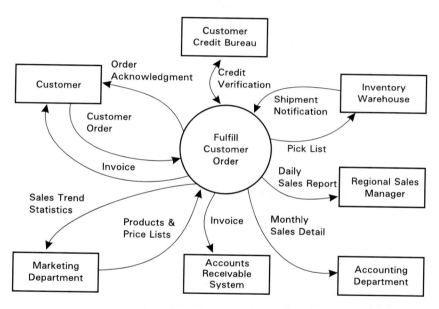

**Figure 3–18.** Sample context diagram for order entry

## EXPANDED VERSUS REDUCED SCOPE

Let's say our charter is to create a new order entry system for Chic Chat Industries (CCI), makers of feline designer rainwear. CCI has typical geographic structure. There are ten regional sales offices around the country and two manufacturing facilities. Corporate headquarters are located on the top three floors of CCI Plaza in downtown Puyallup.

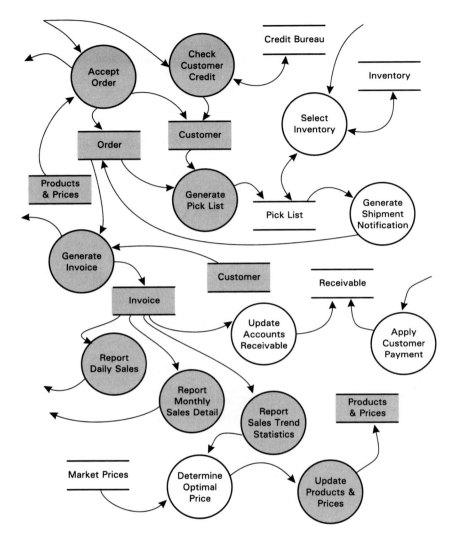

**Figure 3–19.** A flattened DFD for the same subject area

The current order entry system is a COBOL application with a flat file database.[4] There are five terminals located in the corporate office where order entry clerks spend their day keying in orders from paper forms which are faxed, phoned or express-mailed in from the sales offices. On average, it takes about fifteen minutes to enter an order into the system. The key-entry portion can be done in less than five minutes, but the order

---

[4]    COBOL is a third-generation programming language (3GL) which was popular for mainframe business applications throughout the 1960s, 1970s and 1980s. The acronym stands for COmmon Business-Oriented Language.

entry clerks have to spend additional time on the phone clarifying the information with the regional sales office that sent in the order. Each of the five clerks enter about twenty-eight orders in a day. With some quick math, we can see that CCI's total volume is about 140 orders per day (Figure 3–20).

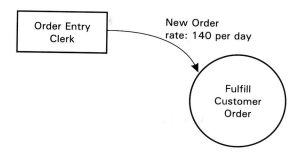

**Figure 3–20.** A context data flow annotated with volume statistics

Over the last fifteen years, this application has been incrementally enhanced, patched and extended to the point where any new change request stabs fear into the hearts of the maintenance programmers. Leopold Morris, vice president of sales, has been enamored with the promise of client/server ever since he read about it in a news magazine on an airplane trip. He wants to deep-six the "dumb terminals" in favor of PCs with a graphical user interface.

We could set our brains to the "off" position and proceed to replace the current technology with fancier technology. Dutifully, we would draw a context diagram showing the order entry clerk as the external agent.

Switching our brains to the "on" position, there are a number of interesting questions that arise: "Wouldn't a set of GUI windows actually slow down the order entry clerk?" "Do we have an opportunity to re-engineer the business process, using client/server technology?" Let's see if we can use the context model to help us explore our options.

Figure 3–21 is an example of a *reduced scope* context diagram. The external agents are the parties which directly transport the information into the system. I like to think of the term *reduced scope* as *reduced options*. You have significantly reduced your options for exploring new ways of doing business.

Figure 3–22 is an example of an *expanded scope* context diagram. The external agents are now the ultimate initiators and consumers of our system's data. The scope of the context bubble has been expanded out to engulf all processes between the data initiators and data consumers. I prefer to create an expanded scope model early in the project to help stimulate new ideas and keep my implementation options open. Client/server technology presents us with a tremendous opportunity to move the traditional automation boundary in our organizations. This cost to re-engineer the business should not be underestimated. It is one of the major hidden costs of introducing client/server.

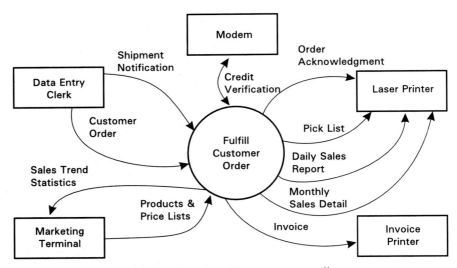

**Figure 3–21.** A reduced scope context diagram

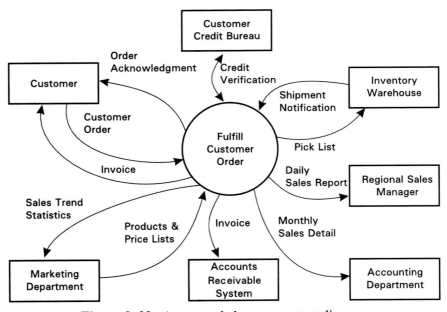

**Figure 3–22.** An expanded scope context diagram

The expanded scope diagram allows us to temporarily ignore who does what, and where it occurs. Now we can delve inside the context and see what data-transforming processes take place for the event *Customer places order.*

What we find is that traditionally there has been a great deal of activity going on at the regional sales offices which fell outside of the old system's domain. CCI's customers are mostly local pet shops and specialty stores. They are visited once a month by a sales rep who attempts to take the order at that time, but usually ends up leaving a catalogue for the store owner. Customers then phone their orders into the regional sales office.

At the sales office, the order is recorded on a preliminary order form. It is standard policy to attempt to sell additional accessories that coordinate with whatever the customer is purchasing. If the customer takes the bait, additional items are added to the order. The order is checked for completeness, the customer's credit standing is checked, and the order is confirmed. In the current system the confirmed order form is sent to corporate headquarters where it is keyed into the system. An order acknowledgment is printed on a line printer and faxed back to the customer.

At this point, you may have already identified some areas for improvement in this business. Many technological limitations from the past have conspired to influence the shape of business organizations today. When the original mainframe order entry system was installed fifteen years ago, it is likely that there would have been tremendous resistance if we had tried to put order entry terminals in the sales offices. Some of the reasons would be due to the available technology at the time. Telecommunications software was immature. Disk space was expensive and traditional character-based screens had very limited real estate. This necessitated the use of cryptic codes and data abbreviations, making the interfaces difficult to learn and use.

Today, our telecommunication capabilities have greatly advanced. Disk space is relatively cheap. Powerful personal computers are widely available, equipped with graphical user interfaces that allow a vast amount of descriptive and pictorial information to be displayed. Our user community is changing too. Nowadays, the PC is a common appliance in most offices, schools and many homes. Virtually any new-hire should already know how to use one.

By moving the order entry process to the regional sales offices, many processes which are currently manual could be easily automated. With a well-designed intuitive interface, the sales people could capture preliminary orders on-line instead of on paper. The volume of orders handled by each office is only one tenth of the volume in the corporate order entry department. The computer could be used to help suggest accessory items that coordinate with the customer's order. Simple editing could validate the order for completeness, as well as do an electronic credit check. By the time the order is confirmed, it's already in the system. We may even explore the possibility of moving the order entry function all the way to the customers.

Our expanded scope diagram also helps us explore possible improvements for response flows. In our reduced scope diagram, the order acknowledgment was sent to the printer. In the real world, each order entry clerk stands up, walks over to the printer, tears off the acknowledgment (being careful not to tear it in half), places it face down on the fax machine, dials the customer's fax number and sends it.

Our expanded scope diagram shows the order acknowledgment flow going directly to the customer. We are now free to explore new technological solutions to this problem. For this situation, there are software packages readily available on the market which can FAX a document directly from the PC, without going to a printer. The new order entry system could look up the customer's phone number and send the document directly to them.

## ONE PROJECT — MANY CONTEXTS

Using the preceding techniques, it is likely that your project will explore many different contexts before settling on the final scope. As your analysis proceeds, your scope may also change. Major scope changes, such as moving data capture out to the field offices also requires rigorous cost/benefit analysis. This type of decision is really part of the chartering phase of the project.

You may start with a reduced scope of the current system, then create an expanded scope diagram showing the ultimate generators and consumers of the data. Later on in the project, as you allocate parts of your model to technology, you may want to create a new reduced scope diagram to depict the context as it pertains to a particular implementation.

There are also some human factors to consider when doing this type of analysis. How do you suppose the order entry clerks are going to react to a context model which clearly eliminates their department? I have seen several projects get themselves into political hot water because no one had prepared the users for the magnitude of change that ensues when a radically new system is introduced. This lack of consideration for the human factors often results in users who begin subversively or overtly obstructing the project by either refusing to participate, or by complaining bitterly about the quality of work being done. Sometimes, animosity quickly deteriorates into open hostility and can actually kill the project. The only way to turn this situation around is to tackle the problem head-on by showing the affected parties what their job will be like when the new system arrives. (Even if they'll be standing in the unemployment line when the new system arrives.) The information technology department is not going to be able to do its job without cooperation of upper management to share the vision of the future with the business, manage user expectations and address their concerns.

## HOW THE CONTEXT MODEL RELATES TO OTHER MODELS

We have already seen how closely linked the context modeling process and the project chartering process can be. For any project contemplating a change to the boundary of the system it is replacing, the context model becomes a crucial element for exploring options and establishing a charter (Chapter 2).

We will see in the next chapter that the context model is directly related to the event model (Figure 3–23), which forms the basis of much of the interface design tasks to follow. Anytime the context boundary is moved, it will alter the landscape of the event model as well (Chapter 4).

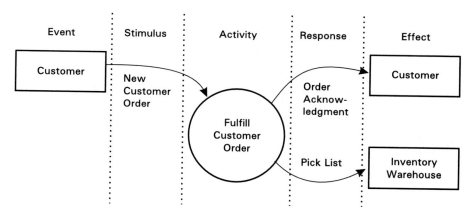

**Figure 3–23.** Events stimulate the system to respond in a predictable manner

When the project's context expands to include geographically distributed business locations, such as the example given in this chapter, then the technical architecture of the target system becomes far more complicated (Chapter 8).

Finally, it is the definition of the data which crosses the system boundary that becomes the system's information model (Figure 3–24). Ultimately, you will have to attribute each data element to its proper entity type, and understand the complex relationships between data (Chapter 5).

## SUMMARY

The context model consists of one bubble in the center which represents the area of study. External agents which fall outside of the control of the system are shown as rectangles. These external agents either send stimulus flows into the system or receive response flows from the system.

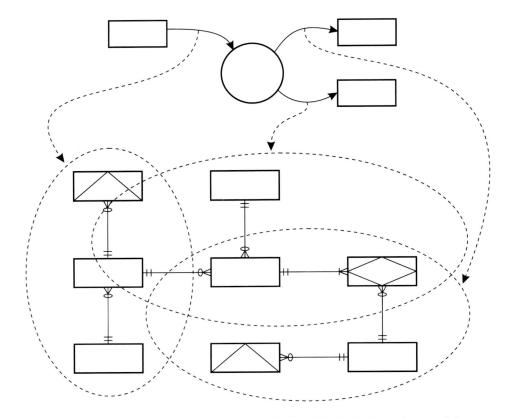

**Figure 3–24.** Data flow elements are defined in the information model

Every object on the context diagram is backed up with clear textual definition. Data flows are further defined by their entities and attributes, which we will cover in detail in Chapter 5 on information modeling.

The process of creating the context model is an important step in exploring the ramifications of moving the automation boundary in any organization. Through expanding and reducing the scope of the context, various scenarios can be explored, and new technology can be exploited to push the capture and presentation of information further out than our former systems were able to accomplish. It is this process of exploration that gives the context model its greatest value.

## EXERCISES

1. Velma is a civil engineer who inspects bridges for the Blither County Highway Department. She carries a clipboard with a pre-printed paper form (Form INSP-B5.2) on which she fills out the bridge number, her county employee

code, and the date of the inspection, checks off items from a list, and makes notes of the bridge's general condition. Each morning, she turns in a stack of completed forms to her cousin Orville, who is the clerk at the county office. Orville divides his morning between entering highway inspection forms into the county's mainframe system and reviewing building permits for the county's unincorporated areas. Blither County is embarking on a project to replace its old mainframe highway inspection tracking system with a modern client/server system. Given what you know of the process, should the external agent which represents the source of bridge inspection data on the context diagram be *Velma*, *Bridge Inspector*, *Orville*, *Clerk*, or *Bridge*? Why?

2. Orville currently manually approves building permits. The new proposed county system will automatically approve 85% of the county's permits within a user-controlled set of parameters. In essence, part of Orville's current job will end up inside the "system." Are people inside or outside of the bubble on context model?

3. Can you think of a system for which you can draw no essential context model? *(Hint: The trick question meter is turned up to "10" on this one.)*

# ANSWERS

1. Velma's role of *Bridge Inspector* is the most appropriate choice for an external agent on an expanded scope context diagram. Orville is not the initiator of the bridge inspection data, and the bridge is incapable of giving the system any information. Furthermore, we don't put people's names on a context diagram. By nominating the inspector as the external agent, instead of the clerk, the project might consider the option of using hand-held devices in the field and eliminating or drastically reducing the data entry function at the office.

2. As strange as this question sounds, I hear it often from people who are drawing their first context diagram. People are outside of the system. Processes and data stores are inside the system. The key is to differentiate between the person and the process he currently performs, or the data store he may possess inside his head. In our example, Orville approves building permits. He manually conducts the process *Approve building permit* by examining some input data (the permit application), checking it for completeness, checking it against a set of parameters or rules that he has memorized and making sure the fee is paid. The process *Approve building permit* can live inside the context bubble, making it inside our area of study and within the scope of potential automation, but Orville, as a person, does not belong inside the bubble. He gets to go home at night. Not all of the processes performed by Orville are in scope. Orville also answers the phone and makes coffee. Unless you intend to include these processes in the new system, it's best to leave them out.

3. The trick part of the question is "essential" context model. The word "essential" has been used in our industry for decades to mean implementation independent. The context model is a top-level view of the system using data flow diagramming as the technique for representation. Data flow diagramming conventions dictate that a process bubble must transform data in some way, not simply transport it. Therefore, applications which only move data from one system to the next will have no essential context model, since they perform no transforming process.

# CHAPTER
# 4

Event
Model

Interface Prototype

Architecture Model

Database Design

External Interface Design

Internal Component Design

Construction & Testing

# THE EVENT MODEL

## INTRODUCTION

Chapter 4 is devoted to the topic of event modeling. Event modeling is a way of defining the system's requirements from a user's point of view. We start by listing the business events for which our users will employ the system. Every event on our event list is given a detailed definition in the event dictionary. The event dictionary lists the data which stimulates the system into action, and the data which comprises the system's response to the event. These data elements are then recorded in the information model, the subject of Chapter 5. Between the stimulus data and the response data, we write a mini-spec definition of what activities the system must do internally to transform the given input into the desired output. The sum of the event dictionary's activity entries form the processing specification for our new system. The event dictionary documents the business policy and rules required to respond adequately to every event in your charter. In this chapter, I will cover the formal definition of an event, and show you how to uncover events as you conduct your analysis. I will provide you with a format for recording the event dictionary for each event, and show you the various ways an event list and event matrices can be organized to aid you in analysis and design. Event modeling is not without its own industry jargon, so dutifully, I will cover different types of events (unexpected, expected, temporal and non-events) and event levels (the conceptual level, business level, dialogue level and design level). Event modeling is a key concept that, when mastered, helps you organize your analysis specification in a manner which is easily consumed in the design of the graphical user interface.

## THE PURPOSE OF THE EVENT MODEL

The purpose of the event model is to describe what is appropriate behavior for a system. It accomplishes this by listing all of the events in the business to which the system is chartered to respond. For each event on the list, an event dictionary entry is created which details the definition, stimulus, activity, response and effect on the business. The event dictionary tells us how the system is expected to behave when the event occurs. It becomes a crucial repository for the business policy which must be executed each time the event occurs.

The event model is completely consumed in the tasks which follow its creation. For the analyst, the event model states the user's business in terms they can easily understand. The event list describes the system from the user's perspective. For the client/server architect, an event model which has been annotated with statistics provides critical information about who uses the system, what data is required at any given time, and how quickly it is expected to respond. For the interface designer, the event model provides the business rationale for navigation and window content. The keystrokes and mouse clicks that are ultimately coded are a direct implementation of the business events in the model. For the internal designer, the business policy stated in the event dictionary provides the rationale for the business logic which will be coded into the system. The event dictionary is the primary place where you will discover the same policy and rules cropping up in different events which lead you to identify and factor out reusable software components in your internal design.

## WHAT IS EVENT-DRIVEN?

If you take a look at the sticker on the shrink-wrap of just about any GUI development tool today, you'll see the claim "Event-Driven." It has become as commonplace in our vernacular as the word "NEW" on a box of laundry detergent. But what does event-driven really mean?

In a graphical-user interface, event-driven means that the program responds directly to mouse clicks and keystrokes *as soon as they occur*. Now, anyone who graduated from high school after 1985 might look at this and say, "duh." For the rest of us dinosaurs, this represents a fundamental change in the way humans communicate with computers.

Hundreds of thousands of mainframe applications still grace the global landscape today, hosted on a technology which has limited portals to the processor. In the traditional "green screen" world, the user types a screen full of data with the main processor blissfully unaware that anything is going on. Only when the user presses **Enter** or a function key does the processor arise from its slumber, get the screen load of data and process it.

Are we led to believe that this technology was oblivious to events? Certainly not! The striking of the **Enter** key or a function key qualifies as a bona fide event (as we will soon see). The distinguishing factor between "green screens" and GUIs is that the sheer number of events recognized by a GUI is inordinately higher than the relatively minuscule number of events recognized by a green screen. This makes the green screen system's morphology favor process-rich structures, while a graphical user interface, although performing the very same processing, will be required to recognize a much richer topography of events.

## WHAT IS AN EVENT?

In a business enterprise, events occur all around us. Customers order products and services, vendors deliver supplies, warehouses ship finished goods, employees go on leave, and so on. Every time one of these things happens out there in the world, the business is expected to respond in some way.

For those of us involved with computers, a good portion of the business activity for any given event may be automated. Event modeling is a way of determining all of the things that go on in the real world that should cause the system to leap into action and do something.

The syntax for stating an event is *Subject-verb-object*. Somebody [subject] does something [verb] to some thing [object]. Later in the chapter, we will see some special types of events which stray from this convention, but the subject-verb-object syntax has proven to be very useful for organizing lists of events.

There are some rules which govern whether any old sentence in subject-verb-object syntax actually qualifies as an event to our system. To achieve membership in the Grand Fraternal Order of Events, a candidate must pass each of the following tests:

1. An event occurs at a moment in time.

2. An event occurs in the environment, not inside the system.

3. The occurrence of said event is under the control of the environment, not the system.

4. The system must be able to detect that the event occurred.

5. The system is supposed to do something about it; meaning it is relevant to the charter of the project.

Failure to comply with any one of the rules is sufficient to disqualify the candidate event.

Notice that this definition relies on the modeler having a clear understanding of what is in the environment versus what is in the system. The list of events for a project will vary directly with any movement of the boundary on the project context model, reflecting any change in scope. This means that as you explore various versions of your project context, the list of events to which the system is chartered to respond will likely be altered as well.

## No Internal Events

This definition does not recognize what some methodologists refer to as *internal events*. Like the context model, the event list assumes a black box point of view. It is compiled from the user's vantage point. Internal events are triggers between two processes inside the system and therefore hidden from the user.

I contend that at this point in the analysis, modeling internal triggers is premature and not relevant to the user. Additionally, the reason any process leaps to life inside our system can be traceable to an external event. We will see later in this chapter that the event dictionary entry for each event provides most of the detail needed to understand requirements for the inner workings of the system.

To be fair to the internal event crowd, let's see how an internal data flow could become a bona fide external event by changing our scope. In Figure 4–1, the process *Add item to order* is executed on the client, and the process *Check customer credit limit* is executed on the server. *Check Customer credit limit* is triggered by a data flow *Validated order item* coming from *Add item to order*.

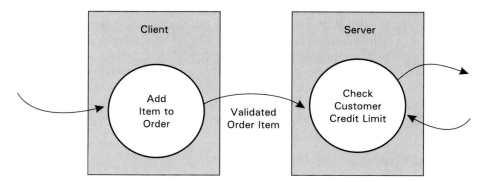

**Figure 4–1.** Two processes inside of the system

During the analysis of the business problem, we do not allocate processes to either client or server. This task is safely deferred until we have a better understanding of the event, data required for inputs, processing or output, frequency, peak volumes and geographic distribution. It appears that the project in our example has progressed into the design phase since someone has decided that *Check customer credit limit* should be executed via a stored procedure rather than running on the client with the rest of the application. If we trace the data flow upstream from this fragment, we undoubtedly will find an event such as *Customer requests additional item.*

If we redraw the context diagram to narrow the scope of study to only those activities carried out by the server, then any formerly internal communications with the server become events which are now external to our narrowed scope (Figure 4–2).

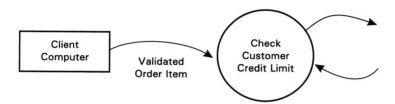

**Figure 4–2.** Context restricted to the server only

With our new context model restricted to the server machine, we can list the event, *Client submits validated order item.* We know this because (1) it occurs in a moment in time, (2) it is outside of the system, as defined by our context (the server), (3) it is not under the control of the system, (4) our process can detect the event, and (5) our system is obliged to react in some manner. When we expand our context back out to the project boundary, this event is subsumed by the system and becomes internal again, dropping off our event list.

## Some Examples of Events

Using a black box example, let's use our knowledge about the common household telephone answering machine to see what is and what is not an event. I'll propose a candidate event, and you can practice using the five criteria to decide whether it belongs on the event list. (Peeking is allowed, but try covering up the answer with a sheet of paper the first time through this exercise.)

*Candidate events:*

1. Caller places call to owner
2. Machine plays pre-recorded greeting
3. Caller falls over

4. Caller hangs up

5. Owner hears message

6. Owner requests messages

7. Owner is not home

*Answers:*

1. *Caller places call to owner* is an event. It occurs, (1) at a moment in time, (2) in the environment around the system. It is, (3) under the control of the environment, (4) detectable by the system when the call is received and (5) relevant to the system charter, in that the answering machine is specifically designed to respond to the call. Congratulations!

2. *Machine plays pre-recorded greeting* is not an event to the system. The playback of the greeting is generated by the system, and therefore, it fails number (2) and number (3), described above. The pre-recorded greeting is an example of a response flowing from the answering machine back to the environment. Responses from the system are not events, however they are evidence that an event has occurred. When you encounter a response flow from the system, trace it back upstream to find the inbound stimulus which caused the system to react. In this case, *Caller places call to owner* is the triggering event.

3. *Caller falls over* is not an event. It does occur at a moment in time in the environment and under the control of the environment, but it fails numbers (4) and (5) in that it is not detectable by the system, nor is it relevant.

4. *Caller hangs up* is an event. My very first answering machine was a big bulky early model in which the machine's designers failed to recognize this event. If a caller hung up during the greeting, the machine didn't turn itself off. When I came home at night, I was greeted with several minutes of recorded dial tone.

5. *Owner hears message.* Sorry, this is not an event. This one is not detectable by the system, so it fails number (4).

6. *Owner requests messages.* This one is an event. It passes all five criteria. The wording is also very specific. It would be very easy to create a definition which describes how the system should behave when this event occurs.

7. *Owner is not home.* This is not an event because it fails number (1). The absence of the owner is a constant state, not a single occurrence. Even if we fix the syntax to read *Owner leaves house*, the event now passes number (1), but fails number (4). When an event fails the test, it may still warrant further investigation. If we dig a little deeper, we find that the analyst was actually groping around for the event, *Owner activates answering machine to answer calls,* which turns out to be a bona fide event that needs to be on the list.

If it seems that I am being overly picky about the name of the event, I am. The most important elements you can put on a model are the words! The words you use convey specific meanings. If the original analyst put *Owner comes home* on the answering machine's event list instead of *Owner requests messages*, who would know what answering machines would be like today? Perhaps our welcome mats would contain electronic devices that blurt out our messages when someone darkens our door. We all know that answering machines don't behave this way, but business systems are far more complex and ambiguous. It is extremely important to get the event named properly so it passes all five criteria in the test.

## THE DELIVERABLES OF THE EVENT MODEL

Business systems are required to recognize a vast number of events. Organizing this wealth of information can be a challenge. The event model consists of two primary deliverables, the *event list* and the *event dictionary*. After the event list is created, a third deliverable, the *event matrices* can be used to relate specific events to other objects in our model of the business.

### The Event List

The event list is exactly what it sounds like, a list of the events to which the system is chartered to respond. The event list catalogues each event by name in subject-verb-object syntax (Figure 4–3). There is no standard graphical notation for an event, nor is one needed. The most readable way to present an event list is by simply writing one event per line.

> **Customer places order**
> **Customer cancels order**
> **Warehouse ships customer order**
> **Accounting invoices customer order**
> **Customer pays invoice**
> **Customer fails to pay invoice**
> **Marketing requests quarterly sales report**
> **Warehouse notifies customer of back-order**

**Figure 4–3.**  A sample event list

The event list isn't just a bunch of words. Each event needs to be recognized in our model as a discrete object which can be related to other, more traditional objects in the model, such as entities, business locations and processes. The event list will also need to be sorted and leveled in a variety of ways in order for it to be truly useful. I'll have more to say about the different ways to dice and slice an event list later in this chapter in the section on "organizing your event model."

## The Event Dictionary

An event list is of little value to the analyst or designer without the event dictionary. The event dictionary entry for each event defines its business relevance and component parts. Figure 4–4 shows an event as it threads its way through the system on a context diagram. This is called an event thread or transaction. It is defined using the event dictionary.

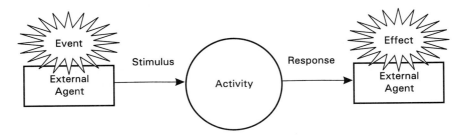

**Figure 4–4.** An event thread

The **event** occurs at a moment in time in the environment, inside the external agent. The system cannot cause the event occurrence; however, we will see later that the system can "bait" the environment for events. The event occurrence is entirely under the control of the external agent. The **stimulus** is the inbound data flow which triggers the event. The **activity** is the processing carried out by the system to produce the appropriate **response**. The response flow consists of data, sent from the system, back into the environment to produce a desired **effect** on the business.

The event dictionary replaces a great deal of the detail that was formerly embedded in the leveled process model in traditional structured analysis techniques. Figure 4–5 shows a sample event dictionary entry for the event, *Warehouse ships customer order*.

The **event id** can be a number, but I recommend against making that number meaningful in any way. A randomly assigned identifier allows you to change the name of the event without changing its identifier. The reader of the event list need not ever see the actual event identifier. Whenever I've tried numbering events chronologically, the method always falls apart as soon as I discover events which can occur simultaneously, or when I forget an event and try to add it in later.

The **event name** is a clear statement of the event in words that the user can understand. It is stated in subject-verb-object syntax whenever possible. We will soon see that this enables us to sort our event lists by subject, or by object. You may want to identify the subject and object of each event as separate properties to facilitate this type of sorting later on.

| Event ID: | 150 |
|---|---|
| Event name: | Warehouse ships customer order |
| Description: | When the warehouse ships finished goods to the customer, the trucking company is identified and the quantity shipped for each item is updated on the customer order. If the total quantity shipped equals the quantity ordered, then the order item is closed out. If all items of the order have been completely fulfilled, then the entire order is closed out. Orders are not typically invoiced until they are fully closed. A trucker's bill of lading is produced by the system to accompany the shipment. |
| Stimulus: | Customer order identification<br>Trucking company identification, vehicle number<br>Ship date, order item shipped, quantity shipped |
| Activity: | Create an instance of order-shipment using customer order id, trucking company id, ship date and vehicle number<br>For each item shipped<br>    Create an instance of order-item-shipment using order<br>    item id and quantity shipped.<br>    If the sum of the quantity shipped for every order-item-<br>    shipment associated with the order item > = the order<br>    item's ordered quantity,<br>        Update order item status = closed<br>    End if<br>End for each<br>If order item status = closed for all items on the order<br>    Update order status = closed<br>End if<br>Print bill of lading using customer ship to, order shipment, order shipment items, trucking company. |
| Response: | Bill of lading |
| Effect: | The trucker can leave the premises once he has a bill of lading in hand. If the order has been fully closed out, then the customer's order is ready to invoice |

**Figure 4–5.** A sample event dictionary entry

The **event description** informs the reader, in clear and simple terms, of the event's business policy. If the users read no further than the description, they should be able to verify whether you've captured the essence of their business. The event description is also reused downstream in the design documentation. For example, when you design a window layout, just like any other object in your model, you have incurred an obligation to define it. The core of any window layout definition is the description of the events which are recognized by that window. There's no need to retype all of the business policy in the design, testing, help and training documentation. Simply steal it from the analysis models, and add the physical design elements.

The **stimulus** section of the event dictionary identifies the data required to trigger the event. All events need some sort of input data flow. This may either take the form of a classic data flow containing discrete data elements, or a control flow, which contains no data, only a message from the environment telling the system to "do it." In the example, we don't have to feed all of the information about the customer's order back into the system. It's already in there, presumably due to a predecessor event *Customer places order*. The stimulus suggests that the order only needs to be identified, and the relevant information from the order can be retrieved by the activities that need it.

The stimulus is *data*. We find this data represented in at least two other related models. On the context diagram, the event stimulus may be represented as one or more data flows into the system. Be careful not to assume that there is a one-to-one correlation between data flows and event stimuli. Data flows can be arbitrarily bundled for graphical convenience on the diagram, but the event stimulus must be very specific to the event at hand. The primary model in which data is defined is the information model. In the next chapter, we will see that all of the data on the stimulus flows, combined with all of the data on the response flows, comprise the system's information requirements.

The **activity** occurs inside the system. This is all of the *processing* that the system must do to convert the stimulus input into the appropriate response for the event. The activity section should look very familiar. It's a process *mini-spec*. There are a variety of ways to document the activity for an event.

In the example in Figure 4–5, I chose to write a short mini-spec, using a pseudo-code style to convey the business policy for the event. For many simple events, all you need is a brief mini-spec and the information model, and you have enough to proceed with prototyping and design. For more complex events, you'll need to define the process in more detail.

For our sample event, *Warehouse ships customer order*, I could have drawn an *event-neighborhood diagram* to specify the activity section. Any solid process modeling technique will work. Data flow diagramming is extremely useful for breaking down complex processes into understandable components. Figure 4–6 shows an event-neighborhood diagram for *Warehouse ships customer order*.

For each symbol placed on the data flow diagram, the modeler incurs an obligation to define it. The data flow diagram graphically depicts the overall process for the event activity, and allows you to partition the activity into manageable pieces by writing a mini-spec for each primitive process on the diagram. In practice, I find that the event-neighborhood diagram is only needed when a detailed mini-spec for the activity section begins to exceed several pages of text. For this example, a lexical activity section should suffice.

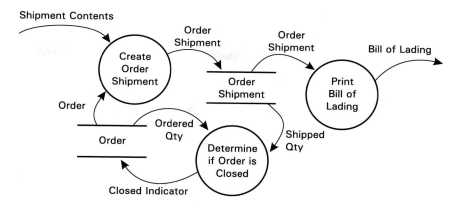

**Figure 4–6.** An event neighborhood diagram

This approach of employing the event model to define a system's process requirements differs slightly from some historical process modeling techniques, however it is solidly rooted in early work by McMenemin and Palmer.[1] The processing required by today's GUI and client/server systems is no less complex than the mainframe systems of old. In fact, these systems do far more in the way of on-screen editing, validation and general user-helpfulness than green screens ever could. When you toss in the likelihood that a system today will automate more of the business than ever before, you've got a significant amount of "processing" to understand. The difference in GUI applications is that much of the processing is far more fragmented than before. Users can execute individual pieces of the business policy by clicking on their window. They don't have to wait until they hit the Enter key.

In my own experience developing large-scale client/server business systems, I have found that the activity section of the event dictionary adequately covers a large proportion of the process model of the information system. There may come a place in any system where the richness of the processing requirement rises above the point where a textual specification alone is no longer adequate. There are a variety of well known, tried and true process specification techniques available. I see no reason to invent a new one. The role of data flow diagramming has diminished in recent years, but the technique can be very useful for imposing an organization on very large systems, or when clarifying particularly complex internal procedures. The data flow diagram makes no assumptions about which program or object will eventually house any particular portion of the business policy, and for that reason alone remains a valuable technique for capturing the essential business requirement prior to designing an implementation strategy.

---

[1]  McMenamin, S. M., and Palmer, J. F., 1984.

The activity section of the event dictionary is neutral as to the target language of the project. Later, in the design phase of an object-oriented implementation, the activity section for each event can be converted into an *object-communication diagram* to depict how activity has been mapped onto object classes (see Chapter 12). The activity section of the event dictionary gives the object-oriented designer much of the analytical basis for creating what some techniques refer to as the *event-trace model* or *dynamic object model*.

The activity section of the event dictionary has proven to be an effective place to document business rules. Let's digress for a moment to a different example to illustrate how you might use the event dictionary to record business rules. Let's say that Dick is married to Jane. Jane is a manager of projects. Dick works on projects as an employee at the same company. There is a business rule that states, "no employee shall manage a project on which his/her spouse is employed, nor shall an employee be assigned to a project on which his/her spouse is a manager." In our analysis, we quickly find at least three events that need to check this policy:

> Employee is assigned to project
>
> Manager is assigned to project
>
> Employee marries manager (and vice versa).

By finding more than one event which carries out the same policy, you have identified a place in the system where the policy could be factored out into a reusable component. In the application design, this policy could be implemented as a separate *Marriage monitor* object in an object-oriented system, or it could be coded as a stored procedure on your database server, or even be designed as a callable library module or function in a more traditionally-structured system. At this point in the analysis, you may elect to record the rule as its own process mini-spec and simply reference it from each event activity section (e.g.: "invoke employee/manager marriage rule"), or leave the policy fully spelled out in each event dictionary entry and comb through your events later, as a separate step with the purpose of locating all potential reusable procedures.

Some simple business rules are very data-centric (e.g.: start date must be greater than or equal to end date), and can fit nicely into your attribute definition in the information model (covered in Chapter 5). Other business rules are more process-centric, and difficult to model using traditional entity-relationship diagramming. Some information modelers advocate a semantic modeling notation which allows you to identify relationships as being mutually exclusive. This works, but tends to add a layer of complexity to the information model that can make it hard to manage on a large scale. Some object-oriented analysis advocates assign business rules directly to objects. I view this as a decision involving design trade-offs and therefore premature in the discovery phase. My preference is to record business rules in the activity section of the events which invoke them.

The **response** section of the event dictionary identifies the *data* required by the user to achieve the desired effect on the business environment. From our user's black box point of view, if you put the stimulus in, you expect a particular response back. Our example in

Figure 4–5 shows a bill of lading as the desired response to the event *Warehouse ships customer order*. Reports, either printed or visually displayed, are typical response flows for business systems. The best way to specify a report is by using a picture of the desired layout and an information model to show how the source data is organized.

Event responses will also show up on the context model, but beware, just like stimulus flows, there is not a one-to-one correlation between a response and an outbound data flow on the context diagram. Many events have decision points which could produce one or more different responses for the same event.

Other events, such as those that simply update internally stored information in the system may have no response flow noted on the context model. An example is a table update event such as *Marketing adds new product*. This event inserts a new instance of product, but there is no apparent response from the system other than to acknowledge that the new product record was saved successfully. In these cases, I like to write "save acknowledgment" in the response section of the event dictionary so the reader knows that I haven't omitted an important response.

The **effect** is the desired post-condition of the environment after having received the response. Like the event, the effect also occurs in the environment. The effect is not part of the automated system, but is of paramount importance to our users. The entire purpose of the system is to produce the desired *effect* in the real world. As technologists, we must never lose sight of the reason we've been employed in the first place. If the business users could get directly from the event to the effect without involving any bothersome computers or programmers, they would be absolutely delighted.

## Event Matrices

Once you have an event list for your project, there are a number of matrices that can relate events to other parts of your business model. I'll cover event matrices in more detail in Chapter 8 on architecture, but I want you to get an idea of where I'm going with this.

Most large businesses operate more than one location. These various locations can be housed in the same building, or may be flung clear across the globe. The whole idea of enterprise client/server computing is to link all of the locations of the business together into one apparently seamless network of computing capability. An important element in this endeavor is understanding which events occur where.

Events can play a key role in determining the data and process distribution requirements for a client/server system. The *event/business location matrix* (Figure 4–7), shows which events are to be recognized at each business location. This tells you that these locations will need access computing capability to capture these events.

The *event/entity CRUD matrix* (Figure 4–8) shows which events create, read, update or delete (CRUD), instances of the entities in your information model. This matrix gives you a good overview of the data operations required to properly respond to each event. By examining the event/entity CRUD matrix, you can see which events perform similar or identical actions on their respective entities, and use this information to identify procedures and rules that would be good candidates for coding as reusable software components. If you find six different events which create or update customer addresses, the rules which ensure the accuracy of addresses should be coded only once. (For example, you might have a restriction which states that post office boxes may not be flagged as a ship-to address, or a rule which makes state or province a required field for cities within the United States or Canada, but optional for all other countries.)

| Event/Business location | New York, NY HQ | Boise, ID Sales | Miami, FL Sales | London, UK Sales | California Plant | North Carolina Plant |
|---|---|---|---|---|---|---|
| Customer places order | X | X | X | X | | |
| Credit dept. approves order | X | | | | | |
| Prod. dept. assigns order | X | | | | | |
| Plant fills customer order | | | | | X | X |
| Plant ships customer order | | | | | X | X |
| Accounting invoices customer order | X | | | X | | |
| Marketing mails catalogue | X | | | X | | |

**Figure 4–7.** An event/business location matrix

| Event/Entity | Customer | Order | Order item | Plant order | Plant order item | Finished goods invt. trns. | Raw materials invt. trns. | Invoice | Invoice item |
|---|---|---|---|---|---|---|---|---|---|
| Customer places order | CRU | C | C | | | | | | |
| Credit dept. approves order | U | RU | R | | | | | | |
| Prod. dept. assigns order | R | R | R | C | C | CR | CR | | |
| Plant fills cust. order | R | R | R | RU | RU | CRUD | CRUD | | |
| Plant ships cust. order | R | R | R | RU | RU | | | | |
| Acctg invoices cust. order | R | R | RU | R | RU | | | CRU | CRU |
| Marketing mails catalogue | R | | | | | | | | |

**Figure 4–8.** An event/entity CRUD matrix

Since you now have an event/business location matrix and an event/entity CRUD matrix, through Boolean matrix multiplication, or by simple inspection, you can derive a *business location/entity CRUD matrix* (Figure 4–9), showing the data distribution requirements for the business. This matrix, combined with the constraints of the available technology, gives the client/server architects much of the raw data they need to determine whether data access for any given business location will need to be local, remote, or some combination of the two.

| Business location/Entity | Customer | Order | Order item | Plant order | Plant order item | Finished goods invt. trns. | Raw materials invt. trns. | Invoice | Invoice item |
|---|---|---|---|---|---|---|---|---|---|
| New York, NY HQ | CRU | CRU | CR | C | C | CR | CR | CRUD | CRUD |
| Boise, ID Sales | CRU | C | C | | | | | | |
| Miami, FL Sales | CRU | C | C | | | | | | |
| London, UK Sales | CRU | C | C | | | | | CRUD | CRUD |
| California Plant | R | R | R | RU | RU | CRUD | CRUD | | |
| North Carolina Plant | R | R | R | RU | RU | CRUD | CRUD | | |

**Figure 4–9.** A business location/entity CRUD matrix

# UNCOVERING EVENTS

Discovering events is easy once you make the mental shift from viewing every problem from an internal processing point of view to seeing the system from a stimulus/response perspective.

## User Interviews

Users will blurt out events faster than you can write them down. The only problem is that users don't typically converse in a neat and tidy subject-verb-object format. A clerk at the receiving dock might say something like, "Acme Supply Company sends a red delivery truck over every Tuesday morning. Bob puts the yellow copy of their tally sheet on the top of my 'in' basket. After lunch, I key the tally sheet into the GURBNIT system."

The business analyst quickly converts this to *Vendor delivers supplies* and writes down the event and a description based on the user's vignette. He then acquires a copy of the tally sheet to examine the data elements which comprise the event stimulus. The next logical question is to find out what the GURBNIT system does with the tally information, what is the user's desired response and subsequent events. The savvy analyst will always ask the user if anything is inconvenient or wrong with the current process, and be on the look-out for new opportunities.

On larger projects, or one where consensus-building is key factor, the analyst may elect to conduct formal JAR sessions (joint application requirements). During these meetings, the first-cut event list and information model are elicited from a selected group of users by a facilitator in a series of group sessions and break-out exercises. For more up-close-and-personal analysis, a great way to uncover events is to sit with the users and watch them do their job for a while. For users who may have problems with the more formal abstractions of analysis, a simple paper prototype can be used to elicit requirements for both the event and information models.

## The Charter

A well-crafted charter will include a set of events at the conceptual level. The event list which typically is included in a charter document paints the system's responsibilities in fairly broad brush strokes. The business analyst inevitably discovers more events and more variations on events during detailed analysis. If your charter doesn't include an explicit list of events, there is undoubtedly evidence of events throughout the document.

Project charters often include a section that I refer to as the "commandments." This is usually a list of requirements beginning with the phrase "The system shall . . . ." Consider these as erstwhile events just waiting for some enlightened analyst to discover them. For example, the charter might say, *"The system shall print a receipt for each cash transaction."* Using what you know of events, what component of an event is the receipt?

A printed receipt is the desired *response* from the system. If the receipt is the response, then what's the event? Somebody, at sometime, is expected to submit a cash transaction to the system, and it looks as though the system is supposed to do something about it.

## Existing System Documentation

If you're lucky enough to have documentation for the legacy systems that you're replacing, you can bet that they're full of events. Every input screen or report represents stimuli and responses, evidence that a business event occurs. Any existing test scripts that might be excavated from the system library should do a good job of mapping the stimulus to the expected response.

## The Context Model

You can also derive events from other existing models. If you already have a context diagram for your system, you can determine the event or set of events which account for every stimulus data flow into the system, and any response flow out of the system.

## The Information Model

Events can even be derived by "interviewing" an information model. If your system is chartered to remember any given data element, some event must put it there. Figure 4–10 shows a small fragment of an entity-relationship diagram (discussed in detail in the next chapter). We can ask ourselves, "What events account for every symbol's existence on the diagram?" We may surmise that a new instance of *Order* is created when the event *Customer places order* occurs. Examining the cardinality that says an order is placed by one and only one customer, we know that the relationship "Customer *placed* Order" is also created at the same time. Now that we've established how an order is created, we can broaden our search for events by asking which events update orders, and start looking for any events which delete orders.

**Figure 4–10.** ERD fragment for the event, *Customer places order*

The cardinality on the right side of the relationship is also a clue to possible events. The information modeler has indicated that a customer may place zero to many orders. The zero is particularly interesting because it implies that an instance of customer can be created without a corresponding instance of order. It may be that this company solicits potential customers with a high probability that they'll place an order. Perhaps they record the customer information, but don't accept an order until the customer passes an authorization procedure. It also might imply that all of a customer's orders could be deleted, without removing the customer. Whatever the reason, the event list should be able to account for anything you see in the information model. If you find entities, attributes or relationships in your information that you can't explain, then you've either missed some events, or your model is in error.

## EVENT TYPES

Events can be classified into several types. Understanding the pattern associated with each event type gives the analyst an added advantage when determining the appropriate behavior for the system, and aids in discovering subsequent events.

Certain types of events have similar characteristics and patterns. Pattern recognition is one of the key elements to reusability. By detecting a familiar pattern that we have seen before, we can reuse our knowledge about the pattern. Reuse isn't just applicable to code. It also applies to business models. In fact, much of the reuse that can be leveraged in an application development project comes from having a *model* of the business problem. Patterns are far more recognizable in models than they are in the installed source code.

## Unexpected Events

The vast majority of events in business information systems are *unexpected*. An unexpected event means that, for any given instance of the event, the system never knows when it will happen, or whether it will happen at all. The granddaddy of all unexpected events for most businesses is *Customer places order*. (The Marketing Department can get rather defensive at this statement and argue that there is a statistical likelihood that any given customer will place an order within a certain time frame. Unless the system is actually chartered to make this prediction, *Customer places order* remains an unexpected event.)

Examples of unexpected events include:

Customer places order

Customer cancels order

Acquisition department purchases new plant

Management requests ad hoc sales report

Marketing department introduces new product line

Sales department announces price increase

The key characteristics that these events have in common are that the system has no responsibility for predicting or prompting for their occurrence. If they never happened, the system would just lie around all day doing nothing. When they do happen, however, the system is supposed to leap to life and do something interesting.

## Expected Events

For an *expected* event, the system has some window of expectation in which it anticipates that the event should happen. An event becomes expected when a predecessor event has set up a deadline within the system before which the expected event should occur. The event still occurs outside of the system, in the environment. The only difference is that the system can identify the particular instance or instances of the events for which it is waiting.

### Temporal Events

The most common type of expected event found in business systems is triggered by the passage of *time*. Time-triggered events are called *temporal events*. Temporal events are always expected because some predecessor event must establish the schedule inside the system. Think of the schedule as the timer. The timer can be set on an *absolute* basis, so that the event is scheduled to occur at a particular date and time, or it can be set *relative* to another event.

Temporal events break the subject-verb-object event naming convention. They are typically named "*Time to [do something]*" (Figure 4–11).

| Event name | Description | Schedule |
|---|---|---|
| Time to create monthly statements | On the last day of each calendar month, the Accounts Receivable Dept. sends out monthly statements to all customers with non-zero balances. | Absolute, Last day of each month |
| Time to notify plant of vessel sailing | Five days prior to scheduled vessel sailing, a final listing is sent to the production plant, showing all orders which must be on the dock. | Relative, Five days prior to scheduled vessel sail date |
| Time to send customer oil change notice | If the customer hasn't returned within 80 days of their last oil change, a reminder notice is mailed to them. | Relative, 80 days after last oil change service. |

**Figure 4–11.** Examples of temporal events

### Event Recognition

Temporal events are particularly interesting because the system has to do some extra work to determine that the event occurred. Figure 4–12 shows the typical pattern of an indirectly recognized event. A schedule has been previously established in the system. The process plays the role of *event recognizer*. It must periodically read the schedule and check it against raw input data from the environment. When the system has determined, based on the input flow and the schedule, that the event has occurred, it leaps into action and fires off another process to manage that event's activity.

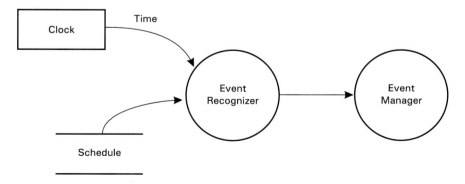

**Figure 4–12.** DFD for an indirectly recognized event

In the case of temporal events, the input flow is *Time*. Even though your computer system contains a clock, the system itself does not control the passage of time. It has been a long-standing tradition in context modeling that we don't show a data flow called *Time* coming into the system. It is declared to be universally available to all information systems.

Indirectly recognized events are not limited to temporal or expected events. Although this book is aimed primarily at the development of business information systems, the concept of events has its roots in real-time systems. Real-time systems are used in the control and monitoring of machinery and have a much richer set of event recognizers than business systems. Events in real-time systems might be set in motion by rise or fall of pressure in a tank, or a product reaching a checkpoint in the production line. These events may be expected or unexpected.

Most of the events in an on-line information system will be directly recognized. This means the onus is on the user to tell the system that the event has happened. Direct event recognition will usually manifest itself as a command button or menu item on the application window.

### The "Non-Event"

The full name for a *non-event* is "the non-occurrence of an expected event." In simple terms, a non-event "occurs" when an expected event fails to occur. On the surface, this appears to violate the first test for an event, "*the event occurs.*" That's why the sentence reads, "*An event occurs at a moment in time.*" It's the "*moment in time*" clause that allows us to keep non-events on our list. For a non-event to pass the event test, its failure to occur must be detectable by the system at a moment in time. The occurrence is determined by the expiration of the time frame, coupled with the failure for the event to present itself at the system's doorstep.

The system cannot create events. The effect of one event, such as *Billing Department invoices customer order* may bait or entice the environment for the next expected event in the chain, *Customer pays order*. Although the system sets up a window of expectation (such as 30 days from invoice date), there is no guarantee that the customer is going to pay the invoice. It is this type of pattern that produces the non-event.

Non-events must have a companion expected event. Like all expected events, they are preceded in time by some other event which has established the expectation. Non-events are often overlooked and omitted from the event list, but they are very important. Quite often, you will find much more complex business policy attached to the non-occurrence of an expected event than to its run-of-the-mill occurrence.

The event *Customer pays invoice* is a ho-hum affair for most systems. The accounts receivable clerk applies the payment and the outstanding balance is reduced. If *Customer fails to pay invoice* occurs after thirty days, the system may have to accrue late charges and send out a polite reminder. If *Customer fails to pay invoice* occurs after sixty days, more late payment interest is accrued and a less than polite reminder is sent out. If the customer still hasn't paid after ninety days, the system may be required to notify the acquisition department for some midnight asset reclamation.

Each event on the event list should be classified as unexpected or expected. For the expected events, you should always ask, "Does the business care if it doesn't happen?"

If the system is responsible for the policy associated with the non-event, it is likely that you will have to do a great deal more work on your project. If the system is not responsible for detecting the non-event, I make a note of it in the event dictionary of the companion expected event. This lets other project members know that the question has been raised and answered.

## Review of Event Types

Events fall into two major types; *unexpected* or *expected*. Most of the events in an on-line business information system will be unexpected. Real-time systems deal with a significantly higher number of expected events. The classification into these two categories is important because it systematically leads the analyst through a set of questions:

> Is the event *unexpected* or *expected*?
>
> If the event is expected,
>
>> Is it a *temporal* event expected *relative* to another event or at an *absolute* time?
>>
>> Does the system care if it doesn't happen (the *non-event*)?
>>
>> What is the predecessor event which establishes the expectation?
>
> For either unexpected or expected events,
>
>> Is the environment (*direct recognition*) or the system (*indirect recognition*) responsible for recognizing the event?
>>
>> What are the predecessor events in the chain?
>>
>> What are the successor events in the chain?

Asking these questions will help you create a more complete model of the system's desired behavior. The distinction between unexpected and expected events will also assist you in determining the proper chronological sequence of events when you begin organizing your event list.

## ORGANIZING YOUR EVENT MODEL

The event model will be completely consumed in all of the subsequent steps of analysis, design and testing. The event model represents a fundamental shift in the organization of business requirements. Traditionally, the hierarchical process model was the primary structure for housing requirements.

The process model was represented as either a decomposition diagram, or a leveled set of data flow diagrams. During the design phase, these essential processes were transformed into a structure chart, which provided an organizational map of the 3GL programs that would be constructed. The shape of the hierarchical analysis model was largely driven by the shape of the chosen solution. Monolithic process-driven programs were easier to design if the analysis models conformed to the same morphology.

As an example, Figure 4–13 shows a typical green screen layout for entering customer discounts. This screen is used to establish discount percentages for a specific customer, for a specific product line. The user types in the customer number, the product line code, the discount amount and associated dates, sales rep. code, and up to four lines of special instructions. When they are through typing, they either press Enter, a function key, or type a string on the command line. Only then does the computer's processor recognize the need to edit, validate and store the information on this screen. The accompanying program running behind this screen might have a structure chart that looks roughly like the one in Figure 4–14. Since the prime deliverable for the programmer was a large program, the structured design and preceding structured analysis models reflected this bias and were organized to be easily consumed by the programmer.

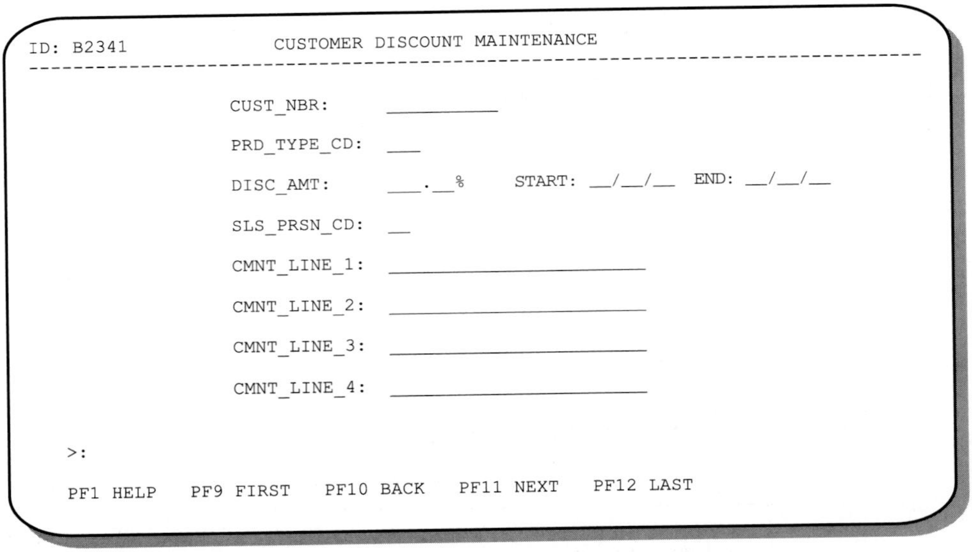

```
 ID: B2341              CUSTOMER DISCOUNT MAINTENANCE
 ---------------------------------------------------------------------

                    CUST_NBR:         _____

                    PRD_TYPE_CD:      ___

                    DISC_AMT:         ___.__%    START: __/__/__  END: __/__/__

                    SLS_PRSN_CD:      __

                    CMNT_LINE_1:      _____

                    CMNT_LINE_2:      _____

                    CMNT_LINE_3:      _____

                    CMNT_LINE_4:      _____


   >:

    PF1 HELP    PF9 FIRST    PF10 BACK    PF11 NEXT    PF12 LAST
```

**Figure 4–13.** Green screen for *Customer Discount Maintenance*

Now imagine taking the large program represented by the structure chart in Figure 4–14 and tearing it up into little pieces, loading it into a shotgun and firing it at a window. The result would be little snippets of code, fragmented like buckshot, scattered among all of the objects contained on the window.

Figure 4–15 shows the same customer discount maintenance application hosted on a GUI window. What once was a structured, predictable program has been broken up into little bits of code which may be independently executed at the user's discretion simply by typing or clicking the mouse.

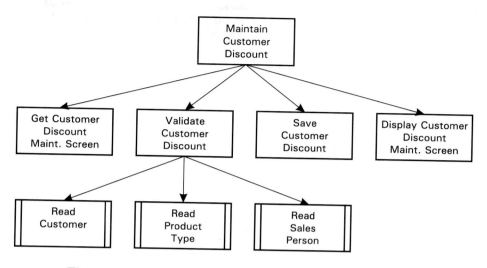

**Figure 4–14.** Structure chart of *Maintain Customer Discount*

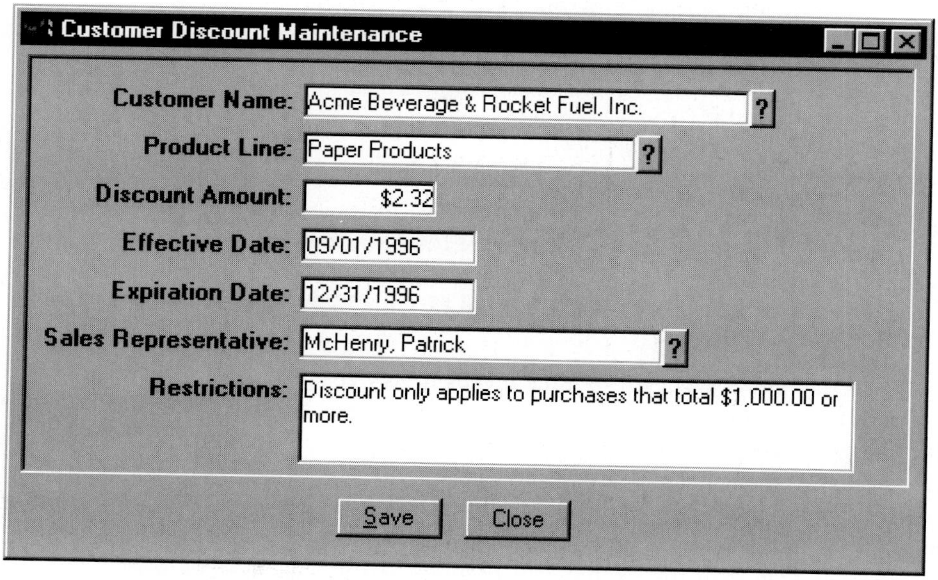

**Figure 4–15.** GUI window for *Customer Discount Maintenance*

The customer ID field has been replaced by a customer name lookup which will accept null, partial or complete strings and pop open a list of matching customer names from which the user may choose. (I use the question mark [?] icon in this book to differentiate this behavior from that of a drop-down list.) The need to remember product line codes has been eliminated by allowing the same manner of selection as the customer field. The window itself contains code to open, close, move and re-size. A command button allows the user to save his work at any time.

The event model provides far more flexibility to the analyst for organizing his model. Since the target environment is far more random and flattened, it is useful to have the same capability in the organization of the analysis models. This section examines different ways that the event model can be organized to aid the analyst and designer toward the goal of building a client/server-GUI system.

## Sequencing Events by Time

One of the most obvious ways to organize an event list is to sequence events chronologically (Figure 4–16). On the surface, the technique is very simple. Events are sorted in the order in which they typically occur. The events on your sorted list are linked together in an *event chain*. All event chains start with an unexpected event.

```
Customer places order
Credit department confirms customer credit limit
Customer pays deposit on order
Sales manager approves order
Production department schedules order
Plant produces order
Plant ships order
Time to issue monthly A/R statements
Customer pays balance due
```

**Figure 4–16.** Event list sorted chronologically

Sequencing an event list by time makes it very easy for the users to read and validate. The order of the events often mirrors how they have explained their job to you. The chronology of events also gives you an excellent opportunity to determine predecessor and successor events, identify expected versus unexpected events, and look for non-events that may be missing from the list. Once you embark on this endeavor, you may find that sorting events chronologically isn't as simple as it initially appears.

Rather than take the example in Figure 4–16 as gospel, let's start asking some questions. This is called "interviewing your model." After making my initial chronological listing, my next step as an analyst would be to start asking the users more questions:

"Does the credit department always have to approve credit on each order, or can customers be pre-approved up to a certain limit?"

"Do all orders require a deposit?"

"Do any customers elect to pay in full in advance (negating the need for the last two events)?"

"What happens if the plant cannot schedule the order in a reasonable time?"

"At what points can the customer cancel their order?"

"Are all orders subject to sales manager approval, or only the big ones?"

"What happens if the customer doesn't pay?"

"What happens if their credit is rejected?"

"What happens if the sales manager doesn't approve the order?"

Depending on the answers you receive, the event list could get far more complicated. You may find that a large percentage of orders advance through the chain in neat and tidy linear fashion, but others follow a variety of exception paths. Non-events can reroute your event chain into alternate detours or dead ends. Some events can occur out of sequence while others must follow a prescribed chronology.

When it comes time to design an interface for this system, the designer needs to be able to facilitate the normal event chain easily, but still handle the chartered exceptions in a reasonable manner. In the next chapter, we will introduce a critical model, the *state transition diagram*, which does a good job of graphically depicting complex event chain paths.

Sequencing events chronologically is very useful as a tool for validating your model with the users. It is unlikely that you will be able to create a single chronology for all of the events in a large business system. For example, table maintenance events such as *System administrator adds new country* have virtually no useful relationship to the events pertaining to customer orders or financial transactions. However, the technique works extremely well within a particular subject area.

By examining the sorted event list, you can tease out which events must precede others and which are optional. The chronological sorting makes it easy to spot expected events and identify non-events which may be missing from the list. Every business has exceptions, and it is these exception paths that will complicate the chronological sorting. Ordering events by time is an excellent way to discover exceptions to the rules early in the project and avoid costly oversights later. Additional models, such as the state-transition diagram, covered in the next chapter, will be needed to sort out particularly tangled event sequencing.

## Sorting by Subject

The subject-verb-object syntax of event names provides us with the ability to group events together by the subject who initiates the event (Figure 4–17). This technique resurfaces the same issue of expanded versus reduced scope that arose in Chapter 3. The event list is directly sensitive to any elasticity in the boundary of the context model.

```
Customer events:
Customer places order
Customer pays deposit on order
Customer cancels order
Customer picks up order
Customer fails to pick up order
Customer pays balance due
Customer fails to pay balance due
Customer changes name
Customer changes location
Customer files quality claim

Plant events:
Plant schedules order
Plant produces order
Plant ships order...
```

**Figure 4–17.** Event list sorted by subject

An expanded scope event list is entirely appropriate in the analysis phase, especially when there are opportunities to change the business organization. In Chapter 3 there is an example of an order entry function which could be moved from the central headquarters to the remote sales offices due to the enabling communications technology and the widespread acceptance of the personal computer. Prior to such a decision being finalized, I prefer to state events using the expanded scope subject, *Customer places order*.

The expanded scope has several advantages. First of all, it doesn't imply the final organizational structure of the people who will use the system. It keeps your implementation options open. It also allows you to sort your event list by subject and group all events which are originated by the same subject (in this case *Customer*) together and examine it for completeness, patterns and possible redundancy.

After the implementation decision has been finalized regarding which user groups will have the responsibility of interacting directly with the system, the subject can be stated in reduced scope fashion. *Customer places order* becomes *Sales office enters order*. Sorting by subject on a reduced scope event list gives the interface designer a wealth of information for organizing the interface. It enables the designer to create custom groupings to locate functions in convenient proximity for the users of the system.

To improve the rigor of the event dictionary, I suggest making two separate properties for the subject of the event. One is the logical *initiator* of the event, the other is the *transporter* of the information to the system which has been nominated by the business (Figure 4–18). This allows you to sort by initiator or transporter without changing the name of the event. The initiator is discovered by examining the event using expanded scope. The transporter is based on an implementation and organizational decision by the business, and may not be known until later in the project.

```
Event:              Customer places order
   Initiator:           Customer
   Transporter:         Sales assistant

Event:              Customer picks up order
   Initiator:           Customer
   Transporter:         Will-call office clerk
```

**Figure 4–18.** Event dictionary entries for *initiator* and *transporter*

Sorting events lists by subject is a powerful technique. Using the expanded scope initiator of the event, the sorted list shows the complete role played by the subject in the system's context. We will see in the next chapter, (The Information Model) that this can be particularly useful for uncovering all of the data elements that the system may be required to remember about the initiator. The list can be easily verified by subject matter experts. It also points out patterns that can be useful in determining which user group should play the role of physically transporting the event's stimulus into the system.

Once the optimal user groups are defined, sorting the event list by transporter becomes a valuable tool for the application designer, as we will see in Chapters 6 (The Interface Prototype) and 11 (External Interface Design). By identifying all of the tasks of each user group, it also allows you to plan for upcoming prototyping, testing, training and documentation efforts.

## Sorting by Object

It stands to reason that if there are benefits to sorting the event list by *subject*, there may also be advantages to sorting the event list by *object* (Figure 4–19). In this case, I am using the term "object" to mean the noun in the sentence which receives the action of the verb.[2] The object of the event represents a real world entity, attribute or information abstraction such as *Order, Invoice, Product, Customer account*. The object may be a single data element as in *Shipping Line changes last receiving date*. Conversely, the object may represent many data elements on many entities as in the case of *Customer places order*, or *Manager requests weekly sales report*.

---

[2] I once saw an event list which was sorted by *verb*. This could yield some bizarre results (especially if the list contains events such as *Accountant **executes** month-end reporting* along with *State **executes** death row inmate*). I think the analyst was attempting to separate events which create information in the system from those which request data. This is better accomplished with an event/entity CRUD matrix.

```
Order events:
Customer places order
Sales manager approves order
Customer cancels order
Customer picks up order
Customer fails to pick up order
Production department schedules order
Warehouse fills order

Price List events:
Marketing department establishes new price list
Sales manager requests current price list
Sales manager requests price trend report
```

**Figure 4–19.**  Event list sorted by object

In object-oriented systems, the term "object" represents a programming construct which mirrors a real world entity or information abstraction in its data, process and observable behavior. I am not implying that every object of the event list syntax will become an object in an object-oriented business system; however, there is a strong likelihood that many of the system's object classes can be found in the event list as both subjects and objects in the sentence structure. I'll have more to say about business objects later in Chapter 12 on internal component design.

The trick to sorting the event list by object is to determine the primary object on which the event acts and to assign object names consistently. This technique isn't going to be applicable for every single event in your system. Its main advantage is to identify all of the events for the major objects in your system. It's OK to have a number of stray events that don't seem to fit in neatly with the others.

A more rigorous method of relating events to objects is by creating an event/entity CRUD matrix (Figure 4–8). Events are listed on one side of the matrix, and the entities from your information model are listed on the other side. In each cell it is indicated whether the event creates, reads, updates or deletes an instance of the entity. As we will see in the chapter on architecture modeling, the event/entity CRUD matrix can be very useful for determining the physical requirements for very large and widely distributed systems. The technique may be overkill for smaller localized applications and you may find that sorting the event list by object suits your needs.

Sorting the event list by object can yield some specific benefits. The sorted list can be trotted around to the object's subject matter experts to see if it is complete and correct. We will see in the chapter on interface prototyping that the on-line designer needs to know which events are capable of being executed by the user, once they have acquired the business object on the window.

For projects which are fully object-oriented (OO), this is the first step toward cataloguing business objects. I strongly suggest, that if your project is going full-blown OO, that you take the time to create an information model, event model, and the event/entity CRUD matrix, and use this as a basis for cataloguing most of your business objects. Without this level of rigor, objects are sometimes determined by "he who shouts the loudest" in a group design session and can be subject to sudden fits of overly creative thinking.

You may have already noticed that sorting an event list by object is easier if you have an information model at hand to which you can refer. It is virtually impossible to create a complete and useful event model without also creating the information model. It is also unlikely that the context model can be created without creating a good portion of the event model as well. This is why I call these models the "big three." They form the foundation of the project's analysis, and are best done iteratively and concurrently.

## Leveled Events

For very large systems, the analyst needs some way of grouping events together in a way that makes sense. Events can be decomposed or *leveled*, just like traditional process modeling. The challenge is that the scope of any given event is subject to the modeler's interpretation.

The analyst must always be aware of the appropriate level of granularity for each phase of a development project. Events, just like traditional process models, have an implied hierarchy. I have defined four major levels of events that I find very useful for helping me organize my models. The *conceptual level, business level, dialogue level*, and *design level* (Figure 4–20).

The conceptual level is useful for project planning. The business level, coupled with an information model is the heart and soul of the analysis effort. Early prototyping on the project introduces the dialogue level, which begins the transition to design. The design level comprises all of the decisions made by the developers about how the system will be physically constructed to recognize and react to the logical business level event.

### The Conceptual Level

The *conceptual level* is appropriate for the project charter and planning phases of a project. Events stated at the conceptual level are intended to define the major functional areas of the system. *Customer places order* is often a conceptual level event in most big companies because the process of ordering products or services can be very complex. As soon as the analyst delves into the details of this event, it will soon become obvious that this event is at too high a level for useful analysis and design. Many projects opt to dispense with the event syntax and label the conceptual level events with a function area name, such as *Order entry, Accounts receivable* and *Accounting*. These functional areas just as easily could be named *Customer places order, Customer pays invoice, Time to account for sales*.

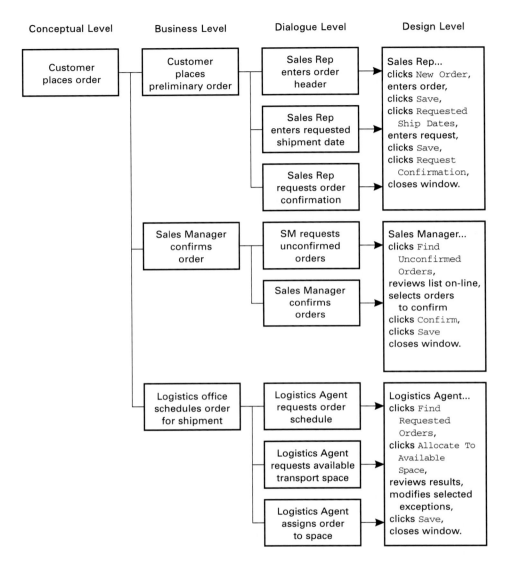

**Figure 4–20.** Event levels

### The Business Level

The conceptual level *Customer places order* points us in the right direction. Detailed analysis of the business area uncovers a rich lode of related, more granular events which fall under its umbrella. These events are at the *business level*. This is the level which is most appropriate for event modeling during the analysis phase because it corresponds to what the business users consider a complete task. At the business level, the prime objective is to uncover all of the system's detailed essential requirements, without designing interface dialogue. When conceptual level events are decomposed into business level events, they may take the form of either event chains or subtypes.

Event chains are multiple events in succession, that comprise the logical conceptual level event. *Customer places order* may break down into a chain such as: *Customer places preliminary order*, followed by *Sales manager confirms order*, *Logistics office schedules shipment*. The business level events were too granular to mention in the project charter, but they clearly fall under the auspices of *Customer places order*.

Event subtypes are variations on the same event. *Bank customer applies for loan* may break down into subtypes of the event, such as *Bank customer applies for car loan, Bank customer applies for boat loan, Bank customer applies for home equity loan*.

The business level will yield many different permutations on the same event. For instance, in a point of sale receipting system, the event *Customer pays for merchandise* can be subtyped into

Customer pays by check,

Customer pays with cash,

Customer pays by credit card.

Subtyping the event dramatically surfaces all of the different flavors of the event that the system will have to recognize. This is important because it leads the analyst to discover that the stimulus data required and the business policy associated with the activity section for each subtype of the event are different. If the customer pays by check, the check number and account number will have to be entered and funds may be verified via a phone line. If the customer pays by credit card, the system needs to know the credit card type, number and expiration date, and the credit balance verified via a different on-line service. For cash transactions, none of that data or processing is required.

As an analyst, you have the option of documenting business events at the subtype or supertype level in your event model. Whichever method you choose, there will be a trade-off. If you create a separate event dictionary entry for each subtype event, you will incur some redundancy for any stimulus, activity or response which is identical between the subtypes. Rolling all of the subtypes up into one event dictionary entry is also acceptable, but you may find yourself having to include mutually exclusive case statements in your stimulus and activity sections.

In the example in Figure 4–21, the stimulus definition has to differentiate which data elements pertain to which subtypes. The activity section will also have to state which processing is exclusive to each subtype. We also see that the check and credit card payments necessitate an intervening event before the logical purchasing transaction can be completed. The system has to dial a verification service and wait for authorization. The outcome of the customer's visit to our store can vary dramatically depending upon whether the subsequent event turns out to be *Verification service authorizes transaction* or *Verification service denies transaction*.

| Event ID: | 37 |
|---|---|
| Event: | Customer pays for merchandise by check, cash or credit card |
| Description: | After the cashier announces the total due to the customer, the customer will remit payment either by cash, personal check or credit card. Checks and credit cards are verified via an on-line service. |
| Stimulus: | If cash<br>    Amount tendered<br>If check<br>    Amount tendered<br>    Check number<br>    Bank account number<br>If credit card (exact amount only)<br>    Credit card type<br>    Account number<br>    Expiration date<br>End if |
| Activity: | Read total amount due<br>If cash<br>    Record amount tendered<br>    Calculate change due<br>    Print receipt<br>If check<br>    Record amount tendered, check number, bank account number<br>    Dial check verification service<br>If credit card<br>    Record credit card type, account number, expiration date<br>    Dial credit card verification service<br>End if |
| Response: | If cash<br>    Receipt = store id, date, time, amount due, amount tendered, change due.<br>If check<br>    (sent to check verification service) amount tendered, check check number, bank account number, store id.<br>If credit card<br>    (sent to credit card verification service) amount due, card type, account number, expiration date, store id.<br>End if |
| Effect: | If cash, the customer has paid in full.  If check or credit card, the cashier and customer are awaiting authorization. |

**Figure 4–21.** This supertype event dictionary entry should be three separate entries

After attempting to create an event dictionary for the supertype (Figure 4–21), it is clear that the differences between the subtypes outweigh the similarities. I would opt to make separate event dictionary entries for the subtype events in this case. Subtyping will also crop up again in the next chapter. The subtyping found in the event model is likely to be mirrored by subtyping in the information model.

How far to level your event model can be a topic for intellectual debate; however, experience soon guides the analyst to a practical solution. Fewer events on the list will yield more complex event dictionary entries; more granular events will have simplified specifications but there will be more of them.

My general rule of thumb is similar to the heuristics for data flow diagramming. When your activity section begins to exceed one to three pages of specification, or when you are introducing numerous case statements into your stimulus and response flows, you probably need to decompose the event further, either through subtyping, or looking for a logical break in the chain. If your event list is gigantic, and the activity section is really skimpy, it is possible that you are starting to design user interface dialogue and have descended past the business level.

### The Dialogue Level

One of the primary tasks of the interface designer is to determine the appropriate level of dialogue between the user and the system. The *dialogue level* takes each business event and breaks it into a dialogue between user and system, based on the power of the technology, the skill level of the user, and the appropriate unit of work for the business task at hand.

To illustrate this point, let's take two events from a department store. The first event, *Vendor signs new pricing contract,* occurs when one of the department store's vendors signs an exclusive agreement to supply the store at a stated discount off their regular price. The terms of the agreement are to be entered into their new computer system. Let's say the agreements are entered by a clerk in the payables department with fifteen years of computer experience. If there are ten data elements in the stimulus for this event, it is likely that the interface designer will be able to put them all on one window. The business event has been implemented in the system without being broken apart into smaller chunks of dialogue.

A second event, *Shopper inquires on back order status*, is to be implemented via a terminal mounted in a kiosk by the entrance of the store. Shoppers can inquire directly on the status of available stock in the store, and even see if the desired item has been back-ordered. This event requires just a handful of data elements as well, such as the department, the garment type, the brand name, color and size.

Since the kiosk terminal is to be used by the general public and not a professional "power user," the designers may break apart the event into more discrete dialogue between human and computer. In this case, the designer may break up the event so the computer asks for each piece of information separately. For instance, the user may first point to the department they want, and the computer asks them what type of item they desire. That fragment alone qualifies as an event at the dialogue level. It is just a small piece of the business event, but the designer has opted to create a dialogue in order to make the computer easier to use for the average shopper.

The *dialogue level* is typically begun in early prototyping (Chapter 6) and is fully fleshed out in detailed external interface design (Chapter 11). At this level, the event list and event dictionary are fully consumed to design the appropriate interface. Each event is broken apart into a conversation between user and computer, based on the available technology, the skill level of the user, and the appropriate unit of work.

At the dialogue level, the events are too numerous to manage in a practical manner through an event list and event dictionary. The navigation diagram, interface prototype and window layouts are far better models for conveying the behavior of the proposed system. By using the event list and event dictionary as a basis for the interface design, the appropriate behavior is engineered into the product. Each window or set of windows developed should be traceable to the logical business level events to which they were designed to respond.

### The Design Level

The last level in the event hierarchy is the actual keystrokes and mouse clicks that will have to be coded to implement the event. At the *design level*, the event's dialogue is decomposed further into the specific action the user must take to fully inform the system that the event has occurred.

The design level incorporates actual navigation, button and menu item names, and specific field positioning on each window. The appropriate tools for this kind of detailed design are the window navigation diagram, the window layout, the GUI design specification which describes the enablement and behavior of each control on the window and the presentation and business rules for the data itself. We will see in the following chapters that the user interface can be engineered from the business event model and information model using a reliable and repeatable process.

## SUMMARY

The event model is the glue that holds all of the pieces of analysis, design, construction and testing together. The event list embodies the reason you have been hired. The business needs to be able to respond to real world events, and it is the responsibility of the information technology staff to supply them with products that service that need.

The event model contains an event list and event dictionary. Whenever possible, events on the list are stated in subject-verb-object syntax. The event dictionary provides the core of the process specification for your system. For each event on the list, the analyst has an obligation to define its meaning in clear, concise text. The technical portion of the event dictionary contains a definition of the stimulus data required to trigger the event, the activity carried out by the system to formulate the appropriate response, and the data contained on that response. Additionally, the effect on the environment is documented so we can understand what the users are trying to achieve.

Most business events are unexpected. The system never knows when a particular occurrence will happen. Some events are expected. A predecessor event has established some window of expectation within which the system anticipates the occurrence of the event. It is very important for the analyst to ask whether the system cares if the event fails to occur, and include the "non-event" on the list. Expected events in a business system can be temporal events, meaning they are triggered by measuring the passage of time against a schedule. Most events in a business system, however, will rely on the user to directly inform the system that the event has occurred.

The event model is a powerful document which is completely consumed throughout the project. The information model, the foundation of the underlying database design, is constructed concurrently with the event model by cataloguing the data requirements for each event. The interface prototype declares candidate window layouts, based on the capability of the technology, the sophistication of the users, the complexity and sequence of the events, and the character of the data required.

Events can also play a key role in architectural decisions. Event matrices can be used to plan hardware requirements based on which events occur at the various distributed business locations. The event dictionary is once again consumed in the detailed design phase as the designer determines navigation paths, menu and button specifications, object classes, background functions and stored procedures to execute the business policy for the event.

The event model also becomes the basis for creating testing plans. The event dictionary already contains a mapping between required stimulus and appropriate response that can be easily expanded into test scenarios.

Event modeling has its roots in traditional structured analysis. The technique has risen to the forefront today because the systems we are building are far more flattened than the hierarchical structures of old. The event list and event dictionary have proven to be powerful GUI development models. The term *event-driven* is used to describe GUI systems because the user's navigation patterns and flow of work are far more unpredictable now that they are armed with a mouse.

The key to good GUI design is understanding how the system should behave when responding to business events, and engineering just enough flexibility into the design to manage multiple events and non-traditional sequencing. This is not to say that GUI window design is a free-for-all. A significant task of the GUI designer is to decide what the user *can't* do at any given time. A solid event model helps to organize this task.

## EXERCISES

1. Which of the following events are expected vs. unexpected in a typical order management system?

(a) Customer places order

(b) Credit manager approves order

(c) Customer cancels order

(d) Warehouse ships order

(e) Customer fails to pay invoice

2. Maureen is the purchasing agent for Villa St. Emily Wineries. Her job is to review purchase orders that have been entered into the system by the field office and approve or reject them. The purchase orders are already in the system, so what's the stimulus for the event dictionary entry for *Purchase order manager approves purchase order*? Is it the *Purchase order identifier* and the *Approval status*, or is it all of the selection criteria Maureen might use to get a list of purchase orders on the window?

3. At Villa St. Emily Wineries, there is a business rule stating that if an in-process order is priced according to a list price, and that list price changes prior to shipment, then the order must be reviewed by a sales manager to either grandfather the old price, or re-price the order at the new price. Where should this business rule be documented in the analysis models?

## ANSWERS

1. (a) *Customer places order* is usually an unexpected event in most business systems. Few businesses know ahead of time which customer will place any particular order at a given point in time.

(b) *Credit manager approves order* is an event which is expected, assuming that it is preceded by the event *Customer places order*, which establishes a window of expectation, within which the order should be approved.

(c) *Customer cancels order* is unexpected.

(d) *Warehouse ships order* is expected, unless of course, your warehouse is given to shipping items at random.

(e) *Customer fails to pay invoice* is actually the non-occurrence of an expected event, *Customer pays invoice*, or in other words, a non-event.

2. The stimulus would be the purchase order identifier and the purchase order status with a value of "approved." The activity for the event would update the identified purchase order to "approved" status. (It is possible that there is no response required from the system for this event.) In the event model, you only need to note that the user needs a way to acquire the purchase order to indicate

approval. You can use the prototype to determine exactly *how* to accomplish that task. In this example, the dialogue level is far more interesting than the rather light-weight business level event. In the design of the interface, you might give the purchasing agent a way to retrieve all purchase orders from the system that require approval, using a variety of selection criteria. Once a list of purchase orders are on the window, you might allow the user to point to one (or more than one if appropriate), and set the status to "approved" via a command button or menu item. I have seen some project teams who are uncomfortable with leaving the "browse" function for this event out of the event dictionary. My suggestion in this case is to create another event, *Purchase agent browses purchase orders*, and list all of the various selection criteria under the stimulus for that event, rather than saddle the approval event with having to articulate *how* purchase orders are retrieved in the system.

3. A good, reliable place to document the rule would be in the business event, "*Marketing department changes current price list*." That way, the business rule is cited in the exact event which will invoke it. If the rule were invoked by more than one event, it could be documented in one place, and simply referenced by name in the event activity sections which execute the policy.

# CHAPTER
# 5

```
        △
     ┌──────────┐
     │Information│
     │  Model   │
     └──────────┘
    ╱ Interface Prototype ╲
   ╱  Architecture Model   ╲
  ╱    Database Design      ╲
 ╱  External Interface Design ╲
╱  Internal Component Design   ╲
╲    Construction & Testing    ╱
```

# THE INFORMATION MODEL

## INTRODUCTION

Chapter 5, in which Christopher Robin discovers entities, attributes, and relationships. We ought to start teaching information modeling skills in grade school, because it is without a doubt, the singular skill which is most vital to the success of your project. I wish that I could make information modeling as easy for you as a stroll through the Hundred Acre Wood, but alas, it's a tremendously complex yet important topic, so we'll have to wade through it together. The concepts and traditions of information modeling form the basis of relational database design and are a core competency for good object modeling. An ill-conceived information model can play havoc with not only your project, but every successive project which attempts to use it or extend it. In this chapter, I will cover the entity-relationship diagram, and the information model's three primary constructs, the entity, the relationship and the attribute. I will cover relationship cardinality and the concept of normalization. Advancing past the basis, we will proceed to attributive entity types, associative entity types and

117

supertypes and subtypes. We'll take a look at a the state-transition diagram, an important link between the information model and the event model. I'll round out the chapter with some advice on strategies for constructing your information model.

## THE PURPOSE OF INFORMATION MODELING

Data is the central core of any information system. It comprises the map of the corporate memory for any organization. If I was limited to only *one* model on a development project, I'd chose this one in a heartbeat. The information model (a.k.a. data model) creates the foundation on which the database is designed.

Most businesses are rich in data. There are literally thousands of facts that computer systems must remember. The trends towards relational databases, open systems and enterprise-wide computing has elevated the importance of proper data modeling because data respects no project boundaries. Chances are, if your project is interested in some information about, say, customer discount agreements, then some other part of the business is likely to be interested in that information as well.

Documenting a business' data requirements is peculiar in that it has spawned so many rival notations and naming conventions. Modeling data is as difficult as is it important. Compounding the difficulty of mastering a technique and notation is the fact that so many disparate parties within the organization are interested in differing facets of the same stuff. If you can get your organization to agree on which style of boxes and lines to adopt, you're only part way there. The real challenge is to agree on what to put on the boxes and lines.

The goal of this chapter isn't to foist a particular notation on you (or heaven forbid, invent a new one), but rather to help the reader understand how to assemble an information model that accurately reflects the data requirements of the system.

### A Brief History Lesson

If you got into information systems as a career after the advent of relational databases, you may not appreciate how things used to be. Back in the old days, you had to walk five miles through the snow to get your data, holding nothing but a baked potato in your hands to keep you warm. Well, maybe it wasn't *that* bad, but understanding where data has been can help us to appreciate the rationale for some of the questionable habits that still exist in the industry today.

In the 1960s and 1970s the predominant method for storing data was in flat files. A flat file is simply a named file on the disk which contains data about a subject. You can imagine the flat file as being comprised of individual records. Each record is made up of individual data elements, such as customer_name, street_address, city, state, zip_code, phone_number. In order to access the data on a record, the programmer would count the number of characters in the record and declare in the program the exact position where each data element begins and ends. By altering the definition of the parsing routine, the designer of the flat file is able to redefine individual records within a flat file, so that the definition of one record can vary from the next.

As abhorrent as this sounds to anyone raised on today's relational database technology, one has to remember that at the time, disk space was far more expensive than it is today. Database management systems were primitive at best, and every programmer had to manually declare the name, length and data type of every data element read from the database. This led to conflicting definitions of the same data element across many programs, and even different naming conventions of the same data element appearing in different flat files.

As the breadth and depth of information stored on disk expanded throughout the world it was clear that a technical and organizational crisis was looming. Businesses needed to get their arms around the type of data that their systems needed to remember. Standards needed to be established and runaway redundancy had to be curtailed.

By the late 1970s and early 1980s, data flow diagramming was gaining favor as a method for analyzing the process carried out within a system and the data requirements flowing into and out of each process. Data for every data flow was defined in the data dictionary using a short-hand notation to describe the relationship between elements. For example, the data flow *customer_order* would be defined as:

*customer_order* = customer_name, customer_address, account_number, current_date + {product_code, quantity}.

The reader would interpret this as "customer order equals customer name, customer address, account number and current date, plus *iterations of* product code and quantity. Additional symbols were included to convey optionality.

Although this technique was cumbersome, it was far better than anything that existed up to this point in time. The translation from data dictionary entries into database design was not obvious, and many early structured analysis projects collapsed under the weight of their own data dictionaries.

Along came Peter Chen's concept of the entity-relationship model to the rescue.[1] He devised an implementation-neutral and process-neutral way to depict the structure of data itself. Logical groupings of data elements about real-world objects were called entities, and were drawn as rectangles. The relationship between the entities was drawn with a diamond on a connecting line. This is commonly referred to as *Chen notation*. The diagram is known as an *entity-relationship diagram (ERD)* (Figure 5–1).

Examining the diagram, we can intuitively see that this system appears to be interested in persons and dwellings. Furthermore, we can deduce that the system is chartered to keep track of which persons reside in which dwellings. Chen notation has not entirely survived in today's world of automated CASE[2] tools. The diamond has largely been dropped in favor of just a single line to represent relationships. The main reason for the diamond falling out of favor is that it occupied too much real estate on the computer screen.

---

[1]  Chen, 1976

[2]  CASE is an acronym for Computer-Aided Software Engineering.

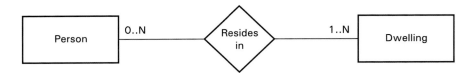

**Figure 5–1.** Chen notation

Some of the early adopters of Chen's technique were very successful in modeling their data requirements. Others experienced problems in the design phase, since relational databases still had not come into their own in the marketplace. The constraints of the flat file or hierarchical databases of the time often prompted dramatic departures from the logical data model when it came time to implement a design.

Today, with the advent of modern relational database technology, it is possible and desirable to implement a database which closely resembles the real world structure of the data. Relational databases have continually improved in their speed and ability to efficiently handle multiple table joins. These improvements, coupled with the availability of cheaper disk space has removed most of the criticisms of data modeling leveled by early skeptics.

The structure of the data model has undergone some improvements since Chen's time as well. Most CASE tools do a reasonably good job of managing the data model, but unfortunately, competing vendors have introduced a variety of notations. The term *information modeling* has come into vogue, since the term *data* implies a collection of facts, but *information* implies that the facts have some business relevance beyond their sheer existence. I'm not too picky about which term you use. The term *object modeling* has been used by some in an attempt to appear more object-oriented, but this term carries with it a more complex connotation of process and behavioral elements, as well as a bending or outright suspension of the traditional rules of normalization. For this reason, even on a project with an object-oriented target language, I prefer to build an *information model* to document my data requirements, especially when a relational database is involved. The activity of cataloguing objects is a natural follow-on task.

## THE COMPONENTS OF THE INFORMATION MODEL

A complete information model which is sufficiently detailed to be useful for subsequent design or software package purchase decisions should include the following. The rest of this chapter will provide detailed definitions of each component.

> **Entity-relationship diagram,** showing all named entities, named relationships and the minimum and maximum cardinality on each relationship in both directions. Large diagrams should be partitioned for readability.
>
> **Volume** and **retention** estimates for each entity
>
> **Attribute listing** for each entity

Clear textual **definition** of each entity, relationship and attribute

**Properties** of each attribute including: optionality, data type, range, unit of measure, precision and restricted values

**State-transition diagrams** for each status attribute or relevant entity life cycle

A variety of **entity matrices**

If this looks like a tall order, it is. This model provides the detailed foundation for all data design decisions which follow, including physical database design, data distribution, even window and report layout. A so-called "high-level" information model which only includes a hastily drawn diagram with no attributes or definitions is of absolutely no use at all to the designer or to the software package purchasing team. Regardless of whether you will build or buy your software, this is where the project must get into the nitty-gritty dirty details of the business requirements. It's better to take the time to build the information model now than have to suffer the consequences of making ill-informed decisions later.

## The Entity-Relationship Diagram

The information model's primary graphic element is the entity-relationship diagram (ERD). It is comprised of the entities about which the system needs to remember specific facts, and the relationships which exist between these groups of facts. Figure 5–2 shows a small piece of an entity relationship diagram. In the following sections, I will cover all of the components represented in the notation.

## Entities

Webster's New World Dictionary defines *entity* as, "*n.* 2. a thing that has definite, individual existence in reality or in the mind." That's a very broad statement, so let's see if we can cast the word *entity* in terms of software engineering.

We see from Webster's that an entity is a noun. Additionally, it can represent a real world construct such as *Customer*, *Order, Sales person* or it can represent an abstraction such as *Order item, Discount agreement* or *Magazine subscription*. Each individual instance of each entity is unique; however, they have similar characteristics and behavior which makes it often advantageous to group them. The system needs to be able to represent entities in a persistent format that can be recalled on demand. Our software-engineering definition of an *entity* is:

An *entity* is a person, place, thing or abstract idea, about which the system needs to remember something. Instances of each entity have similar characteristics and behave in a similar manner.

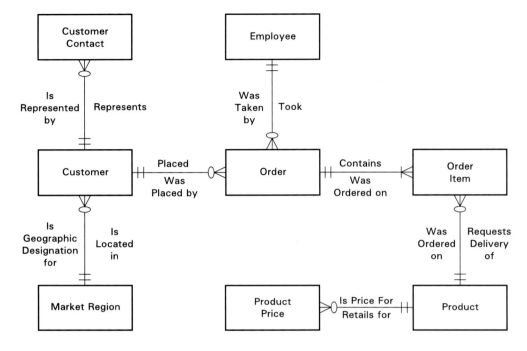

**Figure 5–2.** A sample entity-relationship diagram

Entities are represented graphically as a rectangle. The name of the entity is placed inside the box. Imagine the box as containing a bunch of dots. Each dot represents an individual instance of the entity. No single instance is represented twice (Figure 5–3).

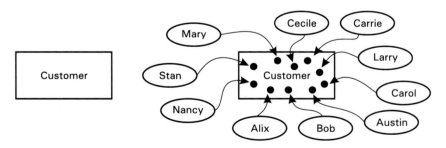

**Figure 5–3.** Each member of the entity is unique

When you create an entity, just like any other object in your model, you have incurred an obligation to define it. Write down the name of the entity, and then write a clear textual definition. Try to picture in your mind if the definition adequately describes the real-world instances of the entity. Read your definition and re-examine the entity name to see if you've chosen the best one.

As you create your model, you may come across entity volume and retention estimates. Volume is the number of instances of the entity that a business might expect, such as number of customers, number of orders placed per year, number of vendors. Retention is how long you need to keep any given instance of the entity on-line. These statistics will become important later in the design of the architecture and application, so if you encounter the information now, it's good to include it with the entity definition.

## Relationships

Entity members are very social. Instances of entities are constantly associating with other entities. Customers place orders, orders may have multiple order items, each associated with a product, which may be associated with an inventory balance, and so on. These associations are called *relationships*. A relationship is drawn as a line between one entity and another. Imagine that the line connects the "dots," or rather the instances of one entity with the instances of another. In Figure 5–4, we see a relationship between the entity *Person* and the entity *Dog*.[3] The relationship can be read in either direction. Reading from left to right, we use the name above the line, "Person *owned* Dog." Reading from right to left, we use the name below the line, "Dog *has been owned by* Person."

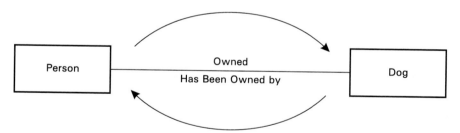

**Figure 5–4.** Horizontal orientation

For relationships which are depicted vertically (Figure 5–5), or at an angle, imagine our horizontal relationship rotated clockwise. The name which was on top is now read from top to bottom down the right-hand side. The name which was on the bottom is now read northbound up the left-hand side.

You may have noticed that I named this relationship in the past tense. Just like any other words we use on a model, the names of entities and relationships need to be very precise in order to convey the same meaning to each reader. If the relationship is supposed

---

[3]   I must give credit to Meilir Page-Jones for his world-famous *Person owns Dog* example, which has been pressed into service many times to illustrate a host of information modeling concepts.

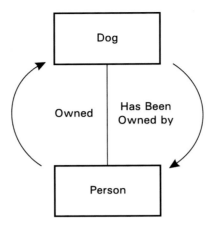

**Figure 5–5.** Vertical orientation

to represent all dogs that the owner has ever owned, past tense is appropriate. If the relationship is restricted to only the dog or dogs currently owned, present tense should be used. Better yet, the relationship name can be modified to be even more descriptive, such as "Person *has ever owned* Dog" or "Person *currently owns* Dog." In addition to naming the relationship, you also have an obligation to define it with a clear textual statement.

Relationship names are extremely important because they are able to convey a great deal of business policy and meaning when named correctly. I beseech you to avoid sloppy names such as *Can have*, *Is related to* or *Is associated with*. The fact that you have drawn a line already informs the reader that a relationship or association exists. This type of lazy name is about as useful as naming each entity *Entity*.

### Relationship Cardinality

There is an important constraint on relationships that is declared graphically on the entity-relationship diagram called *cardinality*. Cardinality is how many of one thing relate to another. Relationship cardinality is particularly important because it forms the basis of many design decisions. Cardinality is expressed with a value for minimum and maximum. The minimum value describes whether the relationship is optional or required. The maximum value describes whether the relationship is singular or plural. Since relationships are stated in both directions between two entities, the minimum and maximum cardinality must also be stated in both directions. This means that for every relationship in your model, *four* points of cardinality are required to express the nature of the relationship adequately (minimum and maximum in both directions).[4] Let's

---

[4]    I will concede that on large, conceptual level information models, which are used for planning but not detailed design, you can get away with stating only the maximum cardinality. However, when you get into detailed analysis and design, you need all four points of cardinality to adequately express the business rules which need to be enforced in the database structure and perhaps on the interface as well.

explore the different facets of relationship cardinality using our example of "Person *currently owns* Dog" (Figure 5–6).

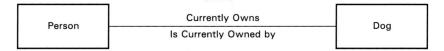

**Figure 5–6.** Relationship without cardinality notation

Once you have established that the system is chartered to remember which persons currently own which dogs, the next four questions to arise are:

1. Must a person own a dog?
2. May a person own more than one dog?
3. Must a dog be owned by a person at all times?
4. May a dog be owned by more than one person at a time?

Question 1 is designed to tease out the minimum cardinality when reading from left to right, entity A to entity B. Is a person compelled to be a dog owner in our system? If so, what happens if their dog dies or runs away? Do we run the dogless individual out of town? Do we hound them until they get a new dog? Should we supply them with a replacement?

Question 2 is designed to determine if the same instance of entity A can participate in relationships with multiple instances of entity B at the same time. When the answers to questions 1 and 2 are determined, the analyst can place the minimum and maximum cardinality on the diagram to express the business rule.

The graphic notation for minimum cardinality is either a zero, meaning "optional," or a one, meaning "required." The notation for maximum cardinality is either a one, meaning "only one," or a pair of crow's feet, meaning "many." Figure 5–7 shows the four possible combinations and their accepted vernacular.

| Min    Max | Graphic notation |
|---|---|
| Zero-to-One | ——————○⊦ |
| Zero-to-Many | ——————○⟨ |
| One-to-One | ——————⊦⊦ |
| One-to-Many | ——————⟨ |

**Figure 5–7.** Notations for relationship cardinality

The cardinality notation is placed directly on the relationship line to the right of the relationship name which it modifies. If we have determined that a person may own zero to many dogs, it would be expressed graphically as in Figure 5–8.

**Figure 5–8.** Relationship with minimum and maximum cardinality in one direction

To read the diagram, you start by saying the name of the first entity, followed by the proper relationship name in the direction you are reading, followed by the cardinality notation, and finally the name of the second entity. In Figure 5–8, we read "Person *currently owns zero to many* Dogs."

We are only half finished with relationship cardinality. We have yet to answer questions 3 and 4 which will tell us the cardinality in the opposite direction. Question 3 starts with the *Dog* entity and reads backwards towards *Person*, asking if the relationship between a dog and its master is optional or required. The business implication of a zero minimum cardinality is that we will allow stray dogs in the system.

Question 4 asks whether we will allow joint custody of dogs, or whether dog owner is always one person only. Notice that the relationship is named *Is currently owned by*. We might get a different answer to our question if the relationship means *Was ever owned by*.

Assuming that the business tells us that a dog may be currently owned by only one person, and that a dog must have an owner to be a dog of interest, we can finish our diagram by placing the minimum and maximum relationship cardinality for the opposing side of the relationship (Figure 5–9).

**Figure 5–9.** Relationship with all four points of cardinality

In summary, relationship cardinality is expressed by the minimum and maximum number of occurrences allowed between an instance of entity A and instances of entity B. To fully describe the nature of the relationship, the cardinality must also be determined between an instance of entity B and instances of entity A. The cardinality pairs are placed on the diagram at the end points of the relationship. When reading the diagram, you start by reading the name of entity A, followed by the relationship name between entity A and entity B, followed by the cardinality closest to entity B, and finally the name of entity B (Figure 5–10). This process is exactly reversed for reading in the opposite direction.

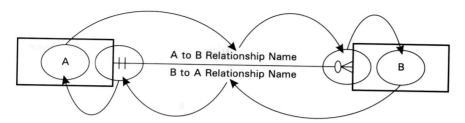

**Figure 5–10.** Reading relationship cardinality

There are several graphic notations for relationship cardinality. I favor the crows feet notation because it is so intuitive for the reader. It uses a "1" for "one," a "0" for "zero" and the "<" sign that we all remember fondly from our second grade introduction to set mathematics. Whichever notation you use, make sure that all four points of relationship cardinality are expressed graphically on your diagram.

The minimum and maximum cardinality must be expressed in both directions to adequately define the business rule. To stress the importance of this point, let me illustrate how the designer consumes this information.

Let's say our business users have told us that a dog must be owned by one and only one person. A person must own at least one dog, and possibly many. The business rule would be expressed as shown in Figure 5–11.

**Figure 5–11.** Persons must own at least one dog

It is the responsibility of the database designer to implement this relationship in a physical database schema. During the relational database design many, if not all, of the entities in your information model will become tables. (More on this subject in Chapter 9.) Given the relationship in Figure 5–11, it is inadvisable (and downright malfeasance) to place the primary key of the *Dog* in the *Person* table as a foreign key, because it would require a repeating group. It is acceptable (and common practice), to place the primary key of the *Person* table in the *Dog* table, since there will only ever be one person representing the owner for each dog. Of course, if the business ever declares that joint custody of dogs is acceptable, your design is blown. Note that the maximum cardinalities on this relationship dictated which physical table got the foreign key. The minimum cardinality between *Dog* and *Person* dictates that the person's primary key will be *required* as a foreign key in the *Dog* table.

Perhaps more interesting is the relationship between *Person* and *Dog*. The minimum cardinality on the "many" side of the relationship is not enforced by referential integrity in relational database management systems. The business rule that a person must have at least one dog will have to be coded into the system. Several possibilities are available to the designer. When entering a new person into the system, the designer could elect to disable the **Save** until the user specifies at least one dog. The user would also have to be disallowed from ever removing the last dog from a person. The challenge of enforcing this rule would certainly move me to explain to the users the ramifications of their decision, and ask them again if they want the rule enforced in their system. Relationship cardinality has an extremely powerful impact on the database and application design. The cost of making a mistake in your model can be very high down the road.

## Attributes

The third major component of the information model is the *attributes* which represent all of the data elements in your system. Each fact about an entity constitutes a separate attribute. There is no standard graphical notation for attributes, since they are often too numerous to list on an entity-relationship diagram. Usually, the attributes are provided on a separate list which accompanies each entity. Some CASE tools allow you to print the attributes listed inside of the entity box on the ERD, however, this can get unwieldy as the list grows.

The following example takes the business event *Customer drops off laundry* and shows how each data element involved in the transaction can be *attributed* to an entity on the information model.

### Example: Attributing Data Elements to Entity Types

Let's take a moment to pry into the private life of traveling salesman, Slick Pitchman. Slick has been touring the countryside selling portable household vacuum cleaners which are reportedly powerful enough to suck up small cats. After having relieved Dodge County's citizens of several of their beloved felines in an ill-fated demonstration at the fairgrounds, he has made a hasty retreat to Winthorp on the other side of the mountains. His first order of business is to drop off his shirts and jacket at the local dry cleaners.

He walks through the door and sets fifteen identical white shirts and a soiled corduroy sport coat on the counter. The clerk eyes him suspiciously and asks him if he's new in town. Slick doesn't know it, but he is about to become an instance of the entity, *Customer.*

The clerk has certain facts that she needs to collect about Slick and his laundry. She takes down his first name, last name and the phone number of his cheap motel. She notes that fifteen shirts need to be laundered and one jacket requires dry-cleaning. She also makes a note of the peculiar red stains and preponderance of cat hair that will have to be removed from the jacket. Slick is issued a dated and numbered claim ticket, with the price marked in the corner. The clerk promises him that his clothes will be ready the next day after 5:00 PM, and politely declines his dinner invitation. Figure 5–12 summarizes the list of data elements required by the system to recognize and respond to this event.

```
Customer's first name,
Customer's last name,
Customer's current phone number,
Date dropped off,
Claim ticket number,
Date promised,
Time promised,
Plus a repeating group of:
    Garment type,
    Number of garments,
    Service required,
    Service price,
    Special instructions.
```

**Figure 5–12.** Data elements for event: *Customer drops off laundry*

The data elements of any business problem can be attributed to entity types through a process called *normalization*.[5] Normalization is a set of heuristics developed by Edgar F. Codd in the early 1970s to extend the life expectancy of applications by representing the data in a non-redundant relational format. Systems with well normalized databases are able to withstand extensions to data, functionality, and changes in the nature of inquiries with minimal disruption.

Codd's principles of normalization are the foundation of relational database design. The goal of the information model is to create a logical representation of system's normalized data requirements; in other words, to store each fact in one place. To this end, Codd provides us with three levels of normal form, cleverly entitled, *First Normal Form*, *Second Normal Form* and *Third Normal Form*.[6]

**Unnormalized** data is a random collection of data elements with repeating record groups scattered throughout. Figure 5–13 shows the data from our dry cleaning example, unnormalized. It appears as though *Claim Ticket* has been nominated as the primary key for this rabble.[7]

---

[5]   Codd, 1972

[6]   There are additional levels of normalization, but in practice most analysts will stop at third normal form.

[7]   The term *primary key* is used for the field or fields which uniquely locate a record in a physical table or file. A *foreign key* is a primary key that is embedded in a different (or same) table, (hence the name foreign), to link two records together by providing a reference back to the table in which it is a primary key. The term *unique identifier* is used for the attribute(s) and relationship(s) which may be used to identify a specific instance of an entity.

| Field name | Value |
|---|---|
| Claim ticket | 1376 |
| First name | Slick |
| Last name | Pitchman |
| Phone number | 555-4567 |
| Drop off date | 6-17-95 |
| Date promised | 6-18-95 |
| Time promised | 5:00 PM |
| Garment type | Men's shirt |
| Service type | Launder |
| Quantity | 15 |
| Unit price | $1.00 |
| Garment type | Sport Coat |
| Service type | Dry clean |
| Quantity | 1 |
| Unit price | $7.50 |
| Special instructions | Stain, cat hair |

**Figure 5–13.** Unnormalized dry cleaning order

### First Normal Form

In *First Normal Form,* there are no repeating groups of attributes.

To achieve first normal form, the repeating records are first moved off to a separate group and associated back to the other data through the use of a relationship. In a physical database design, the primary key of the first group, *Claim ticket number*, is inserted in the second group as a *foreign key* to link the records. In the information model, the graphic relationship between entities suffices to inform the reader of the association. The foreign keys are not shown as attributes in the other entities. This omission adheres to the concept of safe deferral. As long as the database hasn't been physically designed, the primary key of any given entity could be a topic of debate, and therefore, scattering it about the model as a foreign key in other entities is premature and inadvisable.

Figure 5–14 shows our dry cleaning order in first normal form. The *Order* can still be uniquely identified by the claim ticket number, but the individual services ordered require both the *Claim ticket number*, *Garment type* and *Service type* to uniquely identify an instance of *Order item*.

Figure 5–15 shows the entity-relationship diagram for our dry cleaning order in first normal form.

First normal form solves the age-old problem of repeating groups in data sets. In the dark ages of database design, the analyst attempted to guess at the upper limit of the repeating group and establish the requisite number of columns in an unnormalized file. Everyone in the business would swear on their grandmother's grave that no customer had ever brought in more than five garment types at one time. Inevitably, as soon as five repeating groups had been petrified for all time in the system, the first six-garment-type customer would parade through the door.

ORDER

| Claim ticket | First name | Last name | Phone number | Drop off date | Date promised | Time promised |
|---|---|---|---|---|---|---|
| 1376 | Slick | Pitchman | 555-4567 | 6-17-95 | 6-18-95 | 5:00 PM |

ORDER ITEM

| Claim ticket (fk) | Garment type | Service type | Quantity | Unit price | Special instructions |
|---|---|---|---|---|---|
| 1376 | Men's shirt | Launder | 15 | $1.00 | -None- |
| 1376 | Sport Coat | Dry Clean | 1 | $7.50 | Stain, cat hair |

Note: Primary keys are underlined, foreign keys denoted with (fk).

**Figure 5–14.** Dry cleaning order in first normal form

**Figure 5–15.** ERD for the dry cleaning order in first normal form

## Second Normal Form

In *Second Normal Form*, for records with concatenated primary keys, all non-key attributes are fully functionally dependent on the whole of the primary key.

**Second normal form** addresses the problem of records which have primary keys comprised of multiple data elements. When you have concatenated keys, each data element on the record should be functionally dependent on the entire key, and not just part of the key. In our *Order item* in first normal form, the primary key is comprised of *Claim ticket number*, *Garment type* and *Service type*. Notice that the *Unit price* is not entirely dependent on the whole key. The current unit price can be determined using the *Garment type* and *Service type*. It appears that this business is in need of a price list for the services it provides.

We can remove the *Unit price* from the *Order item* and put it in a table with *Garment type* and *Service type*. While this satisfies the syntactic requirements of second normal form, it presents a problem to the business because the *Unit price* could be changed on the *Service type* table, leaving them unable to query historical prices associated with each *Order item*. For this reason, I suggest strongly that we qualify the unit price on the *Service type* table as *Current unit price* charged by the business. We need to also include unit price back to the *Order item* as well and qualify it as the *Order unit price*, which represents the unit price charged at the time the order was taken. The *Current unit price* is dependent only on the *Service type* and *Garment type*. The *Order unit price* is dependent on *Service type*, *Garment type* and *Claim ticket*.

The unit price is an example of *apparent redundancy*. If we named both attributes *Unit price*, they might look redundant but they really are not. I have seen cases where one or the other attributes were removed from the model in the name of eradicating all redundancy. The resulting system was problematic. To avoid over-zealous abuse of normalization, each attribute in your model must be defined. In this case of unit price, only the definition would point out that the unit price on the order is subtly different than the unit price stated on the service type price list. Figures 5–16 and 5–17 show our dry-cleaning order in second normal form.

ORDER

| Claim ticket | First name | Last name | Phone number | Drop off date | Date promised | Time promised |
|---|---|---|---|---|---|---|
| 1376 | Slick | Pitchman | 555-4567 | 6-17-95 | 6-18-95 | 5:00 PM |

ORDER ITEM

| Claim ticket (fk) | Garment type (fk) | Service type (fk) | Quantity | Unit price | Special instructions |
|---|---|---|---|---|---|
| 1376 | Men's shirt | Launder | 15 | $1.00 | -None- |
| 1376 | Sport Coat | Dry Clean | 1 | $7.50 | Stain, cat hair |

SERVICE TYPE

| Service type | Garment type | Current unit price |
|---|---|---|
| Launder | Men's shirt | $1.00 |
| Dry Clean | Sport Coat | $7.50 |

**Figure 5–16.** Dry cleaning order in second normal form

Second normal form removes data elements which are not fully dependent on a concatenated key and places them in their own table. Because the rule for second normal form is limited to data sets with multi-column keys, it is not as obvious a distinction as first or third normal form.

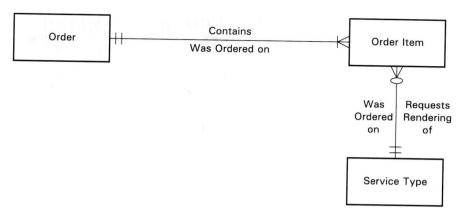

**Figure 5–17.** ERD for the dry cleaning order in second normal form

## Third Normal Form

In *Third Normal Form*, each attribute is functionally dependent on the key, the whole key, and nothing but the key.[8] (Transitive dependencies are removed.)

If we examine our data layout so far, we can still spot a problem. The customer's *First name*, *Last name* and *Phone number* are not really attributes of the *Order*. They are attributes of the *Customer*. From a technical standpoint, we are wasting space when all this information has to be repeated for every order that is placed. From a business standpoint, we lack the ability to accurately query all orders for a given customer since the customer's name could be spelled differently on any given order. We can address the second problem by assigning each customer a unique *Customer number*. The problem of data redundancy, however, still exists until we take the attributes which are transitively dependent on *Customer number* out of the *Order* and move them to their own entity.

Much of your system's data can be resolved to third normal form quickly if you just take the time to play a game that I call "Are you my mother?" *Are You My Mother*, written by P.D. Eastman and first published in 1960, is a book which teaches pattern recognition to small children by relating the story of a baby bird hatched while his mother was away gathering worms. The baby bird proceeds to wander about the yard asking the kitten, hen, dog, cow, car, boat, plane and snort[9] if they are his mother. By simple inspection the bird (and hopefully the reader) can see that these creatures are not birds, and therefore could not be his mother. When the bird finally is reunited with his mother, it is plainly obvious to all that the baby belongs with the mommy because they are both birds.

---

[8]  So help me, Codd.

[9]  Eastman, 1960. If you don't know what a "snort" is, I suggest you acquire a copy of the book. I don't wish to give away the entire plot.

A great number of the attributes floating around your system can be reunited with their mother entities if you simply take the time to use a strong dose of common sense and ask, "Are you my mother?" Is *Customer name* an attribute of *Order*? No, it's an attribute of the *Customer*. Most of our customers were named by their parents long before they decided to drop off any laundry at our establishment. Their name is not an attribute of their dry cleaning order.

Is the customer's *Phone number* an attribute of the *Order*? No, it is the number where the customer can be reached. It clearly is dependent on the customer. With a little common sense, we can quickly get much of the model to third normal form by asking if the attribute *really* belongs to the entity. Take the time to try this with your information model. Many of the attributes in your models represent real-world entities. If you simply visualize the entity and its characteristics, it isn't difficult to pigeon-hole a large percentage of your attributes correctly. Then your team can argue over the hard ones.

Figures 5–18 and 5–19 show our dry cleaning order in third normal form. The attributes which are dependent on the customer have been moved to a *Customer* entity. Since no suitable logical identifier exists for *Customer*, a *Customer number* has been added. Remember that I'm only including the foreign keys to illustrate normal forms. In an information model, the relationships suffice to communicate the linkage between entities. The decision to place the *Customer number* in the *Order* is an implementation decision and would be deferred until database design.

It is important for every professional in the information industry to be at least familiar with the concepts of normalization. I am not suggesting, however, that you must always be ready for a pop quiz on second normal form should somebody accost you with their data layout in an elevator. As your information modeling skills develop, you will find yourself instinctively attributing your entities in something very close to third normal form.

I present normalization in this chapter because it is a foundation on which the information model and relational database concepts are based. In practice, it is not necessary to turn the iron crank of the normalization machine every time you need to organize your data. The analyst must know what his data means and how it is to be used to do a good job of information modeling, or, as Meilir Page-Jones is fond of saying, "Normalization is a syntactic solution to a semantic problem."[10]

A small percentage of the information modeling population will use normalization as a formal technique for organizing a sea of tangled legacy data elements. Most people will simply employ the rules of normalization as a method of testing the completed information model. It is my sincere desire that you will internalize the concept, lodge it in the back of your mind and go about your days subconsciously creating elegantly normalized information models.

---

[10] Additionally, Page-Jones asserts, "Normalization is a proofreading technique for information models, not a construction technique." I agree whole-heartedly.

CUSTOMER

| Customer number | First name | Last name | Phone number |
|---|---|---|---|
| 100 | Slick | Pitchman | 555-4567 |

ORDER

| Claim ticket | Customer number (fk) | Drop off date | Date promised | Time promised |
|---|---|---|---|---|
| 1376 | 100 | 6-17-95 | 6-18-95 | 5:00 PM |

ORDER ITEM

| Claim ticket (fk) | Garment type (fk) | Service type (fk) | Quantity | Unit price | Special instructions |
|---|---|---|---|---|---|
| 1376 | Men's shirt | Launder | 15 | $1.00 | -None- |
| 1376 | Sport Coat | Dry Clean | 1 | $7.50 | Stain, cat hair |

SERVICE TYPE

| Service type | Garment type | Current unit price |
|---|---|---|
| Launder | Men's shirt | $1.00 |
| Dry Clean | Sport Coat | $7.50 |

**Figure 5–18.** Dry cleaning order in third normal form

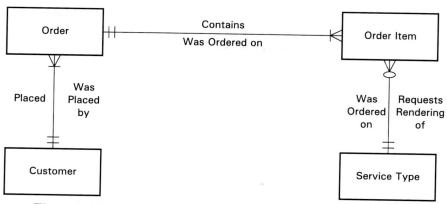

**Figure 5–19.** ERD for the dry cleaning order in third normal form

### Attribute Cardinality

You may have inferred from the section on normalization that each attribute in your model gets a name and a clear textual definition. The textual attribute definitions create a data dictionary that is used throughout the entire life of the system.

Another important property of attributes is *attribute cardinality*. Attribute cardinality declares how many instances of the attribute can apply to one single instance of its entity.

There are two points of cardinality for every attribute, a minimum and a maximum value. The minimum value can be zero or one. A minimum of *zero* declares that the attribute is *optional* for any given instance of the entity. A minimum of *one* says that the attribute is *required*. This is a critical piece of information because it will determine which columns are capable of storing nulls in your database design.

The maximum value may be one or many (or some fixed upper limit number greater than one). The maximum value is designed to tell us whether the attribute is repeating for any instance of the entity. The maximum cardinality is important because it will help you eliminate repeating groups and quickly get your model to first normal form. Many seasoned information modelers reflexively record their model in at least first normal form, so repeating groups are automatically eliminated. In this case, you only need to record whether an attribute is optional or required because the maximum cardinality will always be one.

Returning to our "Person *owns* Dog" example, let's examine some attributes that might be associated with a dog. Our system might be chartered to remember the dog's *License number*, *Name*, *Weight*, *Birth year*, *Vaccination type* and *Vaccination date*. The *License number* has been nominated as our unique identifier.

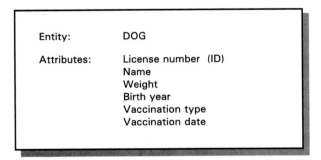

**Figure 5–20.** Attributes of the *Dog* entity

By assigning the attribute cardinality we find that the *License number* is required. We will accept no unlicensed dogs in our system. Each dog will have only one license. The business has also insisted that the *Name* of the dog is required, and a dog may have only one name. The *Weight* is optional and we are only interested in the current weight. The *Birth year* is optional, and again there will only be one birth year for any given dog.

The *Vaccination type* and *Vaccination date*, however, could have no values if the dog has never been vaccinated, but could have multiple values if the dog has received many shots. The resulting attribute cardinality can be expressed using a short-hand notation to the left of the attribute name (Figure 5–21). The minimum value is stated on the left, the maximum value on the right.

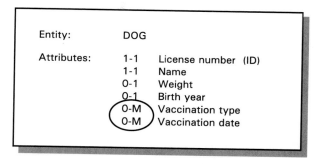

**Figure 5–21.** Attribute cardinality

Your first normal form violation siren should be going off about now. The *Vaccination type* and *Vaccination date* need to be moved off to a separate entity to eliminate the repeating group. When one or more the attributes of one entity get promoted to an entity of their own, this is called an *attributive entity type*.

## Attributive Entity Types

An attributive entity type is an entity which started life as an attribute or set of attributes of another entity. Because it is inextricably linked to its parent entity, it cannot exist on its own. Figure 5–22 shows the entity-relationship diagram for *Dog* and our new entity *Dog vaccination*.

**Figure 5–22.** An attributive entity type

Note that the relationship cardinality between *Dog* and *Dog vaccination* is zero to many. It is the same as the attribute cardinality for *Vaccination type*. The unique identifier for an attributive entity will be a concatenation of the relationship to the parent entity and at least one other attribute. In this case the relationship to *Dog*, plus the *Vaccination type* and the *Vaccination date* is required to identify a unique instance of *Dog vaccination* (Figure 5–23).

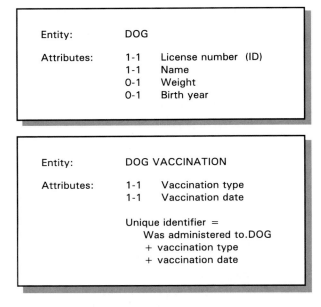

Entity:          DOG

Attributes:      1-1      License number  (ID)
                 1-1      Name
                 0-1      Weight
                 0-1      Birth year

Entity:          DOG VACCINATION

Attributes:      1-1      Vaccination type
                 1-1      Vaccination date

                 Unique identifier =
                    Was administered to.DOG
                    + vaccination type
                    + vaccination date

**Figure 5–23.** Attributes for *Dog* and *Dog vaccination*

The attribute cardinality for *Vaccination type* and *Vaccination date* has now changed. The zero-to-many relationship cardinality takes care of the repeating group. The attribute cardinality now expresses how many occurrences of *Vaccination type* and *Vaccination date* are possible for one instance of the entity *Dog vaccination*. In other words, for any record of the dog getting a shot, how many values could you have for the type of shot and the date of the shot? The answer is one. If the dog receives two types of vaccination on the same date, you record two instances of the entity *Dog vaccination*.

Attributive entity types can be noted graphically on the entity-relationship diagram. Several notations have cropped up. The most common is a pyramid in the box. An alternative is a rounded corner rectangle (or "roundangle") in the box (Figure 5–24). By noting the attributive entity types graphically on the diagram, you convey to the reader that the entity is really a logical extension of its parent entity.

**Figure 5–24.** Two versions of attributive entity type notation

Figure 5–25 shows a common attributive entity type, *Product price*. The product entity has an attribute called *Price* which itself has attributes, *Start date* and *End date*.

Most businesses have a requirement to keep prices past, present and future, causing this attribute group to repeat for any instance of product. The attributive entity type comes to the rescue again as a good solution to this problem.

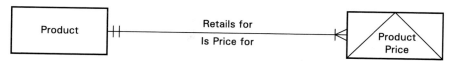

**Figure 5–25.** *Product* and attributive entity type, *Product price*

## Attribute Definition

So far in this chapter, we've seen that each attribute requires the following properties:

**Name:**   A concise, understandable name conforming to your shop's data-naming conventions

**Definition:**  A clear and complete textual statement of the attribute's meaning and its purpose and use in the system. The definition should be verifiable by the intended users of the system. Much of the field-level on-line help and definitions within the written system documentation should be derivable from the attribute definitions.

**Cardinality:**  Attribute cardinality has two values, a minimum and maximum. The minimum value is either zero or one. It determines whether the attribute is optional for any given instance of the entity. The maximum value is either one or many. It determines if the attribute can repeat for any instance of the entity.

In addition to these properties, the analyst should also record,

**Data type:**  The data type describes the length and valid values for the attribute. You may use standard SQL data types such as Char(1), Integer, Decimal(11,2), Varchar(200), in accordance to your shop's standard data type convention.[11] You may also create standard data type abstractions such as:

---

[11] So far in this chapter, I've implied that you have a published set of standard naming and abbreviation conventions and a standard set of data types in your shop. The word "standard" also implies that there is some penalty for non-compliance. If your IT shop does not have these established, there's no point in proceeding any further until you get this in place. Without standards, your information modeling efforts will quickly descend into chaos.

YES/NO:  a one-character field whose valid values are "Y" and "N"

MONEY:  a DECIMAL(11,2) field with nine digits to the left, two to the right, to be used for all domestic currency attributes.

Whichever method you use to assign data types, it is important that you achieve a reasonable level of consistency across the entire model that will serve you well in the database design.

**Range:** If your data is numeric, you must specify the upper and lower limits of the range (e.g., *Dog weight* must be greater than zero and less than 1,000 pounds.).

**Unit of measure:** I like to embed the unit of measure in the attribute name, such as *Shipping weight MT*. This tells the reader that the shipping weight is stored in metric tons, rather than short tons, pounds or kilograms. *Fiscal year* conveys far more explicit information than *Fiscal period*. If your shop's standard does not employ such a naming convention, you must include the unit of measure in your attribute's properties.

**Precision:** Sometimes the precision allowed (number of places to the right of the decimal) is more restrictive than the data type is capable of storing. For example, your standard data type for percentage fields might allow for three decimal places (e.g.: "0.125" for 1/8th), but your application might only allow increments of 1/8th rather than any three digits. If the precision is not readily discernible from the data type, it needs to be explicitly stated.

**Restricted Values:** Many values in GUI systems will become drop-down lists. Their values are restricted to a particular set of words or characters and they are sufficiently invariant that a separate reference table is not needed. For example, the values of order status might be "pending, confirmed, back-ordered, filled, shipped and invoiced." The values must be listed in the information model so they can be designed into the interface and application logic.

There is a lot of information to be gathered about each attribute in the system. This is where most of the detailed definition of your system's requirements resides. A well-crafted information model with detailed attribute definitions, coupled with a robust event model will give you a wealth of knowledge from which you can engineer applications that meet the business' needs. From this point forward in your project, there is little or no use for a "high-level" information model. You need to be down in the details.

## ASSOCIATIVE ENTITIES

If an attributive entity type is an entity which started life as an attribute or set of attributes about another entity, then you may have surmised that an *associative entity type* is an entity which started life as an *association* or relationship between two or more entities. Let's do a simple example to illustrate how associative entity types are derived, then tie it back to a classic example from a real business system.

### Example of Deriving Associative Entity Types

Let's say our firm has been hired to analyze a problem at a local chicken ranch. We find our chicken ranch located at the intersection of four state highways, two running north–south and two running east–west. Due to a recent increase in traffic, and the unfortunate location of the ranch, there has been an unusually high fatality rate as the chickens seem unshakable in their determination to cross the roads. Our job is to create an information system which will track which chickens crossed which roads and gather statistics about the conditions at the time of the crossing, and rate the success of the endeavor. The database will be used to come up with a solution for this vexing problem. (If this project had done a charter, they probably would have figured out that a simple fence would suffice.)

First, identify the event(s) which create the association. In this case, *Chicken attempts road crossing* is the culprit. Record and define the entities which represent fundamental, tangible things in the real world. *Chicken* and *Road* fall into that category (Figure 5–26).

**Figure 5–26.** Begin with the fundamental entity-types

Once you've drawn an entity, it's a good habit to define it right away. Defining *Road* is easy, but *Chicken* can be more difficult. Are you going to create a record for every chicken on the ranch or only those who attempt road crossings? What you're really verifying is which event or events create instances of the fundamental entities in your model. This is very important stuff. Most errors that I have seen on information models are due to sloppy naming and poor definitions, which often lead to various members of the project team making divergent assumptions about the system. By management fiat, I will declare that chicken means "only chickens which have attempted at least one road crossing." (We should cross-check our event dictionary entry for *Chicken attempts road crossing* at this point to ensure we have mandated that novice chickens have their identities established on their first crossing attempt.)

Now that you have settled on the fundamental entities, establish a relationship between them. Name it in both directions, and define all four points of cardinality.

The resulting cardinality (Figure 5–27) shows us that chickens must indeed cross at least one road before they are recorded in the system, and they may cross many roads as long as their luck holds out. Additionally, roads need not be crossed before they are recorded in the system, and any given road can be crossed many times.

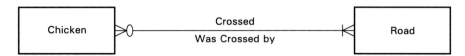

**Figure 5–27.** A many-to-many relationship

This pattern is called the *many-to-many* relationship. It allows for a single instance of either entity to be associated with multiple instances of the other entity.

> A *many-to-many relationship* occurs when an instance of entity A can be related to multiple instances of entity B, and an instance of entity B can be related to multiple instances of entity A.

Many-to-many relationships add a great deal of complexity to the design of a system. The first problem is in the relational database design. Let's jump forward to the design phase and imagine that we have a *Chicken* table and a *Road* table. To implement the relationship, *Chicken crossed road* using foreign keys, the relational database designer can't place the *Chicken number* in the *Road* table, or the *Road number* in the *Chicken* table. To work around this dreadful design, users would have to add a redundant row to either table every time a crossing occurred (or worse, call the IT department and have them splice in some extra columns). Such a relational database designer is likely to be murdered after hours by the programming team.

The last vexing issue is that we have no place in which to store attributes such as: *Crossing date, Crossing reason, Crossing direction, Traffic conditions, Crossing successful.* These are not attributes of the *Chicken* or the *Road*. They are actually attributes of the relationship *Crossed*. The evidence is mounting that we have another entity emerging in our model which is an *associative entity type.*

> An *associative entity type* is used for the following reasons:
> 1. to resolve many-to-many relationships,
> 2. to hold additional attributes which are characteristics of the relationship, not of the participating entities,
> 3. to allow a relationship to participate in other relationships.

Promote the relationship to become an entity. The graphic notation for an associative entity type is a diamond in the box. This is a quaint carry-over from Chen notation which depicts relationships as diamonds. This graphic clue immediately informs the reader that the entity started life as a relationship. The entity must be named and defined. In this case, I've chosen the name *Crossing*, and defined it as "an instance of a single chicken attempting a crossing of one of the four roads surrounding the ranch" (Figure 5–28).

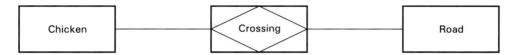

**Figure 5–28.** The many-to-many relationship resolves to an associative entity type

We now have two relationships to define, one on either side of the associative entity. Since we've already used the primary relationship name for the associative entity, naming these secondary relationships can be tricky. The resulting diagram in Figure 5–29 shows that the many-to-many relationship has been replaced with one-to-many relationships.

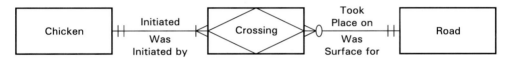

**Figure 5–29.** The resulting cardinality for the associative entity, *Crossing*

An important pattern emerges. Notice that the cardinality connecting *Chicken* and *Road* to the associative entity is "one to one." This is because a *relationship* cannot exist without its end points. Also notice that the original one-to-many and zero-to-many still exist, but they have crossed over. Figure 5–30 shows how the cardinality on a many-to-many relationship typically resolves using an associative entity type.

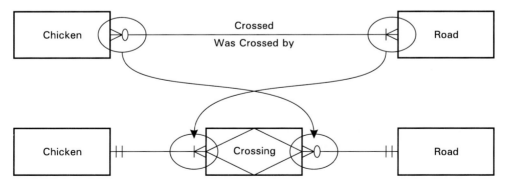

**Figure 5–30.** The typical many-to-many resolution pattern

We now have a suitable home for the attributes associated with the *Crossing*. Notice that the relationships to the originating entities are included in the unique identifier for an instance of crossing, along with at least one other qualifying attribute to distinguish between repeated attempts (Figure 5–31).

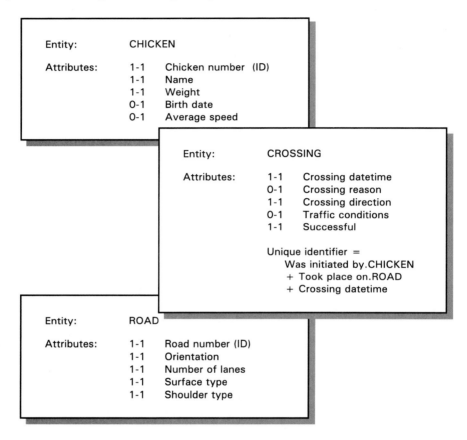

**Figure 5–31.** Attributes for *Chicken*, *Road*, and *Crossing*

Suppose that we decide to promote *Crossing reason* to become an entity so the users can control the list of valid reasons. The associative entity type, *Crossing*, gives us the ability to allow the original relationship to participate in other relationships. We can simply connect the entity *Crossing* to the entity *Crossing reason* (Figure 5–32).

Now, let's see if this pattern holds for more complex systems. Pretend that our *Chicken* has been transformed into *Customer*, and the object of her desire is not a *Road*, but instead a *Product* or *Service* offered by your company.

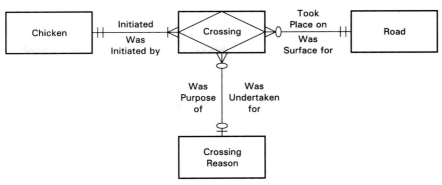

**Figure 5–32.** Associative entity types can participate in other relationships

**Figure 5–33.** *Customer* and *Product* are fundamental entity types

Identify the event or events of interest. In this case, I'll nominate *Customer orders product*. Record and define the entities which represent fundamental, tangible things in the real world, *Customer* and *Product*.

You will recall the wrangle over defining chickens. Defining *Customer* is just as tricky. You must decide when a customer becomes a customer in your system. Is it when they place their first order, when they apply for credit, or will you record potential customers as well? (I don't know the correct answer for your company, but I'll settle this one by saying it's when they place their first order, just so we can finish this book.)

Establish a relationship between *Customer* and *Product*, and determine all four points of cardinality (Figure 5–34). Now you can begin to resolve the many-to-many relationship by promoting it to an associative entity type. What emerges is the famous associative entity type, *Order* (Figure 5–35).

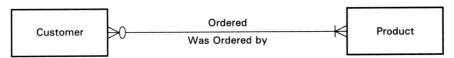

**Figure 5–34.** A many-to-many relationship

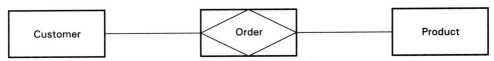

**Figure 5–35.** The many-to-many relationship resolves to the associative entity type, *Order*

We must be very precise when placing the cardinality on these relationships. *Customers* can place one and perhaps many *Orders*. An *Order* is placed by one and only one *Customer*. *Orders*, however can request one or more *Products*, and *Products* can be requested on zero or many *Orders*. We have yet another many-to-many relationship (Figure 3-36)! Many-to-many relationships don't always resolve in one step.

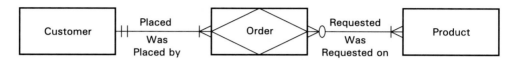

**Figure 5–36.** The resulting cardinality still includes a many-to-many relationship

We repeat the process one more time to resolve the many-to-many relationship between *Order* and *Product*. *Order item* emerges to represent the various *Products* that can be requested on a single instance of *Order*.

Figure 5–37 shows the finished ERD fragment. This important pattern crops up over and over again throughout any system where customers acquire the products or services of business or government. You will see this pattern emerge throughout this book. (I was struck once by the similarities between the information models of a sales system and a superior court system. The only difference was that the customers of the court were not showing up voluntarily, and the court was dispensing prison sentences instead of products.)

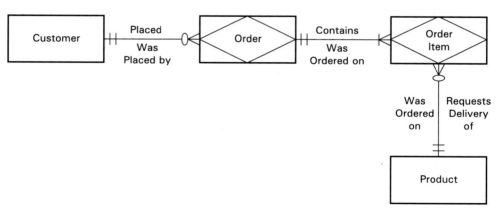

**Figure 5–37.** The classic customer-order pattern

It is important to resolve all of your many-to-many relationships in your logical model prior to designing the database. By uncovering your associative entity types, you create a mother entity for all of the attributes which are characteristics of the relationship.

The associative entity type also allows the originating relationship to participate in other relationships.

Perhaps the most important reason to recognize these objects in the analysis phase is because they can severely complicate your design. Associative entity types will result in intersection tables in your relational database, adding an additional table join to link participating members in the relationship. They will require additional windows and more complex reporting. Associative entity types present the GUI designer with some interesting navigational challenges, especially if the many-to-many nature of the relationship is the exception rather than the rule.

## SUPERTYPES AND SUBTYPES

In the real world, many objects belong to a similar class, but themselves have divergent characteristics. *Planes*, *Trains* and *Automobiles* are all examples of the class *Vehicle*, but they clearly have different characteristics and behavior. Some of the entities in your model will follow similar pattern. Collectively, they fall into a broad category called the *supertype*, within which each instance shares a limited number of similar attributes and can participate in the same relationships. The supertype may break down into several categories called *subtypes*. Subtypes are groupings within the supertype that have attributes which are unique to the subtype, and not shared among all instances of the supertype. Subtypes may also participate in relationships which are exclusive to the subtype.

The most common and often most complex supertype/subtype in most business systems is the entity *Customer*. Customers come in many shapes and sizes. Take, for example, the customers of a typical international manufacturing firm. The data required for export customers is different than that for domestic customers. Customers who are responsible for payment may be different than the customers who actually receive shipment of the goods. Customers may be internal to the organization or external. External customers may be trading companies operating on behalf of the real customer. Understanding and modeling the structure of the customer is often one of the most difficult information modeling tasks facing an organization. Other likely candidates for subtyping including the products and services offered by the company, and the different types of employees, contractors and service providers involved in the business.

There are a variety of notations available for subtyping. Figure 5–38 shows three of the most popular notations. The first is a simple decomposition diagram of the entity, showing that *Vehicle* can be either a *Plane, Train* or *Automobile*. The second notation uses garden-variety relationships to express that a "Vehicle *can be a* Plane," but a "Plane *is a* Vehicle." The third notation nests the subtype entities inside of the supertype entity. This is particularly handy because it saves space on the CASE tool screen.

Attributes which are common to all instances of the supertype are stored in the supertype entity. They are not repeated in the subtype entity. The supertype/subtype relationship declares that any subtype entity *inherits* all of the attributes of its supertype and participates in any relationships attached to the supertype.

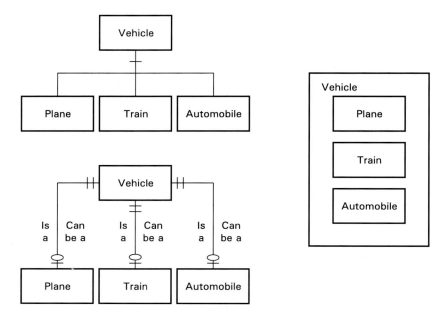

**Figure 5–38.** Three supertype/subtype notations

Attributes which are unique only to the subtype must be listed with the appropriate subtype. Similarly, all relationships which are restricted to the subtype must be attached only to the subtype entity.

In our example, all vehicles may have a *Vehicle ID*, *Passenger capacity* and *Top speed*. These attributes can be safely housed in the supertype entity *Vehicle*. If you need to store *Wingspan*, however, this attribute is only applicable to the *Plane* and should reside only in that subtype (Figure 5–39).

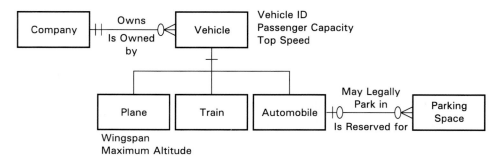

**Figure 5–39.** Relationships and attributes of supertypes and subtypes are depicted at the level to which they apply

A relationship such as "Company *owns* Vehicle," could apply to all instances of the supertype, but other relationships such as a plane's base airport or an automobile's currently assigned parking space should be connected to only the subtypes to which they apply.

In practice, subtyping has to be approached with a strong dose of common sense. If you modeled every possible subtype and permutation of *Customer*, in most large organizations, the number of entities needed to represent *Customer* could be extremely high. The goal of subtyping isn't to eliminate every optional attribute in your model, rather it is to identify the major classes of supertypes which define common behavior for their subtypes, and to separate out specialized subtypes at a reasonable and relevant level.

For determining "how low to go" when subtyping an entity, I prefer to brainstorm all of the different types of the entity. Returning to our manufacturing example, a customer may break out initially to:

*Ship to* versus *Bill to* roles

*Export* versus *Domestic* locations

*Internal* versus *External* ownership.

I'll stop there before this example gets too complicated for the confines of this chapter. The next step is to examine the similarities and differences between the attributes of the different customer types and the relationships in which they participate.

We may find that the attributes for the location to which the product is shipped are very different than those for the customer to whom the product is billed. The shipping location could be the customer's manufacturing location or their warehouse. The bill could be sent to the parent company's corporate office. The *Bill to* customer requires attributes regarding its credit status, the *Ship to* does not. Additionally, we may find that pricing and product specifications are related to the *Ship to* customer, but not to the *Bill to* customer. Conversely, the invoice must relate to a *Bill to* customer.

As a general rule, I find the exclusivity of relationships at the subtype level is a far more compelling reason to model the subtype as a separate entity than is the presence of a few specific attributes. Let's say that the only difference between *Internal* and *External* customers is a few attributes, but no significant relationships are associated exclusively at the subtype level. I find it acceptable and practical to roll these back up to the supertype level and use an attribute such as *Customer type* to make the distinction.

This simple suggestion can save you a lot of grief if someone on your project goes overboard on subtyping. You mustn't ignore subtypes altogether. They are a critically important part of your modeling effort, and there are a variety of ways to represent them in a physical database. Differentiating subtypes based on their participation in relationships will help you keep your model grounded at a practical and consumable level.

## STATE TRANSITIONS

One of the most useful models to the GUI designer is a *state-transition diagram.* Many of the entities in your model pass through a life cycle. An instance of the entity is born, passes through several phases in life, and is eventually laid to rest. The tip-off that your system is chartered to remember the current life cycle phase of an entity is typically an attribute called *Status.*

An entity, such as *Order*, might have a *Status* whose values may be restricted to:

tentative,

confirmed,

canceled,

back-ordered,

filled, or

shipped.

To "kick" an entity from one status value to the next, you need an event. The state-transition diagram forges an important link between the event model and the information model because it graphically shows which events change the value of a given state attribute.

Figure 5–40 shows the state transition diagram for order status. The status values are shown inside the box. The events are shown as arrows which note the direction of the state change. The initial status is indicated by an arrow entering the diagram from the top or side. In this case, the event, *Customer places order* sets the order status to "tentative."

It appears that one of two events may occur next. *Credit department approves credit,* could set the order status to "confirmed," or the customer could call and cancel his order. The state-transition diagram is very powerful and easy to read. We can see from this example that only "confirmed" orders can be "filled" or "back-ordered." This implies that tentative orders cannot be filled or back-ordered. Similarly, a shipped order cannot be canceled, but a filled order can.

As an analyst, you can take the state-transition model to the users and lead them through the possible transitions. What you will often find is that there are additional events lurking out there that have heretofore eluded the project team. You may find, for instance, that the customer *can* cancel a filled order, but is charged a restocking fee. This difference in policy for filled orders should be reflected in the event dictionary.

The rules expressed by the state-transition diagram are critical to the design of a well-crafted user interface. Figure 5–41 shows an *Order Selection* window on which the user can retrieve a set of orders based on the selection criteria he enters at the top of the window. Once the orders are retrieved, he may click through the list and carry out a variety of actions based on the command buttons on the window.

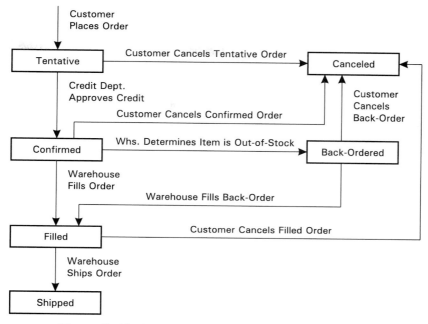

**Figure 5–40.** State-transition diagram for *Order status*

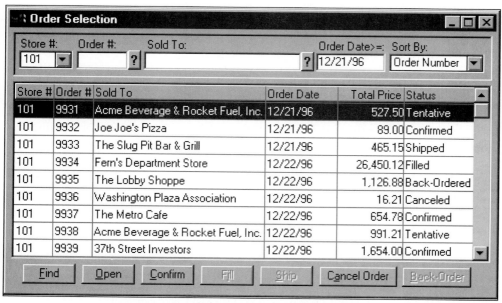

**Figure 5–41.** Window layout for *Order Selection*

Notice the Cancel Order button on the button bar. Command buttons and menu items are enabled or disabled depending on whether the action is a valid one for the user to take. If the user has clicked on, or "set focus" on any given order, should the Cancel Order button be on or off? The answer depends on the status of the selected order. If the status is "canceled" or "shipped," the button should be disabled (grayed out). Our state transition diagram tells the designer that the *Customer cancels order* event is not valid when the order has already been canceled or has been shipped. If the user clicks on a different order in the list which happens to have a status of "tentative," then the Cancel Order button should be enabled once again.

Status fields are not trivial matters in complex business systems. Many entities may have multiple status attributes, each tracking a different aspect of the entity, such as *Production status, Pricing status*, or *Approval status*. Each attribute which holds a state value for an entity should have its own state-transition diagram. The state-transition diagram allows the analyst to model and verify the business rules, prior to the design and coding of the system. It also provides a basis for testing the system's behavior after coding is complete.

The state-transition diagram graphically depicts each restricted value for a status field as a rectangle. The arrows show the events which can move the status from one value to the next. The diagramming technique is extremely useful for those state values which do not proceed in a neat and tidy sequential fashion. An unexpected event such as *Customer cancels order* throws an exception path into the natural progression of the order through its life cycle. Exception paths such as these make simple sequencing of the event list unwieldy. The state-transition diagram rides to the rescue by allowing the analyst to map multiple paths on one diagram.

## ENTITY MATRICES

Once you have a list of the entities in your system, a variety of matrices can be built to relate the entities to other objects in your model. In traditional information engineering,[12] entity matrices are used extensively in the formation of an organization's information strategy plan. These matrices, and variations thereon, are also useful for deriving the distribution requirements for an overall client/server architecture.

We saw at the end of Chapter 4 that an *event/business location matrix* can be created to show which events are to be recognized at each business location (Figure 5–42).

Each event's data requirements can be summarized in an *event/entity CRUD matrix* (Figure 5–43). This shows which events create, read, update or delete (CRUD) instances of the entities in the information model.[13]

---

[12]  Martin, Finkelstein, 1981.

[13]  This model largely replaces the *entity/process CRUD matrix* used in traditional structured analysis for mainframe systems. Since the activity section of the event dictionary contains the system's processing requirements, events are really a "user's perspective" way of identifying procedure, albeit with some redundancy.

| Event/Business location | New York, NY HQ | Boise, ID Sales | Miami, FL Sales | London, UK Sales | California Plant | North Carolina Plant |
|---|---|---|---|---|---|---|
| Customer places order | X | X | X | X | | |
| Credit dept. approves order | X | | | | | |
| Prod. dept. assigns order | X | | | | | |
| Plant fills customer order | | | | | X | X |
| Plant ships customer order | | | | | X | X |
| Accounting invoices customer order | X | | | | X | |
| Marketing mails catalogue | X | | | | X | |

**Figure 5–42.** An event/business location matrix

| Event/Entity | Customer | Order | Order item | Plant order | Plant order item | Finished goods invt. trns. | Raw materials invt. trns. | Invoice | Invoice item |
|---|---|---|---|---|---|---|---|---|---|
| Customer places order | CRU | C | C | | | | | | |
| Credit dept. approves order | U | RU | R | | | | | | |
| Prod. dept. assigns order | R | R | R | C | C | CR | CR | | |
| Plant fills cust. order | R | R | R | RU | RU | CRUD | CRUD | | |
| Plant ships cust. order | R | R | R | RU | RU | | | | |
| Acctg invoices cust. order | R | R | RU | R | RU | | | CRU | CRU |
| Marketing mails catalogue | R | | | | | | | | |

**Figure 5–43.** An event/entity CRUD matrix

Given these two matrices, a third matrix can be derived. If the event occurs at the business location, then the event's required data must also be accessible at that location. The *business location/entity CRUD matrix* displays the data distribution requirements (Figure 5–44).

| Business location/Entity | Customer | Order | Order item | Plant order | Plant order item | Finished goods invt. trns. | Raw materials invt. trns. | Invoice | Invoice item |
|---|---|---|---|---|---|---|---|---|---|
| New York, NY HQ | CRU | CRU | CR | C | C | CR | CR | CRUD | CRUD |
| Boise, ID Sales | CRU | C | C | | | | | | |
| Miami, FL Sales | CRU | C | C | | | | | | |
| London, UK Sales | CRU | C | C | | | | | CRUD | CRUD |
| California Plant | R | R | R | RU | RU | CRUD | CRUD | | |
| North Carolina Plant | R | R | R | RU | RU | CRUD | CRUD | | |

**Figure 5–44.** A business location/entity CRUD matrix

A variation on the event/entity CRUD matrix is the *event/entity currency matrix* (Figure 5–45). The values in the cells show how *old* the data can be for any given event. For instance, the customer's credit information must be 0 hours old for the event *Credit department approves order.* Similarly, the customer's shipping address must be 0 hours old for the event *Plant ships customer order.* On the other hand, the data can be up to 48 hours old for the event *Marketing mails catalogue.* This information will give the system architects a sense of how quickly they need to either replicate or transport data around a widely distributed system.

The *user authorization/entity CRUD matrix* (Figure 5–46) is a variant of the event/entity CRUD matrix. Instead of events, the matrix shows the *user groups* who are authorized to carry out the events. The duplicate entries are distilled down to a matrix which shows which user groups are authorized to create, read, update and delete which entities. The result is a matrix which forms the basis of the user authorization for your relational database management system.

## TOP-DOWN VERSUS BOTTOM-UP STRATEGIES

The information model, event model and context model form the "big three" analysis models. Together, they cover the data, behavioral, process and boundary requirements of the system. All that is missing is to put a face on the interface with some interface prototyping to validate the essential requirements.

I want to stress that even though this book presents context, events and information sequentially in separate chapters, in practice, these models are built concurrently. It

| Event/Entity | Customer | Order | Order item | Plant order | Plant order item | Finished goods invt. trns. | Raw materials invt. trns. | Invoice | Invoice item |
|---|---|---|---|---|---|---|---|---|---|
| Customer places order | 0 | 0 | 0 | | | | | | |
| Credit dept. approves order | 0 | 0 | 0 | | | | | | |
| Prod. dept. assigns order | 24 | 0 | 0 | 0 | 0 | 0 | 0 | | |
| Plant fills cust. order | 24 | 24 | 24 | 0 | 0 | 0 | 0 | | |
| Plant ships cust. order | 0 | 24 | 24 | 0 | 0 | | | | |
| Acctg invoices cust. order | 0 | 0 | 0 | 0 | 0 | | | 0 | 0 |
| Marketing mails catalogue | 48 | | | | | | | | |

**Figure 5–45.** An event/entity currency matrix

| User authorization/Entity | Customer | Order | Order item | Plant order | Plant order item | Finished goods invt. trns. | Raw materials invt. trns. | Invoice | Invoice item |
|---|---|---|---|---|---|---|---|---|---|
| Sales representative | CRU | C | C | | | | | | |
| Credit manager | U | RU | R | | | | | | |
| Production manager | R | R | R | C | C | CR | CR | | |
| Production assistant | R | R | R | RU | RU | CRUD | CRUD | | |
| Invoicing clerk | R | R | RU | R | RU | | | CRU | CRU |

**Figure 5–46.** A user authorization/entity CRUD matrix

is a matter of personal choice as to which one you start first, but it is almost impossible to finish one without having a good handle on the other two. Additionally, we will see in the next chapter that the interface prototype, to a large extent, can be derived from the "big three" models. What I have found in practice, however, is that it also works in reverse. The interface prototype can also help you derive and *finish* the "big three."

So, how do you get started on your information model? There are several ways to approach it. A top-down strategy can be employed by looking around your event model for all of the major things about which the system needs to remember something. This will lead to subject-area entities such as *Customer*, *Order* and *Product*.

Once you have the main entities for your major functional areas, you can start subtyping them and refining them. *Customer* may break out into several subtypes. *Order* will possibly end up as *Order header*, *Order item*, *Scheduled shipment*, *Scheduled shipment item*. Your *Product* entity will decompose into the various subtypes of products and relationships to the pricing structures, bill of materials and manufacturing specifications.

Eventually, the top-down approach progresses from large subject area entities, to more granular refined entities, and eventually to the attributes. A top-down approach works well if you are creating an enterprise-wide information model for strategic information planning. It is also useful at the project level if your legacy system offers few clues to the data elements needed for the new system.

A bottom-up approach starts with the attributes, and using the concepts of normalization (and a good dose of "are you my mother" and common sense) aggregates the facts in the system into entity groups. A bottom-up approach is appropriate when you are confronted with the amorphous sea of data from an unnormalized legacy system. You collect all of the data together and simply grind through it, systematically attributing the data elements to their proper entity types and working out the relationships and cardinality.

A middle-in approach is one that I use, by building my information through accretion. I like to get a rough idea of my major entities first, then start doing some event modeling. I determine the data elements required for each stimulus and response and attribute those to my information model, refining as I go. In the end, I model only the information that the system needs, and I have accounted for how each attribute is created and consumed by the system.

It is important to recognize that information models respect no project boundaries. Data is the core shared asset in any organization. Your information modeling effort must be bound by some sense of scope. The event model and context model provide that boundary. Without setting some sort of limit, the information model can expand infinitely as you creep ever outwards into other subject areas and eventually beyond the borders of your organization.

This caveat goes both ways. At the same time that you are limiting your modeling effort to the scope of your project, you must be aware that other projects need your data. The first client/server project in your organization may also be the first entirely relational database. If this is the case, you are presented with a fantastic opportunity to normalize your organization's data. This is a tremendous responsibility because the database for the first client/server project often is confronted with modeling the core entities such as *Customer* and *Product*. Of course, this means that the first project will get hit with the cost of modeling much of the business' data, which will drive up the cost disproportionally. If you do a good job of information modeling on the first project, however, the subsequent projects will reap the benefits of a solid foundation.

Businesses that already have an enterprise model and significant relational database expertise stand a much better chance of success on their first client/server endeavor than those who have yet to institute sound data resource management.

## SUMMARY

The information model's importance transcends a single project. Data is the central information asset of the business and should be modeled and managed prudently. The primary components of an information model are entities, relationships and attributes.

Entities are persons, places, things or abstract ideas about which the system needs to remember facts. Instances of an entity are grouped together because they share common characteristics and exhibit similar behavior. Entities are represented as rectangles on the entity-relationship diagram (ERD). Each entity should be carefully named and defined.

Relationships represent the associations between entities. A relationship is drawn as a line between one entity and another on the ERD. The relationship should be named in both directions. Reading from left to right, use the name above the line, from right to left, use the name below the line. The rule applies for vertical relationships. Simply rotate the diagram clockwise (Figure 5–47).

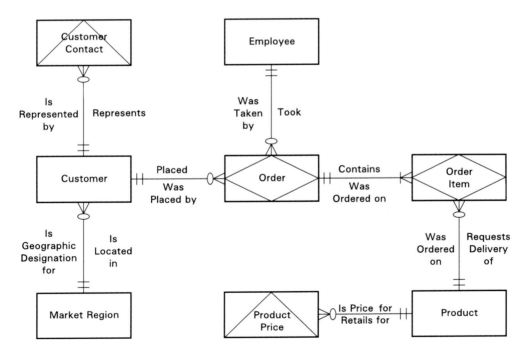

**Figure 5–47.** A sample entity-relationship diagram

Relationship cardinality expresses the minimum and maximum number of occurrences of the relationship that can occur between instances of the entity. A relationship may occur for an instance of an entity one and only one time, one to many times, optionally only once (zero to one), or zero to many times. Relationship cardinality is used to determine the foreign key structure of the physical database. It is very important that your model express all four points of cardinality, minimum and maximum in both directions, for each relationship.

A many-to-many relationship is one which allows multiplicity in both directions. These relationships can severely complicate a system and should be resolved by transforming them into associative entity types. An associative entity type is one which began as a relationship, but is promoted to become an entity so it can hold attributes of its own and participate in additional relationships.

Each fact about an entity constitutes a separate attribute. Attribute cardinality declares how many instances of the attribute can apply to one single instance of its entity. Each attribute should occur only once for each instance of the entity. You must specify whether it is optional or required. If the attribute repeats, then it should be promoted to an attributive entity type. Attributes which are dependent on their entity's key, the whole key and nothing but the key are said to be in third normal form.

Attributes should be carefully named, according to your shop's data naming conventions. Every attribute should have a clear and complete textual definition. In addition to the textual definition, you should specify the data type, upper and lower limits of numeric ranges, unit of measure, precision and restricted lists of values if they apply.

Some entities have groups of instances that themselves share common characteristics and behavior that is not shared by all of the members of that entity. These are called subtypes. Subtypes can have attributes and participate in relationships that are unique to the subtype and they automatically inherit all of the attributes and relationships of the supertype.

The state-transition diagram forges an important link between the information model and the event model. It is used to show which events alter the status of an entity.

Entities can be used in a variety of matrices. The event/entity CRUD matrix shows which events create, read, update or delete instances of each entity. The entity/business location CRUD matrix shows the organization's logical data distribution requirements. The user authorization/entity CRUD matrix depicts which user groups are authorized to create, read, update and delete which entities. The event/entity currency matrix tells us how *old* the data can be for any given event.

The information model can be built using a top-down, bottom-up or middle-in approach. It is important to bound your effort within the context of the project at hand, but be constantly aware that the information model is shared by all projects. If you are interested in certain data, it is more than likely that another application inside or outside of your organization is concerned with the same data. Sound information modeling is one of the secrets to client/server success.

# EXERCISES

1. A developer in a life insurance company once found a curious set of data in the legacy system's database. The column for policy holder's *Age* contained both positive and negative values. Wondering how their customers could be *negative* years old, the developer tracked down the source of the anomaly and was surprised by the reason. Can you guess the reason?

2. In an old mainframe banking system, a developer found an even more curious comment embedded in thousands of lines of undocumented code. The solitary comment read: "*Customer-sex-code: 0 = Unknown, 1 = Male, 2 = Female, 3 = Other.*" The value "3" was actually referenced in the code several times. Can you guess what information modeling problem caused this bizarre situation?

3. Customers very often have many addresses that a system has to keep track of. For this reason, *Customer address* often appears on the information model as an attributive entity type of the *Customer* entity. Employees also have multiple addresses, and so do Vendors. Can you see anything wrong with putting all addresses in the system into one entity called *Address* and linking it to the appropriate other entities, such as *Customer*, *Vendor* and *Employee*?

4. The users at a check printing firm once told me that checks could be purchased with up to six additional options, such as a custom monogram, or the customer's name under the signature line. The *Order Entry* screen dutifully had six columns of option codes next to each order item in which the additional options could be ordered, corresponding to six columns of option codes in the *Order item* table. Loud sirens should be going off in your information modeling minds at this time. What's wrong with this picture?

5. Can an associative entity type exist with only one relationship connected to it?

# ANSWERS

1. The system stored age literally in the database and held the *Date of birth* in a separate field. Each night a batch program ran to determine if anyone had celebrated a birthday and incremented their age one year. Unfortunately, the system analysts failed to recognize either *Date of death*, or *Whether deceased* as attributes of the policy holder, so an intrepid programmer had decided to insert a negative sign in front of the age field to denote policy holders who are no longer with us. That way, the happy birthday batch program knew to skip over these records, since dead people don't get any older.

2. The information modelers had failed to properly subtype customers into human customers and nonhuman customers such as businesses. Because there

was no overt way to distinguish between the two, the programmer needed a way to disregard attributes that pertain to humans that companies do not possess, and vice versa. Since businesses are neither male nor female, he saw an opportunity to create a *Customer-sex-code* value of "3" to identify business customers, thus packing two pieces of information into one field. The result was an unseemly mess throughout the entire application wherever customers needed to be distinguished by type.

3. This is a common information modeling error that I call *aggregation by coincident data type, not by business reason*. The only apparent reason that a modeler would lump addresses together into one grand entity is because they all have a street address, city, state and zip code. It would make no more sense to lump all prices in the system into a entity called *Money*. A true test of whether the concept is valid is to define the entity *Address* and see if it makes any business sense. The definition might be "a physical location on the map at which a person or company of interest to the system resides, makes child-support payments, does business, receives mail, receives invoices or accepts shipments." In most business systems, this definition would be nonsense. Employee addresses have no relationship to customer addresses, and therefore do not belong in the same entity. Few businesses have such a compelling interest in knowing which employees are also customers of the business and further require complete real-time maintenance of related data to make this schema valid. However, it would be perfectly valid to create a reusable address object which retrieves and presents address information on the interface in a standardized manner.

4. The six option codes on the order item form a repeating group, violating first normal form. More important, I found with further questioning, that many people at the company firmly believed that checks only had room for six options. In fact, there was no true limit to the amount of customization you could order on your checks, and customers routinely ordered seven, eight or nine options. The extra options were being keyed into the sixth column on the old *Order Entry* screen as "option code 99-miscellanous," and were being referenced in a comment field and manually priced. As a result, this firm really had no idea how many options of each type they were selling. The solution was to promote *Order item options* to become an attributive entity type and allow for an unlimited number of additional charges on an order item.

5. No. An associative entity type is, by definition, the result of an association (relationship) between two entities (or a many-to-many recursive relationship to the same entity). It cannot exist without explicit references to all of the end points of the original relationship.

# CHAPTER
# 6

Charter

Context Model

Information Model

Event Model

Interface Prototype

Architecture Model

Database Design

External Interface Design

Internal Component Design

Construction & Testing

# THE INTERFACE PROTOTYPE

## INTRODUCTION

Now we get to the fun stuff. Chapter 6 introduces the concept of prototyping. In some shops, prototyping is a euphemism for "code something quickly and see if the users will accept it." You won't find that approach advanced within these pages. Instead, I propose that a prototype can be well engineered. A successful prototype starts with a stated objective of what you want to learn from doing the prototype. Once you understand what it is you're trying to achieve, you can select a prototyping technique (low-tech or high-tech) which is most cost effective for achieving the objective. In this chapter, I will discuss the pros and cons of early prototyping and discuss valid reasons for both low-tech and high-tech approaches. We will then turn our attention to how the analysis models can be used to engineer the system interface. The event model allows you to group events together, based on the user who initiates them, the sequencing of the events, and the objects to which the events apply. The information model provides an organizational map of the data which must appear on the user interface. The relationships in your information model will heavily influence the layout of your windows. We will also see that prototyping can be done at many stages during the project. You can use it as a technique to discover and validate the business event and information requirements to create your "big three" models. During the design phase, you can prototype the various navigation and user control decisions you will have to make before coding the application.

## WHAT IS A PROTOTYPE?

A prototype is generally accepted to be a mock-up or facsimile of the real thing, but not so fully functional as to pass for the final product. Prototypes come in many shapes and sizes. In the auto industry, prototype cars can range in complexity from a model carved from a block of wood to an actual motorized vehicle that you can drive around the back lot.

The same range of complexity holds true for software systems. The prototype can be as simple as a set of paper window layouts taped to the wall, or as sophisticated as an animated software program which allows users to click buttons and enter data.

A prototype can be useful at several phases in a project. At each phase, the objective of the prototype must be clear. During the analysis phase, a prototype can be used to elicit user requirements. In the design phase, a prototype can help evaluate many aspects of the chosen implementation.

### The Purpose of Prototyping

Prototyping should always be done with a specific learning objective in mind. This chapter focuses on how to create window layouts by consuming the context, event and information models for early prototyping in the analysis phase.

In the analysis phase of a project, the prime directive of prototyping is to derive and validate your essential requirements while keeping your implementation options open.

The analysis prototyping effort focuses on window information content and business events. This means that design issues such as final layout, navigation, determining the user's appropriate unit of work and nailing down every command button and GUI control are still premature and can be safely deferred. You will start forming opinions and begin collecting information about the ultimate design of the product, but that is not the purpose of prototyping while gathering requirements. When reviewing an analysis stage prototype with the users, keep them informed of the prime directive. If the users bring up design issues, write their comments down and draw their focus back to content and business events. You will come back to the GUI design later in the project. We will see in Chapters 10 and 11 that there is a lot more to a GUI than window content.

## Benefits of Early Prototyping

More than any of the "big three" models, the interface prototype really draws the users into the project. For the first time, the system has a "face." Inevitably, after seeing the prototype, someone will tell the analyst about an event that heretofore has gone unmentioned. They will also add data items to the window which were not mentioned during interviews, and possibly take some away as irrelevant. For this reason, I find it impossible to really *finish* the information model or the event model until I have a prototype. Taking it to a further extreme, prototyping can be used as an interview tool to actually *derive* the information and event models.

Prototyping will also cause business process issues to surface. When a client/server system begins to intrude into what once was the personal computer's domain, you may find people who perform essentially the same task in radically different manners. The new system may eliminate redundant data entry into spreadsheets or ancillary systems, or alter or eliminate someone's job description. The prototype is often the users' first clear glimpse of their future working environment.

Prototyping will also surface technical issues at a point in the project when there's still enough time to do something about them. Window layouts can be mapped to the information model to get a sense of how complex the data access might be. I recently encountered a dramatic example of a window prototype which surfaced a vexing technical problem. A sales support group required a very densely packed inventory projection window which was capable of displaying past, present and projected future inventory balances. The information model indicated that a massive number of complex table joins and calculations were required to put the data on the display. The potential performance bottleneck had gone undiscovered until the prototype was created. The analyst handed off this window to a technical team that was able to take the time to find a way to make it work, averting a last minute coding crisis.

The prototype also lets you explore possible target environments. It may be that a graphical user interface is *not* optimal for your particular application. You can explore how your interface would look with pen-based systems, hand-held devices, bar-code readers, a web page, or good old character-style green screens.

It is important that your users are familiar enough with the target technology to evaluate your layouts without getting confused. For users who have never seen a GUI, you will need to give them an introduction and demonstration using several standard GUI applications such as a word processor and a spreadsheet, or perhaps demo another GUI application in your shop. Users need to understand that they can have multiple windows open, relevant data in the title bar, and have the ability to drag windows out of the way. Otherwise, your users may insist on practices which were artifacts of the green screen days, such as repeating header information at the top of each screen.

## The Downside of Prototyping

Like all good things, prototyping has a downside. Even though you are still gathering requirements, the prototype starts the project down the road to design. Analysts must constantly mind the prime directive and use the prototype to derive and validate the requirements while safely deferring detailed design decisions. I insist on this separation because analysis is hard enough without being distracted by navigation, ergonomics, or worse, coding issues.

For any portion of your project on which you want to move into design, it is important to get the information model and event models nailed down first. The detailed design of the interface can be done concurrently with the architectural modeling and database design efforts which follow the completion of the analysis models. All of these tasks, however, will be severely hampered and plagued with rework if the information and event models are not well understood.

Be careful in your prototype not to imply features that you can't deliver. The GUI paradigm comes with a plethora of features and controls. The goal is to use the ones which are appropriate, not to use them all. On my very first client/server project, we promised a slick drag-and-drop feature in the prototype. When it came to actually coding it, we found the drag-and-drop function of the development tool to be problematic. We regretted ever promising that particular navigation style, since the users had become enamored with the idea and wouldn't entertain any other alternatives, even though a variety of methods would have worked. Coding took twice as long as expected and testing it was a nightmare. From that point on, we kept the prototypes simple and relatively neutral on navigation issues. In the detailed design phase, we concentrated on those GUI features that we knew we had mastered.

Perhaps the gravest danger of early prototyping is that the project manager may let slip the reins from the programmers. Freed from the shackles of analysis, they may drop all pretense of modeling and start coding the system. On a project of any appreciable size, this spells disaster.

One of the basic premises of this book is that client/server-GUI applications are more complex and require *more* engineering savvy than their mainframe counterparts. Through years of trial and error, I am completely convinced that the current crop of development tools are still more expensive to modify than a well crafted design specification. A discrete design step will yield a specification that allows the project manager to partition the programming effort among multiple coders, and enables independent testing of the application by a quality assurance team. Without a design specification, all subsequent testing and documentation efforts must wait until the programmer delivers finished code. The design specification is one of the most cost-effective deliverables in the entire project.

## How Detailed Should the Prototype Be?

There are two schools of thought when it comes to prototyping. One camp supports a *high-tech* coded prototype which eventually evolves into the finished system. The system is coded incrementally, starting with the interface layout, then adding more and more detail to animate the system.

The other camp believes that so-called high-tech prototypes are still too expensive and that the same benefit can be yielded from cheap *low-tech* layouts made in a word processor, drawing tool, piece of paper, white board or CASE tool.

At this point in the evolution of software development tools, I am a firm believer in low-tech prototypes. Even the low-tech prototype is reused in the design specification and test script. The reason I support low-tech prototyping has to do with the high speed of achieving the learning objective, and the low cost of making changes.

Remember that the prime objective of prototyping in the analysis phase is to gather and validate requirements, while deferring detailed design decisions. Low-tech prototyping is cheap, it's fast and it meets the learning objective. Many of the leading GUI development tools (which I place in the high-tech category) still insist that a relational database be installed prior to making windows which are capable of being reused in the final application. This dependency on tables drives up the cost of making changes to the prototype as well as forces the creation of a database design at a time in the project when the information model isn't complete. While this approach may work on very small applications, it doesn't scale up to a cost-effective methodology for the larger projects.

The low-tech prototyping method minimizes the phenomenon called "pride of authorship." The longer a programmer is allowed to work on a design, the less likely he will be willing to change it. The low-tech prototype ensures that very little emotional investment is made before the product is ready to be reviewed and amended by the users or the rest of the development team.

There are legitimate reasons for building a working, animated high-tech prototype. A small, isolated construction effort can be very instructive if either the development or the users have never before worked with a GUI application. In this situation, the construction of the prototype should be treated as a research and development lab, with clear learning objectives and a scope limited to one small piece of the system. The goal is to get developers and users familiar with the target environment, so in the future, they can recall the abstractions without having to build every piece of the product in order to understand it.

For creating cheap, low-tech prototypes, any drawing tool, or even a word processor can do a reasonable job of imitating a window layout. Project teams have very successfully created templates for objects such as scroll bars, title bars, menus, buttons and fields, making it easy to cut and paste together a new layout in a matter of minutes. Once several window templates have been created in the chosen tool, it is very easy to copy them for subsequent windows, ensuring a common layout pattern throughout the application.

## WHERE DO WINDOWS COME FROM?

Structured software engineering methodologies have been plagued in the past with a deep chasm between analysis and design into which many projects have fallen, never to emerge. I prefer to view the transition from analysis into design as a gradual gradient, in which the models become more design-like with each decision made. The interface prototype is the first step into the realm of design. To begin the prototype, we turn to our analysis models.

Windows are the physical manifestation of the stimulus and response flows from the business events for which you have chosen to implement using a graphical user interface. The first step is to decide which events lend themselves to a GUI. You can start by revisiting the context model. Now that you understand a great deal about your system, you are ready to entertain ideas about the physical transport of data into and out of your application.

Using the context model as a graphic aide, examine the stimulus, response and external agents for each event. Consider whether the interface should be on-line, direct to a printer or fax machine, to an electronic data interchange, to another database or to some other means of transport (Figure 6–1).

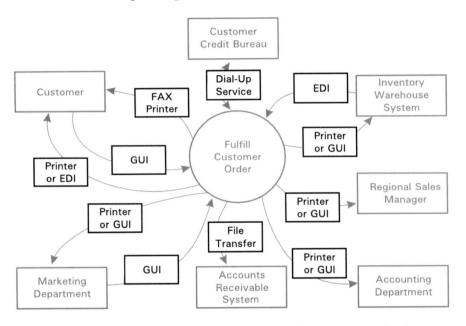

**Figure 6–1.** A context diagram, annotated with transport mechanisms

The context model declares the interface boundary. You will have to design a transport mechanism for each stimulus and response which crosses the boundary. The data which crosses the interface is declared in the event model by the stimulus and response. The organization and definition of that data can be found in the information model.

## THE PROTOTYPE BEGINS THE MAN–MACHINE DIALOGUE

Imagine that we have been hired to design an automated teller machine. (Assume that none of us have left our cubicles for twenty years, and have therefore never seen a cash machine.) We have some sketchy analysis models of the business problem, and have been asked to transform them into an interface prototype. Figure 6–2 depicts the event dictionary entry for *Bank customer requests withdrawal*.

| Event ID: | 005 |
|---|---|
| Event: | Bank customer requests withdrawal |
| Description: | A bank customer may withdraw cash from his account by identifying himself and his account number to the bank, indicating the account type and withdrawal amount. The bank will verify that sufficient funds are available and dispense cash and a receipt showing the amount withdrawn, date, time and new balance. |
| Stimulus: | Account number, PIN (personal identification number), Account type (checking or savings), withdrawal amount |
| Activity: | Validate account exists*<br>Validate PIN<br>Validate sufficient funds<br>Create withdrawal transaction<br>Dispense cash<br>Create withdrawal acknowledgment<br><br>* Methodologist's note: I find it a sensible practice not to break apart events for every possible reject response. By using a key word like "validate", the reader can assume that an invalid data value will be rejected by the system and the event activity will not continue processing. You will, however, need to accomodate each reject response in your final design. |
| Response: | Withdrawal acknowledgment (Account number, Account type, Customer name, Date, Time, Branch, Transaction ID, Transaction type, Transaction Amount, (material = cash) |
| Effect: | The customer has his cash and his account has been reduced by the amount withdrawn. |

**Figure 6–2.** Event Dictionary entry for *Bank customer requests withdrawal*

Our project's technical director has read an article about client/server computing and come up with the bright idea of strapping a monitor, keyboard and mouse to the side of the bank. With our brains in the "off" position, we can create a prototype window to recognize this event simply by arranging the stimulus data elements in the window workspace. The response data will be returned to the user via a printer, therefore no significant response data is needed on the display. The illustration below shows the results of our design masterpiece. Does this prototype satisfy the essential requirements as defined by the analysis models? It appears that it does. Is the prototype design any good? No, it's rubbish!

The analysis models cannot be mechanically transformed into an interface prototype without any additional brain-wave activity. The essential models are silent about the intended user's level of expertise. In the case of our cash machine interface, it is unlikely that the typical bank customer will take the time to type their account number, account type, PIN and withdrawal amount. Many of the bank's customers don't know how to type at all.

Real-world automated teller machine designers are confronted with a quality vector that insists that the interface must be usable by any customer from age five to one hundred and five. To accommodate this requirement, the designers have to break the essential stimulus flow into a series of dialogues. Most modern cash machines have taken the decomposition of business events into dialogue to the logical extreme. They request *one data element at a time*, followed by an editing activity and a system response prompting for the next data element. Each fragment of the dialogue is an event in its own right.

Bank customer requests withdrawal =

    Bank customer inserts account card

    Bank customer types PIN

    Bank customer selects account type

    Bank customer indicates withdrawal amount

The level of granularity of these events is driven by design considerations, and the entire suite of events in the dialogue is required to satisfy the single business-level event. For this reason, an event dictionary entry for each dialogue event is overkill. The interface prototype becomes a superior visual aide. Figure 6–3 shows a reasonable prototype for the event *Bank customer requests withdrawal*, based on the intended user's skill level.

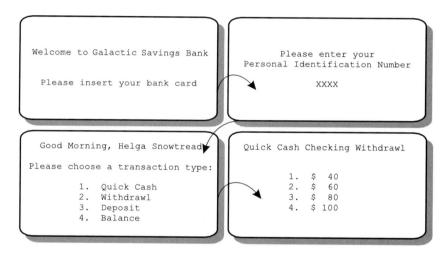

**Figure 6–3.** A prototype respecting the skill level of the intended user

The point of this example is to illustrate that the interface prototype is a *design* activity. It is very difficult to avoid usability issues once you start laying out windows. Be mindful of the analysis prototype's prime directive to derive and validate the essential requirements. You will need to address a certain portion of usability issues so your prototype won't be summarily rejected by your users, but try to keep your design options open. As we will see later in this book, there are a wealth of considerations that go into a well-crafted interface that are deferrable until the detailed design stage. These include determining the user's appropriate unit of work, window type, navigation, and the points at which work must be committed to the database.

## Grouping Events by Subject

Events can be used in a variety of ways to guide the prototype. An event list can be sorted or grouped by transporter, or subject. This technique gathers together all of the events for which a particular user group is responsible. Figure 6–4 is a subset of the many events initiated by a doctor in a family health clinic.

```
Doctor events:
Doctor requests patient history
Doctor records patient diagnosis
Doctor requests prescription dosage
Doctor requests symptom search
Doctor requests monthly sales report
Doctor reviews appointment schedule
Doctor reserves tee-off time
```

**Figure 6–4.** Events grouped by transporter

Traditionally, many systems have been designed following a company's traditional organizational structure. The sales module included the order entry functions, the patient history section would include medical records, the accounting module would contain the financial reports, and so on. Given the list of events initiated by the doctor in Figure 6–5, how many "modules" must the doctor delve into?

| Event name | Traditional system module |
|---|---|
| Doctor requests patient history | Patient history |
| Doctor records patient diagnosis | Patient visit |
| Doctor requests prescription dosage | Medication information |
| Doctor requests symptom search | Ailment information |
| Doctor requests monthly sales report | Accounting |
| Doctor reviews appointment schedule | Reservations |
| Doctor reserves tee-off time | Recreation |

**Figure 6–5.** Events in their traditional "modules"

Organizationally structured systems assume that people's job descriptions are partitioned neatly along political boundaries (Figure 6–6). The interface is structured accordingly. Each window is typically located in one place in the application, for instance, the daily reservation schedule can be found only under the *Reservations* icon on the main menu. The reservations application also includes all functionality required for creating, modifying and canceling reservations.

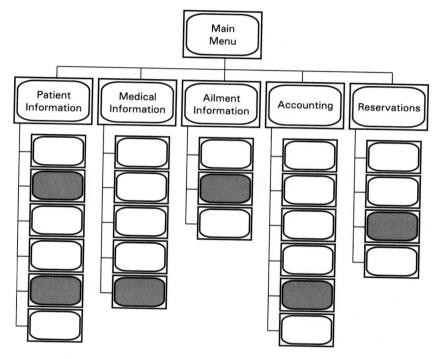

**Figure 6–6.** An organizationally-structured application

One strategy to control user access in an organizationally structured application is to deliver the same application to everybody, but vary their access depending on their authority to initiate various events. This is the most common implementation in the client/server environment because it makes version control very easy when everybody has the same software. The downside is that a single user, such as the doctor, has to become familiar with several major subsystems in order to find the windows they need.

Problems arise in organizationally structured applications when the users' actual job activity strays outside of traditional political boundaries. This is becoming a more common occurrence in today's "empowered" enterprises. An alternative to organizational structure is to package windows together into applications which are targeted to specific event initiators (Figure 6–7). The major advantage of this method is that the user gets one-stop-shopping for the events in which they are responsible. In addition, the size of the application is physically smaller, and the user does not need to learn how to navigate unused portions of the application. The downside is that the on-going version control of software upgrades will have to manage the building and distribution of multiple and disparate executables to different client sites.

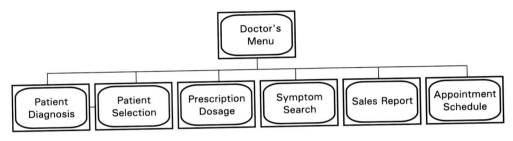

**Figure 6–7.** An application organized by transporter

We will continue to see that design is full of trade-offs and compromises. Grouping events by transporter helps the designer prototype different organizations for the same application, ranging from traditional functional decomposition to heterogeneous packaging based on individual user needs.

Grouping events by initiator, (e.g., "customer") can also be very revealing. By determining the ultimate source of the data, you may be able to extend your data capture or response presentation outside of the traditional organization, and all the way to the customer. Creative examples include electronic ticketing in airline applications, subways and rail stations, and placing orders via the Internet.

## Grouping Events by Object

One of the most powerful ways to consume an event model is to group events by object. The syntax of an event name is *Subject-verb-object*. The object represents the real world *thing* upon which the event is visited. Take our venerable old event, *Customer places order*. The object *Order* may be represented in the data model by multiple entities. In Figure 6–8, we see a typical data structure for *Order*, where a customer can place orders for multiple products and request one or more deliveries of those products over time.

Please recognize that the word *object* is severely overloaded in our industry. *Object* (or more precisely *class*) can be a representation of a single entity type, or an abstraction which represents multiple entity types, or even has no representation in the information model. It can also be a wide variety of programming constructs which are purely implementation-oriented. In the context of this chapter, the word *object* refers to the noun or modified noun in the event name which represents a business abstraction, for which relevant data may be represented within one or more entities in the information model.

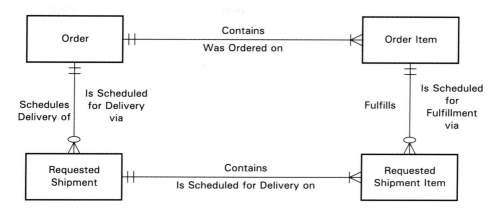

**Figure 6–8.** An ERD of the *Order*

For projects which are targeted to fully object-oriented implementations, this grouping and examination of the event model, in conjunction with the information model is the first step to discovering and cataloguing business classes in an object-oriented design. I will defer a full discussion on this topic until Chapter 12, on internal component design.

Grouping events by object leads to the *object-action paradigm*. The object-action paradigm is a shift in the overall design of user interfaces that has transpired over many years. Early research into the usability of different screen designs revealed that it is more intuitive and efficient when users first acquire an object on the screen, and then tell the computer the action to apply. Early on-line programming languages often encouraged the exact reverse. Figure 6–9 shows the main menu for an action-object implementation.

The main menu for a typical action-object application would have the user declare the type of action they intend to take. They may type UO for "Update Orders" and press Enter. The program would call up a blank order update screen (Figure 6–10). The user would then identify the order they wish to update by typing a key such as the order number at the top of the screen and pressing Enter again. The screen would then retrieve the order and they could get on with their business. This type of design supported an environment where the user's tasks were extremely repetitive. They could stay on the same screen and enter orders all day, keying in data from stacks of input sheets.

Today, we recognize that most user's jobs are more complex. By pushing automation out to the front lines of the organization, the repetitive motion of the data entry departments of old have given way to the more random forces of the real world. Salespeople receive calls from customers asking for new orders, changes to work in progress and cancellation of existing orders. The object-action paradigm states that users should be able to select a list of objects from the database, highlight one or more of them, and then specify the action that they want to invoke.

```
ID: B0001                      MAIN MENU
----------------------------------------------------------------------------

                    TYPE:      FOR:
                    ------------------------------
                    EO         ENTER NEW ORDERS
                    UO         UPDATE ORDERS
                    DO         DELETE ORDERS
                    VO         VIEW ORDERS
                    B          VESSEL BOOKING MENU
                    I          INVOICING MENU
                    X          SOMETHING WE HAVEN'T THOUGHT OF YET
                               BUT WE KNOW WE'LL NEED IT.




     >:

     PF1 HELP
```

**Figure 6–9.** An action-object main menu

```
ID: B0022                      ORDER ENTRY
----------------------------------------------------------------------------

ORDER_NBR: |_____    ORDER DATE: __/__/__  STORE_NBR:__
CUST_NBR:  _____    [CUSTOMER NAME]
ADDR_LINE_1:_____
ADDR_LINE_2:_____
CITY:       _____  ST:__  ZIP:_____-____

ORDER ITEMS:
----------------------------------------------------------------------------
LINE   PRD_CD  PRD_DESC            QTY   UOM   UNIT_PRICE    EXT_PRICE
----------------------------------------------------------------------------

__    _____  _____    ___   ___   $_____.__     $_____.__
__    _____  _____    ___   ___   $_____.__     $_____.__
__    _____  _____    ___   ___   $_____.__     $_____.__
__    _____  _____    ___   ___   $_____.__     $_____.__
__    _____  _____    ___   ___   $_____.__     $_____.__
                                                      TAX: $_____.__
                                                    TOTAL: $_____.__
     >:

     PF1 HELP   PF9 FIRST   PF10 BACK   PF11 NEXT   PF12 LAST
```

**Figure 6–10.** The *Update Order* screen

Figure 6–11 shows a window which supports the object-action paradigm. The user can enter various optional selection criteria at the top of the window which allows them to retrieve a list of orders when they click the Find button. The list displays in the lower portion of the window.

**Figure 6–11.** The *Order Selection* window

By clicking through the rows in the result set, they can select the object of their desire. The command button line (or menu in some applications), contains all of the actions that are capable of being invoked from this window. The user first selects the object, then applies the action. To update an order, the salesperson simply finds the order on the list, and clicks the Open button. The *Order Maintenance* window then opens, with the data prefilled from their selection (Figure 6–12).

The graphical user interface also supports an important extension to the object-action paradigm. When the user has selected the object, the interface is sufficiently intelligent to inform them which actions are legal at any point in time based on the user's authority and the current status of the object. Command buttons and menu items are routinely disabled (grayed out) on the interface when the action is illegal for the selected object. This can be a daunting task to program and virtually impossible to test for correctness without a state-transition diagram.

Figure 6–13 shows a list of events which have been grouped by object. The object of the event can usually be determined by simple inspection. Often, events will affect more than one object. A far more rigorous approach is to produce an event/entity CRUD matrix to determine which entities are affected by each event; however, this level of detail is not always required.

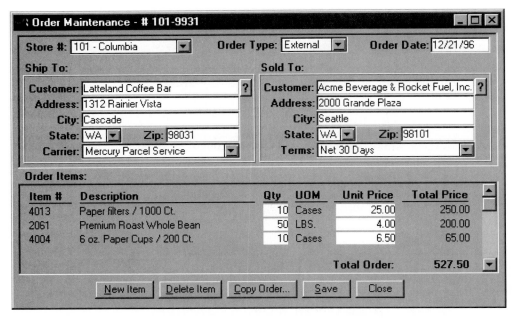

**Figure 6–12.** The *Order Maintenance* window

| Event name | Transporter | Object |
|---|---|---|
| Customer places order | Sales rep. | Order |
| Customer modifies order | Sales rep. | Order |
| Customer cancels order | Sales rep. | Order |
| Prod. dept. allocates order | Production mgr. | Order |
| Trans. dept. books order | Marine booking rep. | Order, Booking |
| Plant ships order | Shipping clerk | Order, Shipment |
| Sales mgr. requests order report | Sales mgr. | Order |
| Customer inquires on order status | Sales rep. | Order |

**Figure 6–13.** Events grouped by object

A sensible method for getting started on a prototype for these events is to first examine the transporter of the events, and then examine the object. We can see in Figure 6–13 that the sales representative is responsible for entering, updating and canceling orders, as well as answering customer inquiries. We may also find that the sales manager is an occasional user of the application, and nine times out of ten, he asks the sales representative to pull reports for him.

Since each of these events is transported into the system by the same user group, and affects the same object, they are likely candidates to be grouped together in the interface. Using the object-action paradigm, we can give the sales representative a window on which he can acquire a list of objects from the database, and initiate these events for the selected items.

In the prototype, we would expect to see a layout of an *Order Selection* window on which the user may browse multiple instances of orders, and as many *Order Maintenance* windows as it takes to capture the information about a single instance of order. In the analysis phase, the prototype can safely defer detailed design issues such as the final navigation, window type and whether the user may have multiple orders open at one time. These issues should be addressed in a design prototype after the essential content of the interface has been validated.

## USING THE INFORMATION MODEL TO LAY OUT WINDOW CONTENT

The information model is a critical guide to window layout. The organizational map of the data is dictated by the relationship cardinality on the entity-relationship diagram. If an order can have multiple order items, one for each product ordered, then one would expect a classic header-detail relationship on the order maintenance window (Figure 6–14).

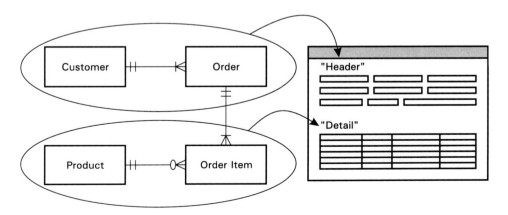

**Figure 6–14.** The information model guides the data layout on the interface

If there is room to display both entities on the same window, then the order entity can be arranged at the top, and a grid style section can display each instance of order item in the lower portion of the window. If there are too many attributes to fit comfortably on one window, then multiple windows will have to be employed to display the information.

For updatable fields, avoid at all costs using scroll bars to view fields which have been hidden to the right or bottom of the window. Users often reject scrollable windows which have updatable fields hidden from view (Figure 6–15).

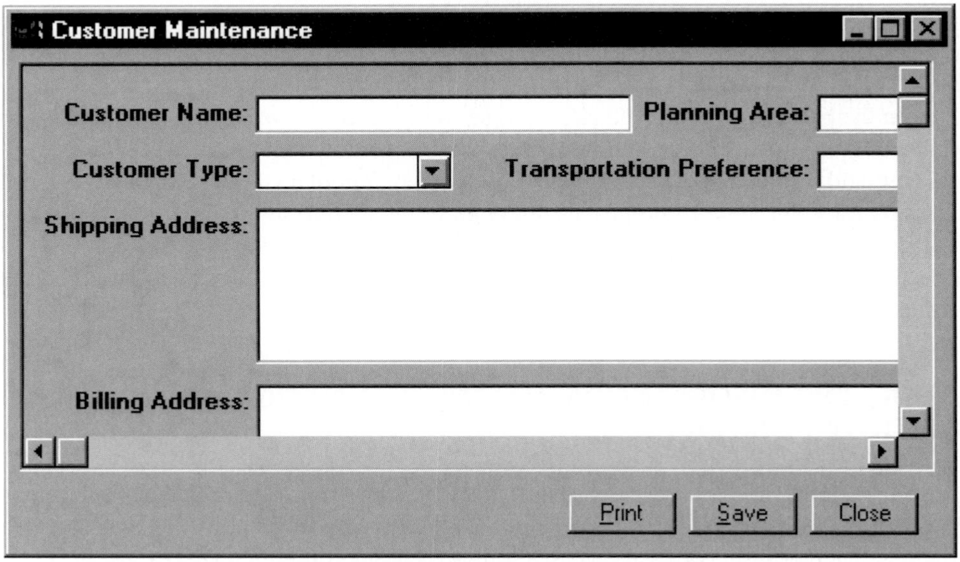

**Figure 6–15.** Improper use of vertical and horizontal scroll bars

Vertical scroll bars are best employed for large lists where more rows are returned than can fit on the screen. Horizontal scroll bars should be reserved also for *non-updatable lists* when the number of columns returned exceeds the width of the display. When using horizontal scrolling lists, it is a polite practice to use grid-style windows which allow the users to rearrange their columns to their specifications and save their format to a local file (Figure 6–16).

Just like the consumption of any of the other models, the information model cannot be consumed in an intellectual vacuum. Consider the following ERD fragment, (Figure 6–17). An *Invoice* can have many *Invoice items*. The prototype designer has dutifully translated each entity on the information model into a window. There is a window for *Invoice Selection*, *Invoice Maintenance*, *Invoice Item Selection*, and *Invoice Item Maintenance*. The user's first reaction to the application is that it takes too many windows to get to the *Invoice Item Maintenance* window. The analyst reminds them that the purpose of this prototype is just to validate content, and not to address navigation, but the users are concerned and won't let it drop.

| Vessel | Voyage | Trade # | Load Port | Disch ▲ |
|--------|--------|---------|-----------|---------|
| Ocean Rider | V24 | B1096 | Vancouver, BC | Taganoura, JI |
| Ocean Rider | V24 | B1096 | Tacoma, WA | Shimizo, JP |
| Ocean Rider | V24 | B1096 | San Francisco, CA | Shimizo, JP |
| Ocean Seeker | V28 | B147 | Vancouver, BC | Taganoura, JI |
| Ocean Seeker | V28 | B147 | Tacoma, WA | Shimizo, JP |
| Ocean Vision | V22 | B12 | Vancouver, BC | San Francisco |
| Ocean Loaner | V34 | BC6 | San Francisco, CA | Vancouver, B |
| Ocean Loaner | V34 | BC6 | Los Angeles, CA | Vancouver, B |
| Ocean Cruiser | V38 | BC12 | San Diego, CA | Seattle, WA ▼ |

Vessel Selection — Vessel: ___ Voyage: ___ LRD>=: 12/15/96 ETD>=: ___

[Print] [Open] [Close]

**Figure 6–16.** Proper use of vertical and horizontal scroll bars

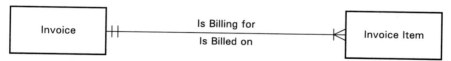

**Figure 6–17.** An ERD fragment from an invoicing system

Even though final navigation decisions will be deferred until the detailed design stage, it is OK to diffuse the situation in analysis by demonstrating the many ways navigation could be handled. The users may be assuming a single threaded navigation from window to window (Figure 6–18).

The analyst should ask, "How many invoices have more than one item on them in reality?" If the users indicate that a majority of invoices have only one item on them, then the designer can help them skip a screen. The information model simply states that more than one item is allowed. It does not address the norm.

When the user clicks the Invoice Items . . . button on *Invoice Maintenance*, instead of blindly retrieving the *Invoice Item Selection* window, the system could first count the instances of *Invoice Item*. (This SQL statement proves to be fairly fast.) If the system returns a count of "one," the application opens the *Invoice Item Maintenance* window, if the system counts more than one item, the user is presented with a list of items from which they may choose one. Figure 6–19 shows the streamlined navigation.

The analyst may also determine that a significant number of invoice inquiries are made at the invoice item level, not the invoice header. The Invoice Items . . . button could also be placed on the *Invoice Selection* window, allowing the users to bypass the *Invoice Maintenance* window entirely and go straight to the item level.

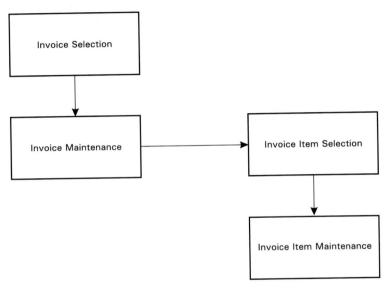

**Figure 6–18.** Single thread navigation

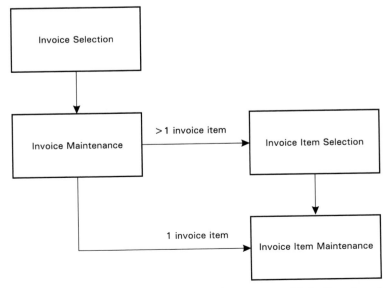

**Figure 6–19.** Navigation paths for single versus multiple-item invoices

Graphical user interfaces allow for such a vast array of navigation designs. This is why I insist on keeping my options open while I'm still gathering and validating requirements. If you find yourself faced with a group of users who are hung up on navigation, demonstrating multiple navigation paths for your proposed window layouts will often assuage their concerns. It will also elicit important design considerations that can be used later, and will help to get the users back on topic.

The information model is a critical guide to window layout. It provides a map of the cardinality between data groups. In addition to the data's structure, the interface designer also needs to understand the real-world statistics behind the cardinality to avoid creating interfaces that force users to follow the rare exception paths, instead of the norm.

## REQUIREMENTS TRACEABILITY

As business events are allocated to windows, an *event/window matrix* can be created to provide a traceability document (Figure 6–20). Events are listed down one axis, window titles across the other. An "R" is placed in the matrix for the window on which the event is first recognized. An "A" is placed in the matrix for additional windows used to support the activity of the event.

| Event/Window | Order selection | Order maintenance | Order item selection | Plant order selection | Plant order maintenance | Invoice selection | Invoice maintenance | Invoice item maintenance | Invoice item |
|---|---|---|---|---|---|---|---|---|---|
| Customer places order | R | A | RA | | | | | | |
| Credit dept. approves order | | | RA | | | | | | |
| Prod. dept. assigns order | | | RA | | | | | | |
| Plant fills cust. order | | | | R | RA | | | | |
| Plant ships cust. order | | | | RA | | | | | |
| Acctg invoices cust. order | | | | | | R | A | A | A |

**Figure 6–20.** An event/window matrix

For events triggered by other methods, such as the receipt of an EDI transmission, the appropriate interface object name can be indicated on the same axis used for window object names. This document provides users, trainers and testers with an index to the windows which initiate and execute business events. It also provides a test for completion of the preliminary interface design activities and assures both users and managers that all chartered events have been accounted for. The manager can also use the completed window count to make estimates for the design and implementation effort required to complete the project. If your model also includes an event/entity CRUD matrix, then a *window/entity CRUD matrix* can be derived, showing which windows need the data services for each entity.

## KEEPING THE MODELS IN SYNC WITH THE PROTOTYPE

The interface prototype is a model which needs to be kept in sync with the other models. When new events are discovered during the prototype review, they should be added to the event model. Errors found in the model for existing events should be corrected. Data elements not represented in the information model should be added, and attributes found to be in the wrong place should be moved to their proper entity.

CASE tools could go a long way to taking the drudgery out of keeping models in sync. A CASE tool should treat a business event as an independent object, capable of having properties and relationships to other objects in the CASE tool repository. The CASE user should have the ability to model the stimulus and response for each event graphically as a portion of the information model. For each attribute, the tool should allow the analyst to specify default label names for use when the attribute is displayed in a free form field or in a columnar format.

The creation of a candidate window layout should be as easy as selecting an event or list of events and declaring that they should be recognized on a window. With the event model and information model already linked, the CASE tool already knows which attributes need to be captured on the display, and also knows the relationship between the entities represented. It should provide, at minimum, a list of known attributes that the designer could drag onto the window layout, or better yet, generate a preliminary layout based on the stimulus and response attributes, and the cardinality between their entity types (Figure 6–21). If the designer drags an attribute from the header area of a window into the detail area, the tool should be polite enough to ask if they'd like to move the attribute in the underlying information model as well. CASE tools will never be able to read our thoughts. The preliminary design generated by a computer might look a lot like that dreadful cash machine interface at the beginning of this chapter. It would, however, give the designer a starting point, and provide much needed traceability and balancing capabilities between the various models.

CASE technology has alleviated many of the mundane activities of system development such as drawing graphics and generating database schema. As of this writing, they have a long way to go in terms of helping us create interface prototypes in the analysis stage, as well as modeling business events in a distributed business environment. In the absence of the CASE tool of our dreams, the analyst still has the responsibility to manage these tasks the old fashioned way.

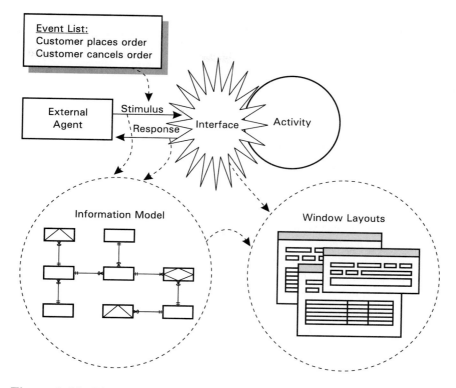

**Figure 6–21.** The relationship between events, entities, and window layouts

## USER REVIEW TECHNIQUES

Prototypes can be instructive to build, but their real value is realized when they are reviewed with the intended users. Inform the users of the specific learning objective prior to walking them through the prototype. It is best to review the prototype in person so you can witness the users' reactions. Don't fall into the lazy trap of simply mailing analysis documents to the users and requesting their approval within a stated time frame. Even if your users are geographically remote, a variety of technologies such video conferencing, remote PC links or even the good old telephone can be employed to help the team review the product together.

Many projects are very successful at reviewing paper prototypes without incurring the cost of having to build a working, coded product. Using an overhead projector with the window layouts printed on transparencies, the users are invited to use colored pens to simulate data entry. As they fill in the fields, the analyst can indicate which data elements will be free-form entry, on drop-down lists or selected from pop-up windows.

Most users will be able to validate window content and ensure you have captured the events properly using this low-tech method of prototyping. Any detailed design suggestions made during the session are written down for later consideration.

Even detailed design issues such as navigation, ergonomics or ease of learning an interface design can be tested on paper. One technique is to give the user no prior training on how to use the interface. The user then fills out the interface design form and "clicks" buttons with a pencil. The facilitator lays a new layout in front of the user to simulate a window opening. By observing the subject attempting to use the interface, the designer can see where the interface is intuitive and where the user has trouble. Changes suggested by the user in a debriefing can be quickly made to the paper prototype and retested.

A good prototyping technique for reviewing navigation is to tape pictures of the window layouts to a white board (Figure 6–22). Using the event model as a guide, the designer walks the users through each business event which uses the various windows. By using colored dry-erase white board markers, the users and designer trace the navigation paths between windows for each major event. By seeing all of the candidate windows at once, the users gain an appreciation for how much data is involved, and can make relevant suggestions as to the optimal way to navigate the application. If one suggestion is ruled out, the path is simply erased from the white board.

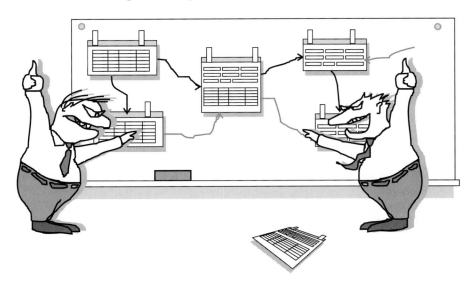

**Figure 6–22.** A white board navigation session

The payoff for using low-tech prototypes is that most of the analysis and a lot of the design information can be gathered without incurring the cost of building a semi-working product. Low-tech prototypes are cheap to build and easy to change. When a product undergoes several iterations of prototyping on paper prior to its initial construction, the beta version of that product is far more likely to be closer to the mark. When reviewing either low-tech or high-tech prototypes with your users, it is also important to implement some level of version control so you can recover the last acceptable version if they don't like your latest ideas.

## SUMMARY

A prototype is a model created to test some aspect of a proposed product design. Automobile designers don't have just one prototyping session and neither should software. Each prototype should have a specific learning objective. Once the learning objective has been established, a good software engineer will look for the most expedient method of deriving the prototype. In most cases, paper prototyping is still cheaper than incurring the cost of building a working interface, even with today's point-and-click GUI tools. When development tools evolve to the point where meaningful prototypes can be derived easily from abstract models such as the information and event models, then the cost scales may tip in favor of animated, working prototypes.

The interface prototype can be used in the analysis phase of the project to validate the information model and event model to ensure that the user's requirements are adequately understood. It can also be employed as a method for deriving the information model based on the data the users ask for on the window. Inevitably, refinement of events and discovery of new events also occurs during prototype review sessions with the users. Prototyping will also surface business process issues, especially when the corporate automation boundary is being pushed into areas that were previously the domain of manual processes and personal computer desktop packages. It may also surface potential technical issues, such as performance bottlenecks, while there is still time in the project to do something to address them sensibly. Prototyping can also be used to explore the look and feel of various different target environments without having to commit to a particular technology.

The event model provides a list of all events to which the system must respond. For those events which are to be communicated to the machine via the on-line interface, a prototype can be developed using the event model as the basis. Each event's stimulus and response contains the data elements that are required to pass across the interface. Additional display elements may be indicated in the activity section, and more data may have to be displayed in order to make the interface polite, informative and friendly. Turning a business event into a window or set of windows often involves breaking the essential event into a dialogue between human and machine. The level of granularity of the dialogue will depend, to a great extent, on the capability of the intended user.

The event model is an important tool for organizing the user interface. Events can be grouped by subject, or transporter, to create overall areas of one-stop-shopping for users. Grouping events by object leads to the object-action paradigm. The user is allowed to acquire a set of objects from the database, and then apply the desired action to selected objects. The state-transition diagram is used to determine which actions are legal, based on the status of the selected object. An event/window matrix can be created to demonstrate which windows are involved in the recognition and activity for each event.

The information model contains an organizational map of the data which will appear on the interface. The relationship cardinality between entity types is used as a guide by the interface designer to group data into header-detail relationships, and shows which information can be successfully joined together on a window.

Interface prototyping starts the project down the path to design. The process requires careful project management to keep it from careening out of control. After the window content and business policy have been uncovered, subsequent prototyping efforts can begin to focus on design issues. We will see in Chapters 10 and 11 that a host of decisions confront the GUI designer. Detailed design prototyping sessions can be used to evaluate window type, navigation, ergonomics, ease of learning, and the user's appropriate unit of work.

Your project might choose to use low-tech paper prototypes in the analysis phase to discover and validate requirements. During design, you might employ navigation diagramming techniques (covered in Chapter 11) to prototype the organization of the application on paper and review it with your peers. Many portions of the system may go all the way through the external design stage without coding anything. Other parts may require that you build a piece and show it to the users to get their feedback. Prototyping can be used as a learning technique during many phases of the project. The most important thing to remember is that you should identify the objective for doing the prototype, and then select the method which best meets that objective in a cost-effective manner.

The prototype should always be reviewed with the intended user group. Face-to-face walkthroughs are far more valuable to the development team than is communicating through the interoffice mail. Always inform the users of the purpose of the prototype, and write down all of their comments, even if they pertain to deferred design issues. After the walkthrough, it is the analyst's responsibility to ensure that the analysis models are kept up to date with any new information discovered in the review.

## EXERCISES

1. List the advantages of low-tech prototyping.

2. Why might you choose a high-tech prototyping method over a low-tech method?

3. Take a look at some of the legacy systems in your shop. Do they support the object-action paradigm or the action-object paradigm?

## ANSWERS

1. Low-tech prototyping methods, such as using a drawing tool or word-processor to mock-up window layouts, have the following advantages over

high-tech methods, such as using the target GUI development tool to "evolve" the application:

Low-tech prototypes are inexpensive to create

They can be created rapidly

They can be modified quickly

They engender low emotional commitment on the part of the developer, making it easier for the author to accept constructive criticism

There is no danger that the development team will start hacking out the final product before they understand the requirements.

2. A good time to use high-tech prototyping methods is when the use, applicability or performance of the target technology is not well known, and building an actual piece of the application can serve as an important proof-of-concept.

3. If your old systems have screens on which the user must first declare a "mode," such as insert mode, update mode, or delete mode, then proceed to a screen which supports just that mode, then the design most likely is based on an action-object paradigm. Old systems which allowed users to first retrieve lists of database items, then apply a variety of actions to any given row that they may have marked, were designed more from an object-action viewpoint.

# CHAPTER 7

# WRAPPING UP THE ANALYSIS PHASE

## INTRODUCTION

Chapter 7 wraps up the analysis section of the book by introducing the topic of business issues. The larger the project, the more likely you will encounter unforeseen issues which could seriously impede your progress if left unresolved. The timely documentation and resolution of issues is key to getting through the analysis effort while there is still time and money to deliver a solution. This chapter offers up some techniques and advice on how to manage that effort. Finally, I close the chapter with a brief summary of the analysis phase, and the models which comprise the analysis deliverables.

## BUSINESS ISSUES

The last topic in the analysis section is uncovering and resolving *business issues*. Business issues are questions raised by the project team that are outside of the realm of automation. They are fundamental procedural or policy questions regarding how the company intends to conduct business. Software does not exist in a vacuum. Instead, it can be viewed as the automated center of a much larger system. Figure 7–1 shows three concentric layers of a business system.

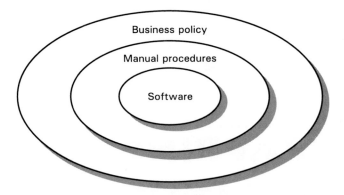

**Figure 7–1.** Software is the automated core of a much larger system

At the core is the software, reliably chugging away to fulfill its robotic duties. The software is surrounded by a layer of manual procedures and business practices. This is the non-automated processing that occurs outside of the system. The direct users of the system inhabit this strata. It is because the manual procedure layer of the organization carries out its duties in a consistent and standardized fashion, that we are able to exploit software to take over more and more of the drudgery of daily business life. In a completely random and chaotic environment, we would have a hard time automating anything useful.

The outermost layer represents the business policy. Policy and direction is set at the highest levels of the organization. The mission and goals of the business provide the reason *why* the business behaves as it does. The policy layer envelops all that goes on within. Together the software and manual procedure exist to carry out *what* needs to be done to execute the business policy.

Now, what does this have to do with analysis?

Client/server systems and GUI applications are often chartered to boldly go where no system has gone before.[1] They wrap or replace existing legacy systems, and then extend the automation boundary outward to the very frontier of the business. If the legacy system is simply replaced, the business may end up with GUI windows over a

---

[1]   Or "to go boldly," for those of you who object to split infinitives.

formerly heads-down data entry system. This would annoy the data entry people tremendously, since a GUI is likely to slow them down. Client/server moves the information capture and presentation directly to the offices of the decision makers, sales force, production workers and accountants.

One of the biggest hidden costs of client/server is the cost to re-engineer the business. In the terms of the diagram in Figure 7–1, when the software boundary moves, there must be changes in the manual procedure layer, and sometimes even in the business policy layer. In the most successful client/server projects, the business has taken the time to redefine its policy and procedures in anticipation of the new software boundary, *prior* to detailed analysis and design of the software system. This strategy gets all of the users aligned to the new business processes, with visible support from the highest levels of the organization.

Unfortunately, not all shops are blessed with such visionary management. Often client/server projects are started with less than full appreciation of the cultural changes they will trigger. Such businesses pay a high price for their process re-engineering when it is done concurrently or after an expensive software development effort.

When the analyst ventures out into Userland, he routinely is confronted with conflicting practices, unstated policy and divergent viewpoints on how business should be conducted. The project charter may call for one consolidated source for customer information, but the plant manager refuses to let the Neanderthals at corporate headquarters update *his* customer records, and the high mucky-mucks at corporate headquarters are indignant at the plant's refusal to recognize their omniscience. This type of conflict is typical. Where people and software meet, the analyst finds blurry, indistinct scope boundaries, a wealth of previously undiscovered personal spreadsheets, divergent reporting requests and stakeholders vehemently defending their version of reality.

Issues which arise in the manual procedure layer and certainly in the policy layer of the business are outside the analyst's authority to resolve. It is *absolutely* the analyst's responsibility to surface them! It is important that we separate in our minds the responsibilities of an analyst versus a programmer. A programmer's responsibility is to write code which meets the specification's requirements and is free of software bugs. The analyst's responsibility is to uncover business problems and define the requirements which will address them. It is OK for a programmer to ignore a business issue.[2] Strictly speaking, it's not their problem. It is *professional malpractice* for an analyst to ignore a business issue!

The analyst is placed in a difficult position. He has the professional responsibility to point out holes in the manual procedure and policy layer of the business that may prevent the software layer from behaving effectively. He doesn't, however, have the authority to resolve those issues. That is why, as part of the project chartering process, the business should establish a business issue resolution process.

---

[2]   This highly inflammatory statement is intended to draw a clear distinction between the role of programmer and the role of analyst. Even though these roles may be played by the same person on a project, the responsibilities are vastly different.

## THE BUSINESS ISSUE RESOLUTION PROCESS

The project charter should contain the names of the *user council.* This team is comprised of system users and their immediate supervisors. These are the best people to resolve issues within the manual procedure layer, at the operational level of the business. By solving their own problems, they are more likely to accept the solutions. For issues which the user council is unable to resolve, or those which require a policy decision, a *steering committee* is needed. The steering committee resolves issues at the tactical and strategic level of the business. It is also the supreme court of issue resolution for operational issues that the user council is unable to resolve. Its members should contain policy makers and system stakeholders at the highest level of the organization who have the authority to make key decisions.

It should be obvious that the steering committee should only be bothered with the most broad sweeping issues such as, "Should invoicing be done at the production facilities or consolidated at corporate headquarters?" The more mundane issues such as, "Should the user be able to credit and reissue multiple invoices at once, or one at a time?" can be left to the user council.

The analyst's job is to document the issue and add it to the project's centralized issues list. The issues list is owned by the project manager. One of the jobs of the project manager is to remove roadblocks which may impede his team's progress. The project manager is responsible for shepherding issues through the resolution process. This involves convening the user council or steering committee periodically, and ensuring that the business reaches resolution on each issue. This often involves a degree of political wrangling and arm twisting.

The project manager will have much more leverage with the business if the issue resolution process is in the project charter and the timely resolution of issues identified as a critical success factor. At some point, if enough issues clog the pipeline, the project manager can publish the fact that the project is dead in the water until the business gets moving on its responsibilities.[3] This will only work if the business is educated about its role in a development project, up front. Otherwise, the manager will look like an ineffective whiner, and the business may never resolve its problems.

The analyst's job is to provide the business with enough information about the issue so those responsible can make an informed decision. For tracking issues, I have found the following format effective. Some project management or defect tracking software packages include similar data elements, or a simple application can be created using any of the popular relational database products.

---

[3]  I have seen good project managers use various tactics, ranging from broadcast e-mail to posting a list of unresolved issues and the people who are sitting on them in the lobby of the building. Although extreme, public humiliation tends to elicit some action.

## BUSINESS ISSUE DOCUMENTATION

For each issue, the following information should be captured:

**Tracking number:** A sequential number is often used. The number serves as the unique identifier of the issue.

**Title:** The title of the issue should be a short phrase which conveys the essential meaning of the issue, often posed as a question, (e.g., "Should invoicing be consolidated at corporate HQ?" or "Will sales agents be willing to pull their own on-line commission reports instead of receiving paper in the mail?").

**Author:** The author is the name of the project team member who uncovered the issue. This is usually the analyst.

**Date discovered:** This is the date on which the issue was uncovered.

**Description:** The issue should be explained in enough detail so that no other research is required to understand the nature of the problem. I prefer to structure the description of the issue as follows:

**Background:** This is the context of the problem. It is safe to assume that the reader is familiar with the business, but may not have the same depth of detail as an analyst who has been immersed in a particular subject area. Include a brief synopsis of the functional area of the business in which the problem exists and the portion of the application affected.

**Problem:** State the problem in clear, concise terms.

**Impact:** State the impact of doing nothing. If the problem is allowed to continue, what will be the result to the project and to the business.

**Solution options and recommendation:** Many people are not fond of making decisions. Making choices is easier. It is very likely that the analyst already knows what should be done, he just needs approval from a higher authority to make the change. If there are several options, assess the pros and cons of each one. Include a recommendation if you have a strong opinion.

**Assigned to:** Name the team or business individual to which the issue has been assigned for resolution.

**Date Assigned:** Record the date on which the issue was forwarded to the resolution team.

**Resolution:** Document the decision made by the resolution team.

**Date Resolved:** Record the date on which the resolution was received by the project team.

**Resolved by:** Sometimes the issue will be resolved by an authority higher than the one to which it was assigned. It is useful to record whether the line-level clerks or the company president made the decision.

You may be experiencing a sense of déjà vu when it comes to the issue description. The problem statement, impact of doing nothing and presentation of solution options come straight from the decision-making framework presented in the charter chapter. In fact, the analyst can strengthen his recommendation by evaluating solution options based on the criteria laid out in the charter, namely, the ability to meet project objectives, cost and application of the quality vectors.

One of the first things I ask for when joining a project is the issues list. In the early analysis stages, a healthy project will have a rich lode of unresolved issues. This is good! It means that the analysts are out there asking questions. If you were to track the number of *unresolved* issues on a project over time, the graph should look similar to Figure 7–2.

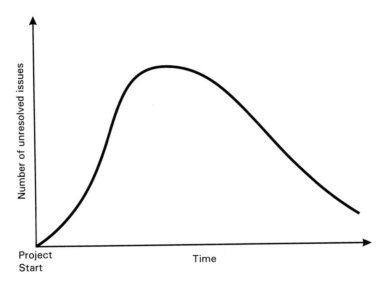

**Figure 7–2.** Outstanding unresolved issues

On the first day of the project the number of unresolved issues is zero. Nobody has asked any questions yet. As the analysts go forth and analyze, plenty of questions should arise which are written down as unresolved issues. On a healthy project, the number of unresolved issues will climb rapidly. As the project manager guides the unresolved issues through the resolution process, the number of resolved issues should start to outnumber the unresolved ones. Eventually, the number of unresolved issues should drop off as the business achieves a common vision of how their new world will operate.

The crux of an analyst's job is to ask questions, to *write those questions down*, go find out the answers, and *write the answers down*. The answers will beget more questions, and each of those are written down. The objective is to get as quickly as possible from a state of profound ignorance to a state of simple ignorance (Figure 7–3).

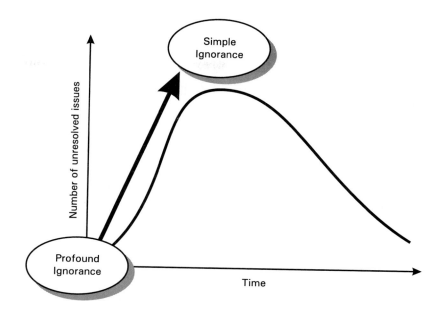

**Figure 7–3.** Moving from a state of profound ignorance to simple ignorance

In a state of profound ignorance, you do not know that which you do not know. In a state of simple ignorance, you *do* know what you do not know. In less twisted words, you cannot manage a state of profound ignorance, because you are completely blind to the issues which may confront you. A manager in a state of profound ignorance comes to work each day to find bombs exploding on all fronts of the project. A manager in a state of simple ignorance has a list of the major issues that have been uncovered, and can manage against that list. He can estimate how badly progress is impeded and develop a plan to get the issues resolved.

The list of resolved issues becomes an important document for the training and implementation phase of the system. The changes made in business policy and procedures reflect the difference between the old way of doing business and the new. The issues list provides a means for the project to remember why it did things the way it did, and who was involved in the decisions. It is probably a safe time to start designing any part of the system where the analysis models are reaching completion, and the resolved issues are clearly out numbering the unresolved issues.

## SUMMARY OF ANALYSIS DELIVERABLES

The purpose of analysis is to define the user's essential business requirements. It is a critical step to understanding the business' needs prior to designing technical solutions. The analysis phase of a client/server-GUI system includes the following activities.

Forge a **charter** with the business which articulates the goals and objectives of the project in clear, concise, measurable terms. Make sure that both parties have reached consensus on the objectives and have agreed to their respective roles and performance requirements in writing.

Further define the scope of the area of study through creating a **context model** and validate it with the appropriate user base.

Define the **events** to which the system is chartered to respond. Events are listed in the event list and defined, in detail, in the event dictionary. For each event, the dictionary entry includes the event's meaning, stimulus data required to initiate the event, activity to be carried out to formulate the appropriate response, and the response data which is expected by the users. The effect of each event is documented to keep faith with what the system is attempting to accomplish in the real world.

Create an **information model** which comprises all of the data elements that your system is chartered to remember. The information model respects no project boundaries, and therefore a strong sense of scope is required to determine which data elements are relevant. The information model can be built through accretion by defining the data required for each event's stimulus and response.

Put a face on the system by creating an **interface prototype**. The prime objective of the prototyping effort, in the analysis stages of a project, is to derive and validate the essential system requirements while leaving your implementation options open.

Please remember that these steps are not necessarily lineal tasks. The best chartering efforts I have seen were done in conjunction with a context diagram, event list and first-cut information model. Without doing some preliminary modeling, there is nothing upon which to base an estimate of the resources required to tackle the problem. It is also unlikely that a project will nail down its information model and event dictionary to the last detail without having done some sort of prototype.

## HOW THE MODELS INTER-RELATE

The analysis models pull the business problem apart into three respective views; data, process and behavior. The **data** requirements are modeled in the information model. The **process** requirements are found in the activity section of the event dictionary. Appropriate **behavior** is defined for the system in the event model by mapping the stimulus to the desired response for each business event to which the system is chartered to respond.

These three views of the business are heavily interdependent (Figure 7–4). The data requirements are the sum of the stimulus and response elements in the event model. The processes only exist to provide the proper responses upon receipt of the stimuli. If you change the scope of the project, you also change the events, processing and data requirements. They are three views of an object, commonly called "the system."

We have seen that the analysis models can be consumed to create a first-cut interface prototype. The rest of this book will focus on the design effort, where the separate views of the analysis models will be synthesized into a solution. The shape of that solution will be dependent to a large degree on the chosen technology. Third generation language solutions will have a clear separation between the process and data elements of the model, while object-oriented languages will have a much tighter coupling of process, data and behavior.

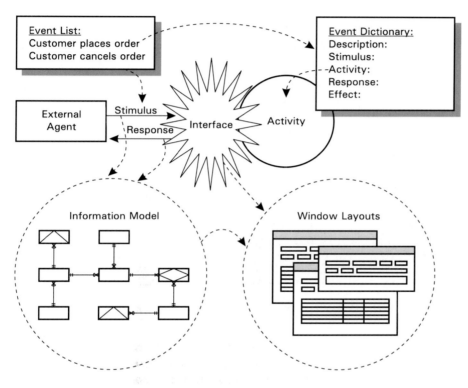

**Figure 7–4.** The inter-relationship of the analysis models

As of this writing, most client/server projects call for a mix of approaches. Some elements of the solution will be heavily object-oriented, while others may be 3GL or 4GL in nature, and the database is likely to be relational. The essential analysis models detailed in this book provide the client/server system designer with the raw material necessary to make sensible engineering decisions, and to exploit a wide variety of technical paradigms.

# CHAPTER

# 8

Charter

Context Model · Information Model · Event Model

Interface Prototype

**Architecture Model**

Database Design

External Interface Design

Internal Component Design

Construction & Testing

# THE ARCHITECTURE MODEL

## INTRODUCTION

Chapter 8 takes a serious departure from the safe haven of analysis and examines how to meet the project's requirements with the sorry rabble of equipment provided by the management. Architecture modeling begins by gathering statistics and constraints about the events and information requirements you have documented during analysis. The architecture modeler will need to know the rate at which the most significant business events occur, and the response time expectations to which the new system must conform. The information model is used to estimate the size of records and predict network traffic and database size for various configurations. The architecture modeling phase makes key decisions about the geographic distribution of both data and processes across the wide-area network. At a more granular level, the chosen programming languages may influence whether a fat client or fat server approach is favored for the construction of the application code. You will find in this chapter that there is no such thing as a perfect solution. Architecture modeling is all about making trade-offs and compromises between sub-optimal solutions. By using the analysis models to aid your efforts, you can choose the least objectionable technical architecture through a process of informed consent, rather than by accident or the time-honored technique of loud shouting and repeated assertion.

## WHAT IS ARCHITECTURE MODELING?

The architecture model maps the essential requirements from the analysis phase onto a technical architecture. Because so many different architectures are possible, the purpose of the architecture modeling effort is to choose the optimal configuration, or perhaps the "least worst." The process of devising an architecture includes gathering data volume statistics and event rates for the essential model, documenting the geographic topology of the business, determining the geographic distribution of computing sites, determining the local partitioning of process and data within each site, and validating the architecture against the essential model.

Up until now, I haven't addressed the issue of hardware. In the essential requirements phase, we allow ourselves to bask in the luxury of assuming infinitely fast processors and infinitely large storage capacity. We make this assumption about perfect technology so we don't cast our statement of the business problem in the form of a solution. Now it's time to figure out how this perfect model is going to run on the sorry collection of boxes that management has given us.

It is unlikely that you would get this far into a project without addressing some aspect of architecture. The reason that the chapter appears at this point in the book is that you can't put it off any longer. The reward to the procrastinators is that you now have far more information on which to base your decisions than you would if you tried to make architectural decisions without the benefit of a model of the business requirements.

This chapter is all about trade-offs. It is not my intention or desire to discuss the gory details of stringing together one type of hardware configuration versus another. For that task, I regret I must leave you to sort through the opinions of other authors, journalists and the claims of the vendors. Instead, I will focus on how to use the essential models to help you make rational architectural decisions by balancing the requirements of the business against the constraints of the available technology. Today, this is no easy task. In the future, perhaps advances in technology will lower the barrier of constraints imposed by technology's own limitations, and architectural modeling may someday become irrelevant. The propensity of software to absorb quickly any improvements in computing capacity, however, makes this rosy scenario unlikely.

Architecture modeling is the allocation of the essential requirements model to specific technology. The architecture modeling effort determines which processes will run on which processors, where the data will be stored, and how much communication is required between processors. It is a major leap into design. At the end of the architecture modeling effort, the team will have determined:

the geographic distribution of computing requirements,

the hardware components for the client machines,

the hardware components for the server machines,

the configuration and number of client/server hardware tiers,

the network communication mechanisms and languages,

the operating systems,

the development paradigm (object-oriented, 4GL, 3GL or mixed),

the presentation language,

the background coding languages,

the database management system,

the location or locations of the processes,

the location or locations of the physical data,

and the synchronization strategies for geographically distributed data.

Many of these decisions will have been made already, either by management fiat, or by the fact that hardware or standard shop languages already exist. For the lucky few projects that have complete control over their choice of architecture, the architecture modeling phase becomes a global quest for the most appropriate technology, based on the requirements of the essential model. For the rest of us, architectural modeling is a search for the least objectionable way to meet the business requirements, recognizing the limitations of what we've been given to work with. In other words, it's an attempt to squeeze ten pounds of requirements into a five pound box.

## OVERVIEW OF THE CLIENT/SERVER ARCHITECTURE

Before launching into a long diatribe on client/server architecture modeling, I feel compelled to attempt to further define the term "client/server." The problem with coming up with a precise definition is that client/server is yet another one of those overloaded words in our industry. It is important that we all share the same view of the term for the remainder of this book, even though the definition in your shop may vary slightly. *For this book:*

Client/server computing is the cooperative processing of business information by a set of processors in which multiple, geographically distributed clients initiate requests that are carried out by one or more central servers.

Primarily, client/server is used to describe software which executes on more than one piece of hardware in order to accomplish a business task. Hardware separation is the norm for client/server applications, although some have used the term to describe disparate software components communicating with each other while running on the same box. The distance between remote processors varies from computers which are located in the same room or building, to those which are located in different buildings, different cities, or even flung across the entire planet.

Today, the different processors are typically a hybrid of types, meaning that a different type of computer is used for the client machines than is used for the server machine. This potpourri of hardware can be compounded when a wide variety of client machines must be accommodated. A heterogeneous mix of desktops, workstations, laptops and palmtops can seriously complicate the client side of the equation.

The idea of client/server computing is to treat a computer like an appliance. Each appliance in a professional kitchen is capable of doing many things, but a master chef will allocate each machine to its most propitious use. For instance, it is possible to cook a piece of toast in a large convection oven. A toaster, however, does a far more reliable job, takes less skill to operate, and requires less power to run. Mainframe computers are very much like the convection oven. They are big and powerful, but require a great deal of skill to operate, and are overkill for a wide variety of mundane requests. Personal computers are far better at managing presentation, take less user skill to operate, and provide cheap and efficient processing for many of the ancillary tasks of the organization.

Now, imagine the users as patrons in your information restaurant. They order up a new report which requires a mix of graphics and data. In the mainframe environment, the programmer would have to don an asbestos suit and venture into the convection oven to fulfill the request. In the client/server world, the requisite data can be sent off to the PC toaster, where the user can decide whether to top their toast with jelly, marmalade, or fresh strawberries. From the users' point of view, they don't care on which appliance their toast was cooked. From the master chef's point of view, the appropriate appliance is allocated to the task without bothering the user with the details.

Client/server applications seek to balance the desire of the users to have their toast and eat it too with the chef's need to keep control over the central kitchen. The client initiates requests from the server, much like our restaurant patron making demands of the waiter. The server manages requests from multiple clients, delivering the appropriate response back to each client machine, much like the waiter taking orders from multiple parties and servicing requests from a single kitchen.

## CLIENT/SERVER HARDWARE TIERS

The most common use for client/server architecture is to exploit the power of the PC for managing the graphical user interface, while still protecting the integrity of the business data on a central host machine. The overriding concern to the user is that the applications

appear seamless, so users remain blissfully unaware as to which processor is working at any given time. In its least complicated form, client/server architecture involves multiple clients making requests of a single server (Figure 8–1). This model shows a two-tier hardware architecture.[1]

The client machine meets the demand for a helpful, friendly, courteous and kind user interface. This demand has probably always been with us. It is just recently that the technology has begun to catch up with the need. Our new challenge is what to do with the rest of the PC's vast processing potential. It's a no-brainer to decide to move the presentation management portion of the application to the client, but what about the rest of the application?

---

[1]  The word *tier* originated as a way to describe levels of hardware, although it has been also used by some authors to describe *layers* of software (e.g., the presentation layer, business logic layer and data management layer have also been called the presentation tier, etc.). To avoid confusion, I will make every attempt to reserve the word *tier* for describing levels of hardware, and *layer* to describe levels of software.

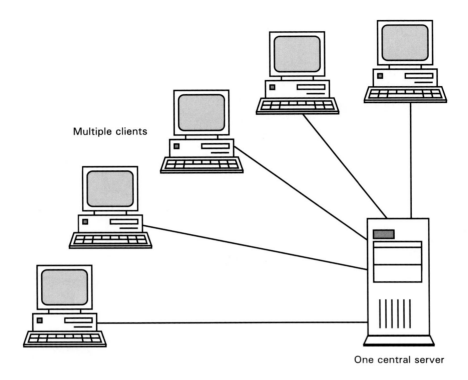

Multiple clients

One central server

**Figure 8–1.** A two tier client/server architecture

Information is one of any company's key assets. Keeping control over the data asset is far easier if you can corral the data into one place to resolve redundancy and ensure periodic back-ups. It's another no-brainer to decide that at some point, data should come back to the safe custody of one or more central servers, but what about the location of data at run time?

There are no easy answers to these questions. Before we explore the possibilities, let's complicate matters once again by introducing more tiers into the client/server architecture. Figure 8–2 shows a three tier client/server architecture, in which client machines are connected via a local area network to a local application server, which in turn communicates with a central database server.

In the three-tier architecture model, the lines between client and server begin to blur. The PC which hosts the interface application is certainly a client, and the central database host which houses the data is certainly a server, but what about the local application server? It's sometimes a client and sometimes a server, depending on the direction of communication. Let's compound the issue further by allowing the PCs to connect directly to the database server, bypassing the local server. How many tiers do we have now (Figure 8–3)?

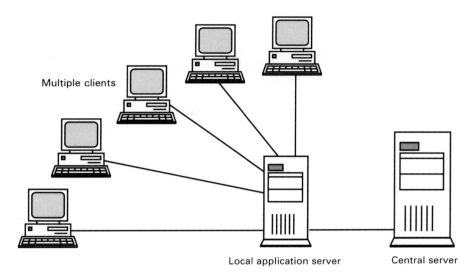

**Figure 8–2.** A three tier client/server architecture

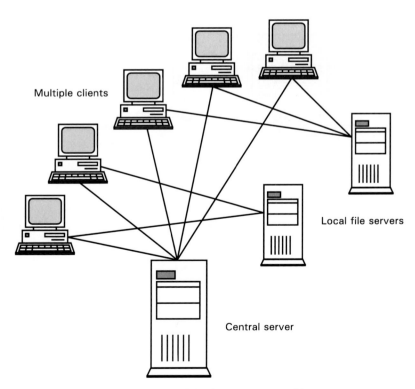

**Figure 8–3.** An n-tier client/server architecture

The n-tier architecture is quickly becoming the norm in most organizations as local area networks, wide area networks, the Internet and the World Wide Web are all linked together. The distinction between strict client and strict server is almost obliterated in such an environment, making client/server more of a conceptual pattern that is applied on a transaction by transaction basis at run time.

For the sake of simplification, much of this chapter will assume a two tier client/server architecture, where multiple PC clients make requests from a central data server. This will allow us to explore some of the most common and fundamental characteristics of the client/server environment without splitting hairs over terminology.

## CLIENT/SERVER SOFTWARE LAYERS

In order to discuss the deployment of software across a multi-tier hardware architecture, we must first dissect the software application into its layers. The innards of a business application can be grouped into at least three major categories; the presentation layer, the business logic layer, and the data management layer.[2] Figure 8–4 shows a business event as it passes through the three layers of a software application.

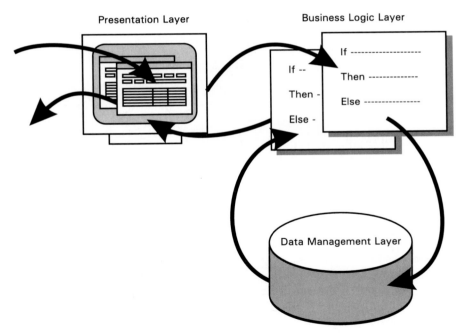

**Figure 8–4.** Software layers

---

2    When you deploy an application across multiple hardware tiers, you incur a fourth software layer, that which manages machine-to-machine communications.

The **presentation layer** resides at the edge of the software system. Its job is to capture external event stimuli and perform some degree of editing on the incoming data. It also is charged with presenting the event response to the outside world. The presentation software is almost always located on a client machine, such as a PC, however, this is not a strict rule. PCs can be used to emulate mainframe screens with very little of the presentation logic resident at the client. The language paradigm of the presentation layer is increasingly object-oriented. The windowing environment of most client operating systems lends itself naturally to object constructs.

The **business logic layer** contains the code which executes and enforces the policy of the business. Rules and regulations, as well as the internal calculations are all found in the business logic layer. Software which executes business logic is the layer which is most mobile. It can be located on the remote clients, the central server, or any place in between. Many of the pros and cons presented in this chapter focus on the location of this layer of the application. As of this writing, the language paradigm for the business layer is a mixed bag. The trend is a movement toward object-oriented constructs. The degree of object-orientation employed in the business logic layer is heavily dependent on the chosen language or development tool. It is entirely possible to have 3GL, 4GL and object components mixed within the same application.

The **data management layer** provides access to the corporate data. It manages concurrent requests to read and write to the database, as well as the synchronization of distributed data elements. Much of the data management layer will follow the physical location of the data. The decision to distribute or centralize the database will determine much of the location of the data management layer. For most business systems, the database paradigm of choice remains the relational database. Most data collected by businesses fits nicely into the column and row format of the relational paradigm. Relational database vendors are also responding to pressure to extend their databases to handle unstructured data such as multi-media, sound, video and hypertext objects.

## FAT CLIENT, FAT SERVER

A somewhat politically *incorrect* term has cropped up that is used to define an application's philosophy regarding where the bulk of the business logic layer of the application lies. *Fat client (thin server)* means that the lion's share of the software is executed on the client machine, and the server is relegated to slavishly doling out data upon request and mindlessly stuffing it back into the database when instructed to do so by the client.

*Fat server (thin client)* describes an allocation of duties in which the client is restricted to the presentation of the interface and minimal editing, while the majority of the business logic and rule enforcement is executed on the central server. Of course, this is an overly simplified view of the world, since n-tier client/server architectures can support vastly complex software layers with fat deposits all over the network, but the term does help us to recognize the philosophical leanings of a particular programming language.

The first generation of many popular client/server-GUI development tools assumed a two tier hardware architecture when they were first developed. The earliest versions of packages such as PowerBuilder® and Visual Basic® absolutely encouraged a fat client approach (Figure 8–5). The business logic was inextricably tied to the presentation layer of the application. Through the introduction of object-oriented concepts such as inheritance (covered in Chapter 12) many of these tools have been very good at exploiting the reuse of object constructs which manage the presentation of the interface.

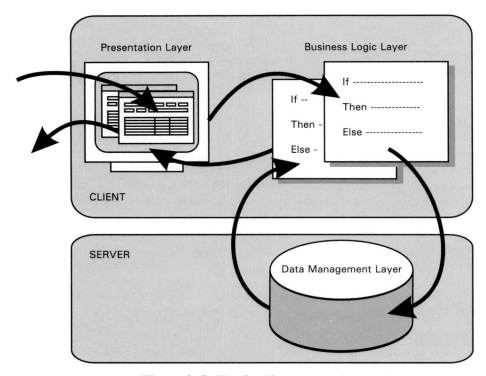

**Figure 8–5.** The fat client approach

Responding to the demands of the marketplace for more flexible development languages, the second generation of GUI development tools recognizes the need to separate presentation from business logic. This partitioning provides several advantages, *reusability, portability* and *maintainability.* The most widely promoted reason is reusability. Presentation classes are extremely easy to reuse because they are very mechanical in nature.[3] Business classes, on the other hand, are highly complex. A business class, such as *Customer,* plays many different roles within the organization. The goal is to create classes which enforce all of the business rules for a particular business class, and also to be able to reuse that code any place in the application which deals with the class. In order to achieve reusable code in this layer, a high degree of software engineering discipline is required.

---

[3]   The word *class,* here, is used to mean a class of objects in an object-oriented system.

Portability is a second compelling reason for separating code which manages presentation from code which executes business logic. Once severed from the interface, the business logic code can be relocated in various tiers of the client/server architecture in order to achieve optimal performance. The ability to move business logic around the client/server architecture enables the business to take advantage of improvements in processing speed of particular machines, and to supplement the hardware architecture with a faster component, without having to rewrite large sections of the application (Figure 8–6).

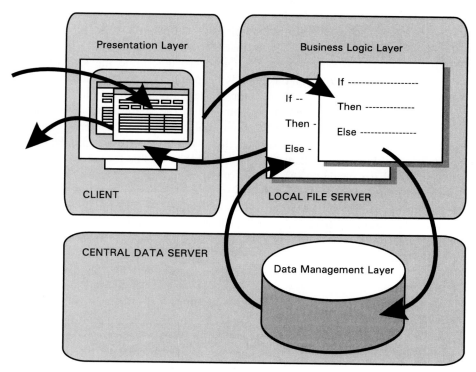

**Figure 8–6.** Business logic moved from client to a file server

A third reason for corralling business logic into its own set of classes is to attempt to keep the business rules in one place, rather than scatter them like buckshot across the interface. The big pay-off of this strategy is the reduction of the ripple effect of making maintenance changes and enhancements to the system.

The trend in development languages is to allow the project to balance the demands of the application against the hardware architecture. Whether the resulting deployment resembles fat client or fat server should be a product of sound engineering decisions, based on the project's quality vectors, and not a result of the constraints of the chosen development language. It is important to recognize the bias of your chosen development language and make sure it fits with the needs of the essential requirements.

## GATHERING STATISTICS AND CONSTRAINTS

Determining the correct architecture for your system involves sizing the computing capacity to the problem. The essential analysis models provide a reliable framework for estimating the computing requirements of the finished system. The first act of architectural modeling is to fill in that framework by counting things.

## Gathering Statistics for the Information Model

Two essential pieces of information are required to estimate the size of a database; the size of the columns, and the number of estimated rows that will accrue over time. These are relatively simple numbers to come up with. To determine the size of the data columns, refer to the data type that has already been recorded for each attribute. Simply add up the number of bytes for each attribute in the entity, and then add the number of bytes for the primary key, and foreign keys implied by the relationships. (We will cover the translation from information model to relational database in Chapter 9.) This yields a very close estimate of the number of bytes that a single table row in the database will occupy. A reasonably good CASE tool should be able to do this for you.

The next statistic needed is the number of expected rows for each table. Some entities will result in the creation of control tables, such as *State*, *County* and *Country*. The number of instances in these entities are relatively fixed, unless the business expands into new market regions, or global conflict alters the geo-political landscape. If your enterprise is only interested in fourteen counties, then one would expect fourteen rows in the county table.

It is far more interesting to estimate volume for the transaction tables. These tables are created from entities such as *Order*, *Order item* and *Invoice*. The event model can tell us which events create an instance of these entity types. In Figure 8–7, we see a fragment of the information model. In this example, the event *Customer places order* always creates one instance of *Order*. To find out how many orders come into the system, we need to know how often the event occurs. Let's say that the users tell us that they receive 100 orders per day, five days a week. The order table is going to get about 500 new rows each week.

**Figure 8–7.** ERD fragment for *Order* and *Order item*

What about *Order item*? Note that the cardinality between *Order* and *Order item* is one-to-many. We know that the event which creates an instance of *Order* must create at least one instance of *Order item*, but the model doesn't tell us how many instances of *Order item* is the norm. We have to do some more research. We might take a look at the existing database, a sampling of customer orders, or talk to the order-takers to find out how many products a customer typically orders at one time.[4] We may find that the average order has three instances of *Order item*. Given this information, we can estimate that the system will add about 1,500 new rows to the *Order item* table each week.

The last piece of information required to estimate the number of rows in a table is the retention period for the oldest row. If the company has a requirement to keep orders on-line for two years, then the average number of rows in the *Order* table will be:

500 rows per week × 104 weeks = 52,000 rows

By using the attribute data types, and primary and foreign key estimates to determine the length of each row, we can now estimate the total size of the order table. Let's say each row works out to be 500 bytes. The *Order* table will occupy about 26,000,000 bytes or 26 megabytes of disk space.

Using our example from above, if a row in the *Order item* table is estimated to be about 300 bytes, then the total size of the order item table will be:

1500 rows per week × 104 weeks × 300 bytes per row = 46,800,000 bytes total

The order table and order item tables will occupy approximately 26 megabytes and 47 megabytes, respectively.

Gather the following statistics for each entity in the information model:

1. estimated length, in bytes, of one instance of the entity (calculated by adding up attribute data types and adding in size estimates for primary and foreign keys),
2. event rate for how often a new instance is created,
3. retention period.

When the information model is used to generate a relational database schema, you will already have the volume estimates for the table sizes. The estimated length tells you much space is required by one row. The event rates tell you how often new rows are inserted, and the retention period declares how long you must keep a row before archiving it off-line.

The statistics that are gathered for the information model are used to estimate the resources needed to adequately house the database. Even if disk space is not a problem for your project, the statistics will also be useful for working out other issues. The business events that the system handles need access to the very same data. As we will see in the following sections, the problem gets more complicated when the physical data repository is geographically remote from the event that needs that data.

---

[4] Be careful when gathering this type of statistic if the legacy system you are replacing is not properly normalized. When you ask an order entry clerk how many items a customer requests per order, he may say "one," since that is all the old system will accept.

## Gathering Statistics for the Event Model

The system is constantly being bombarded with business events. Some events are far more critical than others, in that the ability of the system to respond rapidly is of paramount importance. The event model can be annotated with statistics that capture the rate of the event and the desired response time for the event.

A little common sense can go a long way in terms of how many statistics you take time to gather. The events which affect the mainstream transactions of the business are the most critical. Events such as *Customer places order*, *Passenger books airline ticket*, *Time to invoice order*, *Train approaches station*, *Customer inquires of order status*, *Broker places stock trade order*, *Plaintiff files civil suit*, are the meat and potatoes of their respective businesses.

If an event such as *Trucking company changes address* occurs about once every two years in your area, it probably doesn't need intense scrutiny. A blanket benchmark for performance can be stated for most of the mundane events which simply update control tables.

For the major business transaction events in your system, you need to collect the average rate of the event, the peak rate and the peak time period. Let's take an example from Joe-Joe's Pizza Delivery Company. Joe-Joe delivers pizzas out of several kitchens which are distributed across the greater metropolitan area. To order a pizza, his customers call one central hot-line. Pizza orders are automatically dispatched to the kitchen nearest the customer, to ensure that a piping hot pizza is delivered on time to the customer's door.

Joe-Joe has built a reputation based on good food and fantastic service. Sixty percent of Joe-Joe's customers are return customers, and that percentage is growing. Most call from home or from their car phones, so he has installed caller identification software to search the database for their customer profile as the incoming call is received. By the time the customer service rep picks up the call, the caller's prior pizza ordering profile is already on the screen. Joe-Joe is considering allowing customers to place orders directly from their home computer via the Internet.

The most significant business event for Joe-Joe is *Customer places pizza order*. In Joe-Joe's case, he sells an average of 875 pizzas per day between the hours of ten in the morning and two o'clock the next morning. It is fairly easy to do the math and determine the average event rate is around 55 pizzas per hour. It takes approximately two minutes for a customer to place a pizza order. With a new order coming in every minute, one could extrapolate that Joe-Joe needs a system capable of answering three phone calls simultaneously (one in-coming, one in progress, one hanging up). But is there anything wrong with this? Such an ill-conceived system would probably put poor Joe-Joe out of business in less than a month!

### Irregular Event Rates

Average event rates can only tell you the normal level for an event. We also need to know the peak rates. As you may have suspected, Joe-Joe's customers don't order their pizzas in a uniform pattern from morning until night. There is very little activity before 11:30 AM, then there is a big spike as the lunch crowd descends on the city (Figure 8–8). Business drops off after 1:30 PM, then quickly accelerates at the five o'clock hour, and then trails off again after nine at night. To complicate matters, the ordering pattern varies on Friday, Saturday and Sunday. Friday's evening spike lasts a lot longer into the night, as does Saturday's. Saturday and Sunday have much smaller lunch peaks, but steadier business through the late afternoon.

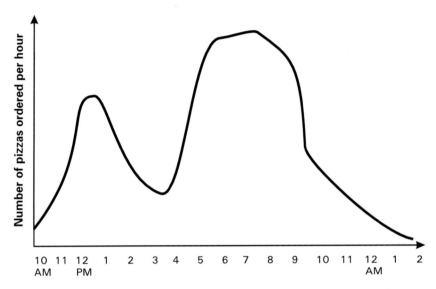

**Figure 8–8.** Event rate pattern for *Customer places pizza order*

## Sizing the System for the Peak Rate

Joe-Joe has a critical architectural dilemma. Should he size the system to be able to handle his highest peak so that no customer ever gets a busy signal or languishes on hold? If he sizes for the peak capacity, then he has unused capacity sitting idle for a great deal of the day. If he sizes the system for less than the peak capacity, he may have customers who will turn to his competitors for their dinner.

These decisions are not easy, and should not be made by IT alone. The example of Joe-Joe's Pizza illustrates an irregular event pattern in which the customer is a major player. If the system can't handle the peaks, then the customer is impacted. Unless the cost is prohibitive, most organizations will prefer to spend the money to size the system close to the peak to avoid inconveniencing or losing customers.

## Move the Peak

Some companies have come up with creative solutions in an attempt to smooth out the peak in some event rates. Some stock brokerages charge their customers a higher commission to move their stock trade orders into the priority queue during peak hours. Customers who don't want to pay the surcharge allow their trade to wait in the regular queue until the computer is available. The phone company does similar load leveling by charging higher long distance rates during business hours, and discounting rates during evenings and weekends. It not only makes good financial sense for the phone company, it encourages customers to make their discretionary calls during off-hours and lowers the number of lines needed to manage peak periods. Our friend Joe-Joe, however, may not be so lucky. People tend to want their pizzas at meal time, so he would be hard-pressed to offer a discount that would persuade customers to eat dinner at three in the afternoon.

You do not have to go hog-wild collecting event rates for the entire system. Concentrate on the major business events with the highest volume, largest amounts of data, most geographically remote locations, and largest customer impact. For each of these events, determine whether the event rate is uniform or irregular. For uniform rates, the average event rate will suffice. For irregular event patterns, you must determine the peak event rates over time and involve the business in the decision of whether to size the system for the current peak traffic, for something less than peak, or for a peak that might even grow.

### Event Performance Requirements

In Chapter 2 (project charters) we discussed quality vectors. One of the recurring quality vectors for information systems is *immediacy of response*, more commonly referred to as *response time*. The requirement for the maximum acceptable response time needs to be stated on an event-by-event basis. You may already have a target benchmark stated in the project charter. If not, you need to know what the target is for the most critical events in the system.

Again, a good dose of common sense is required. The team should concentrate its efforts on the most important business events, those which occur most often and impact the customer or users the most. Response time can be measured either at the business event level or the dialogue level. At the business level, the response time metric measures time between receipt of the initial stimulus to the issuance of the final response. At the dialogue level, the response time metric measures the time it takes the system to respond to a single query, which might be just one portion of a whole business event.

For example, in a customer service department, the most important metric may be *time spent responding to each customer's call*. If the goal of the system is to cut the average call time by fifty percent, then the response time is measured from the time the customer calls, to the time he hangs up. The actual response time of the system to return a single query is just one part of the total transaction time. The designer has a number of creative solutions at his disposal. One option might involve bringing back more information about the customer onto the screen, so that the service rep makes fewer individual queries against the database. The response time of the initial query might be longer, but the total average response time for the business event might be reduced. Another solution might be to optimize certain windows to quickly return the most frequently used queries. By training customer service reps to use the special window for those queries, the average call time may be reduced without having to speed up the rest of the system.

When response time is expressed at the dialogue level, the designer is far more constrained. In this case, the business expects that the computer will respond within the stated time for any of the queries or updates required to execute the business event. For the architecture modeler, this means that the client needs rapid access to the data.

Other events, such as *Time to run monthly closing*, have immense processing needs. These events do not necessarily affect customers directly. CPU-intensive monthly closing routines are legendary in many companies. Lights dim within a ten-mile radius as the jobs are run to post the month's activity to the general ledger. Many companies have decided that as long as their customers aren't impacted, it is acceptable to have poor system performance for the one or two days a month that it takes to close the books. In many shops, closing routines are run at night, in an attempt to move the peak resource drain into off-hours.

The event model can be annotated with statistics to record the average rate of the event, peak rate patterns for irregular event rates, and the response time expectation for the event, either at the business event level or the dialogue level. The next step is to examine the geographic distribution of events. This will lead naturally to the required distribution of data access. Together, the frequency of events, volume of data, response time constraints and the geographic distribution of the business will form the basis for determining an acceptable architecture for your system.

## DETERMINING GEOGRAPHIC DISTRIBUTION REQUIREMENTS

In Chapters 4 and 5, I mentioned several matrices that can be used to map the essential model onto the topology of business locations. These matrices relate each event and the associated data entities to the location in which the event occurs. The purpose of this exercise is to map out your organization's geographic distribution of computing requirements.

Let's take an example from the Nihilist Toy Company, manufacturers specializing in particularly violent and offensive playthings. The firm was the brainchild of Billy Joe Bobcat of Windy Hills, Nebraska, a man of questionable taste, who found himself unable to locate toy weapons that would allow his eight- and ten-year-old sons to engage in realistic war games. Billy Joe's early prototypes proved immensely popular with the local grade school kids, but it wasn't until the CIA placed an order for 30,000 units of the now-famous "Pan-Continental Annihilator," that the company was able to pull up stakes and move to New York City.

Today, the Nihilist Toy Company has sales offices in London, Boise, Miami and New York City. Figure 8–9 shows the geographic distribution of the major order fulfillment events.[5] Orders are accepted in each sales office, with three located in the United States, and one in England. The New York City office serves as galactic headquarters for the operation. Their central credit department must approve each new order before it is allocated for production.

---

5  For this example, I am using conceptual level events. When mapping events to business locations, the use of conceptual level events can be a convenient simplification.

| Event/Business location | New York, NY HQ | Boise, ID Sales | Miami, FL Sales | London, UK Sales | California Plant | North Carolina Plant |
|---|---|---|---|---|---|---|
| Customer places order | X | X | X | X | | |
| Credit dept. approves order | X | | | | | |
| Prod. dept. assigns order to plant | X | | | | | |
| Plant fills customer order | | | | | X | X |
| Plant ships customer order | | | | | X | X |
| Accounting invoices customer order | X | | | X | | |
| Marketing mails catalogue | X | | | X | | |

**Figure 8–9.** *Event/business location matrix*

Toys are manufactured in two plants located in North Carolina and California. The allocation of orders to a particular plant is determined in the New York office. The routing of an order to either plant is based on the size of the order, shipping logistics to the customer and availability of inventory and raw materials.

Orders for Western and Eastern Europe, Mediterranean and the Middle East are invoiced out of the London office. Orders for the Pacific Rim, Asia, South America, Central and South Africa, Australia and North America are invoiced out of the New York office. Twice a year, the company mails a new catalogue to all of its customers. Mailings are done from the New York and London offices.

The event/entity CRUD matrix is derived from the activity section of the event dictionary. For each event, the matrix indicates whether the system needs to create, read, update or delete instances of the named entity. In Figure 8–10, we see that the event, *Customer places order*, can create an instance of *Customer*, and read or update the *Customer* entity.[6] It also creates an instance of *Order* and *Order items*.

Reading through the matrix, we see that the event, *Credit department approves order* has the ability to update the *Customer* entity, reads and updates the *Order* (to set its status to "approved"), and reads information from the *Order item* (most likely the price). The event, *Production department assigns order to plant*, reads *Orders*, *Customer shipping*

---

6   This example has been simplified for teaching purposes. On a real project, the *Customer* entity would likely be represented by several entity types, including subtypes, supertypes and attributive entity types which make up the customer. The project may choose whether to create matrices using discrete entity types from the information model, or aggregate them into conceptual objects, if they are utilized by the event as a logical unit.

*addresses*, each plant's *Finished goods inventory* and *Raw materials inventory*, and creates one or more *Plant orders* and *Plant order items*, scheduling the production and/or delivery orders in the plants. It also appears that the event reserves either finished goods or raw materials by creating *Inventory transactions*. Inspection of the other events in the matrix reveals their respective data access requirements.

| Event/Entity | Customer | Order | Order item | Plant order | Plant order item | Finished goods invt trns. | Raw materials invt. trns. | Invoice | Invoice item |
|---|---|---|---|---|---|---|---|---|---|
| Customer places order | CRU | C | C | | | | | | |
| Credit dept. approves order | U | RU | R | | | | | | |
| Prod. dept. assigns order | R | R | R | C | C | CR | CR | | |
| Plant fills cust. order | R | R | R | RU | RU | CRUD | CRUD | | |
| Plant ships cust. order | R | R | R | RU | RU | | | | |
| Acctg invoices cust. order | R | R | RU | R | RU | | | CRU | CRU |
| Marketing mails catalogue | R | | | | | | | | |

**Figure 8–10.**  Event/entity CRUD matrix

From these two matrices, a third matrix can be derived. Once you know the geographic distribution of events, and each event's data access requirements, then you can derive the geographic distribution of data access requirements, the business location/entity CRUD matrix (Figure 8–11). This important matrix tells you exactly which business locations need create, read, update and delete capabilities for each entity in the model.

We now have a model of the data access requirements for each business location, against which we can begin assessing potential architectural solutions. Before we lock the data centralization fanatics and the data distribution fanatics in a room to shout each other down, a few statistics can help either faction defend its case.

Each business will have different utilization patterns for its system. That is why there is no universally "correct" architecture. The architectural solution which emerges for our Nihilist Toy Company example is appropriate for them only because it takes into account their unique geographic distribution, data volumes and event rates. Before discussing the pros and cons of centralized versus decentralized solutions, let's find out a bit more about our purveyor of fine toys.

| Business location/Entity | Customer | Order | Order item | Plant order | Plant order item | Finished goods invt. trns. | Raw materials invt. trns. | Invoice | Invoice item |
|---|---|---|---|---|---|---|---|---|---|
| New York, NY HQ | CRU | CRU | CR | C | C | CR | CR | CRUD | CRUD |
| Boise, ID Sales | CRU | C | C | | | | | | |
| Miami, FL Sales | CRU | C | C | | | | | | |
| London, UK Sales | CRU | C | C | | | | | CRUD | CRUD |
| California Plant | R | R | R | RU | RU | CRUD | CRUD | | |
| North Carolina Plant | R | R | R | RU | RU | CRUD | CRUD | | |

**Figure 8–11.** Business location/entity CRUD matrix

The matrix in Figure 8–12 shows the intersection between events and entities. But instead of indicating create, read, update or delete in the cells, a number is inserted to show how current the data must be for the event. For those entities which are created or updated by the event, a zero indicates that the database must instantly reflect the most recent update. For entities which are read by the event, the number may be higher than zero, indicating that it is acceptable for the data to be slightly older. A currency matrix can be misleading, and really requires some narrative background before it makes sense to the reader.

In this example, we have discovered that although the production department reads the customer's *Shipping address* in the process of assigning orders to plants, it doesn't care if the address is one hundred percent correct. Production's reasoning is that shipping addresses rarely change so dramatically that producing a customer's order on one coast of the United States versus the other would be affected. The business has also informed us that the shipping address plays a minor role in the allocation of orders to plants, and that frequently a customer's order may be split, with portions manufactured at both plants.

Once the plant has received the *Plant order*, subsequent changes made to the *Order* or *Order item* are not immediately relevant. Customers rarely cancel orders after they have been scheduled for production. If a customer cancels an order at the last minute, the plant managers have found it more cost effective to let the day's production run as scheduled and place the product into finished goods inventory than to interrupt production. Therefore, they need up-to-date plant orders, but the customer's master order can be up to one day old.

| Event/Entity | Customer | Order | Order item | Plant order | Plant order item | Finished goods invt. trns. | Raw materials invt. trns. | Invoice | Invoice item |
|---|---|---|---|---|---|---|---|---|---|
| Customer places order | 0 | 0 | 0 | | | | | | |
| Credit dept. approves order | 0 | 0 | 0 | | | | | | |
| Prod. dept. assigns order | 24 | 0 | 0 | 0 | 0 | 0 | 0 | | |
| Plant fills cust. order | 24 | 24 | 24 | 0 | 0 | 0 | 0 | | |
| Plant ships cust. order | 0 | 24 | 24 | 0 | 0 | | | | |
| Acctg invoices cust. order | 0 | 0 | 0 | 0 | 0 | | | 0 | 0 |
| Marketing mails catalogue | 48 | | | | | | | | |

**Figure 8–12.** Event/entity currency matrix (in hours)

When the marketing department sends out catalogues, they do a mass mailing using the *Purchasing address* for each customer. Unlike the event, *Plant ships customer order*, marketing is willing to accept data which is up to two days old. The cost of mailing a catalogue to the wrong address is insignificant, whereas the cost and customer impact of mailing the order to the wrong address can result in the loss of a loyal customer. Statistically, customers don't change their addresses often enough to warrant real time updates.

Figure 8-13 shows a different view of the currency requirements. In this matrix, the currency for each entity has been aggregated for each event which takes place at a business location. We see that the 48 hour currency tolerance for the marketing department in New York City has been lost in this view because they are located at a site where other departments require instantaneous (less than one hour) updates to customer records. Even the plants, who can tolerate customer information which is one day old for production, require rapid notification of changes to shipping addresses when the order is ready to ship.

We really seem to have painted ourselves into a corner with this view. It appears that every location needs its data to be up-to-date within the hour at all times, even though individual events at those sites can tolerate data which is slightly less than fresh. This viewpoint is too generalized to reveal the fact the only certain *attributes* (or *columns*, if I may switch to the physical vernacular) are needed to be updated or even accessible at certain locations.

| Business location/Entity | Customer | Order | Order item | Plant order | Plant order item | Finished goods invt. trns. | Raw materials invt. trns. | Invoice | Invoice item |
|---|---|---|---|---|---|---|---|---|---|
| New York, NY HQ | O | O | O | O | O | O | O | O | O |
| Boise, ID Sales | O | O | O | | | | | | |
| Miami, FL Sales | O | O | O | | | | | | |
| London, UK Sales | O | O | O | | | | | O | O |
| California Plant | O | O | O | O | O | O | O | | |
| North Carolina Plant | O | O | O | O | O | O | O | | |

**Figure 8–13.** Business location/entity currency matrix

Figure 8–14 shows a matrix of the customer attributes and business locations which need access to them. *Customers* are created and maintained at the sales offices, with the exception of the *Credit limit* and *Credit standing*, which is maintained at the New York office. Customers tend to order through the sales office closest to them, however, there are a few national and international customers who may span multiple sales zones.

| Business location/ Customer attributes | Customer ID | Customer name | Shipping address | Purchasing address | Billing address | Credit limit | Credit standing |
|---|---|---|---|---|---|---|---|
| New York, NY HQ | CRU | CRU | CRU | CRU | CRU | CRU | CRU |
| Boise, ID Sales | CRU | CRU | CRU | CRU | CRU | R | R |
| Miami, FL Sales | CRU | CRU | CRU | CRU | CRU | R | R |
| London, UK Sales | CRU | CRU | CRU | CRU | CRU | R | R |
| California Plant | R | R | R | | | | |
| North Carolina Plant | R | R | R | | | | |

**Figure 8–14.** Business location/customer attribute CRUD matrix

Whether you need to analyze data distribution to the attribute level in your organization will depend on the complexity of your problem, and the span of your geographic distribution. Now let's take a look at the various strategies for ensuring each location has the timely data access they require.

## ONE CENTRALIZED DATABASE

The first solution option to consider for distributing data is to not distribute it at all. Only one master copy of the data is kept at a central location, and all applications which need access to that data must make their queries and updates to the central server (Figure 8–15). The **benefits** are numerous:

It is easy to back up your data when only one copy exists.

The design of the overall system is less complicated, e.g., security is enforced centrally, no synchronization routines are required.

The data is always current.

No data is ever redundant across business locations.

The **downside** can be significant in a geographically remote application deployment.

As of this writing, many data communication technologies are still not fast enough or cost effective for large scale, geographically remote applications. The data volumes and event rate statistics that you gather, when compared to the communication capabilities of your network, can tell you whether remote data access is feasible.

You have a big problem if the central server or the communications lines go down. Your remote sites will effectively be without a computer.

Unacceptable performance, and risk of down-time are the two leading factors that cause businesses to steer away from centralized databases.

## REPLICATED, DECENTRALIZED DATA

On the other end of the spectrum, the database can be completely replicated at all sites that need it (Figure 8–16). Updates to one site can be broadcast to other sites on a real-time basis. Using this strategy, there are some obvious **benefits**:

The design of local applications is simplified by having access to local data.

The response time for each transaction isn't burdened by wide area network traffic.

It promotes local ownership of the data, and provides easy local access.

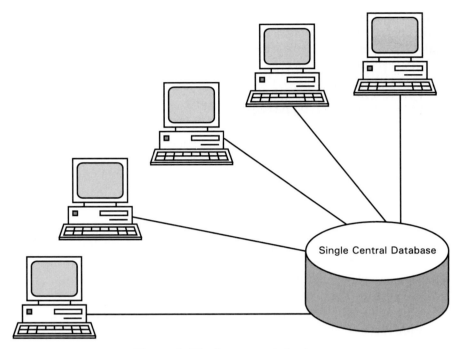

**Figure 8-15.** One central database

The **downside** involves many complications:

The overall traffic on the wide area network is increased due to replication of the data to all sites.

Complex synchronization software is required to keep the various copies of the database updated.

Problems can arise if the same record is updated in two places. These can be exacerbated by time zone differences.

If one of the servers goes down, or the replication software fails, it can be difficult to rebuild the data sets and apply updates in the right order.

Which database is the master? Backup procedures become more complex.

Completely replicated data may incur needless data redundancy.

## Fragmentation

A compromise is often struck between severe centralization and completely replicated decentralization. The distribution of the data is optimized so that only the data which is needed by each site is made local. This is called *fragmentation*. There are several strategies and more jargon associated with this technique.

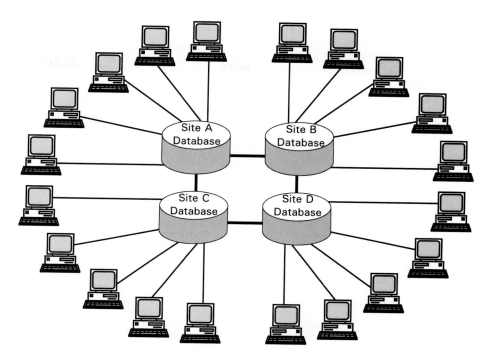

**Figure 8–16.** Replicated decentralized databases

## *Vertical Fragmentation*

*Vertical fragmentation* occurs when only certain *tables or columns* are physically distributed to remote sites (Figure 8-17). Each location has only those tables or columns that are needed by the events which occur at that site. This reduces the wide-area network traffic because only the necessary data elements need to be synchronized with other sites. The downside is that this strategy can be very complex to manage. The replication procedures must be able to synchronize updates on a column-by-column basis to different sites.

Many companies already have a version of vertical fragmentation which has occurred more by historical accident than by design. The corporate systems were constructed separately from the manufacturing systems. Both systems carry some of the same attributes about the customer and order, but many of the other columns are different. Unfortunately, the columns which should be the same, often are not. They vary in both data type and data value. The same customer is represented in both systems, but with different identifiers, sometimes even different names. As many firms try to integrate their operations, they face the daunting task of consolidating and reconciling historically fragmented records which were never designed to be electronically linked.

CUSTOMER - Database A

| Customer ID | Customer name | Credit Limit | Rail Siding | Last unload time |
|---|---|---|---|---|
| H2432 | Curtain Iron Works, Ltd. | $ 500,000 | N | |
| A5345 | Consolidated Industries | $ 450,000 | Y | 14:00 |
| G2412 | Sal's Manila Chicken Farm | $ 120,000 | N | 17:00 |
| N2341 | Day Glo Nuclear Facilities | $ 200,000 | N | 20:00 |

CUSTOMER - Database B

| Customer ID | Marketing Contact | Phone Number | Contact Comments |
|---|---|---|---|
| H2432 | Bill Dunlap | 555-6541 | Call before 10:00 |
| A5345 | Norman Wenwrinkle | 555-8794 | Contact monthly |
| G2412 | Sally Fanrack | 555-4654 | |
| N2341 | Herb Temkey | 555-4612 | Can reach at home |

*Same customers, different columns*

**Figure 8–17.** Vertical fragmentation

## Horizontal Fragmentation

*Horizontal fragmentation* occurs when only certain *rows* in a table are physically distributed to remote sites (Figure 8–18). This is typically employed when locations have their own customers which do not do business in other locations. In our example of the Nihilist Toy Company, each plant would receive only its own plant orders, and not the orders allocated to the other plant.

With horizontal fragmentation, each location has a complete copy of the database schema. All of the table structures are identical in each location, but the rows of data which populate those tables can be different. Usually, there is a master database which contains every row. Like vertical fragmentation, horizontal fragmentation cuts down on the overall wide-area-network traffic by eliminating needless data transfer. It does, however, complicate the synchronization process somewhat. Problems can arise when locations share some rows. For instance, if a customer does business in two sales zones, which one "owns" the customer's record?

There is no easy answer. If both physical locations have their own copy of the record, you will have to manage updates made at either location to keep the data in sync. You may elect to keep only one "official" copy of the row and make one location go out over the network to retrieve the customer from the office in which it is "most used" or "last used."

CUSTOMER - Database A

| Customer ID | Customer name | Credit Limit | Rail Siding | Last unload time |
|---|---|---|---|---|
| H2432 | Curtain Iron Works, Ltd. | $ 500,000 | N | |
| A5345 | Consolidated Industries | $ 450,000 | Y | 14:00 |
| G2412 | Sal's Manila Chicken Farm | $ 120,000 | N | 17:00 |
| N2341 | Day Glo Nuclear Facilities | $ 200,000 | N | 20:00 |

CUSTOMER - Database B

| Customer ID | Customer name | Credit Limit | Rail Siding | Last unload time |
|---|---|---|---|---|
| J2241 | Acme Distribution, Inc. | $ 300,000 | N | |
| B6547 | Austin Toxic Waste | $ 250,000 | N | |
| E2334 | Barry's Gold Water Co. | $ 20,000 | Y | 18:00 |
| W2331 | Steel Belt Supply Co-op | $ 130,000 | Y | 21:00 |

*Same columns, different customers*

**Figure 8–18.** Horizontal fragmentation

## Mixed Fragmentation

Vertical fragmentation occurs when sites have different columns and/or tables, but the same rows. Horizontal fragmentation occurs when sites have the same columns, but different rows. *Mixed fragmentation* occurs when both conditions exist. The distributed databases share the same logical entity types, but have different columns and different rows (Figure 8–19).

Mixed fragmentation strives for the ultimate in distributed data optimization. Each site has only those columns and only those rows which are actually needed by events which occur at that location. Taken to an extreme, mixed fragmentation can be very difficult to manage. Usually, some number of columns and rows which are not necessarily needed at a site are allowed to be replicated in a mixed fragmentation scheme to ease the burden of managing the replication process.

## SUMMARY OF GEOGRAPHIC DISTRIBUTION

The essential models created during the analysis phase provide a wealth of information for determining the geographic distribution requirements of your system. We started by gathering statistics in order to determine the overall size of the database. This is done by determining the record size in bytes for each row, the rate at which rows are created, and their retention period. This information is critical, not only for determining disk requirements, but, when data is physically distributed, the record size and event rates will

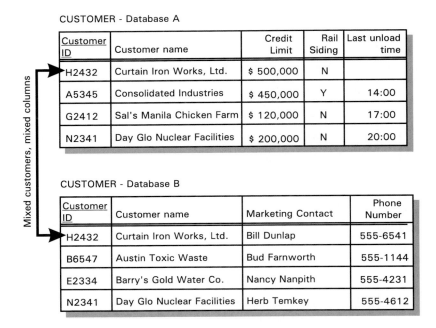

**Figure 8–19.** Mixed fragmentation

enable you to estimate your network traffic. Statistics captured for the event model include the average rate of the event, peak rate patterns for irregular event rates, and the response time expectation for the event.

Armed with these statistics, the next step is to apply them to the site topology of the business. Several matrices have proven useful for modeling this aspect of the system. The event/business location matrix maps events onto the business location in which they are recognized. The event/entity CRUD matrix, derived from the activity section of the event dictionary, summarizes the data access requirements for each event. The business location/entity CRUD matrix is a derived matrix which shows which business locations require what kind of data access, based on the fact that specific events have been allocated to those sites. These are the most useful and important matrices for declaring event distribution, and deriving data distribution requirements.

Once the business requirements for data access have been determined, additional information will help the project team make sound architectural choices. The event/entity currency matrix and business location/entity currency matrix show how "old" an entity may be for any given event and business location. This can help you decide whether real-time synchronization of distributed data is called for, or whether a batch update routine will suffice.

Given the size of your data records, the rate of events which create, read, update and delete those records, and the distance between business sites, the team can now explore their architectural options. Data distribution strategies vary anywhere from complete centralization to complete distribution. For enterprise-wide systems, you are more likely to employ some degree of vertical, horizontal or mixed fragmentation. What ever choices you make, the essential models of analysis allow you to engineer a solution based on balancing the needs of the business with the constraints of your chosen technology.

Once the project has determined the wide-area, or global distribution, it is time to focus on the local area issues of a client/server system.

## DETERMINING LOCAL DISTRIBUTION REQUIREMENTS BETWEEN CLIENT AND SERVER

Once you have determined what data must reside locally, within the reach of a local area network, it is time to tackle the many issues which arise when multiple computers are employed to perform tasks within a geographic site. Just like the wide area distribution decisions that we just covered, there is no "right" answer for the allocation of process or data to a client, departmental server, mainframe or mini-computer server. If one could reduce architecture modeling to a bumper sticker, it might read:

Every solution has a problem.[7]

Every possible deployment of our "perfect" essential model to the imperfect world of technology will have some downside. The purpose of the rest of this chapter is to point out the trade-offs which arise when you move parts of the application from the desktop computer to the server, or vice versa. By understanding the trade-offs, you will be able to make sound engineering decisions by evaluating the impact that any potential architectural scheme may have on your ability to live up to the business requirements.

Many development languages and tools have a predisposition toward either fat client or fat server deployments. As coding languages become more portable, we will see less of this phenomenon. Let's start by looking at the pros and cons of a fat client versus fat server application.

### Pros and Cons of Fat Client versus Fat Server

Fat client applications are those in which the bulk of the processing is done locally, usually on a desktop PC. Most of the popular GUI development tools positively encourage a fat client application since their scripts were designed specifically for the PC. In Figure 8–20 we see a transaction as it passes through a typical fat client architecture.

---

[7]    An old Ruritanian folk saying, unearthed by Meilir Page-Jones.

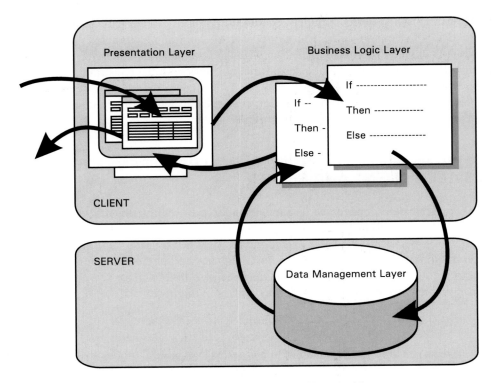

**Figure 8–20.** A transaction in a fat client architecture

The data capture and editing is done on the client. If the user makes an error, he is immediately informed. The interface application edits immediately for proper data type, date and numeric ranges, and valid values for restricted lists. The client application also enforces a wide variety of business rules. This involves giving the user visual cues to distinguish between optional and required fields based on the status of the object being updated. The application also uses the status values and knowledge of the user's level of authorization to turn on and off command buttons and menu items.

An extremely fat client application will also execute any calculations that need to be performed, in lieu of using stored procedures on the server. The server simply receives data and instructions to either create, read, update or delete values in specific tables. The database management system, residing on the server, enforces referential integrity, user authority, correct data type and required fields; however, all of these factors have already been edited by a well-crafted fat client application. On the outbound side of a transaction, say a query, the data is sent from the server back out to the client where it can be sorted, filtered, formatted and displayed to the happy user.

Now that I've painted the fat client scenario, let's pick it apart to expose its strong and weak points. It's pretty obvious that the client machine *must* be capable of putting some sort of display on a monitor, so we can take screen presentation as a pre-ordained duty of the client. Moving on to the editing, the decision to edit for proper data type at the client is low cost, high pay-back. Any decent GUI development tool has the ability to read the data type from the development database and provide data type editing at the client without having to code it by hand. If field has a data type of *date* in the database, then the client application should only accept valid date formats, and inform the user promptly if he attempts to enter a value which doesn't pass muster. A character field, such as *order status*, may only have a restricted set of values. In this case, the presentation application should enforce the setting of the field's values, either by setting it automatically, or by allowing the user to select values from a list. This low-cost editing prevents entry errors at the client from ever reaching the server.

Whether to locate a business rule on the client or server is not as clear cut. A simple rule such as "*a price list's expiration date shall not be less than its effective date*," is a common cross-field edit in business applications. You could get all sorts of weird results if you allowed the user to establish price lists that end before they start. Where should this rule be enforced? On the client's interface application, or on the server's database management system?

Both choices have their merits. To enforce the rule on the client, you might write a line of code that is triggered when the user attempts to save his price list. (You could also put the edit code in the expiration date field, to trap the error as soon as it occurs. However, be aware that when the user is armed with a mouse, he could enter the expiration date prior to entering a start date, making an edit check at the field level tricky and potentially annoying to the user.) By detecting the error at the client, the application is able to give the user a chance to redeem himself before incurring the cost of sending the data over to the server. There is a widespread expectation among GUI users that a modern interface will contain such features, befitting that amorphous adjective, "user friendly."

Enforcing this innocuous date rule on the client reduces the time it takes for the system to inform the user that he has made an error. It reduces the potential network traffic because it eliminates the need for the server to inform the client that bad data has been received. On the other hand, by putting the business rule solely on the client, other applications which access the same data must include an identical rule to ensure compliance.

Herein lies one of the great dilemmas of a client/server architecture. Business rules are designed to protect the integrity of the company's information asset. The client software needs immediate access to such rules to meet the expectations of a friendly interface, but the data on the server needs to be protected from erroneous update by applications which may be ignorant of the rules. If your database can be accessed by a wide variety of applications (e.g., the ominous "end-user computing"), this will drive you toward a fat server philosophy of putting business rules on the server, in either stored procedures or custom code.

Heterogeneity of client hardware may also push a project toward a fat server implementation. Let's say that the database server needs to be capable of fielding queries and updates from workstations, laptops, palmtops, telephones and interactive television. There isn't sufficient processing power on some of these devices to do any serious rule checking. These types of constraints will lead you toward encapsulating your data on the server with a layer of business application logic through which all transactions must pass to access or update the data. Fat server applications have a maintenance advantage over fat client applications in that all of the rules can be found in one place, so are more handily modified. Business logic which is scattered among different client applications can create a version control and maintenance hassle down the road.

Before I start sounding like a fat server bigot, let me return the fat client camp once again. Today's users are simply not going to tolerate an application which slaps them about the head for committing preventable entry errors. They expect the client interface to be aware of the rules and guide them through the use of the application. Today, this often results in coding the same rule in two places, once in the client software to allow for immediate enforcement at the interface, and again on the server to guard against a renegade insurgency from another application. Needless to say, no one is very thrilled about this duplicity. Vendors are working hard to make their coding scripts more portable, so at minimum, the business logic doesn't have to be coded in two different languages.

This problem of maintaining two sets of business rules is partially responsible for the popularity of company intranet technology. The application code resides on the server, and is accessed by the client at run time. The pay-off is one set of rules, but the drawback, of course, is increased network traffic to the web server.

And what of object-orientation? Can OO help us meet the stringent demands of the interface while still keeping the wagons circled around our data? I will cover object-orientation further in Chapter 12, but we must delve into the concept here because it has relevance to the fat client versus fat server debate.

### Business Objects in a Fat Client Application

Much fanfare and hoopla has been made over the use of object-oriented coding techniques to manage business rules.[8] In brief, the programming construct wraps an object's data (known in OO jargon as *variables*) in a veil of publicly known procedures, called *methods*, through which all access to the data is channeled. This is known as ***encapsulation***, meaning that if you want to query or modify the data in any way, you must appeal to the object's methods to do it for you.

Taking this idea and running with it, we can say "Let's take all of the rules regarding an *Order* and stuff them into an *Order* object and make all portions of our application which deal with orders appeal to the order object to do their business!" (This is a

---

[8]   I must note, that much of what I'm about to say can also be achieved with good old structured design and remote procedure calls. Object-orientation is not a prerequisite for solving client/server architectural dilemmas. It is just one of many solution options to the problem.

gross oversimplification of the process, I know, but this will suit our purposes for the time being.) We certainly have the material for deciding what an *Order* object should contain. The information model tells us all of the data that the business cares about for each order. The event model, and specifically the event dictionary's activity section, tells us the procedural requirements for how to manipulate orders. To illustrate, if you were to peruse an event model for a typical order fulfillment system, you might find statements in the event dictionary such as:

> *If an order is canceled, the system must cancel all of the order's pending shipments.*

> *If an update to an order's requested ship date falls outside of the effective dates of the attached price list, the order must be repriced.*

> *All orders must have raw materials allocation prior to being scheduled for production.*

> *Vehicle ID is required for all orders shipped via rail car or truck. Vehicle ID is not required for will-call orders.*

These rules are far more interesting than our mundane date edit. Given these business requirements, a user would be within his rights to expect the interface to behave accordingly. If the user cancels an order, the system should acknowledge that his pending scheduled shipments are also canceled. If he extends an order's ship date beyond the period of the price list, the interface should tell him promptly and clearly that he needs to reprice the order. If he doesn't yet have raw materials allocation, the button or menu item which schedules production should be turned off. Similarly, if he is shipping via rail or truck, it should be visually apparent that the *Vehicle ID* field is required, and if the order is for will-call pick up, the *Vehicle ID* field should be disabled or hidden.

By looking at the mapping of events to candidate windows in the interface prototype, we may find that various aspects of an order are modified on many, many windows within the application. Focusing purely on the client side of an application, the idea of employing object-orientation to manage business rules can be powerful. When an idea as complex as a customer order is scattered about many windows, each window needs access to the business logic which is germane to the tasks conducted therein. The user should expect the rules to be enforced uniformly, no matter which window he is using.

A sound strategy is to partition code which controls the behavior of business classes, such as *Order* and *Customer*, from code which controls the behavior of presentation classes, such as *Window* or *Button* (Figure 8–21). By separating the business logic from the presentation logic, the designer meets two objectives. The business logic now resides in one place within the client application, yet is accessible to each presentation window that needs it.

Thus, the elusive "reuse" of the business class is achieved within the same application by reducing the amount of redundant business logic code required to run the interface. The ability to reuse presentation classes, such as windows, buttons and controls is also increased, because these classes are unburdened with any knowledge of the business, and therefore can concentrate on what they do best, namely the mechanics of managing a graphical interface. Many of today's popular GUI development languages already support this type of application partitioning.

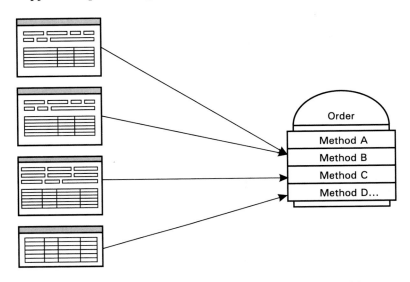

**Figure 8–21.** Many windows appealing to the same business object

### Business Objects in a Fat Server Application

Partitioning the business logic from the presentation logic on the client allows for higher reuse and less redundant code, but it still doesn't address the need to encapsulate data on the server with the same business rules. To solve this problem, you need a language that allows presentation objects on the client to appeal directly to business objects on the server. This is managed with what is known as an ***object request broker*** (ORB). An object request broker is an object which keeps track of the physical location of objects which are deployed throughout a client/server architecture. When a presentation object, such as a window, needs to appeal to the *Order* object, it sends its request to the object request broker, which routes the communication to the appropriate machine on which the target object is located (Figure 8–22).

Object request brokers make business logic portable. The big pay-off is that business rules are made available to the client application, without having to physically locate them on the client. This allows for the central maintenance of one copy of the business class, used by *all* applications which require access to the data. Another huge benefit is that the business logic can be moved from machine to machine, simply by moving the object and updating its location in the object request broker. This allows the system architect to take advantage of new technology as it becomes available to the project, redistributing objects to gain optimal performance without redesigning and recoding large sections of the entire application.

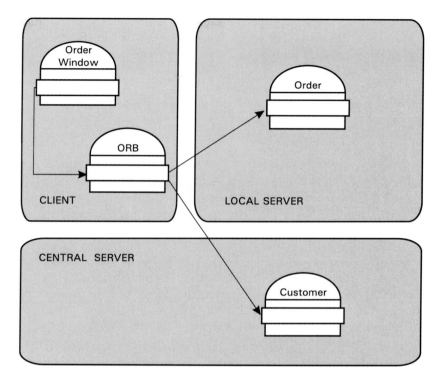

**Figure 8–22.** An object-request broker

Remember, every solution has a problem. The idea of distributing the business logic to the server, *and* still having access to the rules at run time on the client is alluring, but it comes with a price. The design assumes that the speed of the network between client and server is sufficient to handle the additional traffic imposed by insisting that the client go across the line to appeal to the server-based rules.

One-stop-shopping for rules about a suite of complex business objects requires skillful design. No single window or application may ever care about an object such as *Order* in its entirety. To have to instantiate the entire object on the client at run time and populate it with lots of data from the server over a wimpy network is like trying to suck an elephant through a straw. Complex business objects can be compared to the old fable of the blind men and the elephant. The story goes something like this:

Three gentlemen who happened to be sight-impaired were introduced to a pachyderm one fine day, for reasons which escape me. The first sight-impaired gentleman touched the elephant's trunk and proclaimed, "an elephant is like one of those large vacuums that you rent at the car wash. I shall use this elephant to clean my van pool bus." The second man of limited vision walked directly into the elephant's flank. "I beg to differ with you!" he protested. "An elephant is like a large rubber wall. One can charge tavern patrons a fee to bounce against it." The third man, who really wasn't entirely blind, made straight for the elephant's tusks, proclaiming, "Gentlemen, we could make a fortune turning these into piano keys and decorative trinkets," upon which he was promptly arrested under the United Nations Endangered Species International Accord for malicious intent to poach a protected animal.

Interface objects, such as windows which are designed to recognize specific business events are much like the blind men encountering the elephant. A window which creates an order header may be interested in the credit standing of the customer, but may not be interested in the level of inventory for the ordered product. A window which specializes in splitting a requested order into two separate shipments cares nothing about the customer's credit standing, but may depend entirely on the availability of transportation. Each window only needs a portion of the order, much like the blind men require only a portion of the elephant.

The moral of the story is that if your window only requires a portion of the elephant, say a tusk, flank or trunk, then you need not burden the application with any knowledge about the rest of the elephant. The presentation logic should only be aware of those features of the object that are required for the job, and the business object should not encumber the application with having to retrieve data it doesn't need. The designer will, in many cases, need to create services which access only the data required for each task.

Let's look at where your business objects might reside at run time. One option is to locate the business objects on the server. Any presentation object running on the client must appeal to the business objects over the network, usually via an object request broker. The cost of this solution is increased network traffic.

If your network is unable to handle the messaging between presentation objects on the client and business objects on the server, then another option is to instantiate business objects on the client at run time in order to service the interface effectively, assuming there is no appreciable impact on run-time performance to do so. In this solution, the network still must be able to handle a stampede of data from the database required to bring the objects to life. Remember, don't pass the entire elephant across the network for a window that may only require a quick look at the toenail.

A third option is to create two physical sets of the object classes, one on the server and one on the client.[9] The pay-off is that your business rules are resident on the client once again for use by the interface, and an identical copy exists on the server, to protect the data. The penalty is that, once again, we are back to coordinating two physical versions of the rules.

---

[9]   I am still assuming for the whole of this book that the system's data is housed in a relational database, and therefore, some portion of the runtime objects will still be responsible for the retrieval and update of the data.

This scheme is only feasible with languages with true portability between client and server platforms, whether they are object-oriented or not. For development tools with lesser capabilities, we will continue to find ourselves coding business logic in two places to meet the user's demand for visually apparent business rules on the interface, and to meet the need to ensure safe custody of the corporate data.

# REVIEW OF ARCHITECTURAL TRADE-OFFS

The following section briefly covers some of the many architectural trade-offs that must be considered when designing a client/server system. I will state a quality vector, such as *rapid response time at client*, then list the possible ways to achieve it.

## Rapid Response Time at the Client

For systems that demand lightning speed at the client, there are several ways to avoid a sluggish system.

If you have many concurrent users, a fat server application could bog down the server with excessive processing demands. By purchasing very powerful client machines, you can distribute much of the processing to the desktop. This reduces the overall network traffic, eliminating many remote procedure calls. The cost, of course, is that you pay top dollar for the latest client technology. Throwing hardware at performance problems is often cost-effective. It is also important to ensure that there is a high-speed network in place, and sufficient fire power at the server to reduce wait time.

Turning our attention to the data, other solutions include optimizing the database through the use of indices or views to speed up queries on the highest volume transactions. Some data with low volatility may be able to be cached either at the client or on a local file server.

## Heterogeneity of Client Hardware

Some businesses have a requirement that the application must run on any variety of client machines, from a workstation to a laptop, palmtop or telephone. This will force the application toward an extreme fat server architecture, to protect the integrity of the data. Application program interfaces (APIs) will have to be built to allow different client applications with various degrees of intelligence to access the server. For applications which run GUIs on fairly intelligent workstations, you may encounter the demand that many of the business rules housed on the central server also be resident at the client at run time.

For most of this book, I am making the bold assumption that the client hardware is virtually identical for all client machines, or at least, the differences are managed by the IT department. I have found through experience that the subtle differences between even different brands of personal computers can sometimes make the same client application behave unexpectedly. The IT department must wrest control over the purchasing and configuration of personal computers away from the business, and maintain a standard approved hardware configuration for the applications it creates or procures. This includes setting guidelines for the use of a personal computer. It seems that every company has at least one errant manager who is famous for coming in on the weekend and installing a copy of his kid's "Galactic Vomitron Warriors," which just happens to reconfigure his system files, resulting in an angry call to the IT director on Monday morning when his client application aborts after the sign-on window. Business people who are unwilling to give up the historical PC "free-for-all" probably aren't ready for the discipline required for client/server computing. (See Chapter 13, myth #3: PC stands for personal computer.)

## Heterogeneity of Client Software

Not every user is responsible for the same business events, so not every user needs *all* of the software you deploy. Assuming that there are many applications which run over the same database, the designer has the choice of distributing one large application to everybody or many smaller applications to only those who need them.

The second alternative has some advantages. When you break up a large client application into several pieces, the client software occupies less disk space. When the user requests enhancements to the software, you can isolate changes to a particular executable. The pay-off is that you disrupt fewer users with a new software upgrade when you release the enhanced application, and you need not test the pieces of the application which are unaffected. The downside is that all of this partitioning has to be managed with a rigorous version control and distribution process to ensure that IT is acutely aware of what pieces of the application is on each user's PC.

For businesses with a mix of applications sharing the same database, which may be built by different groups within IT or contain some purchased packages, a fat sever solution may be necessary to ensure that the data is adequately encapsulated with the proper business rules.

## Minimal Network Communication

Some sites may not have the network speed, due to either size or distance, to handle large transaction volumes effectively. If this constraint exists, the system architects can turn once again to the essential model for help. Taking the most critical and high volume events, draw an event neighborhood data flow diagram for the event's activity, showing all process and data store access (Figure 8–23).

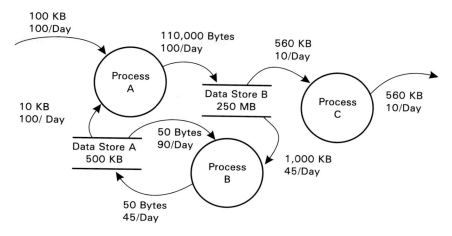

**Figure 8–23.** An event-neighborhood diagram annotated with statistics

Annotate the diagram with the event rates and the number of bytes represented by each data flow. Armed with this kind of information, you can play "what if" games to come up with a client/server distribution of process and data that results in the lowest possible communication. Try separating the client from the server at the point of minimal data flow. Try caching some data locally, at the client or on a client-site departmental server, to reduce the traffic to the central server. By using the model, you can simulate transactions on an endless variety of configurations until you find one that will work.

## SUMMARY

The purpose of architecture modeling is to use our knowledge of the essential business requirements, combined with the constraints of available technology, to come up an adequate distribution of data and processing to the various hardware tiers of the client/server architecture.

The client/server software application can be broken up into layers. The presentation layer is used to manage the mechanics of the interface. The business logic layer contains the code which enforces the business policy, as described by the activity section of the event model. The data management layer manages concurrent access to the database, as well as synchronization of distributed data. The term *fat client (thin server)* is used to describe an application in general terms in which the majority of the business logic layer executes on the client machine. *Fat server (thin client)* describes an application where the lion's share of the processing occurs on the server, and the client is relegated primarily to presentation duties.

Architecture modeling starts by gathering statistics about your business, and documenting the performance expectations that constrain specific events. The size of the database is determined by calculating the number of bytes required for a single row in each table, multiplied by the number of expected rows. The number of expected rows is a function of how often rows are added by an event, and how long you must retain the record. The statistics collected for record size are also relevant when determining the network traffic load between client and server.

Statistics gathered for the event model include the average rate for the business events, and peak rate patterns for events which occur irregularly. Response time constraints are also gathered for the most critical business events.

The geographic distribution of the business is documented in an event/business location matrix. This shows which events occur in the various business locations that are geographically remote from each other. By combining the event/business location matrix with an event/entity CRUD matrix, a third matrix, the business location/entity CRUD matrix can be derived, showing the logical data distribution requirements for the application. By combining this knowledge with a sense of how *current* the data must be at each site, the team can start evaluating whether to have one centralized database, distributed and synchronized databases, or employ a fragmentation scheme for distributing data.

The architect is also faced with local distribution decisions. Users of modern GUI applications demand that many of the business rules be visually apparent to them at run time. The business also has a responsibility to protect the data asset, usually residing on the server, from update by other applications which may not be aware of the business rules. With many development tools and languages, this dilemma can force developers to code rules in two places.

Many of today's popular GUI development tools are predisposed toward fat client architectures. As development languages become more portable, we may see applications trend back toward server-based business logic and Internet/intranet technology, however, this will place even more demands on our existing networks to handle the increased messaging.

Architectural modeling is all about trade-offs. To properly engineer a client/server solution, you should use the model to simulate transactions through various architectural scenarios. The purpose of this chapter is show how the essential analysis models can be used to replace the traditional architecture decision-making method of "he who shouts the loudest wins." The moral of the story is that "every solution has a problem." By becoming aware of the downside for each solution, your team can arrive sensibly at the least objectionable architecture to meet your business needs.

## EXERCISES

1. What factors might push the design of an application toward a fat server implementation rather than a fat client design?

2. What factors might favor fat client design?

3. Why might you choose to implement a replicated database in multiple locations, rather than serve all applications through a single centralized database?

4. Why might you be forced to code a business rule on both the client and the server?

## ANSWERS

1. Client machines with a relatively limited processing power, or a mix of different kinds of client machines with varying degrees of processing capability, would force more of the processing back onto the server than would be the case if all of the client machines had a great deal of processing power. Another situation that favors a fat server model is one where many applications have access to, or can update the same data. By implementing business rules on the server, you avoid having to code them into every application which might gain access to the data.

2. Having limited access to the server from the client is one factor which would favor putting more of the application logic on the client in order to reduce the amount of communication needed between client and server. Furthermore, if the application must remain running, even in the case of network outage or server failure, the entire application logic and data would have to be replicated on the client. The predisposition of your GUI development tool can also influence whether it is easier and more cost-effective to develop fat client or fat server applications.

3. A single, centralized database would be optimal if our technology was perfect. The communication cost, distance, and time required to access data remotely often pushes geographically-distributed organizations to replicate data. Replicated databases can be kept in adequately close synchronization at a low transmission rate that is more cost-effective than is required for real-time, on-line access. Data replication can also ensure that the remote business location's system is still available in the event of a central server outage.

4. This unfortunate reality of client/server systems arises when a business rule is required to be located on the server to protect the database from being erroneously updated by another application, but the users also require the rule to be visually apparent on the interface at the time they are entering transactions. (An example of this would be a data field which may be required under some circumstances, but not under others.) If your development language does not support rapid instantiation of rules on the client from code on the server, you will likely find yourself having to represent a rule in two places in two different languages (for example,

in a script associated with a window on the client and in a stored procedure in the relational database management system). The challenge then becomes to devise some traceability between the requirement for the rule to exist and the various places you may have tucked the rule in your final code. For systems in which requirements traceability is of supreme importance (such as in some government defense systems), each line item in the event dictionary can be numbered and referenced by comments in the final code. While this is overkill for most business systems, it is a good idea to document the location of any business rules or policy in your system which are likely to change or be up for re-evaluation in the foreseeable future. This can be done by amending your event dictionary to note the physical location of key pieces of policy in the final code.

# CHAPTER 9

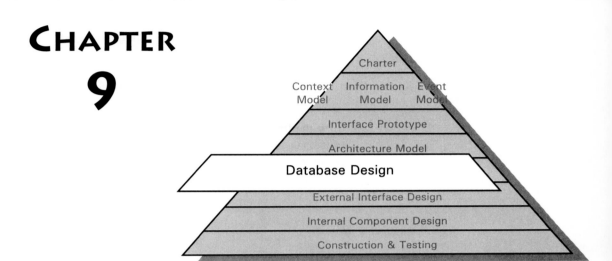

# RELATIONAL DATABASE DESIGN

## INTRODUCTION

In Chapter 9, I provide a brief survey of relational database concepts and demonstrate how an information model translates into a relational database design. I follow with a discussion of the various options you may face when choosing a primary key. I also touch on the options for implementing supertype/subtype relationships. The chapter closes with some tips for performance tuning your database, which could be titled "*Everything you should think about before you decide to denormalize your database design.*"

## RELATIONAL DATABASES IN BUSINESS SYSTEMS

The relational database has enjoyed a tremendous rise in popularity throughout the 1980s and 1990s. It is currently the favored format for storing business data in many organizations throughout the world. Many client/server development tools *assume* that the underlying database will be relational. The strength of the relational model is that it promotes an implementation-neutral and largely non-redundant format for storing information.

Implementation neutrality is important in business systems, because unlike many real-time applications with specific tasks or defined functions, business people are constantly searching for new ways to exploit the information they have collected. Requests to extend the data set or aggregate it in new ways often surface after the initial system is designed and built.

We have seen from the information modeling chapter that data respects no project boundaries. Relational databases are designed to serve many masters. This profoundly powerful concept is often the target of the relational model's harshest critics who point out that performance is impacted precisely because the database layout isn't optimized toward a particular business function. While some early relational databases didn't exactly perform at lightning-fast speed, the modern versions are now performing at rates that are generally acceptable in business systems.

The intent of this chapter is to show how to convert a logical information model into a database design. After covering the basics of the transformation, I will offer some tips on tuning the design for databases where the logical structure has been proven to have a performance problem.

## RELATIONAL DATABASE CONCEPTS

A relational database is made up of a series of tables. Each table consists of columns, which represent individual data elements, and rows which represent data records in the organization.[1] Figure 9–1 shows a table from a dog kennel system. There is no logical implication of the physical ordering of columns from left to right. They may be stored in any order or interchanged at any time.[2]

Rows are also interchangeable, and no two rows are identical. Each is uniquely identified with a primary key (underlined), which may be comprised of one or more columns in the table. Each column should depend on the key, the whole key and nothing but the key, following the rules of normalization, covered in Chapter 5.

---

[1]   The official jargon is that a table is a *relation* and a row is a *tuple*. A column is referred to as an *attribute* or *field*. In the interest of keeping this epic readable, I prefer to use the common vernacular, tables, rows and columns.

[2]   This characteristic of relational databases makes bulk inserts or updates which rely solely on column position a very dangerous practice. I have seen this technique used in batch routines which apply EDI transactions. It works fine until another programmer alters the table structure.

DOG

| License number | Name | Weight pounds | Date of birth | Height inches |
|---|---|---|---|---|
| AE1235 | Mascot | 120 | 12-4-92 | 24 |
| TR578F | Biffy | 32 | 4-7-95 | 17 |
| 7GK342 | Spot | 9 | 3-17-96 | 9 |
| AE980 | Rover | 18 | 5-9-91 | 14 |
| E1TH7 | Martha | 26 | 1-7-89 | 18 |

**Figure 9–1.** The *Dog* table

These concepts should look very familiar by this point in the book. Much of the layout of the database is already achieved when you create a well normalized information model (see Chapter 5). In the next section, I will show how the information model can be converted, in very mechanical manner, into a first-cut database design.

## TRANSLATING AN INFORMATION MODEL INTO A RELATIONAL DATABASE

Most data modeling CASE tools will generate a first-cut relational database from the information model. Each entity becomes a table. The unique identifier for each entity becomes the primary key of the table. Each attribute becomes a column in its respective table, and relationships are implemented by placing the primary key of one table in the related table, as a foreign key, (fk).

Prior to generating a relational database design for any part of your information model, you must first ensure that the model is complete. Each attribute must have the appropriate data type. All of the attribute cardinality and relationship cardinality must be complete and correct. Each entity must have a unique identifier. The unique identifier is important because it will become the primary key when a table is created for the entity, and be used as foreign keys throughout the database.

The notation for a relational database diagram isn't significantly different than that of an information model. Each fundamental, attributive and associative entity type in the information model is translated into a table in the relational database. Where the humble entity is represented with a rectangle on the entity-relationship diagram, we are relieved to find a rectangle representing a table in the relational database diagram (Figure 9–2).

Relationships are replaced with foreign key references. The four points of cardinality from the information model relationship are retained on the diagram. As noted in Chapter 5, only three of these points of cardinality are enforced by the declared database structure. The mandatory nature of the "many" side of the relationship must be enforced somewhere in the application code. The relationship name has been eliminated from the line because the relationship has been implemented by embedding the primary key of one table into the other. An arrow head on the line shows which table has a foreign key "pointer" back to the table in which it is a primary key.

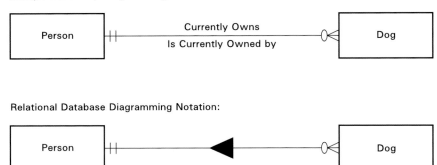

**Figure 9–2.** ERD versus RDB notation

The pattern of the relationship cardinality in the information model dictates which table gets the foreign key. Let's look at some examples.

## One-to-Many Relationships

One-to-many relationships are the meat and potatoes of the relational database. The overwhelming majority of business relationships fall into this category. The rule is simple. The primary key from the "one" side is embedded in the table on the "many" side to implement the relationship. In the example, a person may own many dogs, but a dog must be owned by only one person. To implement the relationship, the primary key from the *Person* table is embedded in the *Dog* table. We cannot embed the primary key from the *Dog* table in the *Person* table because this would result in a repeating group for anyone who owns more than one dog. Figure 9–3 shows the entity-relationship diagram, and the resulting relational database diagram and table schema.

If the "one" side of the relationship is optional, then the foreign key will be optional (Figure 9–4). If the "one" side of the relationship is required, the foreign key will be a required field in the table.

To join a dog with its current owner, *Dog* rows are joined to the corresponding *Person* row by matching the person's foreign key in the *Dog* table to the person's primary key in the *Person* table. The concept of the table join is a basic tenet of Structured Query Language (SQL), which is used to access data in relational databases.

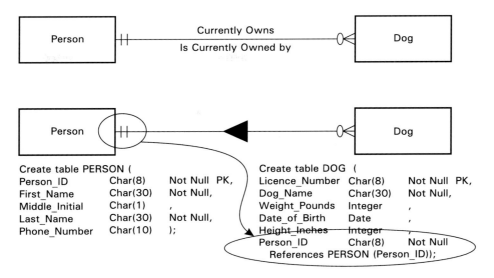

**Figure 9–3.** Required relationship results in required foreign key

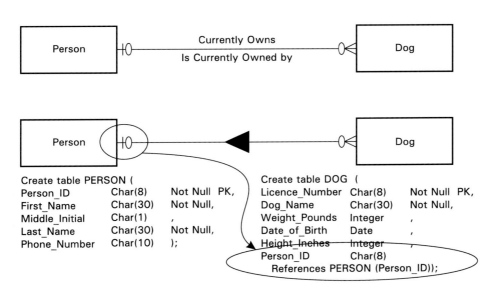

**Figure 9–4.** Optional relationship results in optional foreign key

Foreign keys allow the database management system to ensure that no row can be deleted from the database as long as a row in any table references its primary key. A *Person* record cannot be deleted if a *Dog* row exists which references it. The dogs must be deleted first before the person can be eliminated. This is called *referential integrity*.

## One-to-One Relationships

Figure 9–5 shows a rather odd one-to-one relationship. A person may optionally own one dog, but not more than one. A dog must be owned by only one person. I must say that one-to-one relationships are *exceptionally* rare in business systems. Most of the few one-to-one relationships that I have encountered have turned out to be supertype/subtype relationships in disguise. I seriously doubt that the modeler, in this case, is trying to say that a dog is a type of person, and that a person can be dog. (An assertion that is likely to earn the undying affection of the dog, but could result in a slap in the face from anyone represented in the person entity.) I'll cover the translation of supertype/subtype relationships later in the chapter, so please suspend disbelief just long enough to accept that a person is limited to owning only one dog.[3]

**Figure 9–5.** A one-to-one relationship

A foreign key can be placed in either table to implement the one-to-one relationship. If both sides of the relationship are mandatory or optional, the designer can literally flip a coin, although he should try to imagine which one is more likely to become a one-to-many in the future. In our example above, one side of the relationship is optional and one is mandatory, making our job much easier. The primary key of *Person* table should be placed in the *Dog* table as a foreign key because it is required. By declaring the foreign key to be NOT NULL in the database schema, the mandatory nature of the relationship can be more tightly enforced. Alternately, if the *Dog* key was placed in the *Person* table, it would have to be optional, and the rule requiring a dog to have an owner would not be not addressed.

You might ask, "Why not combine these tables?" This would result in a rather strange object, indeed. A *Person-Dog*, which is part person and, optionally, part dog would be a bizarre creature in the real world and certainly a questionable structure in the database. Combining these two disparate objects degrades the reusability of either, and complicates any code which uses their structures.

## Many-to-Many Relationships

A many-to-many relationship, left unattended, will result in a single intersection table which houses the primary keys of the related tables (Figure 9–6). All many-to-many relationships should be resolved with associative entity types in the information model

---

3   Perhaps we're modeling apartment dwellers who are allowed only one dog.

prior to generating the relational database design. As I pointed out in Chapter 5, there may be additional attributes or even other relationships required to uniquely identify an instance of the association.

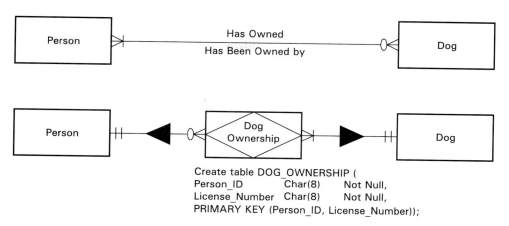

Create table DOG_OWNERSHIP (
Person_ID          Char(8)       Not Null,
License_Number  Char(8)       Not Null,
PRIMARY KEY (Person_ID, License_Number));

**Figure 9–6.** A many-to-many relationship and resulting intersection table

## Attributes

Each of an entity's attributes becomes a column in the associated table. Optional attributes become optional columns. Required attributes become required columns. Repeating attributes are a big no-no. These should be resolved by creating attributive entity types during analysis. The attributes which were nominated as candidate identifiers of the entity become the columns which comprise the primary key.

## CHOOSING A PRIMARY KEY

Choosing a primary key is an important design consideration. The primary key may be a single logical attribute of the entity which has all of the qualifications of a good primary key. It sometimes takes more than one column to form a suitable key. If no decent, upstanding logical key is found among the entity's attributes, then a token identifier may be named as the key. We will see in the following section that primary keys may also be foreign keys to other tables. So what makes a good primary key?

The primary key must be unique. The primary key uniquely identifies a single row in the table. There must never be rows with the same value in the key. This rules out attributes with values over which the business has no control, such as customer name or a person's name.

The primary key must be invariant over time. The primary key of any table is likely to be used as foreign key by any other table which references it. For this reason, columns with values that might be changed or renamed by the users are poor candidates. Name-based mnemonics such as product codes pose particular problems. Let's look at an example to see why they can be such a vexing issue. Figure 9–7 shows a fragment of a *Product* table from a furniture manufacturer in which the designer has used the *Product code* as the primary key.

PRODUCT

| Product Code | Product name | Height inches | Width inches | Length inches |
|---|---|---|---|---|
| CDLD4 | Cherry Drop Leaf Dining Table | 30 | 36 | 48 |
| MDLD4 | Mahogany Drop Leaf Dining Table | 30 | 36 | 48 |
| PLBKC | Pine Ladder Back Kitchen Chair | 36 | 18 | 18 |
| PENCT | Pine Entertainment Center | 80 | 22 | 72 |
| MBWFC | Mahogany Bow Front Chest | 48 | 20 | 28 |

**Figure 9–7.** The *Product* table

Upon preliminary examination, the *Product code* appears to be a delightful candidate for a primary key. It is unique, not too lengthy, and everybody in the organization is familiar with it since it has appeared for years on their screens and reports. But what are some problems that might arise?

The first problem is that the *Product code* appears to contain meaningful data. It is an abbreviation of the *Product name*, which we will see in a moment might change. There are also some suspicious numbers in the first two entries. The "4" which appends the dining table rows represents the seating capacity of the table. This piece of information should have been modeled as a separate attribute of the product. The first letter of the code appears to denote the type of wood used. If the designer fails to provide separate columns for this information, the programmer will be forced to parse the *Product code* to derive them, often with spurious results. Figure 9–8 shows an improved version of the *Product* table.

Data elements such as *Product codes*, *Customer codes* and *Order numbers*, can create a ticking time bomb on any project. An entire generation of workers may have been forced to memorize the old mnemonics. Any attempt to resolve the technical problems that often arise over old codes may put you quickly into political hot water. It may or may not be beyond the scope or authority of the project to re-engineer the code structure. This should be made clear to the team in the project charter, or be raised as a critical analysis issue. Even if you have the authority to create something sensible in the way of a new logical identifier, you may have to carry the old codes as alternate keys in your tables so you can interface with other legacy systems.

PRODUCT

| Product Code | Product name | Material Type | Seating Capacity | Height inches | Width inches | Length inches |
|---|---|---|---|---|---|---|
| CDLD4 | Cherry Drop Leaf Dining Table | Cherry | 4 | 30 | 36 | 48 |
| MDLD4 | Mahogany Drop Leaf Dining Table | Mahogany | 4 | 30 | 36 | 48 |
| PLBKC | Pine Ladder Back Kitchen Chair | Pine | 1 | 36 | 18 | 18 |
| PENCT | Pine Entertainment Center | Pine | | 80 | 22 | 72 |
| MBWFC | Mahogany Bow Front Chest | Mahogany | | 48 | 20 | 28 |

**Figure 9–8.** An improved version of the *Product* table

Another problem with codes is invariance. What would happen if the marketing department found it necessary to change the name of the "Mahogany Bow Front Chest" to the "Hepplewhite Dresser"?

The business has created a rather nasty problem by modifying its product name. In a relational database, the primary key of the *Product* table is embedded as a foreign key in every other table which references it. In this example, the *Product code* would appear as a column in every order item row on which the product was sold (Figure 9–9). To display the *Product name* on an *Order Item* window or report, the programmer would join back to the *Product* table to find the *Product name*.

ORDER ITEM

| Order ID | Order item number | Product Code (fk) | Quantity | Unit Price |
|---|---|---|---|---|
| 3-0031 | 1 | MBWFC | 1 | $ 3,400.00 |

PRODUCT

| Product Code | Product name |
|---|---|
| MBWFC | Hepplewhite Dresser |

**Figure 9–9.** The *Order item* table joined to *Product* table on *Product code*

Several issues emerge when we look at the result of the join. The *Product code*, "MBWFC," no longer makes sense when compared to the name of the product. If the business insists that the code be updated as well, the database administrator must do a global update to all instances of *Product code* which are scattered throughout the database. This solution should be avoided. If the business insists on modifying the *Product code*, it is no longer eligible to be the primary key because it is not invariant. In this situation, a random value (commonly called a **token identifier**) makes a better primary key. A token identifier is a unique value, generated by the database upon insert of the row. The database management system guarantees this value to be unique. It carries no embedded meaning, and is never displayed to the user of the system. Figure 9–10 shows the *Product* table with a token identifier as the primary key. There is no meaning in the value of the token. The structure of the token will vary, depending on the database management system used.

PRODUCT

| Product ID | Product Code | Product name | Height inches | Width inches | Length inches |
|---|---|---|---|---|---|
| X0012 | CDLD4 | Cherry Drop Leaf Dining Table | 30 | 36 | 48 |
| H2432 | MDLD4 | Mahogany Drop Leaf Dining Table | 30 | 36 | 48 |
| A5345 | PLBKC | Pine Ladder Back Kitchen Chair | 36 | 18 | 18 |
| G2412 | PENCT | Pine Entertainment Center | 80 | 22 | 72 |
| N2341 | MBWFC | Mahogany Bow Front Chest | 48 | 20 | 28 |

**Figure 9–10.** The *Product* table with a token identifier

Even with the token identifier, we still have a problem. Every order placed prior to the product name change was for a "Mahogany Bow Front Chest." Documents printed at that time would show the old product description. The same order, reprinted after the name change, will show the new name, "Hepplewhite Dresser." This can cause all sorts of confusion, especially for the customer who placed an order just prior to the name change, only to have an entirely different name appear on his bill of lading when the product is shipped.

There are several solutions to consider and the IT department must help the business understand the ramifications of each. The first solution is to allow the business to modify product names and codes, but to preserve history, the product code and name would have to be carried redundantly on each table which references the product. This preserves the fact that the row represents a single product in the real world that has undergone a name change. Figure 9–11 shows the *Order item* table with redundant *Product code* and *Product name* columns which reflect the code and name at the time the product was ordered. The *Product* table, however, reflects the current code and name.

The advantage of this solution is that historical reporting for the actual product is uninterrupted, because the token identifier has not changed.

ORDER ITEM

| Order ID | OI # | Product ID (fk) | Product Code | Product name | Qty | Unit Price |
|---|---|---|---|---|---|---|
| 3-0031 | 1 | N2341 | MBWFC | Mahogany Bow Front Chest | 1 | $ 3,400.00 |

PRODUCT

| Product ID | Product Code | Product name |
|---|---|---|
| N2341 | HPLDR | Hepplewhite Dresser |

**Figure 9–11.** The *Order item* table with redundant historical *Product code* and *Product name*, joined to current *Product* row

If the business or IT finds this solution undesirable due to the amount of redundant information that must be carried in the database, another option is to disallow any updates to the product code and, perhaps, to the name. If the business wishes to change the name of its product, it may either do so with full knowledge that history will be changed, or the old product row must be retired and a new one created. This can be achieved by adding an *Active status* column to the *Product* table (Figure 9–12).

PRODUCT

| Product Code | Product name | Active Status |
|---|---|---|
| CDLD4 | Cherry Drop Leaf Dining Table | Active |
| MDLD4 | Mahogany Drop Leaf Dining Table | Active |
| PLBKC | Pine Ladder Back Kitchen Chair | Active |
| PENCT | Pine Entertainment Center | Active |
| MBWFC | Mahogany Bow Front Chest | Inactive |
| HPLDR | Hepplewhite Dresser | Active |

**Figure 9–12.** The *Product* table with an *Active status* column

Since the product code may not be changed, it's back in the running as a primary key.[4] However, as we saw with architecture modeling, every solution has a problem. The problem with this solution is historical reporting of the actual product. Our real-world product, an artfully proportioned mahogany chest of drawers with a gracefully curved face, is now represented twice in the database. To get a report showing how many of these lovely items have been sold, the programmer must aggregate history for the two separate product records. To avoid hard-coding the product codes, a recursive *Used to be* relationship must be added to the *Product* table which allows the records to be joined together (Figure 9–13). The price paid for this solution is a serious complication of any reports which are required to show a contiguous history for real world objects, due to the recursive join.

PRODUCT

| Product Code | Product name | Active Status | Old Product Code (fk) |
|---|---|---|---|
| CDLD4 | Cherry Drop Leaf Dining Table | Active | |
| MDLD4 | Mahogany Drop Leaf Dining Table | Active | |
| PLBKC | Pine Ladder Back Kitchen Chair | Active | |
| PENCT | Pine Entertainment Center | Active | |
| MBWFC | Mahogany Bow Front Chest | Inactive | |
| HPLDR | Hepplewhite Dresser | Active | MBWFC |

**Figure 9–13.** The *Product* table with a recursive *Used to be* relationship

## Multi-Column Primary Keys

Some tables require more than one logical column to uniquely identify a row. Typical examples are tables created from attributive entity types and associative entity types. You may have noticed that the *Order item* table from our furniture manufacturer had a two-column primary key. It required both the *Order ID* and the *Order item number* to uniquely identify a line item row on the order. The designer must decide whether to use

---

4   In limited cases, codes which are visually recognizable to the user have an added bonus, a primary key. In cases where the code is referenced as a foreign key, the programmer does not have to join back to the primary table if the code is the only column needed from the table (e.g., If the freight code is obviously recognizable to the user, a listing of shipments need not join to the freight table, since the freight code is already resident on the shipment record as a foreign key.). I must note that in most organizations, the product code is *not* immediately recognizable to the user without a great deal of memorization. The elimination of a join in the code should be viewed as an added bonus but not the prime directive for using a code as a primary key.

the multi-column logical identifier or a single-column database token. Many designers favor tokens for any multi-column keys simply because multiple column keys get unwieldy when used as foreign keys. As a rule of thumb, I always use a token for multi-column identifiers of three or more columns and tend to settle two column keys on a case-by-case basis. If the two-column key is invariant and easily identifies a row, I find it acceptable to use that instead of a token. The hidden danger that lurks in the order item example in Figure 9–14 is that the order items appear to be numbered sequentially. If the user is allowed to delete an order item, the line items either make no sense, or the program must re-assign numbers. A token would be safer in this case.

ORDER ITEM

| Order ID | Order item number | Product Code (fk) | Quantity | Unit Price |
|----------|-------------------|-------------------|----------|------------|
| 3-0031   | 1                 | MBWFC             | 1        | $ 3,400.00 |
| 3-0031   | 2                 | PLBKC             | 4        | $ 225.00   |

**Figure 9–14.** A multi-column primary key

Some tables have no suitable identifier whatsoever. Tables with a date range in the logical key are a classic example. Our *Product* table from the furniture manufacturer probably has an associated *Product price* table. Figure 9–15 shows the *Product price* table. The same product code appears on multiple rows because the price varies over time. The marketing department has entered prices for the first three calendar quarters for 1996. Due to an unexpected increase in the cost of mahogany, the first quarter price for the "Mahogany Drop Leaf Dining Table" was increased by adding a new row effective 1-16-96.

PRODUCT PRICE

| Product Code (fk) | Start Date | End Date | Unit Price |
|-------------------|------------|----------|------------|
| CDLD4 | 1-1-96  | 3-31-96 | $ 2,495.00 |
| CDLD4 | 4-1-96  | 6-30-96 | $ 2,549.00 |
| CDLD4 | 7-1-96  | 9-30-96 | $ 2,595.00 |
| MDLD4 | 1-1-96  | 1-15-96 | $ 2,695.00 |
| MDLD4 | 1-16-96 | 3-31-96 | $ 2,795.00 |
| MDLD4 | 4-1-96  | 6-30-96 | $ 2,849.00 |
| MDLD4 | 7-1-96  | 9-30-96 | $ 2,895.00 |

**Figure 9–15.** The *Product price* table

What is the primary key of this table? A *Product price* is uniquely identified by its *Product code*, (a foreign key to the *Product* table) and a date range during which the price is effective. You could nominate the *Product code*, *Start date* and *End date* as the primary key to *Product price*, but you still have a problem. What happens if I add a row for "CDLD4" which starts on 2-1-96 and ends on 2-29-96 without changing any other rows (Figure 9–16).[5]

PRODUCT PRICE

| Product Code (fk) | Start Date | End Date | Unit Price |
|---|---|---|---|
| CDLD4 | 1-1-96 | 3-31-96 | $ 2,495.00 |
| CDLD4 | 2-1-96 | 2-29-96 | $ 2,515.00 |
| CDLD4 | 4-1-96 | 6-30-96 | $ 2,549.00 |
| CDLD4 | 7-1-96 | 9-30-96 | $ 2,595.00 |
| MDLD4 | 1-1-96 | 1-15-96 | $ 2,695.00 |
| MDLD4 | 1-16-96 | 3-31-96 | $ 2,795.00 |
| MDLD4 | 4-1-96 | 6-30-96 | $ 2,849.00 |
| MDLD4 | 7-1-96 | 9-30-96 | $ 2,895.00 |

**Figure 9–16.** Conflicting price rows

This action would result in two prices for product code "CDLD4" effective during the month of February. The new *Product price* row contains a date range that overlaps an existing row. A selection for the *Product price* for "CDLD4" during the month of February would return two rows instead of one. Uniqueness for this table cannot be managed by the declarative structure of the database. A token identifier will have to be used on this row. To ensure uniqueness, a fairly complex set of procedures must be written to enforce the business rule which states that no set of date ranges shall overlap. An additional rule might state that a product's price rows shall be contiguous so that no gaps appear between the end date of an old row and the start date of the subsequent row. All inserts, updates and deletes to the table will have to evaluated by the procedures to ensure that only one price per product exists for any given date.

The issues we have just examined are endemic to the selection of primary keys. There are no perfect solutions. Instead, the designer needs to make informed decisions based on the pros and cons that come with each solution.

---

5   This isn't a trick question. 1996 was a leap year.

# IMPLEMENTING SUPERTYPE/SUBTYPE ENTITIES

Supertype/subtype entities require far more design attention than your regular garden-variety entities. There are three solution patterns for implementing supertype/subtype entities. The designer must choose which pattern best fits the situation on a case-by-case basis.

1. **Supertype/subtype tables.** Implement the logical supertype and each subtype as separate tables.

2. **Supertype only.** Roll the subtypes back into the supertype and implement the entire structure as one table.

3. **Subtypes only.** Push the supertype attributes and relationships down into the subtype and implement only the subtypes as tables.

## Supertype/Subtype Tables Solution

The first solution option implements the physical database in the exact same shape as the logical model. In a typical manufacturing organization, the *Customer* entity will often subtype into at least two major roles, the *Ship to* role represents the party who will take possession of the goods, and the *Bill to* role represents the party who is responsible for payment of the invoice (Figure 9–17).[6]

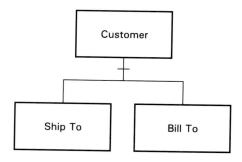

**Figure 9–17.** *Customer* subtyped into *Ship to* and *Bill to*

The *Ship to* and *Bill to* entities have different attributes, and participate in different relationships. For example, the *Ship to* entity may have information about the customer's unloading equipment, rail sidings, acceptable delivery times, while the *Bill to* entity requires information such as a credit rating and invoicing preferences. The *Customer*

---

[6]  I have simplified this example to fit within the confines of this book. The actual subtyping of customer on a real project is often far more complex.

supertype has only those attributes common to both subtypes, such as the name and iden-tifier. Many customers double in both the *Ship to* and *Bill to* roles, since they take pos-session of the goods and pay their own bills. A significant number of the business's customers may have their bills paid by a centralized corporate office, making their entries either a *Ship to* or a *Bill to*, but not both.

If the designer chooses to implement this logical structure as three tables, then the primary key of the *Customer* table can also be used as the primary keys of both the *Ship to* and *Bill to* tables. The advantage of the multi-table structure is that customers who play in the *Ship to* role do not have their records cluttered up with empty credit rating fields. Figure 9–18 shows fragments from the resulting three table layouts.

CUSTOMER

| Customer ID | Customer name |
|---|---|
| H2432 | Curtain Iron Works, Ltd. |
| A5345 | Consolidated Industries |
| G2412 | Sal's Manila Chicken Farm |
| N2341 | Day Glo Nuclear Facilities |

BILL TO

| Customer ID (fk) | Credit Limit | Credit Rating |
|---|---|---|
| H2432 | $ 500,000 | Solid |
| G2412 | $ 120,000 | Paltry |

SHIP TO

| Customer ID (fk) | Rail Siding | Last unload time |
|---|---|---|
| A5345 | Y | 14:00 |
| G2412 | N | 17:00 |
| N2341 | Y | 20:00 |

**Figure 9–18.** Separate tables for supertype and subtypes

The disadvantage of the multi-table structure is that it takes at least two tables to fully describe either subtype of the customer. To display the *Bill to* customer, you must join the *Bill to* table to the *Customer* table to get the customer's name. Since this is a fairly inexpensive join, many designers choose to implement their major subtypes using the multi-table structure.

## Supertype-Only Solution

In the supertype-only solution, the subtype entities are combined with the supertype entity and implemented as one table. A *Customer type* field is added to the table to distinguish between members of the subtypes. Figure 9–19 shows a fragment of the *Customer* table structure which results from the *Bill to* and *Ship to* entities being rolled together in the database design.

CUSTOMER

| Customer ID | Customer name | Customer Type | Credit Limit | Credit Rating | Rail Siding | Last unload time |
|---|---|---|---|---|---|---|
| H2432 | Curtain Iron Works, Ltd. | Bill To | $ 500,000 | Solid | | |
| A5345 | Consolidated Industries | Ship To | | | Y | 14:00 |
| G2412 | Sal's Manila Chicken Farm | Both | $ 120,000 | Paltry | N | 17:00 |
| N2341 | Day Glo Nuclear Facilities | Ship To | | | N | 20:00 |

**Figure 9–19.** Supertype-only table

The developers enjoy the simplicity of having only one table to manage for *Customer*, however, we can see some complicating factors right away. The *Credit limit* and *Credit standing* attributes apply to only customers who play the *Bill to* role. The *Rail siding* and *Last unload time* are only applicable to *Ship to* customers. Whether these columns may be populated by the user depends on the value placed in the *Customer type* field. The code which manages the insertion and update of this table must know that a type of "Bill to" or "Both" makes the *Credit limit* and *Credit standing* fields mandatory. A type of "Bill to" makes the rail-siding and *Last unload time* fields prohibited, and so on.

Another issue involves how these tables are used by the application. A window which allows the user to specify the *Bill to* customer on an order will undoubtedly include a mechanism by which he can select from a list of candidate customers. The list must only include customers where the *Customer type* is "Bill to" or "Both." The select statement to retrieve the list might look like this:

```
Select customer.customer_id, customer.customer_name from customer where
customer.customer-type = "Bill to" or "Both"
```

If the *Bill to* customers were in a separate table, as in our first solution option, the order entry application would only have to retrieve the contents of that table to allow a user to choose the party responsible for the bill. The select statement need not include a parameter limiting the *Customer type*. The downside of this solution is that the select must join the *Customer* and *Bill to* tables to display the *Customer name*.

```
Select bill_to.customer_id, customer.customer_name from bill_to, customer where
customer.customer_id = bill_to.customer_id
```

## Subtype-Only Solution

A third solution option for implementing supertype/subtype entities is to eliminate the supertype and create tables for only the subtypes. This solves the problem of having to join the supertype and subtype together to get a complete picture of the object. However, this solution creates a problem for subtypes which are not mutually exclusive. In the case of our customer example, for any customer playing a dual role, a row would exist in both the *Bill to* table and the *Ship to* table. Some cross-reference link would be required to keep track of the fact that these two rows represent the same real-world customer.

Separate subtype-only tables are more suitable when the subtypes are mutually exclusive, and very little behavior is shared. Let's take an example from a business which owns over 3,000 automobiles and four company airplanes. *Automobile* and *Airplane* are both valid subtypes of *Vehicle*, but it may turn out that very few parts of the business, if any, actually care about vehicles in the aggregate. It would be very poor design, indeed, to encumber over 3,000 *Automobile* records with attributes such as *Wingspan* and *Recommended cruising altitude*.

## PERFORMANCE TUNING

During the information modeling phase, we are able to bask in the luxury of the perfect technology assumption. All processors are infinitely fast, all data stores are infinitely large, and data is universally accessible at all business locations. Once we start designing the physical system, we have to bring our information model out into the harsh light of day and see how well it holds up.

If the information model truly reflects the logical shape of the business, then it is the most desirable shape for a physical database design. I am continually amazed by the number of projects that indulge in a frenzy of denormalization in the anticipation that they *might* have a performance problem. Remember that an information model respects no project boundaries. Your relational database contains valuable information that is needed by many other sectors of the organization. If you pollute the structure to optimize the system for the needs of your particular program, you are more than likely to make it difficult for anyone to sensibly access that data in the future. The first step of performance tuning is for the database designer to see how well the database will perform if implemented as is.

Don't try to solve imagined problems. Good performance tuning relies on being able to measure exactly where and why the database is running slowly. If you have good statistical information about your target environment, you can estimate system response time based on your event rates and data volumes. If you don't have historical metrics for the database management system, you can install some tables, load them up with data, and benchmark the response of the critical parts of your application.

Significant denormalization should only be considered as a last resort for database performance tuning. The sins of denormalization vary in their severity, with *cardinality sin* being the worst sin of all. Let's take a look at some of the techniques a development team can use to address unacceptable database performance.

**Additional Indexes.** An index is used by the database management system to quickly look up the physical location of a given record. When your relational database is first created, indexes are automatically established for the primary and foreign keys of each table. For tables which are routinely accessed using columns other than the primary key or foreign keys, adding additional indexes those columns may speed retrieval.

**SQL query structure.** You can get significant performance improvement from your application simply by understanding how your database optimizer processes queries and structuring your SQL accordingly. This statement may seem to fly in the face of the industry push for standards which should someday eliminate the differences in SQL dialects. The reality is that each database management system (DBMS) has its own warts and wrinkles, and a development team needs to understand the strengths and weaknesses of its particular brand of database.

Your GUI development tool and your database management system are likely to have come from different vendors. If you use the GUI tool to generate your queries, you may find that the GUI tool doesn't structure the SQL in the most efficient manner for the database optimizer, despite all vendor claims to the contrary.[7] Compounding the issue, in many projects, developers who have finally figured out the strange proclivities of their optimizer, find it behaves differently after a version upgrade! At least one of the project's developers needs to take the time to master the DMBS to the level where he understands which queries return the fastest, and which ones bog down. I have seen programmers squeeze tremendous performance improvements out of their code by restructuring complex queries so they process more efficiently when they reach the server.

**Physical location on the disc.** Some degree of optimization can be achieved by the way the data is physically located on the disc. Much like a car needs a regular oil change, your database should be rebuilt periodically to reorganize data which has been fragmented due to the wear and tear of row modifications and deletions. Many database management systems allow the system administrator to assign portions of the database to different physical disks to take advantage of concurrent access of different tables at run time.

**Data distribution and replication.** A common reason that people yearn to denormalize their tables is that the physical access to the data takes too long. A possible solution is to examine a more effective partitioning of the database across the client/server architecture. In Chapter 8, I covered how to use the essential model to arrive at the least objectionable partitioning. There may be additional tables that weren't considered in the initial round of architecture modeling which are frequently accessed, but invariant enough to safely download to the client machine or departmental server. Some tables may even be small enough to load completely into memory on the PC.

---

[7] This problem can still be present, even when the GUI tool and database are from the *same* vendor!

**Process distribution.** Another common client/server performance problem emerges when a client-based application attempts to bring a large amount of data across the network, only to summarize it prior to display or reporting. The performance problem is probably due to the volume of data traversing the network, not to the structure of the database. By sketching a quick event-neighborhood diagram, the designer can determine if a more effective partitioning can be achieved. Response time may be improved by employing procedures on the more powerful server to summarize the data, and pass only the smaller result set across the network.

**Redundant foreign keys.** One of the least intrusive denormalization steps is to include extra foreign keys in certain tables to reduce the number of table joins required to find a record. This technique works in cases where a header/detail relationship exists that extends for more than two levels. Figure 9–20 shows a common example of an *Order* which is shipped on many *Shipments*, each with an additional level of *Shipment details*.

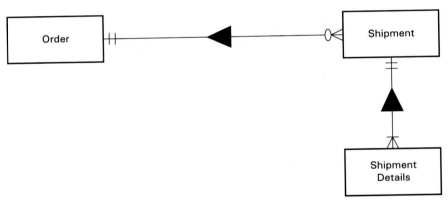

**Figure 9–20.** ERD fragment of *Order*

An instance of *Shipment detail* describes one and only one *Shipment*. An instance of *Shipment* is for one and only one *Order*. Therefore, it is derivable from this structure that an instance of *Shipment detail* is for one and only one *Order*. Imagine a query that must return the *Shipment details* associated with a given *Order*. Assuming that the *Shipment* table uses a token for its primary key, the primary key for the *Order* isn't resident in the *Shipment detail* table. The query must join the *Shipment detail* table to the *Shipment* table to get the order's primary key, since it resides in the *Shipment* table as a foreign key. If the application developer finds that joining the *Shipment* to *Shipment details* would be otherwise unnecessary, it is a safe practice to place the primary key for the *Order* table in the *Shipment detail* table as well to eliminate the cost of a join (Figure 9–21). This type of denormalization is low-risk when limited to adding additional references that are invariant and otherwise derivable.

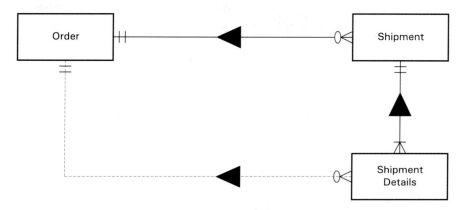

**Figure 9–21.** A redundant reference to the header

**Calculated columns.** While information modelers traditionally don't specify derivable attributes to be stored, it may be in the best interest of performance to store some values which are continually recalculated by the application. Some queries can sum a set of detail rows at lightning speed, but others may prove to have an unacceptable response time. Storing calculated values is a trade-off. It shifts the cost of calculating the number from the read function to the create, update and delete functions. The result will be that selects are faster, but the time it takes to insert, update or delete rows will be slower, because each action which affects the detail values must update the calculated value. For any derived column that you decide to store, you must be able to guarantee the accuracy of that number to anyone who may choose to read it at any time.

**Flattened views**. The last resort of denormalization is to create flattened views of the data. Denormalization is most effective when limited to the high-volume reporting functions of an application. It is particularly cumbersome and dangerous when employed in areas of the application which undergo constant and dynamic updates.

One method for creating views or extracts for reporting is to pre-join tables together, such as adding information from the customer table to the invoice table. The technique focuses on chasing up the "one" side of a one-to-many relationship to bring derivable information closer to the target table. This creates redundant columns in the database, but is designed to avoid joining a vast number of tables to arrive at a single result set (Figure 9–22).

Another method is to flatten header/detail relationships (Figure 9–23). This technique chases down the "many" side of a one-to-many relationship. It results in redundant row information data values for the header columns that must be repeated on each detail row.

This type of radical denormalization should be reserved for the high-volume reporting functions of the application. It should be avoided in the processing of live transactions. Once a transaction has reached a certain point in its life cycle, such as when it is invoiced, much of its data is invariant and can no longer be changed. Creating large, flat-tened extracts of this type of data is a good solution for many of the month-end reporting functions, which work from a "snapshot" of the data taken at a fixed point in time.

INVOICE (flattened view)

| Invoice Number | Customer ID (fk) | Customer name | State Code (fk) | State Name | Invoice Date |
|---|---|---|---|---|---|
| 12-001 | H2432 | Curtain Iron Works, Ltd. | OH | Ohio | 12-21-96 |
| 12-002 | A5345 | Consolidated Industries | ID | Idaho | 12-21-96 |
| 12-003 | G2412 | Sal's Manila Chicken Farm | ID | Idaho | 12-21-96 |
| 12-004 | N2341 | Day Glo Nuclear Facilities | OH | Ohio | 12-21-96 |

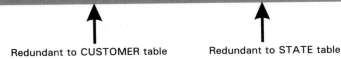

Redundant to CUSTOMER table     Redundant to STATE table

**Figure 9–22.** The "one side" in a flattened view

INVOICE ITEM (flattened view)

| Invoice Number (fk) | Item Number | Invoice Date | Customer ID (fk) | Product Code | Quantity | Unit Price |
|---|---|---|---|---|---|---|
| 12-001 | 001 | 12-21-96 | H2432 | DP42 | 100 | $ 1.56 |
| 12-001 | 002 | 12-21-96 | H2432 | DP56 | 200 | $ 3.55 |
| 12-001 | 003 | 12-21-96 | H2432 | INK23 | 3 | $ 1.23 |
| 12-001 | 004 | 12-21-96 | H2432 | LJ567 | 45 | $ 3.44 |

Repeating information from the INVOICE table

**Figure 9–23.** The "many side" in a flattened view

This idea of decoupling the tables required for reporting from those used for trans-action processing is a central theme in the concept of a *data warehouse*. A data warehouse is a separate database from the production system (or systems), which is kept synchronized with production data, or updated on a periodic basis. The data warehouse is designed and optimized specifically for queries and reporting. There are many new and exciting data warehouse tools that allow users to easily retrieve their own data, manipulate it on the client, create reports, and forward information to others via e-mail or over the Internet.

Data warehousing tools have become popular for several reasons. If the transaction processing system is highly normalized, the data warehouse can be partially denormalized to provide faster access and support end-user queries. If there are multiple old transaction processing systems in the company, rife with denormalized files and tables, the data warehouse might be designed to be even more normalized than the production systems, offering a place where users can find consolidated and scrubbed data without having to dig through the rabble of their legacy systems.

By separating the tables used for data warehouse queries from those used for production, you reduce the resource stress on the production database, and lower the number of concurrent users who may try to get at the same production data. It also gives you the option of locating the warehouse on another machine entirely, to completely eliminate the impact that large report jobs can have on the transaction processing machine.

**Throw hardware at the problem.** One obvious but often overlooked solution to poor performance is to throw more hardware at the problem. Today, hardware is usually far less expensive than the cost to develop the software which runs on it. Often, when a business refuses to spend enough money for adequate hardware, it will spend the money many times over attempting to get its software to run at an acceptable speed.

The problem stems from the law of cost migration.[8] The law of cost migration states that money will tend to flow from a strictly monitored budget to a poorly monitored budget. Hardware acquisition is a classic case of a strictly monitored budget. Hardware is typically a capital expense, carefully controlled and doled out by the company's upper management. Capital expense overruns are often considered capital offenses. Most performance tuning occurs on a system after the initial software is delivered. This makes it a software maintenance cost, usually paid for out of the amorphous blob of the IT operating budget. The operating budget is almost never monitored as carefully as any capital project. Much of the cost incurred in maintenance is simply due to the under-funding of either the hardware acquisition or software development capital budgets, making it difficult to assemble an adequate system in the first place.

Another cost which is rarely considered is the lost productivity of the vast number of users who sit staring at inert computer screens waiting for their systems to respond. Client-based performance problems can often be fixed by purchasing a more powerful desktop machine. It makes no sense to have an expensive group of accountants loitering in front of sluggish old PCs when new ones can be purchased for less than the department's coffee budget. Managers that came from the days when you had to be stingy with hardware need to rethink their bias in light of the staggering costs of software development and maintenance. Get the biggest, fastest, most powerful hardware you possibly can.

---

[8] DeMarco, 1982

## OTHER RESPONSIBILITIES OF THE DATABASE ADMINISTRATOR

Depending on the size and implementation strategy of the project, the database may be installed all at once, or in pieces. Along with the design and implementation of the database schema, the database administrator has other responsibilities which include devising user authorization groups to implement the CRUD authority specified by the essential model in the user authorization/entity CRUD matrix.

Additionally, there are activities which need to take place which are beyond the scope of this book. They include (but are not limited to) implementing log-on procedures, database logging strategies, and back-up and recovery plans; instituting the replications mechanisms; establishing loading and unloading procedures for physical data; and devising the legacy data conversion plan.

## SUMMARY

Whether you are a fan of relational databases, or yearn for the good old days of the flat file, the relational database is here to stay; at least for a while. Its strength lies in the ability to store the information close to its real-world form, and defer the decision about how to aggregate it until run time. As time progresses, it is likely that relational databases will embrace more of the concepts of object-orientation, providing tighter coupling between the data and processes which enforce business rules. It is also likely that object-oriented databases will become more relational, offering flexible query languages that allow data to be grouped in ways not anticipated by the class designers.

A relational database is comprised of tables. Each table has a series of columns which represent the individual data elements. The actual data records in the table form the rows. Each table has a primary key. Tables are related to each other by embedding the primary key from one table into another as a foreign key to implement the relationship. Foreign keys enable the relational database management system to enforce referential integrity. Referential integrity ensures that no row in a parent table can be deleted if it is still referenced by a child row.

The design of a relational database should look startlingly like the layout of the information model. The information model can be translated directly into a first-cut relational database design. Each entity becomes a table. Each attribute becomes a column. Relationships are implemented by placing the primary from the "one" side of the relationship into the table on the "many" side of the relationship.

The selection of primary keys is an important design consideration. The key may be a single logical attribute which is invariant and unique. It may also be more than one column. If a fine, upstanding logical identifier cannot be found, a token identifier can be generated to serve as the primary key.

Supertype and subtype entities can be implemented one of three ways. The most direct method is to create a table for the supertype and additional tables for each subtype.

Another option is to combine the subtypes back into the supertype and implement just one table. The last option is to eliminate the supertype and implement separate subtype tables.

Relational databases are under constant pressure to perform at ever-increasing speeds. When it comes to performance tuning your application, there is an old saying in the industry that, "It is far easier to make a working application fast than to get a fast application working." Applied to database design, this means, start with a design which maps to your logical structure and *then* see if you have a problem.

There are a variety of techniques that you can use to get an application to run faster. The key to success is to identify and measure the problem first before you start coming up with solutions. Just some of the solutions that I have offered in this chapter include, adding additional indexes, restructuring your SQL statements, optimizing the physical storage on the disk, replicating and distributing data, or redistributing processes across the client/server architecture. Upgrading the hardware is a solution that should be near to the top of everyone's list.

When it comes to tinkering with the structure of the database, some levels of denormalization are safer than others. Adding redundant foreign keys in sub-detail tables is a low-risk method for eliminating joins. Storing calculated values shifts the cost of the calculation from the read functions to the create, update and delete functions of the application.

Flattened views or extracts of the data are the most extreme levels of denormalization and should be undertaken with great caution. Flattened tables are particularly useful in cutting down the overhead of joining many tables for high-volume reporting. Extract tables can pre-join information that would otherwise have to be derived, or flatten out one-to-many relationships by carrying header information redundantly with the detail.

Broad-based flattening of the normalized structure is a technique that should be used to augment the normalized tables, but not to replace them. Your database is a crucial company asset, which contains information shared by many parts of the organization. The best way to ensure the on-going value of that asset is to keep the information as normalized as possible so it can be easily utilized by other applications.

## EXERCISES

1. Fenwick Prescott was hired to design a new information system for an auto repair shop. One of the requirements was for the mechanic to note the air pressure and condition of each of the tires on each vehicle serviced. Fenwick dutifully placed four pairs of columns in the *Vehicle service visit* table (*Left front pressure*, *Left front condition*, *Right front pressure*, and so on). On the entry screen, he cleverly arranged the data over a diagram of the vehicle, with the left tire data in the upper left, right tire data to the right, and the rear tire data beneath. Fenwick installed the new system on a Sunday afternoon. On Monday morning the first customer pulled into the repair shop with a monster truck sporting double pairs of rear tires. Fenwick had made a grave error in his database design. Can you suggest a better design solution than Fenwick did?

2. Under what circumstances should a logical primary key be avoided for use as a primary key in favor of a system-generated primary key?

3. Your beautifully normalized order entry system is running too slowly. The primary irritation is the order selection window on which users retrieve large lists of orders. The system must execute a multi-way join to bring together data from several tables for the display. One of the developers suggests creating a flattened table which maps more closely to the window layout from which lists of orders can be more quickly retrieved. Order transactions will be saved to the normalized tables, and the flattened tables updated via stored procedures. If every solution has a problem, what is the potential problem with this solution?

## ANSWERS

1. Fenwick had assumed that all vehicles serviced by the shop had only four tires. If he had done a more thorough job of analysis, he would have found that the shop serviced all manner of vehicles, from monster trucks to recreational vehicles to school buses. Instead of embedding the tire information in the *Vehicle service visit* table, he should have normalized it out to a separate *Tire condition* table (an attributive entity of *Vehicle service visit*). With a little extra work on the interface, he still could have presented the user with a clever diagram of the vehicle by allowing the user to select from a variety of wheel configurations when they entered the basic data about the vehicle. The screen would then display the appropriate number of *Tire condition* fields depending on how many tires were on the vehicle.

2. Some database administrators would say *always* use system-generated keys. In general, a logical unique identifier should not be used as the primary key if it represents information that might change, for example a mnemonic code which is an abbreviation of the product description. Any field which can be changed by the user should be disqualified as a candidate for the primary key since the key could end up embedded in other tables as a foreign key.

3. The idea of retrieving selection windows from a flattened physical table speeds the retrieval of the selection window because it eliminates costly joins on the retrieval. However, since the flattened tables have to be kept in sync with the normalized transaction tables from which they are derived, the scheme simply shifts the cost of joining tables from the retrieval to the save, where the stored procedures must execute the join to keep the flattened tables in sync. The key to deciding whether a scheme will improve performance is to benchmark the database management system to see if the system performs better while maintaining extract tables through stored procedures, or while joining the data during retrieval. A study of the user's data access habits is also needed because, if they execute more saves than retrievals, the proposal could actually slow them down

# CHAPTER
# 10

# GRAPHICAL USER INTERFACE CONCEPTS

## INTRODUCTION

Chapters 10 and 11 are devoted to the design of the graphical user interface. Chapter 10 introduces the key concepts behind what makes a GUI a kinder and gentler interface than the green screens of old. In this section, I cover some the industry accepted standard criteria for good design, and offer some advice from my own experience regarding user control, responsiveness, customization, directness, consistency, clarity, aesthetics, forgiveness and the awareness of human strengths and limitations. For the latter half of the chapter, I have applied terms which have traditionally been used to describe the level of module cohesion in a structured system to the manner in which business events are grouped together on a window. The result is a familiar vocabulary for "window cohesion," a rough measure of the complexity, usability and long-term maintainability of the window's design.

## THE RISE OF THE GRAPHICAL USER INTERFACE

The graphical user interface represents a tremendous advance in the way people communicate with computers. Early research at Xerox's Palo Alto Research Center produced the first point and click graphical user interface in 1980. The mouse-driven interface was marketed as the Xerox STAR®, but commercial success eluded the concept until Apple adopted it in 1984 for the Macintosh® and Lisa® personal computers. The Apple's intuitive visual cues, ease of use and graphics capabilities made it very popular with people who were previously not users of any type of computer. The Apple Macintosh was a big hit and was soon a fixture throughout businesses, schools and homes.

Meanwhile, Microsoft Corporation's MS-DOS® operating system for the IBM personal computer was winning the war for market share because of liberal licensing agreements which allowed DOS to be installed on virtually any IBM clone. The MS-DOS interface was character based, and daunting to all but the bravest of non-technical users. It was the power of software packages such as Lotus 123® and early word processors that secured MS-DOS's foothold in the market. It was obvious to Microsoft, that to hold onto their lead, they would have to come up with a GUI operating system. The result was Windows®, first released in 1985.

As the inevitable lawsuits raged on between Microsoft and Apple over who owned the look and feel of the interface, the graphical interface itself became engrained into the computing psyche of the entire world. Graphical interface technology has won the battle over character-based technology. The debate over whether to use it is all but moot. The challenge now becomes how to craft graphical user interfaces that are well designed, meet the business' needs, and live up to users' ever-rising expectations.

Many of the thousands and thousands of GUI applications already in use around the world are brilliantly designed. Others are utterly dreadful. So what makes one design "better" than another, and how are they different from the old mainframe terminal designs?

For developers who have spent significant career time in the mainframe world, the shift to a windowing interface can be somewhat uncomfortable. Newcomers to the industry, who were raised with their own Macintosh in the nursery, may wonder what the fuss is all about. This chapter is intended to explain the basics about what makes a "good" GUI. In many cases it may put names to concepts that you have already internalized. Wherever possible, I will attempt to contrast the capabilities of the GUI to the venerable "green screens" of old, and explain both the cultural differences and technical capabilities that persuade us to design things differently today than we would have in the mainframe world.

## WHAT MAKES A GUI DIFFERENT FROM A GREEN SCREEN?

Let's take a walk down memory lane to the good old days when life was simple, screens were green and the users weren't armed with a mouse. The "green screen" got its name from the emerald color of the characters on the monochrome monitor, although some models featured amber or white characters on the black screen. The typical mainframe "green screen" was character based. This means that the screen was divided up into a grid 80 characters wide and 24 lines high. Each cell in the grid was capable of displaying a single character. The programmer would have to declare which characters were to appear in each intersection of each column and line position. Some of the characters were used for field labels, others would be used as user-entered data fields.

Because only a limited number of fixed-sized characters could be displayed, the screen afforded very little real estate for communicating information to the user. This limitation lead designers to abbreviate many of an application's data labels to save precious space. The data values were also abbreviated to save real estate on the screen and to save disk space (Figure 10–1). Since disk space was expensive, the fewer characters you stored, the more real savings in hardware dollars.

```
ID: OE002                     ORDER ENTRY                          14:10:11
-----------------------------------------------------------------------------
PSSWD:      XXXXXXX
ORDER_NBR:  12-0034      ORDER DATE: 12/21/96      STORE_NBR:10   INV_CD:  STMT
CUST_NBR:   88-3421-H  [JAVA'S HUT COFFEE SHOP]    SLS_PRSN: BST  PMT_TRM: N30
ADDR_LINE_1:700 N 34TH STREET                      ORD_TYPE: DIR  DLV_MTH: FOB
ADDR_LINE_2:SUITE 100                              DISC_CD:  4M5  CRR_CD:  103
CITY:       SEATTLE                ST:WA  ZIP:98010-0123

ORDER ITEMS:
-----------------------------------------------------------------------------
LINE   PRD_CD  PRD_DESC             QTY   UOM    UNIT_PRICE     EXT_PRICE
-----------------------------------------------------------------------------
01     WBN20L  WHOLE BEAN - 20 LB BG  100   EA    $  95.00      $ 9500.00
02     PFL100  PAPER FILTER  1000 CT   50   EA    $  25.00      $  250.00
03     PPC6OZ  PAPER CUPS 6 OZ/200CT   10   EA    $   6.50      $   65.00
                                             SUB_TOTAL:         $ 9815.00
                           TAX_CODE: EX          TAX:           $    0.00
                                              TOTAL:            $ 9815.00
AUTH_CD:  P340  XMIT_CD:  67  RCPT: Y

>:

PF1 HELP    PF9 FIRST    PF10 BACK    PF11 NEXT    PF12 LAST
```

**Figure 10–1.** Limited real estate forced the use of abbreviations and codes

By the end of the 1970s, just about everything in corporate life had an abbreviation, number or mnemonic. Many of these codes and abbreviations literally became engrained in the corporate culture. This brand of folklore has taken up residence in most of the world's legacy systems like a secret corporate language. The shift to client/server-GUI systems gives us a rare opportunity to challenge the need for such encryption (Figure 10–2). Sizable fonts, pop-up windows and drop-down lists have vastly increased the available real estate on the interface and the plummeting cost of hardware has made it unnecessary to be a miser with disk space.

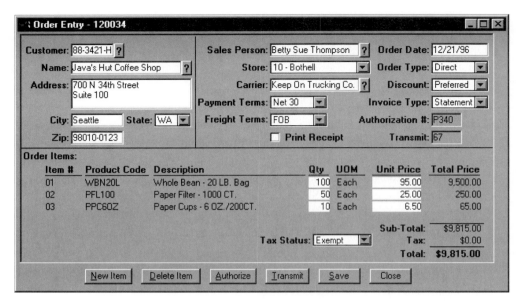

**Figure 10–2.** Same screen in a GUI environment

Character-based terminals also had limited graphic capabilities. Many of us remember with some degree of nostalgia the attempts to fashion a respectable company logo out of zeros, dashes and vertical lines. Today, graphics are only limited by the ever-increasing resolution of pixels on the color monitor.

On mainframe terminals, screens were presented to the user one at a time. Procedural code was written to "put" the screen on the display terminal. The processor, unable to detect individual keystrokes, would wait until the user hit the Enter key or a Function key before waking up to "get" the contents of the screen and process the results. This differs dramatically from the PC, where the window object contains code to detect events as they happen. Each keystroke and mouse click has the capability of communicating information to the processor. Significant local processing power is needed at each terminal to make this possible.

## CRITERIA FOR GOOD GUI DESIGN

Many of the principles behind good GUI design aren't necessarily new. Most users would prefer to use a well crafted green screen over a poorly designed GUI. So what makes one design better than another? These general principles are briefly described in Microsoft (1992),[1] and more extensively in Galitz (1994).[2] In the interest of conformity, I have borrowed their terminology, but targeted my definition for developers who are designing core corporate applications rather than general-use applications for the shrink-wrap market.

**Criteria for good GUI design:**

User control
Responsiveness
Customization
Directness
Consistency
Clarity
Aesthetics
Feedback
Forgiveness
Awareness of human strengths and limitations

## User Control

Much ado is made about giving the user complete control in a graphical user interface. Immediate and obvious feedback for every action enhances the user's feeling of control, and reduces frustration with the system. While the user has far more control than he did on a green screen, too much of a good thing can be dangerous. Taken to the extreme, the user has the ability to move freely from window to window and do anything he pleases.

The mouse renders the control of tab order irrelevant, since there is no guarantee that one field will be input before another. Obviously, in a business application, serious corporate data integrity is at stake and the user simply cannot be given the free reign that one would expect in, say, a word processing package. Since the windowing environment lets you "do anything," the task of the business application designer is often one of restricting where the user *can't go* at any point in time. The user should be in control, but not to the degree that he can make a total botch of the corporate data.

Some users will adore their new mouse, and others will secretly loathe it. The mouse is great for point and shoot selection and navigation, but it can degrade the typing speed of a savvy keyboard user. A good GUI application should be equally usable by a "mouser" or a "power typist" with the prowess of a concert pianist. For this reason, always include tab order and accelerator keys,[3] so that any action that can be taken with

---

[1]   Microsoft, 1992

[2]   Galitz, 1994

[3]   Accelerator keys are the underlined letters in a menu item or command button that provide the keyboard equivalent of clicking on the item. Some GUI tools call these mnemonics and use the term accelerator for shortcut keystrokes that provide quick access to certain tasks, such as Ctrl+C for Copy.

the mouse can also be achieved with the keyboard *sans mouse*. The downside of this is that the interface must now be tested for both keyboard and mouse actions, significantly increasing the required quality assurance effort.

The application should clearly indicate whenever it seizes control away from the user. This is often achieved by turning the mouse pointer into an hourglass or wait indicator, and trapping any additional mouse clicks the user makes which are not trapped by the operating environment.

I once had the misfortune of testing an application in which the programmer had failed to stop the user from clicking ahead while the application was processing. As I saved my work, I expected the ubiquitous hourglass. Instead, I was presented with a pointer. There is one thing you can always count on. A user with a pointer will continue clicking.

In the absence of any hourglass, I gleefully clicked hither and thither on the unresponsive window. When control returned from the server to the client machine, I observed some singular results. As chance would have it, the first untrapped mouse click closed the active window. The second untrapped click hit the delete button on the window underneath, and the third untrapped click fell in the vicinity of the confirmation message box. With a little bit of luck, in addition to saving my update, I was able to accidentally delete an entire suite of transactions. The programmer grumbled that he couldn't make the application entirely idiot proof, at which I took great offense and promptly called upstairs to the users to assemble a volunteer group of higher caliber idiots. After a little practice, they were able to click ahead enough to exit the application entirely and initiate a rousing game of Solitaire.

"Sorry General, I must have double-clicked. We just deleted Kansas."

## Responsiveness

Today's MTV™ generation of users bores quickly. If the application is processing for very long at all, consider adding a sliding scale to indicate the percentage of the job which is done, or distracting them with some informative message on the status bar. When the system fails to respond quickly, many users interpret it as a system failure and will reboot their PCs in the middle of your job.

On one of my first client/server projects, the users were unhappy with the time it took to sign on to the system.[4] We had made every attempt to optimize the database log-on procedures and simply couldn't speed it up any more. Late one night, one of the lead developers got the bright idea of adding a status bar to the sign-on window. He quickly coded up some officious looking messages which were changed every five seconds by the program. After the new window was released, several users actually took the time to thank us for "speeding up the sign-on window." In fact, it didn't run any faster than before, but it did provide them with some distraction which kept them from getting impatient and noticing the passage of time.

The system should provide tangible and immediate feedback for every action. This can be as simple as turning a pointer into an hourglass or highlighting a selected row. Sometimes, validation may require server support, so the user may not find out he has made an error until the database refuses his update. Message boxes are used to interrupt the user to inform him that an error has been detected. When adding a message box to the application, convert any cryptic computer-generated messages into polite, understandable feedback to the user (Figure 10–3).

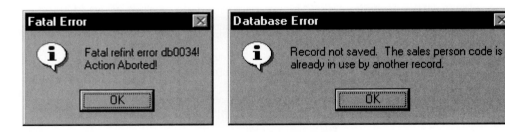

**Figure 10–3.** Cryptic versus understandable error messages

---

4   The real problem was that our early version of the GUI development tool had violent disagreements with the Windows operating system, resulting in sudden system failures. The users quickly learned that "reboot" tended to fix 90% of their problems (an unfortunate habit that sadly persisted even after the root cause was remedied). Therefore, the daily sign-on routine was being invoked several times a day instead of once in the morning, thus the request to "make it faster."

## Customization

Customization is an important feature of graphical user interfaces. Not every user has the same needs, and the programmer can leave many of the personalization tasks to the users. I have found it very useful to allow users to reorder and resize the columns in a large result set. Figure 10–4 shows a window on which there are too many columns retrieved to display on the screen. A *grid* style of data presentation has been employed which allows the users to resize and reorder the columns in the result set, depending on which columns are most important to them. They are able to save their preferences so the next time they retrieve the window, their ordering is intact. At any time, they can snap the column order back to the default set by the programmer. This technique is particularly useful in read-only result sets. I caution the use of the grid for data-entry windows, simply because the user can eliminate a critical column from view.

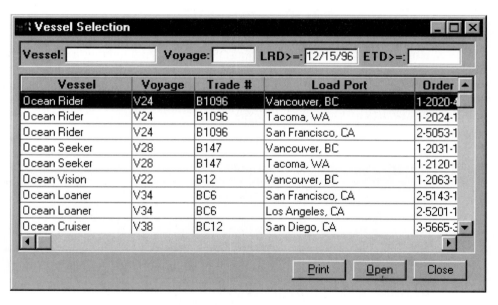

**Figure 10–4.** A typical grid-style window

Many published GUI guidelines say that users should be able to customize colors on the interface. I have encountered some problems with this. It seems that just about every company has a group of users who engage in an "ugly color day" contest. The person who gets the most revolting color combination on his interface wins a free donut. This may be fine for the operating system, but people using the core business application should not be allowed to obscure key information on the interface. I have had users call the help desk to complain that their windows have gone blank only to find that they have changed their field labels to the background color.[5]

For critical applications, lock the colors down. Color can be used as visual cues to inform the user if a field is optional, required or forbidden. A reasonable scheme is to make optional fields white, forbidden fields light gray, and required fields a recognizable but passive color such as pale cyan. The data fields are arrayed on a soft gray background which is easy on the eye. Under these circumstances, modifying the colors changes the meaning of the application. I once heard of a salesperson who extolled the virtues of color customization while selling a GUI emergency response application. If I ever need to dial 911, I hope the operator who answers isn't the winner of ugly color day.

## Directness

The concept of directness is nicely supported by the object-action paradigm (Chapter 6). It is far more intuitive to locate the object of your desire and manipulate it than it is to issue a cryptic command and declare the object to which the command applies. The mouse is an excellent tool for this type of "point and shoot" dialogue. Consider the difference between deleting a file in the old MS-DOS environment and deleting a file with a GUI operating system. In the old days, you issued a command at the C:\> prompt which had to be 100% syntactically correct:

    DEL C:\DIRNAME\FILENAME.EXT

In a GUI environment, you find the file on a list, click on it with the mouse, and drag it over to the trash can or recycle bin (Figure 10–5).

The structure of the command is exactly reversed from the days of old. Instead of issuing the command first, the user is allowed to browse a list of objects, in this case, files on the hard drive. When he has selected the desired object, he may initiate a variety of actions. Every action he can take should be available to him on either a menu item or command button. The drag-and-drop feature goes one step further by adding a visual cue, the trash can, so the user doesn't have to search the menu for the delete feature.

Directness can be applied in business applications as well. A typical layout for an object-action window is one where the user can retrieve a list of objects, say orders, invoices, or personnel files, and apply actions from a button bar or menu to whichever rows he has selected (Figure 10–6).

Visual cues such as icons and tool bars can also be added to business applications to enhance the usability and directness of the applications. Be careful not to go overboard

---

[5] The best help desk call came from a new GUI user who called to inform them that a "light was burned out behind one of the buttons." Rather than try to explain button enablement and disablement over the phone, someone was promptly dispatched upstairs to "change the bulb."

with insufferably cute icons in your business system. Colorful icons can quickly clutter up an application. Picture icons and tool bars should be added to a business application only when they enhance the ability for the intended user to accomplish his tasks. You must once again turn to your quality vectors for each part of the system to decide if you are designing for *speed of input* for the frequent user, *ease of learning* for the casual user, or *flexibility of information manipulation* for the "what if" user, and so on.

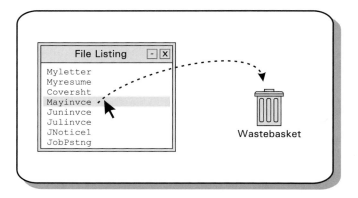

**Figure 10–5.** Drag-and-drop file deletion

| Store # | Order # | Sold To | Order Date | Total Price | Status |
|---|---|---|---|---|---|
| 101 | 9931 | Acme Beverage & Rocket Fuel, Inc. | 12/21/96 | 527.50 | Tentative |
| 101 | 9932 | Joe Joe's Pizza | 12/21/96 | 89.00 | Confirmed |
| 101 | 9933 | The Slug Pit Bar & Grill | 12/21/96 | 465.15 | Shipped |
| 101 | 9934 | Fern's Department Store | 12/22/96 | 26,450.12 | Filled |
| 101 | 9935 | The Lobby Shoppe | 12/22/96 | 1,126.88 | Back-Ordered |
| 101 | 9936 | Washington Plaza Association | 12/22/96 | 16.21 | Canceled |
| 101 | 9937 | The Metro Cafe | 12/22/96 | 654.78 | Confirmed |
| 101 | 9938 | Acme Beverage & Rocket Fuel, Inc. | 12/22/96 | 991.21 | Tentative |
| 101 | 9939 | 37th Street Investors | 12/22/96 | 1,654.00 | Confirmed |

**Figure 10–6.** A typical object-action window

## Consistency

A business application should be consistent with the world in which the users live and work every day. When client/server technology starts to invade areas of the company which were previously not automated, this can be a challenge for the analyst and designer. Business units performing the same function in different geographic locations often have completely different industry jargon and terminology for essentially the same ideas. Companies built through mergers and acquisitions find this problem particularly vexing. The analyst has two choices, either customize the application to map to each location's historical culture, or re-engineer the business to reach a consensus on terminology and business processes (Figure 10–7). These types of issues usually require guidance from the steering committee.

**Figure 10–7.** Consistency involves bringing users to concensus on terms

To achieve consistency of data labels throughout the application, the project should have a set of standard label names for each attribute in the information model. Many of the leading GUI development tools support these types of data modeling extensions. Include a standard label for use when labels are to the left of the field in a free form format and above the field in a columnar format. For attributes such as money, percentages and phone numbers, default formats and masks should also be specified. When a data label must be abbreviated, a standard abbreviations list should be used so the labels are always consistent throughout the application.

Another important aspect of consistency is that applications should be functionally consistent within the application. This is achieved by adhering to standards for look and feel, menu names, command button names and placement, and consistent and rational use of other GUI features. Many of these GUI standards can be purchased today from third party vendors, or simply lifted from another project. A new GUI project shouldn't be wasting any time arguing over the font size for the title bar. When it comes to standards, remember the designer's commandments:

> ***Thou shalt beg,***
> ***Thou shalt borrow,***
> ***Thou shalt steal,***
> ***Thou shalt covet thy neighbor's application.***

Your business applications should also be consistent with the look, feel and language of other applications. It is far easier to train a user how to use the corporate application if it is visually and functionally consistent with the user's word processor, spreadsheet and e-mail. With client/server computing, the "application" isn't just the piece you build. It is everything the user needs on his desktop to do his job.

You can always turn to popular packages such as word processors and spreadsheets for guidelines on how to define menu items and command buttons, however, you will find that the vendors aren't always consistent within their own packages. Some defacto standards have emerged that should always be followed, such as reserved words and placement of certain menu items such as File, Window and Help.

Violating accepted industry standards can result in downright bizarre applications. I observed a project at the Grim Reaper Life Insurance Company which was engaged in a raging debate over whether to locate the Save command under the File menu or the Edit menu. The Edit faction actually won, supported by the opinion that since Save really updated a single row in the database table and didn't actually create a new physical file, it was really performing an edit. Never mind that almost every other GUI application in the *world* has the command listed under the File menu! The project eventually descended into anarchy and was mercifully euthanized by upper management.

## Clarity

Information presented on the interface should be immediately comprehensible, and the use of the application should be visually apparent. Clarity can be a significant challenge for GUI applications which are replacing green screen technology. A GUI application should have limited and consistent use of abbreviations for both data values and labels. Herein lies our opportunity to begin to dismantle the mountain of cryptic codes, abbreviations and mnemonics that have built up since computers were introduced into the organization.

The concept of consistency says to use the real world language of the users. The concept of clarity acknowledges that some of the users' language is downright surreal, and usually the result of legacy system design. You must attempt to wean users away from legacy system jargon. It has no meaning in the new system.

Developers often encounter users who say things like, "The new system must include the 4250 Report." Do you really want to use this name on your new report? Of course not! The number 4250 was the batch report number from the old system that some programmer had placed squarely in the center of the green bar paper report. The number became culturally ingrained in the organization's lingo by generations of users staring at the batch number every day. When you dig deeper, you find that the 4250 is really the "Weekly Sales by Manager Report." Your new report should use the real world title, and by the way, perhaps you can give them on-line access to generate their own copy of the report on demand rather than make it a batch routine.

The old system is likely to be peppered with codes. Many of these codes have worked their way into the everyday language of the business. Not all of them are bad, but they certainly should be questioned. Let's look at an example from an order entry system for a manufacturing firm. Figure 10–8 is an excerpt from the old system's *Order* table. If we examine the database structure, we will find that the *Customer number*, *Transportation code*, *Plant number* and *Salesperson code* are all foreign key references to the *Customer* table, *Transportation method* table, *Plant* table and *Salesperson* table, respectively. The old *Order Header* screen is shown in Figure 10–9.

ORDER

| Order_nbr | Cust_nbr | Trnsp_code | Ord_date | Plant_nbr | Sls_prsn_code |
|-----------|----------|------------|----------|-----------|---------------|
| 102304    | 56023    | 03         | 12-21-96 | 12        | BST           |

**Figure 10–8.** A partial row from the order table

```
ID:OE023                 ORDER HEADER                     08:10:11
------------------------------------------------------------------

ORDER_NBR:      102304

CUST_NBR:       56023      [MANUFACTURING INTL. CORP.]

TRANSP_MTH:     03         ORDER_DATE: 12/21/96

PLANT_NBR:      12         SLS_PRSN:   BST


>:

PF1 HELP    PF9 FIRST    PF10 BACK    PF11 NEXT   PF12 LAST
```

**Figure 10–9.** The *Order Header* green screen

I don't have any particular problem with the *Order number*, but I would complain if the only way to get an order on the screen was to type in the exact number. In a well-crafted system which supports the object-action paradigm, the users should be able to acquire a list of orders by a variety of selection criteria, in case they don't have the luxury of an order number in front of them.

Moving on to *Customer number*, it appears that the way to get a customer on an order is to type in their number. The *Customer name*, which is poorly abbreviated in the old system, displays to the right only when you type a valid number. This causes the user to refer to a list of customer numbers, or worse, memorize them. Again, I don't have a problem with giving customers numbers, per se. It is a handy way to protect yourself against the customer changing its name. On a modern interface, however, the user should have the ability to search by *Customer name* to identify the customer. A reasonable method is to allow a partial string entry in the *Customer name* field, and return a list of candidate customers in a response window from which the user may choose one (Figure 10–10). If the user types the whole name correctly, and it is found in the database, don't bother him with the response window at all. The *Customer number* can either be used as an alternative entry field, set to display only, or entirely removed from the window.

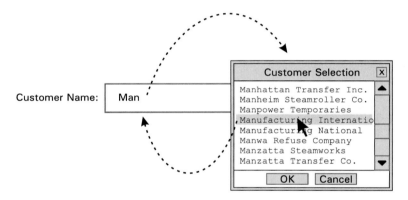

**Figure 10–10.** The *Customer name* look-up method

The *Transportation method* is the most suspicious code on the screen. There are several ways this firm ships its finished product. If you look up the control table for transportation methods, you will find the entries found in Figure 10–11.

TRANSPORTATION METHOD

| Code | Description |
|------|-------------|
| 01 | Truck |
| 02 | Rail |
| 03 | Container |
| 04 | Breakbulk |
| 05 | Air |

**Figure 10–11.** *Transportation method* table

Control tables that contain only a code and description are good candidates for further study. Before we kill off these codes, we must set down some ground rules. To implement a set of restricted attribute values without using a control table, the following conditions must apply:

1. **The data values must be invariant.** Codes are widely employed in places where the name has some likelihood of changing during the life of the system. If the values are *extremely* unlikely to ever change, then a code may not be necessary.

2. **The data values must not be too long.** Another reason codes are employed is because the description prattles on for many characters, making it difficult to fit on windows and reports. Remember that today we have the expanded real estate of windows and sizable fonts on laser-printed reports, so the upper limit of what is an acceptable field length has been raised. In the past, some organizations created a code for any description over six to ten characters. Today, many projects have raised that limit as far as twenty or even more. The decision should be made based on real estate on windows and reports, not on disk space.

3. **The data values must have no other attributes.** If the attribute in question has additional attributes of its own, then it is a bona fide entity, and should remain in a separate table. Whether you use the literal data value as the primary key, however, will largely depend on items 1 and 2.

4. **There is code in the application dependent on the values.** A primary reason for creating control tables for data values is so the user can extend the set of valid values. User-defined extensibility will only work if there is *no code* dependent on the actual values. In the case of the *Transportation method* table in our example, we might find some code in the system which enforces the following business rules:

```
If transportation method = "truck"
   Transportation Company Name is required
Else if transportation method = "rail"
   Transportation Company Name is required
   Vehicle Routing plan is required
Else if transportation method = "Container"
   Container Booking is required
Else if transportation method = "Breakbulk"
   Breakbulk Booking is required
   Shipping Dimensions, (height, length, width) are required
Else if transportation method = "Air"
   Weight must not exceed System Parm [Air weight limit]
End if
```

When you have this type of value-dependent code in your system, there is no way that the users can add more values to the table without significant intervention from the IT department to alter the application code.

5. **The new system does not need to retain code translation for communication with other systems.** If the new system must communicate with other legacy systems that demand the old codes, then code translation tables will have to be part of the new system. Even so, please don't saddle your users with having to use the old codes. Store and display the literal data values and use a translation table to communicate with the old systems.

Given this set of criteria, it looks as though we can kill off the *Transportation method code*. A drop-down list on the interface will allow the users to pick the method without having to memorize the code. The drop-down list won't slow down the touch typists because items can be selected from the list simply by typing the first letter in the field. The list of values can be loaded from a table maintained by the system administrator, or if it is completely invariant, hard coded.[6] Another advantage of this method is that the order rows now contain the literal value, which makes reporting and end-user queries much easier by eliminating a table join.

Returning to our order entry screen, using a number for a primary key in the *Plant* table is a common occurrence. It may be that in the real world, people refer to the plant in Humptulips, Washington as plant number 12 because it really was the twelfth facility to be built. Furthermore, there may be a gigantic 12 painted on the front of the building. In the new GUI system, I would at least expect that the *Plant name* be displayed along with the *Plant number*, and like the *Customer name*, allow the user to select it from a list. Two of the disadvantages of using numbers is that new employees have to memorize the list and you get awkward gaps in the sequence as plants are shut down or sold off.

The last code on our green screen is the *Salesperson code*. It looks as if the designer of the legacy system used the salesperson's initials as the primary key. "BST" stands for Betty Sue Thompson. Unfortunately, Betty Sue's late husband, Mr. Thompson, a wealthy oil baron, fell to his death from their honeymoon suite on board a cruise ship. His estate is still hopelessly snarled in litigation due to spurious claims from distant relatives and the reluctance of the insurance company to disburse funds. In the meantime, Betty Sue has remarried and is now Betty Sue LaCrosse, wife of T. Harmond LaCrosse, a ninety-seven-year-old real estate tycoon with a heart condition. Betty's name has been changed in the database, but her salesperson code can't be updated because it is peppered throughout the system as a foreign key on every order she placed.

---

6   Having been a normalization fan for so many years, I never thought the words "hard-coded" would ever pass my lips, but there are some cases where projects have gone completely overboard, tabling everything in sight. The worst case I've seen of codes-gone-mad was a system in which a reference table held codes for the values "yes" and "no." "Yes" was "01," and "no" was "02." Presumably, the programmer used a two-digit code to leave the door open for at least ninety-eight shades of "maybe."

Name-based mnemonics make for lousy primary keys for any table in which the name is likely to change. In the new system, the salespeople should have entirely random identifiers which are never displayed to the users. These can be generated by the database management system upon insert of a new row. The interface should allow selection from a current list of names. For reports on which names are too lengthy, a concatenation of their current initials can be used (Figure 10–12).

SALESPERSON

| Salesperson ID | Last Name | First Name | Middle Name | Initials |
|---|---|---|---|---|
| DV001X | LaCrosse | Betty | Sue | BSL |
| DV023X | Garnrod | Russell | David | RDG |
| DV104X | Butterfield | Arthur | James | AJB |
| DV055X | Wonrottle | Wendy | Ann | WAW |

**Figure 10–12.** The new *Salesperson* table

Figure 10–13 shows the new *Order Header* window as it would appear in a graphical user interface. The clarity is enhanced by using real-world language for items that previously required memorization of codes. We have hidden the codes from view in places where there is no reason to subject the user to them. With the *Transportation method*, we have eliminated the code entirely and stored the literal value in the database because we found the data values to be invariant over time, not too lengthy, they had no other attributes, there is code dependent on the values, and we don't have to maintain a translation table to other systems using the old codes.

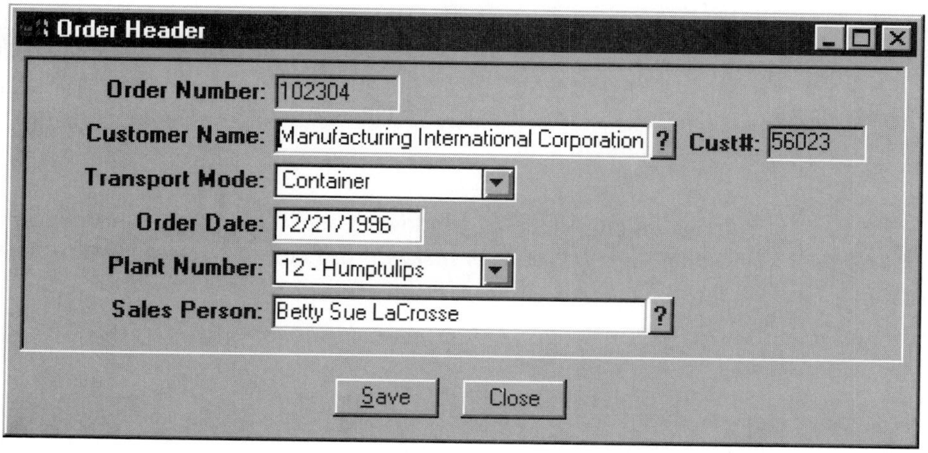

**Figure 10–13.** The new *Order Header* window

## Aesthetics

The composition and layout of a window should be visually pleasing. It should draw the eye toward the information which is most important. Studies on the fixation and movement of the human eye show that most people look first in the upper left center of the screen and quickly scan in a clockwise direction.[7] Through extensive research, design experts have derived principles which define a sense of pleasing aesthetics for the Western cultures.[8] These principles include a sense of balance, use of regularly spaced and aligned elements, symmetry, predictable patterns, economy of styles, colors and techniques, sequential arrangement of elements to guide the eye, unity of related ideas, a sense of proportion, simplicity, and grouping related elements together.[9]

A lot of what these studies learned, artists and photographers have known for years. Scenes which are aesthetically pleasing to the eye place the most important subject near the center of the frame. The *negative space*, or *white space* is the area of the composition which is empty (Figure 10–14). Take a look at the paintings in the next starving artist sale in your town. You will note that the shape of the negative space as well as the peripheral elements of the composition tend to point the eye like an arrow toward the main subject.

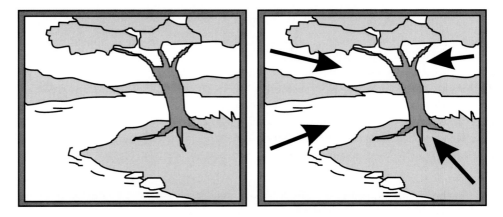

**Figure 10–14.** Negative space is where the image is not. Negative space can lead the eye to the image.

Figure 10–15 shows a highly cluttered window layout which has ill-defined negative space and poor balance and alignment. This makes it difficult to draw the eye to what's most important. The sheer volume of information presented to the user has created a visual mess on the screen.

---

7   Steveler, Wasserman, 1984

8   Taylor, 1960 and Dondis, 1973

9   For an in-depth study of these principles, see Galitz, 1994.

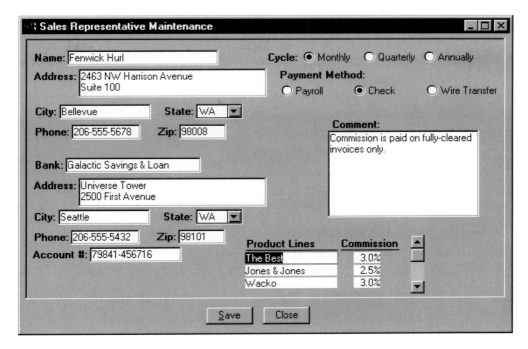

**Figure 10–15.** A window with poor aesthetics

When your windows start to get too busy, there are several good techniques for cleaning them up. You can turn to the information model to see if there is a logical break between two different entities that comprise the window. A relationship, such as the classic header/detail, is an obvious place to break apart a window.

If the window manages more than one business event, perhaps it can be partitioned into separate windows. It may be that the window manages different permutations of the same business event. Look to see if all the data is needed for the normal transaction. Data which is required for the exception event, rather than the norm, can be hived off to a separate window.

If the user truly must have all of the data resident on the screen, perhaps it could be broken into two synchronized, but overlapping windows, with the most important data located on the top window. A judicious use of graphic lines can also create borders around groupings of data on a cluttered window. This reduces the number of elements the eye must perceive at first glance (Figure 10–16).

Artists and photographers also learned over the years that color, as well as composition, can lead the eye. No color draws attention to itself like red. A window with a panoply of colored icons scattered about is likely to create visual tension. Use color economically and judiciously, and reserve icons for areas where visual cues are really needed.

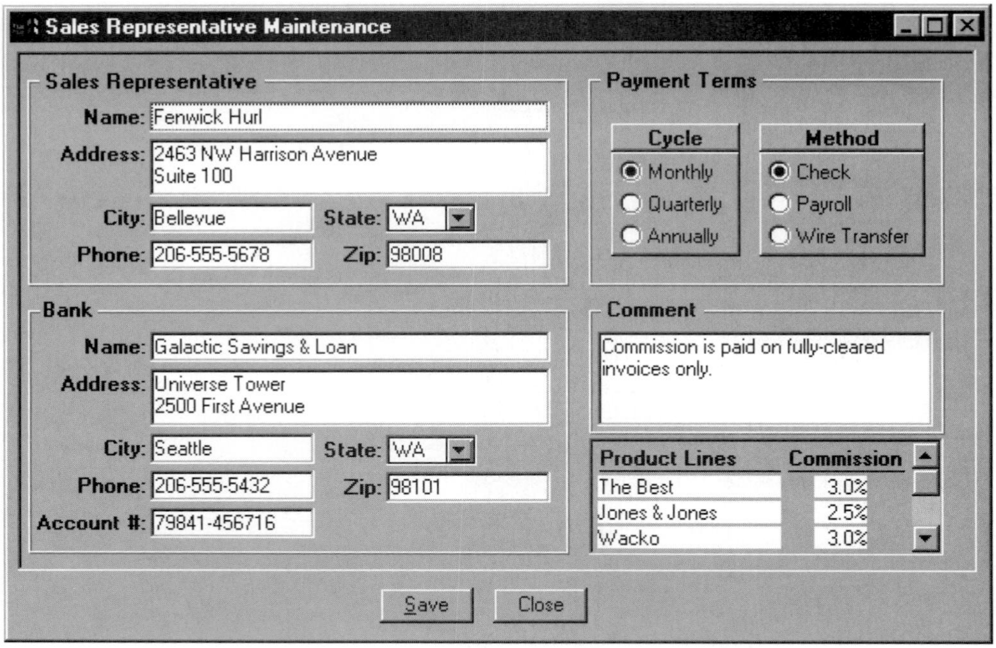

**Figure 10–16.** Possible solutions to improve the layout

Some of the craziest windows I've encountered are ones where the programmer has attempted to use every feature available in the GUI tool. While this may provide a fascinating learning experience for the programmer, it can create an aesthetic and navigational nightmare for the user. The GUI designer needs to place limits on the number of different features he chooses to place in an application, and use them in a consistent manner.

## Forgiveness

A good interface design should encourage exploration. The user should feel free to mouse around the application and take a peek at the various windows and features. This is fairly easy to achieve, but it takes a little more work than what most business application designers are used to.

A user's access level is usually governed by a set of tables on the server. When the application is running, these tables are queried to determine if a user is authorized to make various actions, such as place an order or create an invoice. One way to enforce these rules is to let the user attempt an action, and then either reject it or accept it when the transaction is sent to the database server. Although this scheme is easy to program, it is highly impolite to the poor user who gets penalized long after he initiated the action.

A second scheme is to read the user authorization tables when the user signs on to the system, and use them to enable or disable items on the main menu for the duration of his session. Users are only given access to those parts of the application in which they're authorized to work. Many organizations find this perfectly acceptable, and it is an easy technique to manage. The only downside is that it discourages exploration in areas that are outside of the user's current job description. Remember that the clerk of today is tomorrow's manager. The most liberal scheme is to let everybody into any window, but simply turn off the buttons and menu items to prevent them from taking actions on windows in which they have no authorization. Some users will never stray from their beaten paths, but others will explore the entire system and learn much more about the business and the jobs which take place around them.

You always want to give the user a graceful way out if he decides to abandon his transaction. Figure 10–17 describes several features of a forgiving system.

| Feature | Description |
| --- | --- |
| Undo | The Undo feature is usually placed under the Edit menu. In business applications, it is commonly used to return a single field to its original value, as long as the user has not saved his work. Field level Undo is nice to have, but is not a mandatory feature in business applications. |
| Cancel | Cancel is used on response windows where the system asks the user whether to proceed with the selection action or abandon the action. Cancel is usually paired with an OK button, or YES and NO buttons. It is vital that you give the users an opportunity to cancel these types of actions. |
| Confirm changes on Close and Exit | The Close command is used to close windows within an application. The Exit command is used to leave an entire application. When the user clicks Close or Exit, the system should always check to see if there are any unsaved changes. If there are unsaved changes, the system should ask the user if he wish to save his work before closing the window or shutting down the application. |
| Confirm on Delete | The Delete command is used to remove data from the database permanently. When the user clicks Delete, the system should always ask, "Are you sure?" and allow him to continue or cancel the deletion. |
| Explicit Save | Every Save to the database should be explicit and obvious. Never save data with an OK command. The user should always be aware of when he is updating the permanent corporate record. |

**Figure 10–17.** Features of a forgiving GUI

The explicit **Save** is an important consideration. Many GUI tools allow, or even encourage committing changes to the database on a row focus change. The user is allowed to update a spreadsheet-style window, and every time the cursor leaves a row, that row is updated permanently, without explicitly notifying the user. This violates the concept of an explicit **Save**.

The technique might be useful for reducing the number of keystrokes for a desktop application, but it leaves the database wide open to error in a serious corporate application. It fails what I call the "cheeseburger test." The user should be able to drop a cheeseburger on his keyboard at any time and be able to recover. If you drop a cheeseburger on an updatable window that commits work on a row focus change, you have no idea how much data you have permanently damaged.

A far more forgiving method is to allow the user to update as many elements as he likes on the window, and then have him save his work explicitly, committing changes to all rows at once. This allows him to close the window without saving if he wants to bail out at any time.

## Awareness of Human Strengths and Limitations

One of the most important considerations to keep in mind is that computers are designed for use by real people, and as people, we all have limitations. Recognition is easier than recall. It is far easier to recognize a visual cue or command than it is to memorize how to type it. For this reason, the command line is a thing of the past. The green screen command line forced users to memorize dozens of cryptic commands and mnemonics to use the system effectively. On a graphical user interface, no such memorization is required. Every possible command or action should be available to the user via a button, menu item or icon. Micro help, on-line help and effective use of the status bar can all be used to help the user navigate the system without having to memorize action codes.

One must also respect the human *hrair* limit. *Hrair* is a word used by Robert Adams in *Watership Down*[10] to describe how rabbits count: one-two-three-four-*hrair*. Any number over four is just too large for a rabbit to imagine. It turns out that humans have a *hrair* limit as well. Studies have placed the human hrair limit somewhere around seven, plus or minus two.[11] It appears that the human mind contains about seven "registers" in which it can manage disparate concepts or topics. To squeeze another one in, it must temporarily take one out. An application with six items on the menu bar is going to be far easier to use than one with eleven items. A window with five command buttons will be easier for people to comprehend than one with thirteen.[12]

---

[10]  Adams, 1974

[11]  Depending on whether you're having a good *hrair* day or a bad *hrair* day.

[12]  So far, the award for hrair limit violation goes to a project that placed twenty-two command buttons on a single window, along with dozens of entry fields. The window required at least two sets of horizontal and vertical scroll bars in order to view the masterpiece.

Similarly, the number of business events that can be recognized by a single window should respect the human hrair limit as well. As the number of separate topics managed by a window increases, a person's ability to use the window effectively diminishes. The complexity of the window is also inversely proportional to a programmer's ability to maintain and test the application over time. In the next section, I examine how the way the designer aggregates business events together in an application impacts both the usability and maintenance of the system.

## WINDOW COHESION

In 1979, Larry Constantine and Ed Yourdon published their book, *Structured Design*, in which they established criteria for well designed program modules.[13] They specifically promoted the idea that modules which executed one highly cohesive idea tended to be easier to understand and cheaper to maintain over time than modules which contained many different ideas. They also discovered that higher internal cohesion tended to reduce the communication or coupling between modules. High cohesion and low coupling became the goal for well designed modules. This also increased the likelihood of code reuse.

These concepts are still applicable today in the object-oriented environment of a windowing interface. I have discovered from my own experience that the cohesion of a window can dramatically affect the user's ability to understand and use it, and the programmer's ability to maintain it over time. Window cohesion can be evaluated by the number and type of business events which are recognized and managed within a window or set of windows in an application.

With a nod of thanks to my predecessors, I have adapted Constantine's original terms of module cohesion to describe the level of cohesion on a window. The levels of cohesion, in rough order from the most desirable to least desirable are:

Functional

Sequential

Communicational

Procedural

Temporal

Logical

Coincidental.

---

[13] Yourdon, Constantine, 1979

## Functional Cohesion

A functionally cohesive window or set of windows handles one business level event. Let's take an example from a point-of-sale system. Tidy Tim Household Supply Company sells cleaning supplies over the counter and through an aggressive direct-mail campaign. When a customer purchases supplies from their store, the clerk carries out the following events:

> Clerk enters/updates customer name and address
>
> Clerk places customer order.

The customer can either pay by cash or check, or he may put it on his charge card and be billed later. Depending on the customer's method of payment, the final events are either:

> Clerk applies cash/check payment to order, or
>
> Clerk charges order to customer's account.

There are many ways to design a set of windows to manage these transactions. Using the concept of functional cohesion, we could design a discrete window for each of the events. This would probably result in four windows, one to maintain customer name and address, another to enter the order, a third which serves as a point-of-sale receipting window for cash, and a fourth to capture the customer's charge account information (Figure 10–18).

The advantage of functionally cohesive windows is that you have specialized, efficient windows that are less complex and therefore easier to use. The internal code exists to execute one singular idea which makes it easier to comprehend and cheaper to maintain. The potential for reusability is also greatly increased. In our example, by factoring out the receipting window and charge account functions to separate windows, these windows can be reused with very little effort in virtually any point-of-sale system. The customer maintenance window can be reused in any other part of the business in which a customer's name and address may need to be corrected.

The disadvantage of functional cohesion is that it often increases the number of windows on the interface. This requires the user to navigate between windows to accomplish the entire suite of tasks.

I must be careful to state that since the definition of a business level event leaves a bit of wiggle room, a window can manage several highly related permutations of the same business event and still qualify for functional cohesion. For example, the event, *Clerk enters/updates customer name and address*, would include functions for creating a new customer and updating an existing one. I would rate this as a functionally cohesive suite of activities, even though one could argue that they could be stated as separate events. I don't want to lead any reader to the conclusion that since functionally cohesive windows are "good," one should design separate create, read, update and delete windows for everything. Given today's technology, that would be overkill.

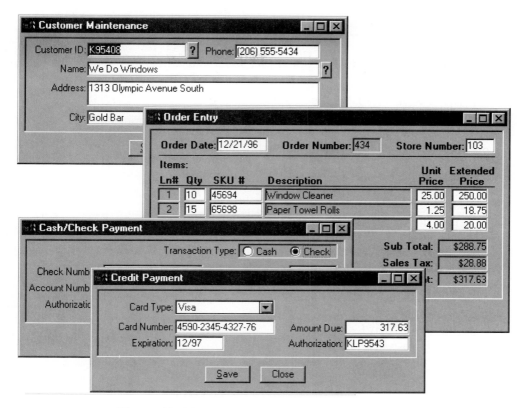

**Figure 10–18.** Four functionally cohesive windows

## Sequential Cohesion

A sequentially cohesive window is one in which events are grouped because they occur in sequence. The first event occurs as a predecessor to the next, and that to the next, and so on. Returning to our example from Tidy Tim's Household Supply Company, let's take the same point-of-sale events, and group them together on a single window.

> Clerk enters/updates customer name and address
> Clerk places customer order
> Clerk applies cash/check payment to order
> or
> Clerk charges order to customer's account

First the clerk makes sure that the customer's name and address are current, then he enters the order, then he applies the payment or charge. By grouping these events on a single window, we get the result shown in Figure 10–19.

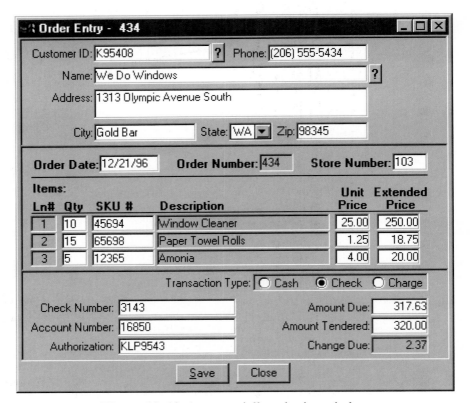

**Figure 10–19.** A sequentially cohesive window

The reward of sequential cohesion is that it maps very closely to the manual work flow. The application conserves navigational keystrokes by putting all of the related events on a single window. Sequential cohesion is suitable for windows which manage highly repetitive tasks where *speed of entry* and *conservation of keystrokes* are the primary quality vectors.

The downside of this type of window is that it is now a highly complex mix of unrelated code. The upper portion of the window must manage the creation of new customers or the retrieval and update of existing ones. The middle section creates new orders, and the bottom applies payment or captures the charge account information. The designer must decide whether the Save action applies to both the customer and the order, or if two saves are required.

The window is more complicated to use, and more costly to maintain. Aesthetically, the window is far more cluttered, and it is unlikely that any portion of it is reusable without some degree of reconstructive surgery. Sequential cohesion assumes that the sequence of events is always orderly. When exceptions occur, the designer must provide either a different window, or the user is forced to make do with the normal sequence that has been hard-wired into the system.

## Communicational Cohesion

A communicationally cohesive window is one on which events have been aggregated because they affect the same object. One could have a functionally cohesive, or even a sequentially cohesive window on which all events affect the same object. The difference with communicational cohesion is that sharing data is the primary reason for grouping the events.

The reward for having communicational cohesion is that events share the same data access code and client-based business rules. Communicationally cohesive windows also fit nicely into the object-action paradigm of selecting an object and then displaying a choice of actions to a wide audience of users.

The problem with communicational cohesion is that the windows often serve more than one master. Several different user groups, responsible for different aspects of the same object, are forced to share an application which attempts to satisfy all parties. This results in highly complex windows on which no single user has the authority to do everything. For each user of the application, a subset of the fields may be irrelevant, and some portion of the buttons or menu items are always disabled.

Figure 10–20 shows an *Order Selection* window with buttons enabled for the events a salesperson may execute.

Figure 10–21 shows the same window enabled for a credit manager. Internally, the program has to keep track of all of the various functions and individually manage button and menu item enablement for a wide audience of user authorization groups.

## Procedural Cohesion

A procedurally cohesive window organizes tasks according to a particular user's job description. Events are aggregated to give the user everything he needs on one window.

Imagine a window on which a user may initiate the following events:

Production coordinator approves order

Production coordinator arranges transportation for order

Production coordinator transfers order from one machine to another

Production coordinator opens phone-message application

The first three events are highly related. Taken alone, they fail the test for functional cohesion, and probably sequential cohesion, since neither transportation arrangements or machine scheduling need to occur in sequence. If the window only managed the first three events, it would probably qualify for communicational cohesion, since each event updates some aspect of the order.

The fourth event simply doesn't fit. The only reason that it's on the window is because the production coordinator also doubles as the receptionist in this small office, and the designer decided to save a keystroke by allowing the user to pop open the phone message application from his most frequently used window.

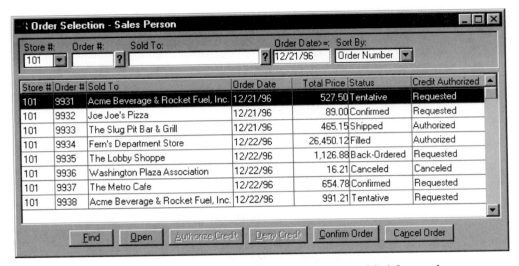

**Figure 10–20.** A communicationally cohesive window enabled for a salesperson

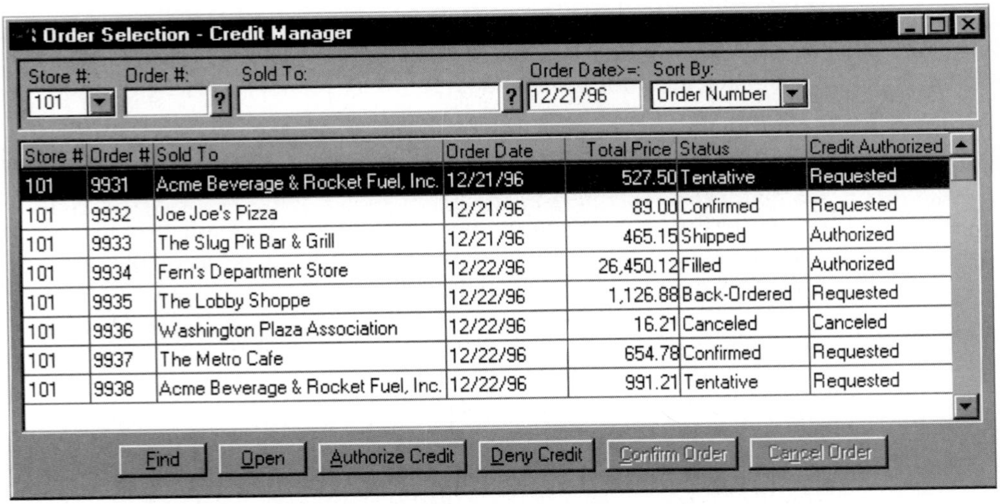

**Figure 10–21.** The same window enabled for a credit manager

Procedural cohesion begins to tread on dangerous ground. Users who are accustomed to the old green screens will often pressure a project team to keep the number of windows "as low as possible."[14] The attempt to give one-stop-shopping on a single window can lead

---

[14] This situation calls for immediate GUI training for the user community to eliminate the fear factor from their input to the design.

to amazingly weird cohesion of unrelated topics. This results in windows which are complex, cluttered, sluggish in their response and overly sensitive to organizational change within the business.

A better way to achieve one-stop-shopping for your users is to aggregate a suite of functionally, sequentially or even communicationally cohesive windows together under a customized menu. Under this scenario, your individual windows will be less complex, easier to reuse, and have an increased chance of withstanding changes in the user's job description. It is far easier to change an applications menu structure than it is to cut apart individual windows.

## Temporal Cohesion

Temporal cohesion occurs when events are grouped together on a window simply because they occur at the same time. For example:

Sign on to the corporate system

Check your e-mail

Print yesterday's sales report.

The developer put these activities on a single window because they are "things the user does when he arrives in the morning." The thread that holds these tasks together is extremely weak. The window could just as easily include a button which orders a latte from the local espresso stand in the lobby.

Temporal cohesion is rare. It usually appears in business systems only to initiate month-end accounting activities, which are related only because they need to occur at a specific time. These windows are almost impossible to reuse and exist for the convenience of a narrow band of users at a particular point in time.

## Logical Cohesion

Logical cohesion occurs when events are grouped together to share the same code. Figure 10–22 shows a general purpose report selection criteria window. The window contains just about any field a user could ever need to dice and slice the data for various reports. The user first indicates the report he desires from a large list of available reports. The selection criteria allows him to narrow the result set before launching the report job. The purpose of the window is to prevent the proliferation of similar report selection windows throughout the application, and is intended reduce the ripple effect of changes which might affect multiple windows.

The problem with this example is that not all of the selection criteria fields apply to every report. Those which are irrelevant are simply discarded by the program. If the designer finds this unacceptable, then the application will have to manage which fields apply by enabling and disabling update capability for each report which uses the selection criteria window.

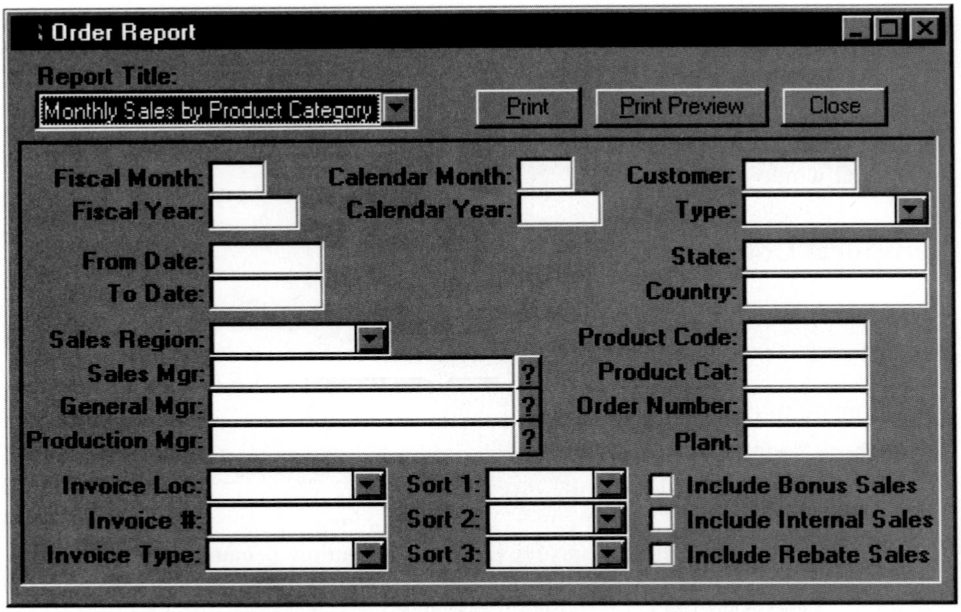

**Figure 10–22.** Logical cohesion: A general purpose report selection window

Logical cohesion can create unorthodox behavior on the interface and vexing maintenance problems. The maintenance programmer must constantly evaluate the effect of any requested change against every event managed by the window to ensure that the change doesn't create spurious results due to the shared code. In many cases, this added complexity negates the intended benefit of reducing the ripple effect. It is often easier to make clear and simple changes in more than one place than to untangle and retest a rat's nest of complex code.

## Coincidental Cohesion

While the other measures of cohesion have at least some discernible design goal, coincidental cohesion is nothing short of bizarre. Whatever relationship there is to be found between events on a coincidentally cohesive window exists only in the mind of the programmer who created it.

While coincidental cohesion is fortunately rare in business systems, it is not hard to find on the Internet. Let's take an example from our friends at Tidy Tim's Household Cleaning Supply Company. It turns out that Tidy Tim's nephew is majoring in computer science at the local community college and designed a home page for his uncle as part of his summer internship. Figure 10–23 shows the Tidy Tim home page layout.

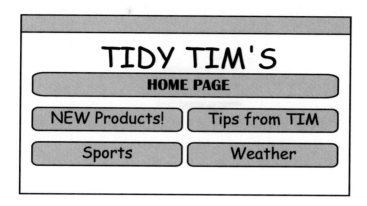

**Figure 10–23.** Coincidental cohesion: Tidy Tim's Home Page

The first two buttons, **New Products**, and **Tips from Tim** are reasonable. The other two, **Sports** and **Weather**, are included only because the programmer thought it would be convenient to let the user jump to some of his favorite web sites. The resulting cohesion can be summed up as *"things Tim's nephew thought were neat."*

Tim's nephew has also violated a crucial principle of home page design. The corporate home page is your electronic billboard. You want to make it enticing and easy to access, but you don't want to encourage people to leave. Tim's Internet advertising message has been fatally compromised to the level of nonsense akin to, *"Try our new jiffy floor wax, and how about those Yankees? Do you think it will rain?"*

## Ranking Levels of Cohesion

Any large corporate application is going to have a healthy mix of cohesion levels among the various windows. Most of the windows in a well designed business application will tend to fall into the top three levels of cohesion. Functional cohesion yields the most reusable, understandable and maintainable windows of all, but would result in far too many windows if used exclusively. Sequential cohesion is an excellent method for designing windows where the user executes a series of tasks on a regular basis. Communicational cohesion does a good job of keeping data access and visually apparent business rules corralled in one place, but increases the complexity of managing enablement and disablement on the interface.

Windows with procedural cohesion engender the added risk of being inflexible to changes in the job description of the user. This doesn't make procedural *bad*, per se. The developer may be under tremendous pressure from the users to employ procedural cohesion. Before aggregating loosely related events based on the user's job description, consider carefully the consequences for both the user and the maintenance programmer of the resulting complexity.

The next two levels of cohesion have limited utility. Temporal cohesion is handy for windows which launch month-end routines or similar time-related tasks. For other areas of the system, it should be avoided. While logical cohesion starts out with the best intentions of sharing code, it usually results in awkward behavior of the interface and ends up being more hassle than it is worth. A logically cohesive window should probably be redesigned into several windows, each with a higher level of cohesion.

The last level, coincidental cohesion, has no place in a serious business application.


## SUMMARY

This chapter attempts to put terms and definitions to the more esoteric aspects of user interface design. The purpose is to offer you some guidelines against which to evaluate the various choices that will confront you as a designer.

The next time you are in a walkthrough and you don't like your peer's window layout, you no longer have to resort to "*I don't like it because that's not the way I'd do it!*" Instead, you can offer a more constructive comment such as, "*Your window, while aesthetically pleasing, violates the fundamental concepts of clarity and forgiveness and appears to be procedurally cohesive. If you remove the cryptic codes, add a confirmation message box and move this event to a second window, you will have a sequentially cohesive window that is clear, forgiving, and pleasing to behold.*" (After which your project team will parade you around on their shoulders proclaiming you the czar of all window design and nominate you to fix every one of their layouts over the upcoming holiday weekend.)

The elements of good interface design have always been with us, even in the days of the green screen. The graphical user interface vastly expands the tool set available to the designer to meet the goals of a user-friendly system. Transitioning a corporate system from the green screen environment to a GUI creates a rare opportunity to eliminate abbreviations, codes and jargon that evolved due the historical limitations of the old systems.

In this chapter, I offer several generally accepted criteria for good interface design. The concept of *user control* dictates that the system always indicates when it has seized control away from the user. *Responsiveness* increases the user's sense of control by immediately acknowledging every action taken. *Customization* is useful in many aspects of the graphical user interface, but should be carefully mitigated when users are entering critical business information.

*Directness* supports the manipulation of objects. Heads-down data entry departments were often organizational solutions to the lack of technical capability of capturing information at its source. Client/server technology moves the information system boundary out to the frontiers of the business. The object-action paradigm recognizes that events occur in a far more random pattern in the real world, and allows users to select items before dictating the action or event that they wish to execute.

Applications should be internally *consistent* in their look and feel. They should also be consistent with other shrink-wrapped applications on the user's desktop. Consistency requires standards. Fortunately, many de facto industry standards are emerging, but every project needs to settle the standards issues *before* attempting to construct the interface.

*Clarity* is achieved by using real-world language and eliminating cryptic commands, mnemonics and codes. Window layouts which are *aesthetically* pleasing draw the eye to the information which is most important. Spatial grouping and judicious use of lines and borders can separate windows which are dense in content into sensible blocks of data which can be better perceived by the human eye.

A good interface provides polite and informative *feedback*. Exploration is encouraged by making the system *forgiving*. Always give your user a way to abandon his work if he hasn't explicitly saved it.

Most of all, a good interface is designed for people, who have certain basic *human strengths and limitations*. Recognition is easier than recall. Don't make the users memorize how to use the system. Keep the number of disparate ideas on a window within the human *hrair* limit. The mind's ability to assimilate different topics significantly degrades when the number of ideas exceeds seven, plus or minus two.

The number of different events managed by a window affects both the user's ability to understand the interface, and the programmer's ability to maintain the window as the system is enhanced. The levels of cohesion, first defined to rate the design of internal program modules, can be adapted to rate the aggregation of events on windows.

*Functional cohesion* limits the window to managing one business level event. *Sequential cohesion* groups predecessor/successor events together on a window. *Communicational cohesion* groups events together which communicate with the same object. *Procedural cohesion* aggregates events on to one window because they are initiated by the same user as part of his job description.

*Temporal cohesion* groups otherwise unrelated events together which occur at the same time. *Logical cohesion* brings events together on the interface to share code. Finally, *coincidental cohesion* is a polite term for utter nonsense. One can only guess at what was going through the developer's head when he coded a coincidentally cohesive window.

This chapter lays a foundation of general interface design principles. The next chapter offers specific techniques for the creation of the external design specification.

## EXERCISES

1. When might an action-object design be more appropriate than an object-action GUI?

2. Some GUI tools encourage **Save** on a row focus change. What concepts does this violate?

3. Nelson was hired to create a purchase order tracking system for an office supply store. The users were accustomed to their old mainframe systems, and told him to keep the number of windows in the new system to a minimum. Dutifully, he created a *Purchase Order Selection* window, and placed 24 command buttons on it (two rows of twelve buttons each). Each button represented an action that a user could take against one or more selected purchase orders. Can you name at least one GUI concept that Nelson violated?

4. Can you guess what level of cohesion Nelson's *Purchase Order Selection* window might be?

## ANSWERS

1. During repetitive activities, such as heads-down data entry, it may be more appropriate to declare a "mode" such as "update mode" and pound in transaction after transaction. For the most part, people are growing accustomed to the object-action paradigm instead and, as information systems push ever closer to the frontiers of the business, the random nature of business events tends to favor selecting an object first, then applying any variety of legal actions to it.

2. Surreptitious saves (when the application commits work without the user explicitly ordering a **Save**) violate the GUI concepts of *forgiveness*, *user control* and *consistency*. The interface is unforgiving because it is difficult to back out of a transaction you may not know you committed. It takes control away from the user and conducts database updates in an inconsistent manner from most standard GUI applications.

3. With 24 actions available on one window, Nelson has failed to respect the *awareness of human strengths and limitations*. The human brain can process seven, plus or minus two, concepts at a time. His purchase order selection window is likely to be difficult for the average user to understand without significant training and practice. One possible solution might be for Nelson to group similar actions together under cascading menus so that the window sports fewer available actions at the top level. Nelson should determine which buttons are pressed most often, leaving them at the top level, and group commands that

are requested less frequently together under a cascading menu. For example, the New or Open button could remain on the window, but all of the various month-end reports could be grouped and listed under a single Reports button or menu item.

4. It is probably communicational cohesion, since it appears that Nelson grouped all of the business events which affect the same data together on one window, namely, the purchase order.

# CHAPTER 11

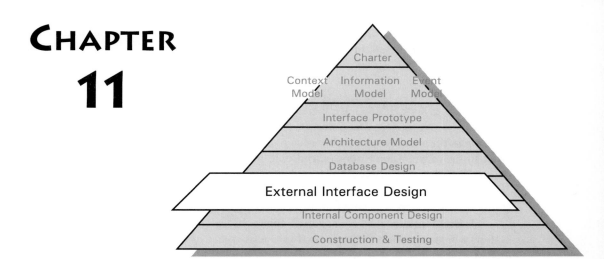

Charter

Context Model    Information Model    Event Model

Interface Prototype

Architecture Model

Database Design

External Interface Design

Internal Component Design

Construction & Testing

# EXTERNAL INTERFACE DESIGN

## INTRODUCTION

Chapter 11 is about the external interface design of your system. The chapter provides you with three valuable concepts. The first is the suggested layout of an external design specification for a graphical user interface. The bigger your project, the more critical the need for a detailed *written* design. (Sorry, GUI code is *not* self-documenting.) This chapter gives you a format to follow for documenting the system and application overview, window navigation, window layout, window descriptions and mini-specs and field level specification. The second key point of value in this chapter is the section on window navigation diagramming. Of all of the techniques in this book, this one is probably the least expensive, and yields a tremendously high payback. Just a few rectangles and arrows and you and your peers can have a substantive discussion of how to navigate your complex application *before* you attempt to code it. The third and final point in this chapter is about the challenge of testing a graphical user interface. Adequate testing begins with a good test plan, and a good test plan is derived from a detailed, written design.

## WHAT IS EXTERNAL VERSUS INTERNAL DESIGN?

The design for a large client/server system can be vastly complex. To bring structure and order to the effort, I have chosen to divide the application design into two broad categories. The first category is the external design of the interface, which is the topic of this chapter. The second category of application design is the specification for the internal componentry, which is covered in the next chapter.

External interface design specifies the look, feel and behavior of the portion of the system which is visible to the user. It is a refinement of the interface prototype which includes elements such as window type, navigation, button specification and definition of the appropriate unit of work for the user. The external design of the system is dependent largely on the industry conventions for the chosen interface technology.

In the next chapter, we will see that the structure and techniques employed to create the specification for internal componentry depend to a large part on the paradigm and capabilities of the target language. The internal component design may be object-oriented, 4GL forms-based, 3GL or a hodgepodge of all of the above. The structure of the *internal* design specification is the model most vulnerable to change as client/server development tools evolve.

## WHY DO A WRITTEN DESIGN SPECIFICATION?

The written design specification serves several purposes. It gives you a method for documenting and reviewing your ideas with your peers that is faster and cheaper than coding. Even the briefest of design specifications goes a long way toward enforcing standards for look and feel throughout your application, and it is far cheaper to modify a model than a partially-finished system.

Window layouts, descriptions and navigation diagrams are excellent tools for validating the design proposal with the user community. Most users who have become familiar with GUI systems are quite capable of abstracting the behavior from the pages of a succinct, well-written external design.[1]

The design specification is also a powerful management tool. It allows the application to be partitioned among multiple programmers for construction at a level of granularity

---

[1]   Many RAD proponents argue that users are incapable of understanding a system unless they can actually operate an animated prototype. I have only found this to be the case with users who are completely unfamiliar with GUI or computers in general. Effort should be made to bring these people up to speed rather than tailor an entire design methodology to the lowest common denominator.

which is lower than the partitioning required to achieve a cohesive design. In this book, I assume that most large business system projects will design and deliver the system in phases. In Chapter 6 we saw that the event list is a useful tool for determining the partitioning of the overall system into logical units or applications. By breaking large systems into separate applications (such as *Order entry*, *Invoicing*, *Pricing*, *Sales forecasting*) the design work can be allocated to more than one designer. Each designer can concentrate on his logical area, and the results of their respective designs can be reviewed to ensure a consistent product across the entire system.

Once a written design specification exists, the programming effort can be further partitioned, even within the same application, to more than one programmer (Figure 11–1). With a written design, you can assign several programmers to build specific windows and their underlying functions within the same application. Their code is easily integrated because they are working from one cohesive specification. The end result is faster delivery of a high-quality finished product.

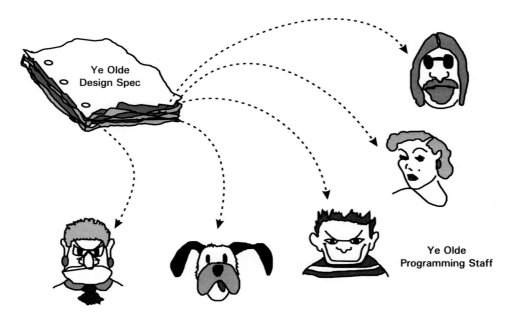

**Figure 11–1.** A large application design can be distributed to multiple programmers for coding

Without the written specification, the developer must design and code at the same time, forcing the manager to partition the programming effort into larger chunks. This can cause serious bottlenecks because the design of the application is buried in the head of the programmer. Without a written specification, the manager is unable to add any more programmers to the team to speed up construction at a point in the project where time is running out. If the manager attempts to partition the programming workload at a level of granularity lower than is appropriate for design, with no written spec, the resulting code may require the efforts of all the king's horses and men to reassemble it into a coherent application.

The written design specification allows the application to be independently tested. Without the specification, any attempt to test the finished product is seriously impaired. A good design specification need not require any fancy CASE tools. Any word processor and a simple drawing tool will suffice. A good CASE tool can make your life easier, but one poorly suited to your specific tasks can make your project a living hell.

## EXTERNAL INTERFACE DESIGN DELIVERABLES

The components of an external interface design for a graphical user interface include (see also Figure 11–2):

**System overview:** A textual description which orients the reader to the purpose and function of the entire system.

**Application overview:** A textual description for each application contained within the system (e.g., *Order entry*, *Invoicing*, *Sales reporting*, *Inventory management*) which defines the features available within the application.

**Window navigation diagram:** For each application within the system, a window navigation diagram declares which windows are available and shows the possible navigation paths between them.

**Window layout:** For each window on the navigation diagram, a window layout depicts how the window will appear to the user.

**Window description:** The text which accompanies each window layout describes the window's function and features clearly, such that a potential user can understand the behavior of the design.

**Window mini-spec:** The window's technical specification defines the behavior for opening and closing the window, and the enablement and execution of each button, control and menu item.

**Field specification:** The field specification defines the fields and associated edits for any data element which appears on the window. The field specification should include a mini-spec of how the data is to be acquired, listing table names, column names, indicating how to join tables, and describing how to apply any selection criteria.

The internal design, covered in the following chapter, includes specifications for all internal classes, functions and procedures and the components which manage the communication between the database management system and the interface.

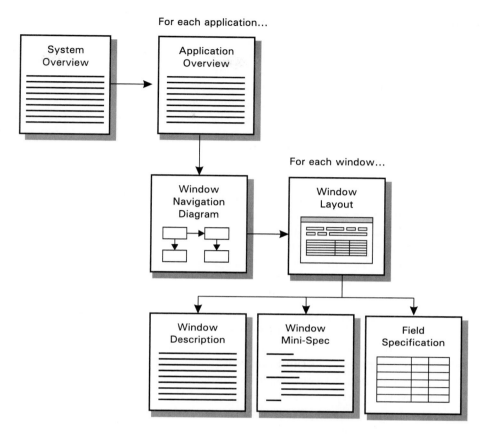

**Figure 11–2.** The external interface design

## System and Application Overviews

The system overview is a textual description of the business purpose and scope of the entire system. It includes a brief statement of the business need, intended users, and how the application fits into the overall strategy to meet that need. If you are designing a large system which is partitioned into multiple applications, an application overview should be written for each sub-section of the system which is implemented as an identifiable application.

Much of the material needed to write the overview already exists. The project charter will include the goals, objectives and scope statements for each section of the system. The event model will include descriptions of all of the major business events managed by the application. Only a brief summary of events is needed at the application overview level. Detailed event descriptions are included at the window description level of the design specification.

The majority of the overview, therefore, can be compiled from existing documents, rather than written from scratch. The only information that is new is a brief description of the structure of the on-line application and a review of some of the technical features contained within. Overviews should be written for a broad audience. They will be reviewed by the users prior to construction. They will be read by the programmer to become familiar with the subject. The overviews are often the first place testers turn to understand the purpose of the system.

The system overview, application overviews and window descriptions also become important documentation tools after the system is installed. These textual descriptions of the system can be included in the on-line help and printed system documentation for both the users and subsequent maintenance programmers. The structure of the overview, therefore, should be consistent throughout the system design documents. A template can be created for the project for designers to use which will ensure consistency and completeness in their writing, and increase the ability of the design text to be used as the documentation suitable for the end-users.

## Window Navigation Diagramming

Window navigation diagramming is a form of prototyping. In Chapter 6, I postulated that the first iteration of prototyping in the analysis phase need not concern itself with nailing down the navigation between windows. Instead, discovery of the correct window content and business policy was the prime objective. I also suggested strongly that a non-animated prototype was the most cost effective means for achieving the learning objective at that point in the project.

During the external design phase, we take the window layouts from the initial prototype and refine them further. The objective of this iteration of prototyping is to determine the correct window type and navigation paths and to define the appropriate unit of work for the user. These objectives can also be achieved very cost-effectively without cutting a single line of code. An interface designer, armed with some window layouts, the event model and information model, can use the navigation diagram to quickly map out a plan for building the interface. Of all of the modeling techniques covered in this book, this one is perhaps the cheapest, and the payback can be tremendous.

### Window Navigation Diagram Notation

After years of trial and error, an international committee of the world's leading methodologists finally concluded that a window shall be represented as a rectangle on the navigation diagram.[2] Each window within the application is placed on the diagram. The

---

[2]   The only hold-out was the delegation from the University of Mulvania, who fervently supported the triangle, a topic of heated debate at the prior year's conference. I can only attribute their unyielding position to their isolation from the rest of the software engineering community during the long Mulvic winter season.

name of the window is placed within the rectangle. You may use the internal name of the window, or the name which appears in the title bar, depending on your intended audience. Some project teams like to put both on the diagram, so it can be easily read by both programmers and users. When the application's windows are too numerous to fit on one diagram, partition the diagram to show the navigation paths for a specific suite of events.

The navigation path between two windows is shown by drawing an arrow from one window to the next (Figure 11–3). A single-headed arrow denotes that return to the calling window is not required. A double-headed arrow is used to show that the user is compelled to return to the calling window after completing his task.

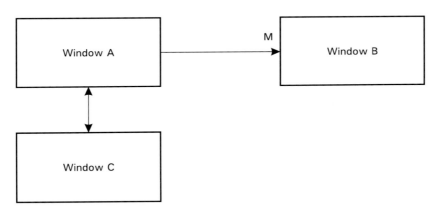

**Figure 11–3.** Window navigation diagramming notation

Sometimes, the designer will allow the user to open multiple instances of the same window. To show this on a navigation diagram, note the maximum number of instances that may be opened at one time on the arrowhead end of the line (read in a clockwise fashion, just like ERD cardinality notation). If there is no logical limit, use the letter "M" to convey "many." In Figure 11–3, we infer that multiple instances of window B may be opened from window A without having to close previous instances of window B.

There are many other useful extensions that can be made to the basic notation (Figure 11–4). If a button is used to open another window, the button can be placed on the diagram and the navigation arrow can originate at the button. If the navigation is the result of a menu selection, the arrow can originate on the frame of the rectangle. Another useful convention is to label the arrow with the name of the button or menu item from which the navigation is executed. Some designers choose to keep their navigation diagrams as uncluttered as possible and elect not to show buttons or arrow labels.

### Window Types

An annotation in the corner of the window denotes the *window type* (Figure 11–5). The window type defines the behavior of the window frame in the target GUI environment (e.g., whether it is movable, resizable or can be overlapped by other windows). Most

GUI development tools come with predefined behavior for various kinds of windows. By simple declaration, you can make a window a member of a particular window type thereby inheriting all of the window type's predefined characteristics. Most GUI development tools further allow you to override individual characteristics to make certain windows behave differently from the rest of their window type ancestors.

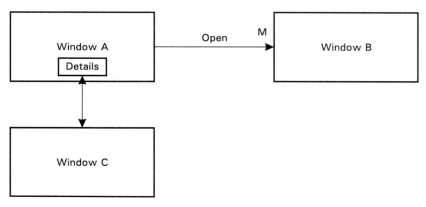

**Figure 11–4.** Various WND notations

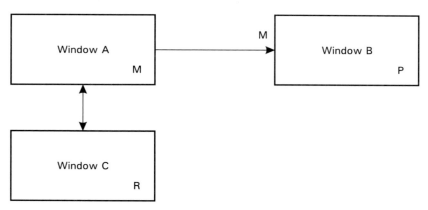

**Figure 11–5.** WND annotations for window type

The following definitions are from the Microsoft Windows environment, and specifically from GUI development packages such as PowerBuilder. Actual terms and window behavior varies slightly between GUI packages and across development platforms, but the concepts are fairly consistent. I will not take offense at all if you scratch out these terms and substitute it with a word that is more meaningful to your development language.

**Main or application window:** A *main window*, also known as an *application window* is the most common garden-variety window available (Figure 11–6). It exists on the screen independently of other windows. It can overlap other windows, and it can be overlapped. It is movable, meaning it can be dragged out of the way to reveal what lies beneath. It is resizable by the user and can be minimized to an icon on the desktop. Main windows normally have a menu, although this feature can be suppressed with most development tools.

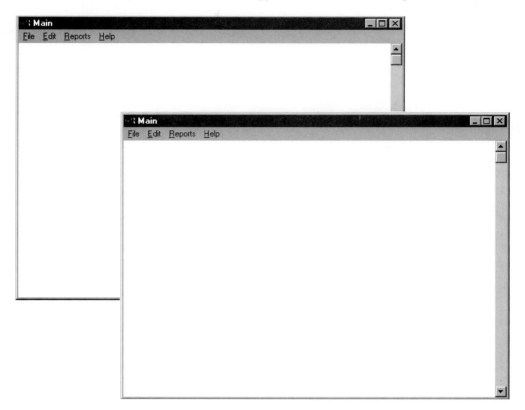

**Figure 11–6.** Main or application windows

**Pop up window:** A *pop-up window* earns its name from the way it pops open on top of the window from which it is summoned (Figure 11–7). A pop-up window is opened from an existing window, commonly referred to as the *parent* window or *calling* window. Unlike a main window, it may not be overlapped by its parent. If you need to view the parent window beneath, you may drag the pop-up out of the way. For example, in Figure 11–7, you can see that if you drag the pop-up window in a south-easterly direction, away from the parent, it remains on top but can be dragged entirely to the side of the parent window, allowing you to view both simultaneously.

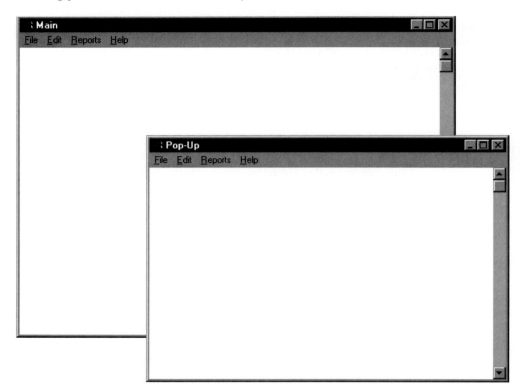

**Figure 11–7.** A pop-up window

When the pop-up window is minimized, it becomes a separate icon on the desktop from the parent window's icon. The pop-up can also exist after the parent is closed. This can be an issue if the pop-up contains any uncommitted data that was required by the parent. Often, the developer will add some code to the parent to clean up any orphaned pop-ups.

**Child window:** A *child window* is very much like a pop-up, but is slightly more restrictive (Figure 11–8). A child window is also opened from a parent window, and like the pop-up window, a child window cannot be overlapped by the parent. The major difference between them is that a child window may not be dragged outside of the confines of the parent's window frame. For example, if you drag the child in a south-easterly direction to reveal the parent beneath, it appears to slide *under* the parent's window frame, but does not emerge on the other side.

When a child window is minimized, it becomes an icon on the workspace of the parent window, not on the screen's desktop. The child cannot exist after the parent is closed. When you close a parent window, all of its open children will also be closed.

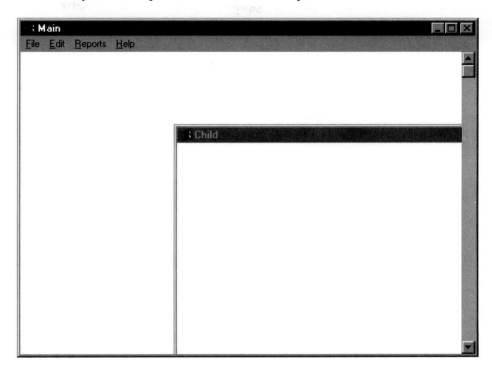

**Figure 11–8.** A child window

**Response window:** The most restrictive type of window behavior is that of the *response window* (Figure 11–9). The response window seizes focus when opened and does not relinquish it until it is closed. It is not minimizable or resizable. A designer will employ a response window in the application when he wants to force the user through a particular path with no deviations. Message and dialogue boxes, used for displaying error and confirmation messages, also exhibit this restrictive behavior.

**MDI frame/MDI sheet:** One of the most useful window constructs in large business applications is the *multiple document interface frame* (MDI) (Figure 11–10). The MDI frame is a resizable, self-contained workspace which operates very much like a main window, but has some special built-in features. Much like a main window, the MDI frame comes with a menu. The windows which are opened inside of the frame are called *MDI sheets*. The MDI sheets behave like child windows. They may not be dragged outside of the confines of the MDI frame, and they minimize to an icon within the frame. The MDI frame, itself, minimizes to an icon on the desktop. MDI frames contain optional built-in functions to tile, cascade, layer and arrange icons for the open sheets inside the frame.

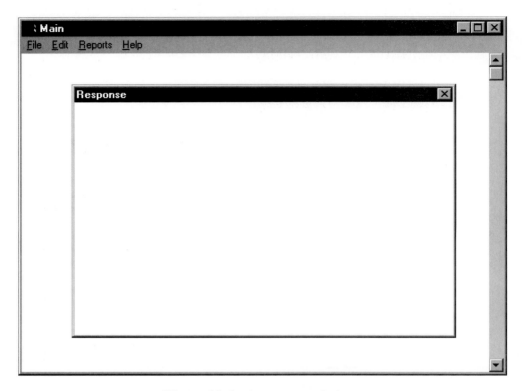

**Figure 11–9.** A response window

The designer also has the option of allowing the user to open multiple instances of the same sheet within the frame. This feature is often disabled in corporate data-entry applications, but is commonplace in packaged software. Examples of well-known applications hosted within MDI frames are Microsoft WORD® and EXCEL®.

MDI frames are particularly useful to partition large systems into separate applications. Because the MDI sheets may not be dragged outside of the frame, the frame forms a nice fence around a suite of windows which may be aggregated to serve a common function, such as order entry. By hosting different parts of the system into their respective MDI applications, the user is able to have multiple applications open at the same time, yet he runs no danger of interleaving unrelated windows between each other. The invoicing windows cannot be mixed up with the order entry windows or the customer profile windows. The MDI frame is a powerful organizational tool that prevents the user from playing 52-card pick-up with a deck of disparate windows.

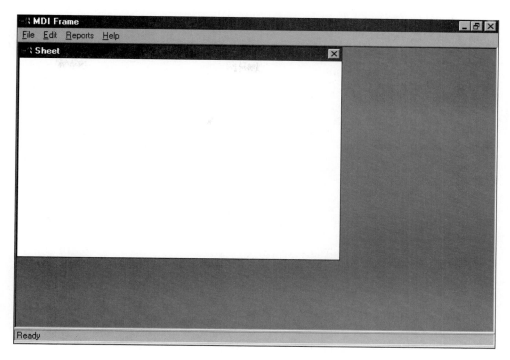

**Figure 11–10.** An MDI frame and MDI sheet

**Tab folder:** The *tab folder* is a special type of window which behaves much like a layered set of MDI sheets or child windows. The look of the window frame has been modified to resemble an old-fashioned file folder with a protruding tab on which the name is written. Tab folders are particularly useful when there are too many data elements to display on one window, and the subject matter to be presented breaks apart logically into distinct subject areas. Figure 11–11 shows a tab folder hosted within an MDI frame. The folder could be used to represent the dossier that the business keeps about a given customer. Each subject area like, *Credit rating*, *Product preferences*, and *Shipping addresses* could be accessed by clicking on the appropriate tab, bringing the selected sheet to the top of the stack.

### Unit of Work

The window navigation diagram is extremely handy for exploring the boundaries of the users' appropriate unit of work. The unit of work is defined as how far you decide to let them go before they must save their work to the database. The navigation diagram allows you to play around with the placement of the **Save** and discuss the merits of the various options with your users and your peers.

The **Save** can be marked on the navigation diagram in several ways. If it applies to just one window, it can be noted directly on the window. If it applies to work done on

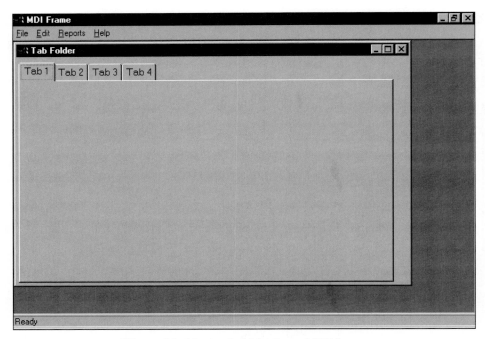

**Figure 11–11.** A tab folder in an MDI frame

several open windows, a dotted line can be drawn around the entire suite of windows whose contents are committed on the **Save**. For applications in which the unit of work spans multiple windows at once, the windows are often hosted within a multiple document interface frame (MDI) and the **Save** is placed on the menu bar of the frame. An MDI frame is noted on the navigation diagram as a solid frame drawn around a set of windows. A **Save** placed on the frame is assumed to commit the contents of any window open in the frame to the database. In some designs, this unit of work may be too liberal and the **Save** command will be moved from the MDI frame menu to individual windows within the frame. Figure 11–12 shows the notation for all four options.

### *Window Navigation Diagram Example*

Now that the window type definitions are out of the way, let's take an example from a simple price table maintenance system and see how one essential requirement to maintain prices could yield vastly different interface designs.

**Specification:** Our hypothetical business requires a price maintenance application that will allow the marketing department to establish new price lists for its products in the future. After information data modeling, event modeling and a prototyping session to determine the window layout, the project team has come up with the database table structure found in Figure 11–13.

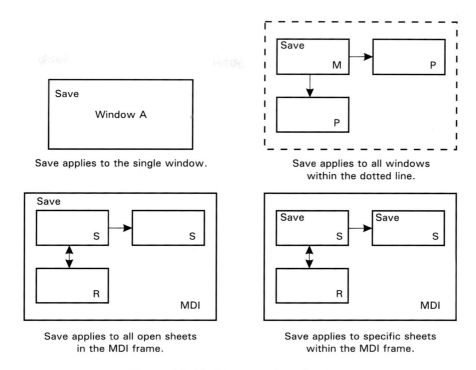

**Figure 11–12.** Four notations for Save

The prototyping session yielded at least three windows for the on-line application (Figure 11–14). One window, *Price List Selection*, allows the user to browse through the price lists already in the system. Another window, *Price List Maintenance* displays all of the price list details associated with the price list. A third window, *Price Detail Comment*, may be needed to update the comment on a price list detail row. Some of the project team argued that a fourth window would be needed to establish a new price list prior to filling in the prices, others argued that it could be combined with the *Price List Maintenance* window.

**Assignment:** Given the table layout, window layouts, and what little we know of the business, how many different navigation models can you come up with? What is the appropriate window type for each window in your model, and where does the Save go? What are the strong points of each design? Assuming each solution has a problem, what are the weaknesses of each design?

Here are some possible navigation paths. Each design has its merits and its shortcomings.

**Design #1:** In the first design (Figure 11–15), the user opens the *Price List Maintenance* window directly from the main menu. When it opens, the fields are empty. To retrieve a price list, the user selects File and Open and the *Price List Selection* window opens, presumably presenting all of the price lists previously saved in the system. The designer has made *Price List Maintenance* a main window and *Price List Selection* a response window. The *Price Detail Comment* window is opened from a button on the maintenance window. We might surmise that the button is enabled only when focus is on a single price detail row.

Table Name:   PRICE LIST

Description:   The price list table specifies the geographic region for which the prices are effective, plus the effective date and expiration date of the price list.

| Column name | Data type | Not null? | PK or FK? |
|---|---|---|---|
| Price_List_ID | (Token ID) | Not null | PK |
| Market_Region | Char(10) | Not null | FK to Market Region table |
| Effective_Date | Date | Not null | |
| Expiration_Date | Date | Not null | |
| Active_Status | Char(8) | Not null | Values = ACTIVE, INACTIVE |

Table Name:   PRICE LIST DETAIL

Description:   The price list detail table specifies the price in effect for each product on the price list. The table has a unique constraint on Price_List_ID + Product_ID such that no product may be listed more than once on a given price list. The marketing department has asked for a comment field at the price list detail level so they can explain how they arrived at certain prices or make notes regarding prices which they intend to revisit prior to the list becoming effective.

| Column name | Data type | Not null? | PK or FK? |
|---|---|---|---|
| Price_List_Detail_ID | (Token ID) | Not null | PK |
| Price_List_ID | (Token ID) | Not null | FK to Price List table |
| Product_ID | (Token ID) | Not null | FK to Product table |
| Unit_Price | Decimal(9,2) | Not null | |
| Price_Detail_Comment | Varchar(200) | | |

**Figure 11–13.** *Price List Maintenance* table definitions

The application appears to be favoring *ease of training* and *consistency among other applications* as the primary quality vectors because the navigation looks very much like other commonly used shrink-wrap applications. It is likely that any user familiar with the Windows® paradigm will need no additional training to learn how to navigate this application.

**Price List Maintenance**

Market Region:      Effective:    Expires:     Active Status:

Price List:

| Product Code | Product Description | Unit Price | Detail Comment |
|---|---|---|---|
| | | | |
| | | | |
| | | | |
| | | | |
| | | | |

**Price List Selection**

Market Region:    Effective:   Expires:

**Price Detail Comment**

Enter notes regarding the selected price:

**Figure 11–14.** Window layouts for *Price List Selection, Price List Maintenance* and *Price Detail Comment*

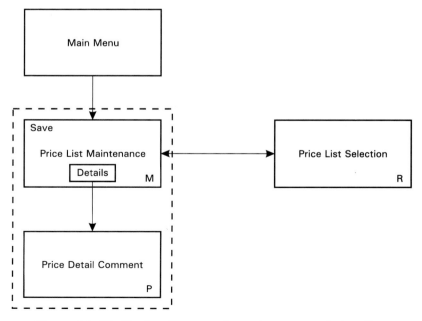

**Figure 11–15.** Design #1 opens the maintenance window first

The designer has defined the user's unit of work to be one entire price list. The application allows the user to enter a price list, all of its price list details, and detail comments before saving any work. The designer has decided that it is not appropriate for the user to open multiple instances of the *Price List Maintenance* window at one time from the main menu, evidenced by the lack of a "many" notation on the arrow.

A possible weak point of this design is that it takes an extra keystroke to get a previous list of prices onto the window. If the users modify prices more than they add new ones, then the navigation isn't optimized to their most frequent task. Another problem is that the *Price List Selection* window retrieves any price list ever entered into the system. This could yield an entirely unwieldy and large result set. Adding some selection criteria by which the users can narrow the selection would avoid the retrieval of historical and superfluous rows.

**Design #2:** In the design in Figure 11–16, the navigation has been reversed. The selection window is the first one to present itself to the user upon entering the application. The designer will need to decide whether this window shall retrieve automatically when opened, displaying a roll-call of every price list ever entered, or whether some selection criteria should be added to the window to allow the user to cut the list down and execute the retrieval on demand.

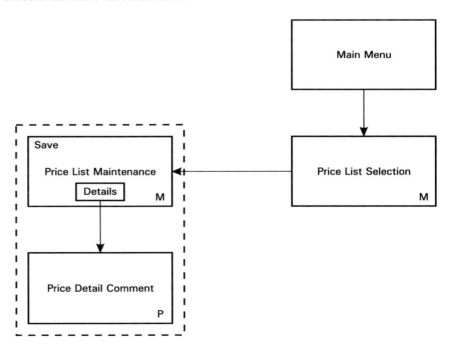

**Figure 11–16.** Design #2 opens the selection window first

This design better favors the object-action paradigm by allowing the user to acquire a set of price lists, and then decide which actions he wishes to apply. To update a price list, the user simply selects one from the list and opens the maintenance window. The downside of this design is that the user must click past the selection window in order to enter a new price list, where in the previous design, he could start typing right away.

In the second design, as in the first, the designer has once again defined the user's unit of work to be one entire price list by placing the **Save** on the price list maintenance window. While I think this is entirely sensible, let's explore our other options.

The design can be easily extended to allow the user to modify multiple price lists at once by placing an "M" on the arrow between the selection and maintenance window (Figure 11–17). This would create an extremely liberal update capability in which the user could have multiple transactions open with the database for countless numbers of price lists.

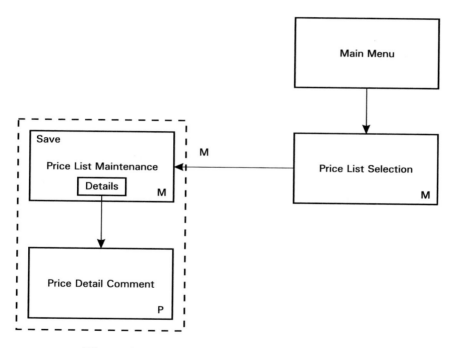

**Figure 11–17.** Unit of work = multiple price lists

If the most unrestrictive unit of work allows for the update of multiple price lists, let's examine the merits and mechanics of the opposite extreme. We might declare that the update of prices is such serious business that the user must save each and every price detail row individually. This can be achieved by disabling the ability to update the price details on the maintenance window, and compelling the user to enter each price on the *Price Detail Comment* window and save it before continuing. (Let's change the name of this window to *Price Detail Maintenance* to reflect its new purpose in life.)

Figure 11–18 shows our new restrictive design which places the **Save** at the lowest level possible. The users must now click on a price detail row in the *Price List Maintenance* window to open the updatable *Price Detail Maintenance* window. At this point, they may enter a price and detail comment, and they must save their work before proceeding to the next price. The most restrictive design would be to make *Price Detail Maintenance* a response window, forcing the users to close it after each use. It might be a bit more friendly to make this a child or pop-up window which would allow the users to click behind it the next price detail row of *Price List Maintenance*, after saving, to refresh its contents with the next price detail.

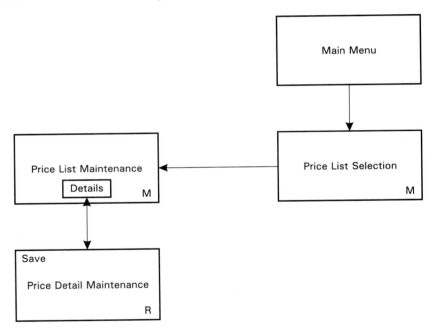

**Figure 11–18.** Unit of work = single price detail

### An Interesting Experiment

If you remain unconvinced of the power of the window navigation diagram to save you time and money, try this little experiment. Take the specification portion from the above example and give it to at least three GUI programmers. Ask them to build the tables and code up an interface using the window layouts. They'll have to come up with their own navigation mechanisms and decide where to place buttons or menu items. They may use whatever window types they deem appropriate. They may even add additional windows, dialogue and message boxes as needed. The only rule is that they are not allowed to see each other's work or talk about their ideas with each other. (This rule is very much like the "heads down and code" decree often issued by panicked managers late in the project.)

You don't have to actually conduct this experiment to imagine the results. It is highly likely that you'll be presented with three interfaces with differences ranging from the subtle to dramatic. Now imagine that these three talented developers are turned loose on a large project, each responsible for producing the interface for various subject areas within the system. The number of navigational and stylistic differences in the completed application could be enormous. The inauspicious window navigation diagram is a powerful communication tool that allows developers to avoid much of this type of divergence.

The window navigation shows how the user may navigate between windows in an application. It is a powerful design and communication technique which helps developers declare the appropriate navigation paths, window type and the appropriate unit of work for the user prior to committing their ideas into code.

The navigation diagram is one of the most cost-effective models available. By taking just a few minutes to draw one, the designer can quickly convene a meeting of his peers and discuss the merits of the model.

### Establish Standard Navigation Models

Each project should have several standard navigation models established for various kinds of on-line activities. One navigation template may be best suited for areas where conservation of keystrokes is of concern. Another template may be better suited to adherence to shrink-wrap navigation norms. For each new area of the application that needs an on-line interface, the designer can shop through the pre-existing patterns and select the one that best fits his problem. Most of the application can be applied to standard navigation models, leaving only the unusual or complex areas of the system open to debate.

Window navigation templates should include project standards for the window title name, internal window object names, standard button names, window types and recommendations for where to place the **Save**. Many GUI development tools support object inheritance for presentation objects, such as windows and buttons. Much of your navigational behavior can be coded directly into the ancestor class library.

### Techniques for Reviewing Window Navigation

Window navigation diagrams can also be used to simulate navigation with your users. Navigation diagramming is another form of prototyping. The learning objective is to determine the appropriate navigation paths, unit of work and window type. The technique is designed to achieve the learning objective without incurring the cost of coding.

To convey your design to the user community, you may want to spruce up the presentation a bit. I have done this several ways, each with great success. Using a windows-based drawing tool, I have quickly pasted bit-map pictures of my window layouts over the boxes on the navigation diagram. This way, the users can see the window layout and the navigation arrows at the same time. (This is usually unnecessary for the technical audience, who is more accustomed to reading abstract specifications.) In the absence of a suitable drawing tool, a low-tech approach is to reduce your window layouts on a copy machine and affix them to a wall chart version of the navigation diagram.

In a more creative session, I taped the window layouts to a large white board. I gave a different colored dry-erase pen to each user in attendance and asked them to approach the board and trace how they might envision navigating the suite of windows to accommodate each event on the event list. The result was fantastically illuminating, and quite a bit of fun. Within an hour, you could clearly see patterns emerging. The normal path taken for most events looked like a psychedelic express freeway on the white board, where the exception paths strayed off to the side in single and paired strands. We never would have discovered this information had we coded an interface prototype for their approval![3]

## Window Specification

Each window on the window navigation diagram requires a specification. The window specification has both a technical and a non-technical audience. The users will need to review the window layouts and their descriptions. Programmers will consume the entire document, including the mini-specs. Testers and trainers should be able to glean the desired behavior from the specification and begin constructing their test scripts and training materials, without having to wait for the final product.

The external interface design articulates the system's visible behavior. The internal design specification will detail how this is accomplished behind the scenes. There are four parts to a window's external specification: Window layout, Window description, Window mini-spec, and Field specification.

### Window Layout

I have already covered much about the window layout. By this point in the project, the initial window layout prototypes have been reviewed by the users and the design team. You should be fairly confident that the content is correct, and the arrangement of the data on the window will fit within the frame and is aesthetically pleasing. The programmer will make final adjustments to the field length and positioning when he creates the window.

The layout can be made using any drawing tool, or even a word processor. The designer should indicate the proper field labeling and relative positioning. The position of all buttons and menu items should be finalized. Title bars should read exactly as

---

3   A significant improvement in CASE tools could certainly sway me away from paper prototyping, but only if the tools were at least as quick and effective as the techniques I have employed.

desired, and all dynamic portions of the title bar should be noted. I have found it useful to indicate required fields and non-updatable fields with a color scheme. I also note fields which will require drop-down lists or look-aside functions by placing a special character in the field on the layout and providing the user with a legend. Figure 11–19 shows a window layout created quickly with a simple desktop drawing tool.

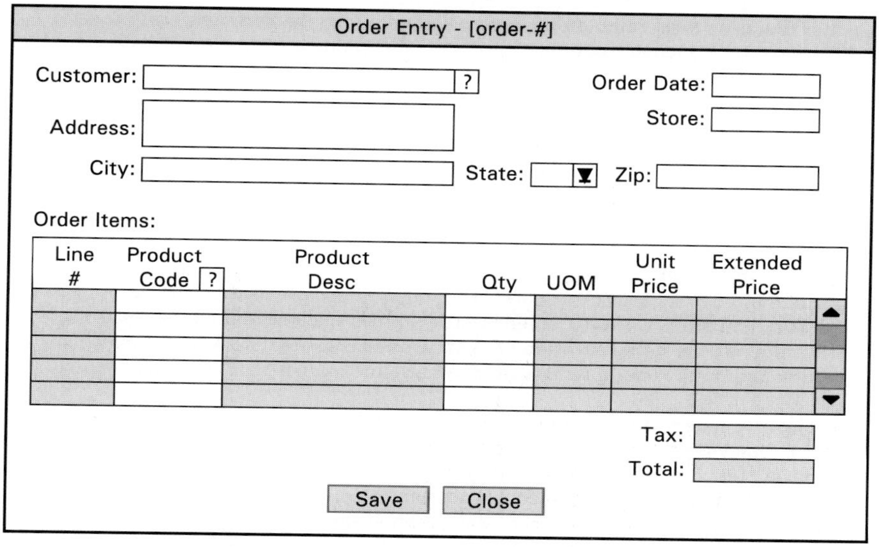

**Figure 11–19.** A window layout diagram

## Window Description

Just like any other object you have created in your model, you have an obligation to define the window layout in clear text so that everyone looking at your picture understands what you are trying to convey. The window description should include an overview of the purpose of the window and a description of the business event or events which are managed by this interface. Much of this text already exists in your event model and in the initial descriptions which accompanied your first paper prototypes. All you need to do is add descriptions of the buttons, menus and ergonomic decisions that you have made in the design phase. Figure 11–20 shows a window description for the window in Figure 11–19. I have not included detailed field descriptions for every field on the window, since this information is already documented in the information model. You may want to include definitions for some fields if they behave in an unusual manner that warrants further explanation, or attach the attribute definitions.

Window Description

Title Bar:       Order Entry - [order #]
Menu:            none
Window Type:  Main

The *Order Entry* window is used by the ACME CORPORATION sales staff to
enter orders at their sales offices, (also known within the company as "stores").
The window is opened from the *Order Selection* window. If the user has
opened a previously entered order, the selected order will display on the window,
with the order number appearing in the title bar. If the user is placing a new
order, the window opens empty, with the cursor positioned in the customer
field.

The customer field is a partial-string look-up on the customer name, using the
system's standard customer look-up function. When the customer is selected,
his default address, city, state and zip code prefills from the customer table.
The salesperson may change any part of the address on the order if the customer
wants the order shipped elsewhere. The order date is prefilled by the system, but
the user may alter it if he is entering orders taken manually on another day.
The store number defaults to the workstations designated store, but it may also
be changed by the user if he is entering a sale on another store's behalf.

The lower section of the window contains a tabular listing of order items. The
system will assign the order item line number automatically. The user can quick-
type the product code, or do a partial-string select to pick it from a list. Some
stores will be equipped with scanners to read the product code directly from the
item. To delete an order item, the user simply blanks out the product code.
The system prefills the product description, unit of measure, unit price and
calculates the extended price based on the quantity entered by the user. Sales
tax is calculated, based on the tax-exempt status in the customer table, and the
order total is displayed at the bottom.

The save button commits the order to the database. The close button returns the
user to the *Order Selection* window.

**Figure 11–20.** A window description example

### *Window Mini-Spec*

The window's mini-spec focuses on the behavior of the window frame and all of the buttons, menu items and controls that you have placed on that window. At minimum you
must specify what happens when the window opens and what occurs when it closes. For
each button, menu item, tool bar push button, or any other control, you must state the
conditions under which it is enabled, and what happens when it is executed. (Standard
controls which are inherited from the window type, such as maximize and minimize, do
not need to be re-specified.) Figure 11–21 shows a mini-spec for the window in our
example.

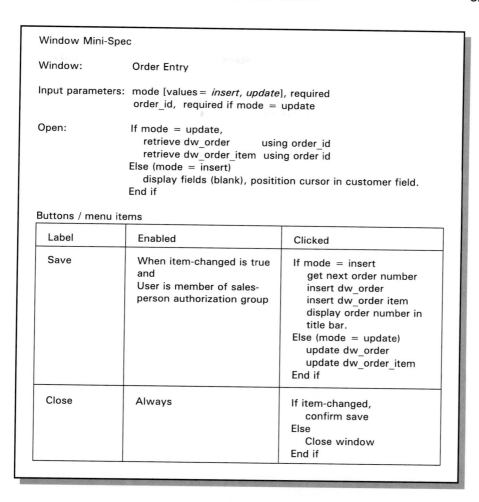

Window Mini-Spec

Window:                 Order Entry

Input parameters:  mode [values = *insert, update*], required
                         order_id,  required if mode = update

Open:                    If mode = update,
                              retrieve dw_order        using order_id
                              retrieve dw_order_item  using order_id
                          Else (mode = insert)
                              display fields (blank), positition cursor in customer field.
                          End if

Buttons / menu items

| Label | Enabled | Clicked |
|-------|---------|---------|
| Save | When item-changed is true and<br>User is member of sales-person authorization group | If mode = insert<br>　get next order number<br>　insert dw_order<br>　insert dw_order item<br>　display order number in<br>　title bar.<br>Else (mode = update)<br>　update dw_order<br>　update dw_order_item<br>End if |
| Close | Always | If item-changed,<br>　confirm save<br>Else<br>　Close window<br>End if |

**Figure 11–21.** A window mini-spec example

The rules regarding enablement of buttons and menu items are derived from two primary sources, user authorization rules, and event state-transition models. The event/user authorization matrix shows which user groups are authorized to execute which business events (Figure 11–22). This is one of the many matrices that can be built when you first create your event model.

As a designer, you need to decide whether to allow a user into a window on which events are recognized but for which the user has no execute authority. In most businesses, the vast majority of users will have read-only access to most of the database. Rather than construct special "view-only" windows, it is far easier to simply let read-only users into the regular maintenance windows and disable all but the selection functions. This tactic encourages users to explore the entire system and leads to a greater understanding of the various tasks that go on around them.

| Event/User authorization | Sales representative | Credit manager | Production manager | Production assistant | Invoicing clerk |
|---|---|---|---|---|---|
| Customer places order | X | | | | |
| Credit dept. approves order | | X | | | |
| Prod. dept. assigns order | | | X | X | |
| Plan fills customer order | | | X | X | |
| Plant ships customer order | | | X | X | |
| Accounting invoices customer order | | | | | X |
| Marketing mails catalogue | X | | | | |

**Figure 11–22.** Event/user authorization matrix

Windows which employ communicational cohesion often require button or menu item enablement based on user authorization. With communicational cohesion, various events are aggregated because the share the same data or business object, but may be executed by different parties. In communicationally cohesive windows, you will have to enable and disable buttons and menu items based on knowing the signed-on user's full authorization. This is usually accomplished by reading the user's authorization levels from the database management system or a set of tables maintained by the system administrator when the application is started, and storing them in the memory of the client machine for the duration of the session.

Along with the event/user authorization matrix, the other primary sources for button enablement are the state-transition models. State-transition diagrams and their accompanying events indicate which transitions are legal from one status to the next (state-transition diagrams are covered in Chapter 5). In Figure 11–23, we see the state-transition diagram for the attribute, *Order status.*

Figure 11–24 shows an order selection window which includes the command buttons used to execute these events. As the user clicks through the items listed in the window's result set, the buttons will enable and disable based on the status of the order he has selected. For instance, if the user selects an order which is "Tentative," the Fill, Ship and Back-Order buttons will be disabled because these actions are not legal for a tentative order. The state-transition model is an invaluable source for the GUI designer. It provides a map for the complex tangle of rules that can result when one or more states are represented on the interface.

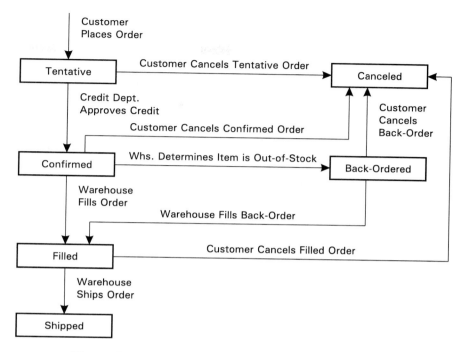

**Figure 11–23.** State-transition diagram for *Order status*

**Figure 11–24.** Window layout for *Order Selection*

### Field Specification

So far we've concentrated on navigation, the window's type and behavior, and the behavior of the controls placed on the interface. Now it's time to turn our attention back to the whole reason for the application in the first place. Let's take a look at what needs to be specified for the actual data content presented by the external interface.

Most GUI development tools provide methods by which the developer can define the display characteristics, edits and functions associated with each data element on the interface. This portion of the specification may represent an internal component such as a business object, 4GL form or DataWindow™ that manages the characteristics of data displayed externally on the window. [4]

Complex windows are often broken up into several display areas. In some development tools, these constitute separate objects on the interface, each with its own display characteristics. For instance, the *Order Entry* window shown in Figure 11–25 has a *free-form* area in the upper portion which is retrieved from one instance of order. Because only one instance of order can be displayed on the window, the designer is allowed to place the data fields in any position that pleases him, hence the name "free-form." The lower portion of the window displays the order items associated with the order header. This section of the window is capable of displaying multiple instances of order item. The *tabular* display style arranges the data in fixed rows and columns. The *grid* display style also arranges data in columns and rows, but it allows the user to rearrange the order of the columns and alter the column size to suit his needs.

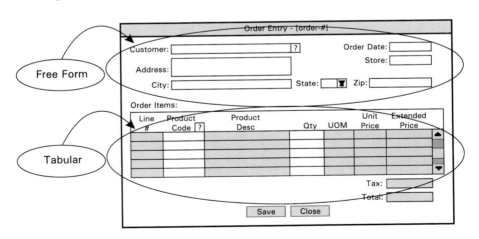

**Figure 11–25.** A window layout with two presentation styles

---

The general characteristics of each display area of the window should be specified first, followed by a listing of the fields contained within. The technical term for the display area will vary from tool to tool. PowerBuilder developers will recognize this as a *DataWindow*. ACCESS® developers might call it a *form*.

For each distinct display area on the window, the specification should include the following:

State the **name of the internal display object**, if supported by your tool.

Declare the **presentation style** (free-from, tabular, grid, graph, bit-map, etc.).

For *tabular* or *grid presentation*, define the applicable characteristics:

> **sort order** (if more than one sort option, define each),
>
> **filters** (conditions under which certain rows may be hidden),
>
> **suppression of repeating values** (e.g., If row 2 has same product name as row 1, display blank),
>
> **selection method** (single select, multi-select),
>
> **grouping** (method by which rows which may only be selected as a group).

For every data element present on the window, the field specification should include the following:

**Label name** to appear on the window.

Include the **table name** and **column name** for all database fields.

Indicate whether the field is **required** or **optional**, and note the circumstances under which optionality may change (e.g., If *Transport mode* = "Container," *Discharge port* is required, else *Discharge port* is optional).

Indicate whether the field is **visible** or **not visible**, and note the circumstances under which visibility may change (e.g., *Rail carrier* is visible only if *Transport mode* = "Rail").

Indicate whether the field is **updatable** by the user, and note the circumstances under which the user's ability to modify the field may be changed (e.g., *Credit manager* field is disabled after order is approved).

Define any **special calculations**, **edits** or **rules** that apply at the field level (e.g., *Net sales* = *Gross sales* less *Shipping costs*).

Note **cross-field dependencies**, edits which depend on other field values (e.g., *Start date* <= *End date*).

Figure 11–26 shows an example of the field specification for the window in Figure 11–19.

Field specification

| Object name: | dw_order |
|---|---|
| Presentation style: | Free Form |

Fields:

| Column Name | Table Name | Rqrd | Vis | Upd | Rules |
|---|---|---|---|---|---|
| Order_ID | Order (pk) | Y | N | N | Get next ID on NEW |
| Order_Number | Order | Y | TB | N | Get next # on NEW |
| Customer_ID | Order (fk) | Y | N | N | Set by f_cust_select |
| Customer_Name | Customer | Y | Y | Y | f_cust_select |
| Address | Customer | N | Y | Y | Set by f_cust_select |
| City | Customer | N | Y | Y | Set by f_cust_select |
| State_Code | Customer (fk) | N | Y | Y | "    / DDL State_Code |
| Zip_Code | Customer | N | Y | Y | Set by f_cust_select |
| Order_Date | Order | Y | Y | Y | Default to current date |
| Store_Number | Order (fk) | Y | Y | Y | Default to user's store |

| Object name: | dw_order_item |
|---|---|
| Presentation style: | Tabular |
| Sort order: | Line #, ascending |
| Filters: | None |
| Suppression: | None |
| Selection method | Single cell only |
| Grouping: | None |

Fields:

| Column Name | Table Name | Rqrd | Vis | Upd | Rules |
|---|---|---|---|---|---|
| Order_Item_ID | Order_Item (pk) | Y | N | N | Get next ID on new row |
| Order_ID | Order_Item (fk) | Y | N | N | FK to order table |
| Line_Number | Order_Item | Y | Y | N | Auto number |
| Product_Code | Order_Item (fk) | Y | Y | Y | f_prod_code select |
| Product_Desc | Product | Y | Y | N | Set by f_prod_code_select |
| Quantity | Order_item | Y | Y | Y | 0 < qty < = 1000 |
| UOM | Order_Item | Y | Y | N | Set by f_prod_code_select |
| Unit_Price | Order_Item | Y | Y | N | Set by f_prod_code_select |
| Ext_Price | Order_Item | Y | Y | N | Unit_Price x Quantity |
| Tax | Order | Y | Ftr | N | f_calc_sales_tax |
| Total | Order | Y | Ftr | N | Sum(Ext_Price) + tax |

**Figure 11–26.** A field specification example

The field specification completes the external design. When this is finished, you have adequately defined the observable behavior of the interface. The remaining design task is to specify the internal componentry that will make this all possible. For many client/server development tools that communicate with the server primarily through SQL, this will simply entail specifying the retrieval for each window from the database, and any stored procedures resident on the server.

While the data access specification technically falls into the topic of internal design, I prefer to include the specification for each window's data access requirements along with the field specification of each window in the external design specification. The data retrieval mini-spec for a window should express enough detail to adequately describe the data access method to the programmer and testers. It doesn't need to be syntactically perfect. You can use you GUI tool's SQL generator for that. The mini-spec for each window's data retrieval requirements should include:

a listing of all input arguments,

a list of all fields and the tables from which they are selected,

directions on how to join the tables,

and instructions on how to apply any input arguments to get the desired result set.

The purpose of the mini-spec is to validate that the database is capable of the selection, identify any potential performance problems, and guide the programmer through complex joins. It also allows the project manager to partition the coding effort among programmers of varying ability, and gives test planners a map of the data needed to adequately test the window retrieval.

Some GUI development tools couple the data access code tightly with the window itself. The next generation of client/server development tools are becoming far more sophisticated, and more object-oriented. For these tools, the designer will have the opportunity to craft a more elegant degree of separation between objects which contain the business policy from those which manage the presentation, communications and database access.

## TESTING A GRAPHICAL USER INTERFACE

Finally, a few words about testing a GUI application. A graphical user interface is far more difficult to test than traditional character-based screens. The most obvious difference between them is that in a GUI application the user is armed with a mouse. Almost every action that can be taken with the mouse also has a keyboard equivalent. This seriously increases the number of individual tests that need to be run. It is not unusual to find errors where the mouse properly executes a command button or menu item, but the keystroke equivalent action fails.

Another complicating issue with windowing environments is that the users can take paths that may have been unanticipated by the developer. They may close windows unexpectedly or shift focus to another application. Users can run your software concurrently with their word processor, spreadsheet, or any number of other PC applications that may be vying for the system's resources.

The external design specification is a crucial document for testers. An application that has a written design specification is far easier to test that one that was constructed without one. The external design tells the tester exactly how the system is supposed to behave. It gives them a basis for writing the test scripts which are used to compare expected behavior to the actual behavior of the finished application. Without a design specification, the tester can run the software repeatedly to determine if the application behaves consistently, but he will not be able to determine whether it is correct.

Each individual programmer should be responsible for unit testing his code. After each is convinced that the application meets the specification, the code should be turned over to independent quality assurance (QA) personnel for further testing. Your QA staff can be made up of testing specialists, or even other programmers, analysts or designers. The only hard and fast rule is that every application must be tested by somebody other than the original programmer before it is released to the users. It is very important that the graphical user interface be rigorously tested. This is the part of the system that the user sees. Even the smallest anomalies on the interface can shake the user's confidence in the integrity of the entire system.

There are many ways to structure test scripts. My preferred method is to create a table which contains four columns (Figure 11–27). The title of the table states the purpose of the test. Column one briefly describes the action to be taken. Column two lists any specific data that must be input, or notes whether the tester can make up his own. Column three describes the expected result of the action. The fourth column is available for the tester to note if the actual system behaved differently than expected.

Test: Customer retrieval

| Action | Data | Expected Result | Actual Result |
|--------|------|-----------------|---------------|
| Fill in selection criteria on Customer Selection window and click Find. | Partial customer name, sales region (optional). | System should return a listing of all customers where the name begins with the first letters typed in the customer name field. If a sales region is also entered, only customers from that region should be retrieved. | Error: System returned customers regardless of the sales region specified. |

**Figure 11–27.** A sample test script

When deriving a test script from a design specification, I like to approach the problem in several passes, devising tests at four different levels, the pixel level, field level, window level, and business event level. The levels of testing move in an ever-increasing expansion of scope from examining individual characters and graphics, to the data field, then out to the window, and then finally to the business event. One word to testers: Even though you may devise the test script in this manner, please execute your testing in reverse order. Test the major transactions first, and then get picky about spelling and punctuation. Programmers will be more appreciative if you find a major system failure on the first day of testing rather than the last.

Pixel level testing is really checking to see if the interface complies with project standards regarding the display, look and feel of the application. This type of testing can be done by virtually anyone on the team. Each project should have a check list of standard items that can be verified by visual inspection of the windows. These are things like font size, use of color, label justification, data justification, spelling, proper use of colons, field alignment, label alignment, button placement, button size, accelerator keys, and standard placement of names of menu items and command buttons.

Moving out from the pixel level to the field level, things get a little more interesting. Every data field should be tested for what I call "stand-alone" properties and edits. This is where you attempt to break individual fields by testing valid versus invalid characters, field length, upper and lower case, numeric ranges, restricted values, required versus optional versus prohibited fields, default values and edit masks. This type of testing is common fare for anyone who has ever tested on-line systems.

What makes the graphical user interface more complex than its green screen counterparts is what I call "cross-field dependencies." This type of test checks all data fields which may change their properties, edits, optionality or updatability depending on the values in other fields. The personal computer's processor allows the GUI application to change field properties instantly when the user types a keystroke or clicks the mouse. Fields may appear and disappear. List values may change. Fields which were optional in one case may be required in another. This feature makes the PC interface far more dynamic than the static green screen. It also makes it more challenging to test. Without a design specification that states the intended behavior, the tester is left to stumble across these features, and has no way of knowing whether the application's behavior is correct or even intentional.

Some common examples of cross-field dependencies are:

**Cross-validation of ranges:** *Start date* field must be less than or equal to the *End date* field. *End date* must be greater than or equal to *Start date*.

**Changes in optionality:** *Credit authorization number* is required for orders over $5,000.00, but optional for orders under that amount.

**Changes in visibility:** *Vehicle routing* field is visible and updatable if the *Transportation mode* is "Rail car," but is not visible if the *Transportation mode* is "Truck."

**Changes in restricted list of values:** The drop-down list for *Customer classification* changes depending on whether the *Customer type* is an "Internal" or "External" customer.

**Default prefills:** When you select the *Customer name*, the *Default address* automatically prefills in the *Shipping address* fields.

The window level test checks the behavior of the window itself, and every control on the window, against the design specification. The external design should include a specification for what happens when the window opens, and when the window is closed. For instance, the window might retrieve data automatically when it opens, or instead position the cursor in a specific blank field. When the window closes, it might be required to check for uncommitted changes and ask the user if he wants to save his work.

Additionally, the tester should check the behavior of the window type against the window type in the design. If the programmer substituted a response window when the spec called for a child window, then the tester should raise the question of which is correct, the program or the design? The navigation paths should also be tested against the navigation diagram. The tester should attempt to break the application by closing down parent windows, attempting to orphan uncommitted changes on any pop-ups.

Each control on the window should also be tested. The external design contains a mini-spec for every button and menu item, stating the circumstances under which they are enabled, and what happens when they are clicked. Once again, without a design specification, the tester would be in the dark as to why certain commands enabled and disabled.

The final level of testing is to devise tests for each of the business events identified in the event model. The event model is a wonderful tool for testing because it is already organized to match the system inputs with their desired outputs. Using the event dictionary as your guide, you should be able to trace each business event to the windows on which it is executed, and write test scripts to verify that the system meets the charter.

These are not the only tests which are run on the application. Once the test scripts are established, they can be loaded in a variety of automated record-and-playback testing tools and used quite effectively for regression testing anytime a change is made to the application.

One of my colleagues uses the term "twister testing" for a scenario where she tries to emulate the "user from hell." She literally clicks anywhere she can, as fast as she can, typing ahead, running multiple applications, leaving e-mail, word processing and spreadsheets open, to try to get the application or operating system to crash. The idea is to see how well the application recovers in a worst-case scenario when the client's resources are stretched past the logical limit.

Another devious test scenario is to get four or five users gathered together on separate PCs and have them try to retrieve the same record at once, or run the same report job. The objective is to see how well the server manages concurrent reads of the same record. Don't forget to test on the exact same machines on which you will deploy the application. There is no sense in performance testing on the latest and greatest workstations in the IT department if your users' PCs are steam-driven.

When you have an external design specification, the preparation of the test script can be done concurrently as the application is being coded. The design is turned over to programming and QA at the same time. With this strategy, the tester fully understands the design intent and is ready to test the application from the moment the code is complete.

## SUMMARY

A vast amount of the time and cost to develop a client/server system is concentrated on the GUI portion of the application. The external interface design is a technique for reducing this cost by working out many of the details of the application prior to coding. In practice, I have found that the design step is not nearly as time consuming as the actual coding. I believe this is due to the overwhelming complexity of the GUI development languages and tools that confront programmers. By having a written design, the project manager can partition the programming effort among multiple developers with the assurance that the various parts can be quickly assembled into a cohesive application that can be independently tested. A written design also allows testers, trainers and technical writers to begin working on their respective deliverables without waiting for the final code.

The external interface design specifies the look, feel and behavior of the portion of the system which is visible to the user. It refines the interface prototype, and continues to consume the models of the analysis phase such as the event, state-transition and information models. The external design specification includes written overviews for the entire system, and additionally, each separate application area within the system.

For each application area, a window navigation diagram is drawn which maps out the navigation paths between windows, and allows the designer and his peers to determine the correct window type. The navigation diagram is then used as a communication tool to discuss the appropriate unit of work for the user and decide where the changes made by the user on the interface must be committed to the database.

For each window on the navigation diagram, the designer has an obligation to define it with a window layout and description. The layout is a refinement of the window prototype, showing the content and positioning of the data fields, as well as the buttons, menu items and other controls required to use the window. The description explains how the window allows the users to manage the various business events for which they are responsible.

The remaining portion of the external interface design document constitutes the technical specification. The window mini-spec includes pseudo-code-style structured text to describe what happens when the window opens and closes. It also includes a brief specification for each button, menu item and control which details the circumstances under which it is enabled, and what happens when you click it.

The field specification rounds out the external interface design by defining the display characteristics for each portion of the window, including sorting, filters, suppression, selection and grouping characteristics for displayed lists. At the data element level, each field on the window is listed, along with the rules regarding its optionality, visibility and the user's ability to update it. The field specification should also include any calculation algorithms, single field and cross-field edits. The window's data access requirements should also be detailed as part of the field specifications.

The external interface design specification is a flexible and negotiable document. The level of detail to which you go in the specification may vary with the complexity of the application that you are attempting to build. Even with the smallest desktop application, it is amazing how much value can be gained simply by spending a few minutes sketching out your thoughts with a navigation diagram. Each design specification should also include some level of version control. This can be as simple as a change log in the front of the document, or as rigorous as formal check-in/check-out procedures.

The external interface design specification states how the application should behave, but still leaves the door open for the programmer to make many decisions about how to achieve that behavior. The design is not the code. If your design spec comes close to compiling, you have gone too far! The programmer will often make aesthetic adjustments to the layout that are too minor to warrant updating the design document. Many times, however, the programmer will come up with an idea which improves the navigation or ergonomics of the design while coding the application. These types of changes should be agreed upon with the designer and updated in the specification. Once the design has been turned over for coding, a change log should be kept so testers, trainers and technical writers can be kept abreast of any alterations.

Testing a GUI can be extremely difficult. The task is made much easier when you have a detailed external design upon which to base the tests. Test scripts can be derived from design spec at various levels. The pixel level consists of a check list from which the tester can verify that the application meets the project's look and feel standards. The field level verifies the properties of each data field. Field level testing needs to verify both the stand-alone attributes of a field as well as any cross-field dependencies that may make a field's behavior change under certain circumstances. The window level test verifies the behavior of the application when the window opens, and when it closes. It also verifies the window type and tests the navigation paths against the design. Every button, menu item and control on the window is also tested against the specification for both enablement and execution. At the business event level, test scripts are organized to verify each business event specified in the event model.

I have presented this material to enough audiences to be able to predict that some readers will think I've gone too far with the detailed interface design. Others will say, "This would be great, but it will never happen in my shop!" My response to those of you who say this is, "Try some of these techniques on your next application." Chances are very high that the clarity of thought you achieve by doing the design will save you countless hours of rework in the long run and yield a product far closer to the mark than you would have otherwise delivered. Every project that I have seen abandon the written design specification has paid for it later either in delayed delivery, astronomical testing costs, or by a torrent of enhancement requests after the system is installed.

## EXERCISES

1. List ways in which the window navigation diagram can be used effectively in the external design phase of a project.

2. What are the two main behavioral aspects of a command button or menu item that should be included in the design specification?

3. Who is your audience for the external design spec?

4. Nelson has been asked to re-host a small warehouse receiving system into a client/server application to support multiple users. The old single-user program was built in the early 1980s using "DodoBase," a now-extinct relational database product for the PC. The database structure of the old system is well defined, but the old interface is a mess. Nelson's manager has assured him that there is no business reason to re-engineer the business process or integrate this system into other applications. Furthermore, he wants Nelson to get this job done in a timely manner. Using the techniques described in this book, quickly outline the steps Nelson should take to re-host this system.

5. What model or models are a big help for figuring out proper button enablement?

6. Edgar develops GUI applications using a tool which communicates with the database almost exclusively through SQL in which the select statements to retrieve windows are closely associated with each window in the final code. Edgar has stated in a staff meeting that he doesn't believe he needs an internal design specification. He is good enough to simply code the select statement for each window using his GUI tool's SQL painter, based on the field content of the window and a layout of the database. Now that you have read most of this book, can you think of any reasons why Edgar, or another designer, should be required to write a mini-spec for each window's retrieval before he codes, and if so, to what level of detail should the retrieval be specified?

## ANSWERS

1. Window Navigation Diagramming can be used to:

   model and discuss the navigation paths between multiple windows in an application prior to coding,

   discuss the appropriate window type for each window,

   determine the appropriate unit of work for the user by deciding how the user will save his work and the scope of the save, discuss whether the user should be able open multiple instances of any given window at one time, and

create templates of standard navigation models which can be used throughout the project.

2. For each command button and menu item on a window, you must state: under what circumstances the control is enabled or disabled, and what happens when it is executed (clicked).

3. The external design specification has many audiences:

Users read the overviews, navigation diagram, window layouts and window descriptions to approve the design or suggest changes to the design before coding.

Programmers use the specification, along with any internal specification provided, to construct the final code.

Testers use the external design spec to devise test scenarios for the interface.

Technical writers and trainers use the specification to create training material, on-line help and user documentation for the final system.

Project managers use the specification to partition the coding work among multiple programmers, and as a basis for revising their project estimates for the work remaining on the project.

4. The first thing Nelson should do is spend a few hours meeting with the users of the system and the project sponsor to determine the problems with the current system, and their objectives for wanting it replaced. He should also gather some quality vectors which reflect their expectations of the new system (e.g., it should support multiple users, the interface should be intuitive, etc.). From this information, he should write himself a short project charter and present it to his manager and users to get clear consensus on what he is about to do. He could count the number of tables and the number of windows he expects to design to help him make an estimate of the effort required to complete the project. Being that this is a re-hosting project and the current database is in pretty good shape, Nelson should reverse-engineer a model of the database and then spend most of his time devising a new interface. Nelson might start by listing all of the business events supported by the current system, and review how the old interface accommodated every event. He should write an event dictionary entry for each event and reference any specific modules of code in the existing system that he will have to replicate in the new system. Once he understands the events supported by the system, he should prototype some layouts and review his ideas with the users. He

could use navigation diagramming on the white-board to let the users help him design the navigation of the new system. Once the layout and navigation of the new system is determined, he can write an external design specification, including the behavior of each button and menu item, and an internal specification which states the retrieval for each window and any internal processing required by the system. After a final review by the users of the specification, he can start coding (and if any other programmers are available, they can help him code as well). While he is coding, his manager has the option of having somebody else devise test plans and create training materials from the design.

5. The state-transition diagram, which links the event and information models, tells you which events are legal or prohibited, depending on the status of the object to which the action applies. An event/user authorization matrix can also be created for the project to help you determine which user groups (e.g., sales people, credit managers, invoicing clerks, etc.) are authorized to carry out specific events.

6. Edgar should write a mini-spec for the data access requirements of each window. The purpose of the specification is to validate that the database is capable of the selection, identify any potential performance problems, guide the programmer (who may be someone other than Edgar) through complex joins, allow the project manager to partition the coding effort among programmers of varying ability, and give test planners a map of the data need to adequately test the window retrieval. Each data retrieval mini-spec should include a list of all input arguments, a list of all fields and the tables from which they are selected, and directions on how to join the tables and apply any selection criteria.

# CHAPTER
# 12

Charter

Context Model · Information Model · Event Model

Interface Prototype

Architecture Model

Database Design

External Interface Design

**Internal Component Design**

Construction & Testing

# INTERNAL COMPONENT DESIGN

## INTRODUCTION

The final technical chapter in this book deals with the task of designing the internal components which dictate the organization of the code within your system. The manner in which you choose to organize the insides of your application will depend heavily on the capabilities of the development languages that you choose. Not all of you will be creating object-oriented constructs in your systems, but since languages are trending rapidly in that direction, I devote most of this chapter to the subject. In this chapter, I cover the key concepts of object-orientation, including encapsulation, information/implementation hiding, persistent state, object identity, classes versus objects, messages, inheritance and polymorphism. After the basics, I promote the idea of creating separate domains of classes in your application to separate foundation classes from those in the architectural, business and application domains. Our overview of object-orientation concludes with a discussion on deriving business and application domain classes from the information and event models. The chapter ends with a brief overview of the type of design documentation that should exist for database triggers and stored procedures, as well as a quick reference to structured design techniques that can be employed on more traditional components in the system.

## WHAT IS INTERNAL COMPONENT DESIGN?

The internal component design is the blueprint for the application code. The shape of the blueprint will be greatly influenced by the paradigm and capabilities of the target languages employed to build your system. Today, it is highly likely that a large client/server system may include some object-oriented code, some SQL, some stored procedures and even a smattering of good old 3GL-style procedural code. The designer should choose the mix of design techniques that best define the structure of the system he intends to construct.

This means that a designer in today's client/server environment needs to understand object-orientation, relational database access (SQL), database triggers and stored procedures, as well as traditional structured design. Since relational database access, triggers, stored procedures and structured design are widely understood and well documented in our industry, I will focus this chapter mainly on object-orientated concepts.

## OVERVIEW OF OBJECT-ORIENTATION

It is not my intent to try to convey everything you'd ever need to know about objects in one chapter. I would have to get in line behind a hundred other authors who have devoted entire volumes to the subject. I also don't intend to promise that OO will solve all of your business problems nor will I imply that objects can help you get a date on a Friday night. Rather, the purpose of this chapter is to cover some of the basic principles of object-orientation and show the models presented earlier in this book that are consumed in the design of an object-oriented system.

Over the last thirty years, programming languages for business systems have evolved into two distinct species, those which do the *processing* (e.g., COBOL), and those which manage the storage and retrieval of *data* (e.g., SQL and the relational database management systems such as Oracle® or SYBASE®). These creatures have survived where others have fallen extinct by specializing in one particular aspect of business software. While "survival of the fittest" may be debated, we could probably agree that "survival of the best marketed" creates its own odd form of Darwinism. This dichotomy of language specialization has created a parallel rift in IT shops. Traditional teams of programmers cut code, the database administrators tend to the corporate repository of all knowledge. The two camps seldom occupy the same vicinity except during the perennial Christmas party or company picnic.

Object-orientation forces the process and data back together. It recognizes that processing only exists to manipulate data, and the data only exists to support the process. Most of all, process and data only are needed in the first place to enable the system to respond properly to business events. Perhaps object-orientation will draw the process fanatics and the data fanatics back together to work toward a common purpose. Failing that, it runs the risk of creating a new class of object fanatics, convinced that the other two groups are a bunch of dinosaurs standing in the path of the on-coming asteroid.

Object-oriented languages have been with us for many years. Early research in the 1960s and 1970s made object-oriented languages a commercial reality before the end of the 1980s. Many early adopters found instant applicability in real-time systems where software is chartered to manipulate real-world objects such as robot arms for factory assembly, or airplane flaps and landing gear. It wasn't until the wide-spread acceptance and demand for the graphical user interface that OO made a big entree into business systems.

A window is such a natural object. Let's use it to illustrate some of the major principles of object-orientation, then we'll take a look at how these concepts can be generalized to apply to objects that are more applicable to running the business.

## BASIC PRINCIPLES OF OBJECT-ORIENTATION

By now, you should be familiar with the concept of the window. Ignoring the content of the window's display area, the window itself has some definite observable behavior. Much of this behavior is made available to you by the good offices of your GUI development tool, whose creators have taken the time to code the basic window classes for you. Just think of the things you can do with a window. You can open it. You can close it. It can be maximized or minimized. You may elect to move it or resize its dimensions.

Donning our programmer's hat, we might pretend that we have just been asked to code the world's first window. We can easily see that we'll have to write some code for the following functions: *Open*, *Close*, *Maximize*, *Minimize*, *Move*, and *Resize*. Having practiced structured design over the years, we may have naturally assumed that we should create separate modules for these functions in order to lower the burden of understanding and maintaining any one function, and to increase the likelihood that functions could be reused by other programs that might have similar requirements (Figure 12–1).

We will need some manner of data to represent our window, its dimensions, state (whether it is maximized or minimized, or is active versus inactive), and its location on the display monitor. There are many ways to represent the window's dimensions and position. One perfectly good way is to remember the x and y coordinates of two diagonal corners. Another alternative is to remember the coordinates of one corner and the height and width dimensions of the window (Figure 12–2). Enter the power of object-orientation. Assuming that a window is always going to be a rectangle, it really doesn't matter which one you use.

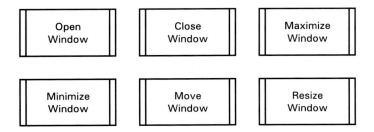

**Figure 12–1.** Modules for the window functions

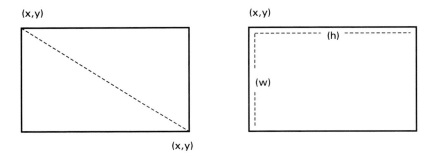

**Figure 12–2.** At least two good ways to represent a window

## Encapsulation

In OO languages, an object's data are called its *variables*. The processes that I represented as little modules are called *methods*. In object-orientation, methods are grouped around the object's variables. The methods can be appealed to directly by other objects, but the variables can only be manipulated by the methods of the object itself. This is called *encapsulation* (Figure 12–3). In our example, the processes you might want to invoke on a window are methods, clustered around the variables used to represent the window internally. Thus, the window's data has been encapsulated by the methods which are allowed direct access to the data.

## Information/Implementation Hiding

The next thing that makes a programming construct an object is the fact that the names, content, and structure of the object's variables are not visible to the outside world.[1] The

---

[1]   I am making the assumption in this chapter that variables are private and methods are public, although many languages support the concept of public variables and private methods.

information contained within is hidden. Even if one were to surmise the information contained within the object, one could never be sure of its specific implementation. This is called *information/implementation hiding*. As long as we know how to appeal to our window to resize or move itself, we can live forever in happy ignorance over how it represents its size or position internally. Encapsulation, combined with information/ implementation hiding makes well-crafted object classes far more resilient to the devastating ripple effect of maintenance and enhancement changes than traditional procedural code. The platoon of methods which surround the variables guard the data from insurgency from the outside world.

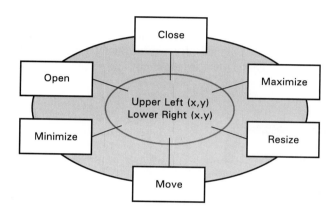

**Figure 12–3.** Window methods encapsulate the window variables

## Persistent State

You may be asking, "What's so different about objects? I could have done that with traditional code!" You would be entirely correct in your assertion, but here's where objects begin to diverge from traditional programs. When you make a program or subroutine call in a language such as COBOL, you pass it some input parameters, it leaps into action, executes its procedure and dutifully returns some output parameters before it lays down to die. Even if the module is called into service again, it has no memory of being called before.

If your family dog behaved like your subroutine, you would be greeted by a different dog every night when you came home. It would act the same, bark at you, knock you down and lick your face, but it would have no memory that it had ever done such a thing in any previous incarnation. After you were through saying hello to your dog, it would vanish and a new dog would be provided to you at the beginning of tomorrow evening's welcome ritual.

Unlike the traditional subroutine or program module, an object hangs around and remembers who it is long after it has finished executing. While this is desirable behavior in dogs, it is particularly convenient in windows so that when you decide to leave the *Order entry* application and go play Solitaire, your original window doesn't develop a fatal case of amnesia in your absence.

## Object Identity

In order for an object to know who it is, it must have a unique identity. An object's identity card (or dog tag) is called the *object handle* (Figure 12–4). Object handles are assigned by the application when an object is created. As for how the handle is generated—only the computer knows for sure. The program will assign a variable to represent the object handle, which affords us the convenience of a unique identity without boring us with the implementation. No two object handles are the same, and an object will carry its handle for its entire life.

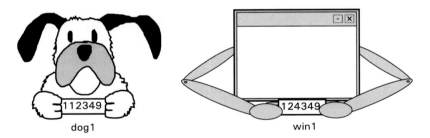

**Figure 12–4.** Object handles

## Classes Versus Objects

Objects are the things which exist at run-time. Classes are the templates from which objects are wrought. Classes are what you design and code. The pattern for creating our window is stored in the class *Window*. If we were to create two instances of our class *Window*, the system would assign two distinct object handles, one for each object. The following statements would result in the creation of two new windows, *Win1* and *Win2*, each pointing to unique object handles in memory (Figure 12–5).

```
var win1:WINDOW := WINDOW.new;
var win2:WINDOW := WINDOW.new;
```

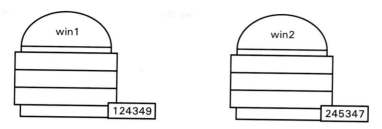

**Figure 12–5.** Win1 and win2 with their object handles

Our two instances of class *Window*, objects *Win1* and *Win2*, are both equipped with all of the variables and methods that come with the class. They can, however, lead entirely separate lives. *Win1*'s set of variable values are entirely separate from *Win2*'s. Although they contain an identical set of methods, the code executes independently on each object.

As a seminar instructor, I often wonder with a degree of dread what a student will remember after a week's worth of pontifications and small exercises. I encountered a co-worker one day who had just returned from a seminar on object-oriented design. He gleefully announced that *"objects are like cookies, and classes are the cookie cutters."* Inwardly, I heaved a sigh of relief that he came home with both clauses of the statement intact. I shudder to think what would have happened if he only remembered the first half.[2] The student's instructor was successful in conveying the difference between objects and classes.

## Messages

So far, we have created skillfully encapsulated constructs of process and data that can be created on demand from classes and can carry out independently fulfilling lives, but I've said nothing about how objects communicate. As you may suspect, it requires a con-spiracy of many objects to conduct any meaningful activity in a software system. Objects collaborate at run time by sending messages to one another.

A message is the way one object appeals to another object to execute one of its methods. In order for an object to send a message to another object, it must know the identity (variable name or handle) of the target object, the name of the desired method, and optionally, any arguments that must be included in the message, (input and output arguments, also known as the *message signature*). Although an object's internal vari-ables are hidden from view, the method name and message protocol must be plainly known by all other objects that wish to communicate with it.

---

2   A less attentive student may have remembered, "Object are like cookies. Cookies are good. There-fore, objects are good." His manager may have run out and hired a pastry chef for the project.

To tell our window to move itself, the object sending the message (perhaps a mouse) must know the name of the object (*Win1*), the name of the method (*Move*), and the arguments required (say, new x,y coordinates for upper left corner). The result would be a message:

```
win1.move (x,y)
```

Whether the move method requires new x,y coordinates, or perhaps a vector and distance, must be known to all objects that might ask the window to move. Thus, changes made to a method's required arguments can have a dramatic ripple effect in an object-oriented system.

Messages between objects can be shown in the *object-communication diagram* which graphically depicts the messaging between the methods of various objects at run time (Figure 12–6). Similar variants of object communication are referred to in some OO methodologies as the *dynamic object model*, or *event-trace diagram*.

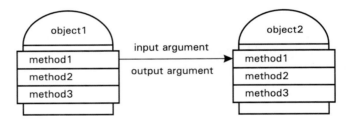

**Figure 12–6.** An object-communication diagram

For this book, I have chosen Object-Oriented Design Notation (OODN) by Page-Jones, Constantine and Weiss because of its expressiveness, simplicity and consistency with traditional design notations.[3] Classes are shown on the diagram as rectangles with a domed top. The part-circle, part-rectangle symbol reflects the fact that objects are part-process, part-data. The "tombstone" shape is also easy to draw and is clearly distinguishable from the entity type symbol. Methods are listed vertically on the rectangular portion of the class. The class can be drawn with or without its methods listed, or you may choose to show only the methods which are relevant to your diagram. By listing the methods on the class, the arrows which denote messages can be drawn directly from the method which sends the message to the method which receives the message. The message's arguments can be shown on the message arrow, or listed on the target method. The internal specification for a class is textual. The specification should include a listing of all the variables, and a process mini-spec for each method.

---

3   Page-Jones, Constantine, Weiss, 1990. For a more complete review of OODN, see Page-Jones, 1995

## Inheritance

Let's say that as we are analyzing our window, we discover some small differences between various types of windows. Some windows need to check to see if any of the display contents have been changed, so when the users attempt to close the window, the windows can prompt them to save their work. While this reasonable and polite behavior for an *updatable* window, it is not behavior which is required from a *non-updatable* window.

Rather than clone all of our window code over and duplicate it in another type of window, we can exploit *inheritance* to keep the code resident in one object class, yet make it available to other object classes. In this example we can make our updatable window a *subclass* of our generic window (the *superclass*). By declaring that the superclass *Window* is the ancestor of the subclass *Updatable window*, all methods and variables defined on the superclass are made available to the subclass without having to replicate them in the code.

If this concept is sounding familiar, it should. The same underlying principles that guide the supertyping and subtyping of entities in the information model also apply to the superclasses and subclasses of objects. While entity supertypes and subtypes focus on data, namely, which attributes and relationships apply in the type hierarchy, object superclasses and subclasses add the complexity of determining which methods should reside at various levels of the class hierarchy.

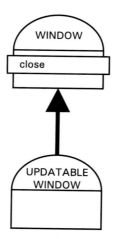

**Figure 12–7.** Inheritance

The OODN symbol for inheritance is a thick arrow drawn from the top of the descendent class, pointing upwards to the bottom of its ancestor. In Figure 12–7, we see that the class *Updatable window* inherits from the class *Window*. The generic class *Window* may have a method on it called *Close*. The subclass *Updatable window* need not have a corresponding method for *Close*. When we create an object, *Win3*, as a member of the class *Updatable window*, it automatically inherits all of the capabilities previously defined by the class *Window*.

```
var win3.UPDATABLE_WINDOW := UPDATABLE_WINDOW.new;
```

If you tell *Updatable window* to "close," it can execute the *Close* method of its ancestor. If, however, you want the class *Updatable window* to behave differently, you can add a *Close* method to *Updatable window* that checks to see if the user has made changes and holds the closing of the window in abeyance until the user has either saved his work or expressed his intent to close it anyway (Figure 12–8).

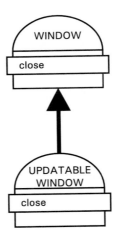

**Figure 12–8.** *Updatable window's Close* method will override the ancestor's *Close* method.

If *Updatable window* has its own version of the *Close* method, the subclass method will override any like-named methods in the superclass.[4] In this example, inheritance has allowed us to extend our application's capabilities by creating subclasses that behave in a slightly different manner than the superclass, without altering the ancestor class code.

Inheritance as a facility for extensibility, combined with its ability to factor out common behavior, makes it one of the most touted features of object-orientation. Like any powerful concept, it has its challenges. Reuse seldom happens by accident, and uncontrolled extensions to a class hierarchy can quickly send any semblance of a reasonable, maintainable design "out the window." Supertyping and subtyping are among

---

[4]   Some languages give the programmer the option of appending code in the subclass method to the code in the superclass(es).

the most difficult crafts to master in information modeling. The modeling of superclasses and subclasses isn't any easier.

## Polymorphism

Imagine that a user attempts to exit an application that has many windows open. The *Exit* code sends a message to all of the open windows, instructing them to close themselves. The sender of the message doesn't need to know whether the target windows are of the updatable or non-updatable variety. The behavior of each window's *Close* method will be determined at run time by the target object's position in the class hierarchy. The ability of object-oriented environments to determine the exact piece of code to be executed at run time rather than when the program is compiled is called *dynamic binding*. The result is that the same message to an object may result in differing behavior, based on which methods actually execute. This characteristic is known as *polymorphism*, a term derived from the Greek words meaning "many forms."

## WHY OBJECTS?

An object is a natural coupling of both process and data into a single programming construct which carries a unique identity, presents a defined interface to the outside world, but hides its internal implementation. The purpose of the technique is to separate the implementation choices from the service the object provides. By hiding design decisions, we can reduce the potential ripple effect of making changes to the system. A well-crafted suite of object classes can promote reusability by factoring out common behavior. Separating classes into domains of service providers, such as presentation, data servers, communication, and business classes promotes specialization and increases the chance that classes can be reused by other applications requiring the same functionality. The ability of an object to retain its identity makes object-orientation languages especially well suited for distributed systems which have lots of messaging between physically remote software components.

Please note that at no time have I implied that object-orientation is easy. It is not a panacea for all of your software problems, and it comes with a steep learning curve and demands rigorous design and documentation.

In the previous section, I briefly covered the basic principles of object-orientation so that we can move on to a discussion of deriving business classes from our essential models. For a detailed discussion of object-oriented terms and an excellent reference on design concepts and notation, I highly recommend Meilir Page-Jones' book, *What Every Programmer Should Know About Object-Oriented Design*.[5]

---

[5]  Page-Jones, 1995

## HOW OBJECT-ORIENTED IS YOUR PROJECT?

In this section I will attempt to put object-orientation in perspective by addressing questions that are commonly raised when developers move from a mainframe environment to the world of client/server.

### "Our application will have a GUI.
### Does that make us object-oriented?"

Not necessarily. Windows, buttons and menus are natural objects on the interface. The business application logic that resides behind the windows may or may not be object-oriented. It depends entirely on the capability of the development language and how you design it. In general, the current crop of client/server development tools fall into two rough categories, those which have limited object-oriented capabilities, and those which are full-blown object-oriented development environments. This distinction is not always readily apparent. If the tool embraces any one of the principles I have outlined in this chapter or contains anything that vaguely resembles a button or window, the vendor is likely to put the words "object-oriented" on the box.

Many popular GUI tools were first written to take advantage of graphical user interface objects, but the business logic is executed with a fairly standard mix of SQL and 3GL-like scripts. These tools are gradually embracing more and more of the OO principles, making them more object-oriented with each subsequent version.

The second wave of client/server development tools have been written from the ground up specifically for object-oriented development. They include fully object-oriented languages which allow for complete separation of business objects from the mechanics of the interface. In truly portable languages, this enables the designer to create object classes which are platform-independent and can be moved from client to server or to any tier in between to achieve optimal performance.

### "Are we object-oriented, even though
### we have a relational database?"

If you use an object-oriented language over a relational database, you are living in both worlds. Objects exist in your run-time environment, but when you store information, the objects unload their data into a relational database. Bridging this paradigm gap is known as *impedance mis-match*, a term borrowed from electrical engineering. Many of today's client/server development tools manage this impedance mis-match skillfully by supplying classes of data service objects that handle the communication between the application and the database, relieving the programmer of this burden.

Having a relational database doesn't make a project inferior to one that uses an object-oriented database. The relational database is very popular in business systems, largely because it allows the organization to collect a broad range of information and defer many of the decisions of how to use it until later. While this makes less sense for real-time systems, it is a reality in business systems simply because of the ever-changing competitive nature of business itself.

## CHOOSE THE TARGET, THEN MAP THE TECHNIQUE TO THE TARGET

If I had to summarize my design philosophy, it would be, "Chose the most appropriate target languages to meet your charter, then map the design technique to the target." The design document is the blueprint for the as-yet-to-be-built system, and like an architectural blueprint, you want the plan to look very much like that which you intend to construct. What this all means to you today as a business systems developer is that you will need to be well grounded in the concepts of information modeling and relational database design, as well as understand the principles of object-orientation.

I have chosen information modeling and event modeling as the primary essential models in this book specifically because the client/server target environment remains such a mixed bag of tricks. The models are well suited to modeling all three aspects of the system; data, process and behavior. The techniques also affords the analyst the ability to defer the declaration of business classes until the design stage, and bases the design on the capabilities of the target environment. One of the key differences between information modeling and object modeling is that in object modeling, the analyst must also find the single best home for the methods, whereas, with information modeling, the system's processing requirements are housed in the event model and not coupled with the data until you begin to declare business classes.

For projects which will be using relational databases coupled with object-oriented languages, I believe it to be a sensible approach to employ information modeling to arrive at a solid database design. A good object class modeler may also arrive at a similar, if not identical, database design, but they will have to do so by extracting the structure of what data needs to be stored out of a static class model. As long as runtime environments continue their trend toward object-orientation and if business systems continue to rely heavily on a relational data repository, analysts, designers and developers will need keep their feet firmly planted in both camps.

For many shops, object-orientation is creeping into business systems through the back door, rather than sweeping in like a tidal wave. OO requires such a dramatic mental shift at the line level of code, that it takes time for a programming team to be retrained. Once the programming constructs are mastered, the developer can move on to higher levels of abstraction of object-oriented design principles. All of this takes time, and is hitting many IT shops concurrently with the shift to relational databases from flat file technology, and with the shift to GUIs and client/server architectures. OO should be undertaken carefully, soberly and with a clear understanding of the required learning curve and costs versus the expected benefits.[6]

---

[6]   See Page-Jones, 1992, "The Importance of Being Ernest"

## DOMAINS OF OBJECT CLASSES

In Chapter 8, I introduced the concept of software layers which separate components into areas of specialty, presentation, business logic and data management. While the notion of a three-layered software cake is useful for modeling architecture, the internal componentry requires a more granular taxonomy.

Objects classes can also be grouped into domains, according to the role they play in the system. The domain levels are the *foundation*, *architectural*, *business* and *application* domains (Figure 12–9).

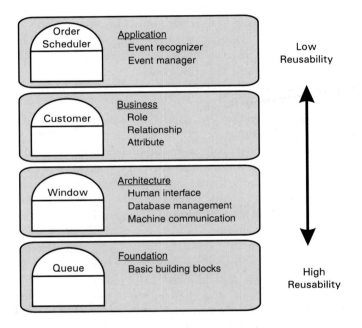

**Figure 12–9.** Domains of classes

## The Foundation Domain

The foundation domain classes form the basic building blocks from which all applications are constructed. In purely object-oriented languages, even traditional data types are classes (e.g., *Integer*, *Boolean*, *Time*, *Money*). Classes in the foundation domain enjoy a higher level of reuse than any other domain. They are widely employed to accomplish tasks by members of the higher domains. For almost all projects, the entire suite of foundation classes should be purchased, ready-to-use from your development tool vendor.

## The Architectural Domain

The architectural domain includes classes which communicate with the hardware. This domain includes classes which manage the human interface (including all of the graphical user interface objects such as windows, buttons, icons, and menus). Also grouped into the architectural domain are those classes which manage the storage and retrieval of information in the database, machine to machine communication across the client/server architecture, and communication with peripherals such as faxes, printers and other electronic interfaces. Classes in the architectural domain are often specific to the chosen hardware. Keeping all of the hardware-specific code corralled in the architectural domain enables you to take advantage of the rapid advances in technology by changing the hardware box without having to rewrite code in your business or application classes.

Mixing components from different domains together in a single class is called mixed-domain-cohesion (or *domain poisoning*, as I like to put it). You should be able to appeal to a business class, such as *Invoice*, and tell it to print itself. The business class is responsible for knowing what information to print but should *not* be encumbered with any awareness of the type of printer to be used. The protocol for communicating with the printer should be managed by an architectural domain class, say, *Printer*. The two separate classes should work together to accomplish the print job.

Many of the architectural domain classes will also come to your project, courtesy of your development tool vendors. These companies have taken the time to code up windows, command buttons, print previews and device drivers so you don't have to.

## The Business Domain

The business domain includes classes which are germane to conducting business within a specific industry. Your business domain will include classes that many of your competitors would find useful. Classes like *Customer credit limit, Invoice, Pizza order* and *Scheduled shipment* all reside in the business domain. There is a movement afoot among several enterprising vendors to create off-the-shelf, industry-specific business classes that can be purchased and extended to suit your needs. This is based on the observation that patterns which show up in one company will tend to surface in other companies in the same industry. Patterns at a higher level of abstraction will even appear in companies from different industries. This also holds true in information modeling. Recognized patterns such as these have been the basis for the success of many of today's enterprise-wide relational manufacturing packages. As we will see in the next section, the classes in the business domain have strong correlations to the information model. The reuse of business classes rarely happens without careful planning. If reuse of business classes is important to your shop, then it should be stated as a primary quality vector from the start of the project.

## The Application Domain

The application domain object classes are seldom reusable. They carry out roles which are limited to a specific type of application. While business domain classes tend to be centered around the business' fundamental data, application domain classes are more rich with processing. Classes in this domain are often culled from the event model, playing the roles of *event recognizer* or *event manager*. In Chapter 4, we saw that some events require the system to determine that the event has occurred. For these events, some manner of event-recognizer classes will have to be constructed. In business systems, the most common event recognizer is temporal. One would expect to find class such as *Delinquent account monitor* in a system which periodically checks the aging of receivables.

Classes are created to play the role of *event manager* for those events which require the coordination of several classes in order to execute the business policy. Examples in an export transportation system would include *Shipment splitter*, which would manage the highly specialized requirement of responding to customer requests to split their pending order into two separate shipments. While this activity may be critical to providing full customer service, it is highly unlikely to be reused in any other application.

## DERIVING BUSINESS AND APPLICATION DOMAIN CLASSES

Object-oriented design is not an activity which is independent from much of what we have already covered in this book. In the analysis section, we analyzed the system's expected behavior and documented the business rules using the event model. We recorded the data requirements using the information model, and we specified the processing requirements in the activity section of the event dictionary. Process, data and observable behavior; we have defined the entire system very much like an object.

The essential models of the analysis phase provide the material for weaving the threads of the business problem back together again into a suitable design, based on the capabilities of the chosen development languages. The information model is vital for designing the relational database. The event model and information model are crucial for devising the interface. Once again, we will find that the analytical models provide a mother lode of raw material from which object classes can be wrought.

In the next section, we will see that some classes in an object-oriented design can be derived from the information model. These include *role classes*, *relationship classes*, and *attribute classes*. In addition to these, additional classes are derived from the event model including *event recognizer classes* and *event manager classes*.

## Deriving Business Classes from the Information Model

The most obvious sources of object classes are the entities on the information model (although these are not the only sources, as we will see in a moment). If you turn to

Webster's Dictionary[7] you will find striking similarities between the definition for *entity* and the definition for *object*:

> *entity, n.* 2. a thing that has definite, individual existence in reality or in the mind.

> *object, n.* 5. anything that can be known or perceived by the mind.

The dictionary definitions are a bit vague for our purposes. It seems that any noun that can be conceptualized by the human mind could qualify as an object. Taking a literal approach, we might invite a group of programmers into the conference room to brainstorm "nouns in the problem domain" and list them as potential classes. While the group would probably discover many of the same nouns that grace your information model, the technique has also been known to generate such candidates as "mouse pad," "thunder" and "lunch."

A more sensible approach to discovering business classes is to methodically survey the information model to see how the entity types (for which you have already determined the system needs to remember something) might translate into object classes suitable for run-time operations. Although there is a strong correlation between entities and objects, you will find that it is not necessarily a one-to-one mapping. We will also see, later in this section, that an object-oriented class model will include many classes which have no representation on the information model at all.

### Entities as Role Classes

Entities form the basis for what are known as *role* classes. These classes play major roles in the business system and include classes such as *Customer*, *Order*, *Product* and *Invoice*. There are some fundamental differences between modeling entities and objects that need to be respected. In Chapter 5, I submitted that information modeling is based on the concept of data normalization. We remove all repeating groups of data from our entities until the information model represents a well-normalized data set.

In object-orientation, the concept of information/implementation hiding provides the designer with a license to denormalize if they so choose. Objects need not hold just a single "row" of data. Indeed, an object's internal variables may be represented by complex arrays. While this notion may horrify normalization purists, you must remember that completely object-oriented languages are not constrained by the relational paradigm.

To illustrate this point, let's say that Marcia, Jan and Cindy each order three pest control items from the Lilly & Vermin mail-order catalogue (Figure 12–10). In a few days time, Marcia is greeted by a large cardboard box on her doorstep which contains her three ordered items packed in styrofoam chips. Marcia is a professional COBOL programmer, maintaining a system which uses flat file data storage. She visualizes her order as a single shipment record which contains a repeating group of shipment-items which occurs three times. The styrofoam chips represent "filler."

---

[7]   Webster's New World Dictionary of the American Language, 2nd College Edition, 1978.

Jan, on the other hand, has spent her entire career designing relational databases. She is an expert in data normalization and SQL. Jan's order arrives in the same fashion, three items packed in a single box. Jan visualizes her order as one instance of *Shipment* which contains one to many instances of *Shipment item*. To her, the shipment of the box and the contents of the box are distinctly separate entities, although she recognizes that for any *Shipment item*, you must be join back to the *Shipment* to learn the shipping date, and whether the item was sent first class.

Cindy has been developing object-oriented applications using Smalltalk™ for several years. When her order arrives, she pauses to reflect on the fact that she can view her box as a single object which is capable of enumerating its contents on demand, or she can visualize her box as a container which transports three distinct instances of ordered-item, her attic mouse trap, rat poison and decorative arachnid-motif doormat. She chuckles briefly as she imagines what a debate this problem could stir up on her project team at work.

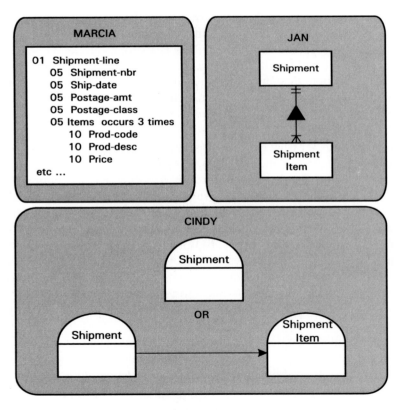

**Figure 12–10.** Marcia, Jan and Cindy each imagine their order differently

The point is that object modelers are not beholden to the laws of normalization. Cindy can represent her order as a single object, *Shipment*, which holds an internal array of its contents, or she may model her order as an instance or *Shipment* which holds the object handles of the *Shipment items*, which are separate objects that can be appealed to independently. She is very likely to choose the later scenario, but the point is she doesn't *have to*. Considerations that would guide the design include whether any other part of the application needs to appeal directly to methods on *Shipment item* without having to bother with the *Shipment*, or whether the inclusion of *Shipment items* with the *Shipment* degrades the reusability of either class.

You can take two approaches to class modeling. You can treat normalization as irrelevant and model objects as you perceive their innate structures, or you can start with a normalized model as the default and make decisions to aggregate entities for specific design reasons. My preference is the latter. By starting with a well-normalized information model, all decisions to denormalize information in the class model are done deliberately by informed consent, rather than by accident. Object-oriented applications which operate over relational databases have the additional burden of having to unload their data into normalized tables, which may also cause you to favor normalized structures within your object classes.

We have seen that object-orientation may lead you to aggregate more than one entity into a single class. The reverse can also occur. You may decide to split a single entity into multiple classes. The most common situation is when the object modeler decides to introduce more levels of class inheritance than the information modeler chose to depict in the subtype/supertype hierarchy in the information model. Let's look at an example of where this might crop up in a real business system.

In Chapter 8, we visited the Nihilist Toy Company, international purveyors of violent and offensive playthings. If we were to examine their information model, we might find an entity such as *Order* lurking about. As it turns out, there are distinct differences between orders placed by customers for shipment domestically within the United States, and those bound for export overseas. There are a modicum of additional attributes required for an export order that have no bearing on a domestic order, and several relationships to export vessel booking entities which are prohibited for domestic orders. Figure 12–11 shows subtyping notation for export and domestic orders in an information model.

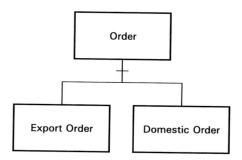

**Figure 12–11.** An ERD showing *Order* subtyped into *Export order* and *Domestic order*

Now, what if the information modeler chose *not* to subtype the *Order* entity into *Export order* and *Domestic order*. Instead, he has represented both domestic and export orders as a single entity *Order*, and distinguished between them with an *Order type* attribute and a set of business rules governing the optionality of certain attributes and relationships?

Before any of you data modeling purists reach for your e-mail to send me a nasty-gram, remember the assertion in Chapter 5 that "normalization is a syntactic solution to a semantic problem."[8] A savvy information modeler would be perfectly within his rights to roll these two subtypes together if he divined that the everyday accessing of the data within the business didn't warrant the added complexity of making a structural distinction.

Enter stage right, the object class modeler. The object class modeler has the added responsibility of assessing the business usage of both the data and the processing that occurs around the data. Looking at the code that will need to be written for the *Order* class, he might determine that there are significant process and behavioral differences in the system between domestic and export orders that warrant the creation of a class hierarchy. The common methods and variables are promoted to the superclass *Order*, and the singular proclivities that distinguish export from domestic orders (such as the ability to name the vessel on which they will sail) can be hived off to the subclasses *Export order* and *Domestic order*, respectively (Figure 12–12).

The divergent conclusions drawn by the object class modeler and information modeler are due to the slightly different set of heuristics on which they base their decisions. The information modeler tempers his normalization with an assessment of data access needs, while the object class modeler is striving for factoring out reusable code, clean coupling[9] between objects, and reducing unnecessary encumbrance.[10]

### Supertype/Subtype Entities as Superclasses/Subclasses

You may have noted in the last section that there is an obvious parallel between the information model and the OO class hierarchy when it comes to supertype and subtype entities. The information modeler distinguishes between entity types which share *some* but not all of the same attributes or may participate in *some* but not all of the relationships. This can lead to supertype/subtype structures such as the example we saw in Chapter 5 of the *Vehicle* supertype with subtypes of *Planes*, *Trains* and *Automobiles* (Figure 12–13).

---

8   Page-Jones, 1991.

9   *Coupling* is a measure of the dependency of one software component on another. First introduced in *Structured Design* (Yourdon, Constantine, 1979), the concept has been expanded by Meilir Page-Jones into a concept called *connascence* which is a more robust measure of dependency between encapsulated structures. (See Page-Jones, 1995).

10  *Encumbrance* is a measure of a class's indirect class-reference set. (See Page-Jones, 1995). In other words, if you traced all of the other classes that a class may directly reference (either through inheritance, messaging or holding the variables of another class), and then all of the classes that *those* classes may reference, and so on, you get a measure of a class's sphere of influence and dependency throughout a system. Encumbrance is an important element in tracing the ripple effect of making changes to a class interface.

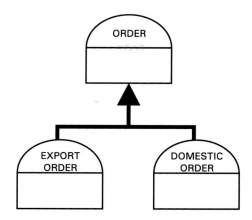

**Figure 12–12.** A class diagram showing superclass/subclass inheritance.

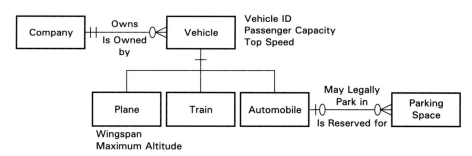

**Figure 12–13.** An ERD of *Vehicle* supertype and its subtypes

The object class modeler employs the miracle of inheritance to express the relationship between the generic superclass *Vehicle* and the subclasses *Plane*, *Train* and *Automobile*. He must also concern himself with the placement of methods in their best home in the class hierarchy (Figure 12–14).

Again, the object class modeler may be faced with complexities that were easily glossed over by the information modeler. For instance, what if our fictional system were responsible for tracking both passenger vehicles and cargo vehicles? Company employees could book passage on the firm's fleet of passenger vehicles, but the cargo planes, freight trains and delivery trucks are expressly prohibited from carrying passengers.

The information modeler might simply put an attribute in the *Vehicle* entity which indicates whether the vehicle is allowed to carry passengers. Under this scheme, the event model would contain the business policy for any event which needed to discriminate between passenger and non-passenger vehicles. In a non-object-oriented system, the application designer might add a stored procedure which enforces the business rule that cargo vehicles cannot participate in relationships which transport passengers. The interface would be coded such that only passenger vehicles appear on the user's list of available vehicles for booking passenger trips.

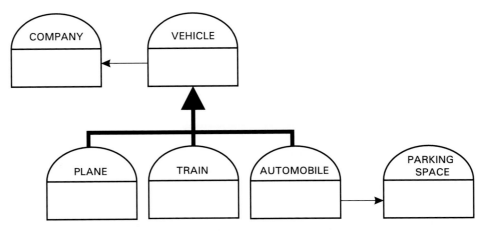

**Figure 12–14.** A class diagram of *Vehicle* superclass and its subclasses

In an object-oriented system, things can get far more complex. The designer may wish to isolate those behaviors of passenger vehicles or cargo vehicles into reusable classes. By employing multiple inheritance (the ability to inherit directly from more than one class),[11] the class designer can come up with a structure in which methods on each class apply to all instances of the class or subclasses (Figure 12–15).

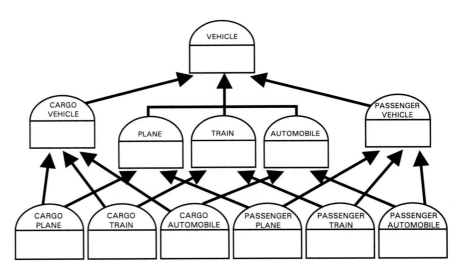

**Figure 12–15.** *Vehicle* subclassed to differentiate between *Passenger vehicle* and *Cargo vehicle*

---

[11] Multiple inheritance is not supported by all object-oriented languages.

On the surface, this might look like quite a mess. If passenger and cargo transportation is the core of our business, it might be entirely reasonable to create such a complex structure.[12] However, if transportation is only a small adjunct to a much larger business system, the class designer may decide that such complexity is unwarranted and collapse the structure of the class hierarchy back to our original *Vehicle*, *Plane*, *Train* and *Automobile* (Figure 12–14). This more simple hierarchy will necessitate a "type" variable in *Vehicle* which distinguishes whether an instance of vehicle is allowed to haul cargo or carry passengers, just as was done in the information model. Methods reserved for either type will need to respect the variable so as not to allow an operation which violates the business policy.

The lesson, once again, lies in the distinction between modeling data alone, and modeling data and process together. The information modeler is largely concerned with creating a flexible, non-redundant data structure that reduces the ripple effect of making changes to the database. The object class modeler is also concerned with creating flexible, non-redundant structures, but must consider both process and data, with the objective of isolating the ripple effect of making changes to the entire application. The database designer may make decisions based on efficiency of data access. The class designer may reach different conclusions based on reusability, maintainability, complexity and efficiency of the application code.

We have just examined some of the similarities and differences between entity types and their object-oriented counterparts, role classes. Let's move on to classes where object-orientation appears to depart further from traditional information modeling.

### Relationships in Class Models

Objects participate in relationships, much in the same way that data is related on the information model. Relationships between classes are grouped into three categories; *inheritance*, *aggregation* and *association*.

*Inheritance* is analogous to the information model's supertype/subtype relationship. The subclass object automatically inherits all of the variables and methods available to the superclass. The notation for inheritance is shown in Figure 12–16.

*Aggregation* is analogous to the header/detail kinds of relationships that are common fare in most business systems. An example is *Order* and *Order item* in a business where a customer may order many products at the same time. These classes will be acutely aware of each other. To implement an aggregation relationship, one object will hold the handle of the other object in its variables. An object of class *Order* might hold the handles of all of its *Order items*, or the *Order items* might hold the handle of its *Order*. In some cases, the designer may choose to implement the relationship with references in both directions. The aggregation relationship is shown in OODN by a normal thin arrow drawn between the objects. The direction of the arrow points from the object

---

[12] For those of you actually in the transportation business, I realize I have actually over-simplified this example.

which holds the handles back to the other object which it references. A bi-directional arrow indicates that both objects hold each other's handles. Users of OODN have found it convenient to place the variable name assigned to hold the object handle directly on the reference arrow, even though this violates the idea that an object's internal variables are hidden. The cardinality of the relationship can be annotated on either end of the line, (0..1, 1..1, 0..M, 1..M). It is read in the same order as an entity-relationship diagram. In Figure 12–17, you would read, *Order* aggregates one-to-many *Order items*.[13]

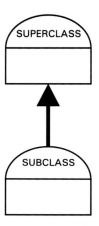

**Figure 12–16.** Inheritance notation

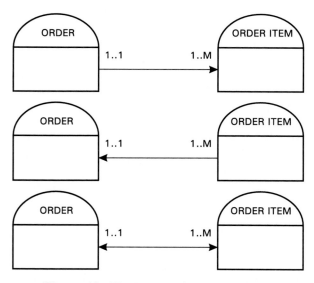

**Figure 12–17.** Aggregation relationship

---

[13] The 1..1 side of the relationship is often left off of the diagram because it is so common.

The last category of class relationship is *association*. Association is the weakest type of link between classes. An example of association is shown in Figure 12–18, our venerable example of "Person *currently owns* Dog." From the cardinality, we can deduce that our system is required to remember the dog's current owner, not the full history of dog ownership, making this relationship a "one-to-many." OODN does not make a distinction between aggregation and association in its notation. The same thin arrow is used to note the direction of the reference.

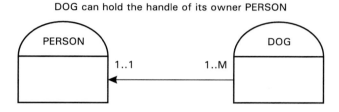

DOG can hold the handle of its owner PERSON

PERSON can hold the handles of its DOGS

**Figure 12–18.** Association relationship

In a relational database, the *Person ID* column would be embedded in the *Dog* table as a foreign key to implement the relationship. In an object-oriented system, a similar approach could be used by having the *Dog* object hold the *Person* handle of its owner, or have the *Person* object hold the handles of their dogs. We can surely rule out inheritance as a way to implement ownership. People aren't subclasses of dogs, and dogs aren't subclasses of people.[14] The relationship isn't one of aggregation. Dogs are not a component part of people, yet we have implemented the relationship in much the same way. Is this the only solution?

Co-mingling dog handles with *Person* or person handles with *Dog* degrades the reusability of both classes, especially if persons or dogs make other appearances in the system where they are not related. Another solution is to create a special *relationship class*, let's call it *Dog ownership*, which manages all of the policy for owning dogs (Figure 12–19).

The concept is similar to the associative entity type in information modeling, except here it is employed in one-to-many relationships as well. By using a relationship class, such

---

[14] Although I have met several dogs that would take issue with the last statement.

as *Dog ownership*, the *Dog* class is no longer burdened with people stuff, and the *People* class is no longer polluted with dog stuff, increasing the reusability of both classes.

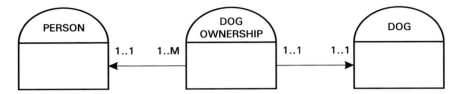

**Figure 12–19.** *Dog ownership* is a relationship class.

You can see that the information model provides a great deal of the classes that appear in the class model, but it is not always a straight transformation. Entities become role classes. Supertype/subtype relationships are indicative of inheritance, which may or may not include all of the same levels articulated in the information model. Relationships can also be promoted to become classes to manage the policy of the relationship and insulate the participating classes from having to know too much about each other.

Even attributes can become classes. For example, an attribute such as *Customer credit balance* might be implemented as a class, coupling the business rules regarding customers that exceed their limits with the data itself.

## Deriving Application Classes from the Event Model

The information model, alone, is not enough to derive a class model for an object-oriented design. The object-oriented designer can systematically account for all of the data in the information model by allocating it to its best home in the class design. He must also account for all of the processing requirements stated in the activity section of each event dictionary entry by allocating them to their most appropriate home as methods on the object-oriented model.

Each statement in the activity section represents some piece of processing that needs to occur within the system in order to transform the event stimuli into the appropriate responses. The information model gives you the data side, the event model articulates the business rules and processing requirements. We saw that many of the transformations from information model to class model were fairly straightforward, as in the case of entity type to role class. Likewise, the allocation of event activity to methods has both straightforward transformations as well as more complicated design issues.

Many of the processes specified in the event dictionary are simple create, read, update and delete statements that are executed on the system's entity types. For the bulk of these statements, they can be handled by methods which are allocated directly to the corresponding role, relationship and attribute classes which were derived from the information model.

For example, an event such as *Marketing Department sets new product price* would have activity which includes the statement:

"create new instance of product price."

The policy for this business activity is likely to be simple enough to be managed entirely within the methods of the role class *Product price*, setting the price value and effective date and inserting a new row in the database.

### Event Manager Classes

Let's take a look at an event who's activity doesn't fit neatly into the classes derived from the information model. The event *Customer places order* at a typical company might have an activity section that looks something like this:

```
If Customer does not exist in database
    Create new instance of Customer
End if
Create an instance of Order
For each Product ordered
    Create an instance of Order item
    Check Product availability
    If Product unavailable
        Create an instance of Back-order item
    End if
End for each
Calculate Sales tax
Calculate Total price
```

It is safe to surmise that the information model, at minimum, contains entity types for *Customer*, *Product*, *Order*, *Order item* and *Back-order item*, and that corresponding role classes have been identified for an object-oriented design. Our mission is to allocate the activity in the event activity to the most appropriate methods on the various classes. Which method should manage the policy for placing orders?

CUSTOMER.Place-Order?

ORDER.New?

PRODUCT.Order-Me?

The answer is none of the above. The process of placing an order requires a conspiracy of many objects at runtime to execute the policy. You may need to create a new instance of *Customer*, you will be creating a new *Order* and new instances of *Order item*, checking availability of *Products* and possibly creating *Back-order items*. The *Customer* object has no business monkeying around with *Back-orders*, any more than the *Product* object has any business demanding the creation of a new *Customer*. The solution is to create a new type of class, called the *event manager* class, (or event-activity-manager) which acts as a director, coordinating the activities of many other classes to execute the business policy for the event. The result can be expressed in an *object-communication diagram* (sometimes called an *event-trace diagram* or *dynamic object model*) such as the one in Figure 12–20 which shows the messaging between the event manager and its co-conspirators for the event *Customer places order*.

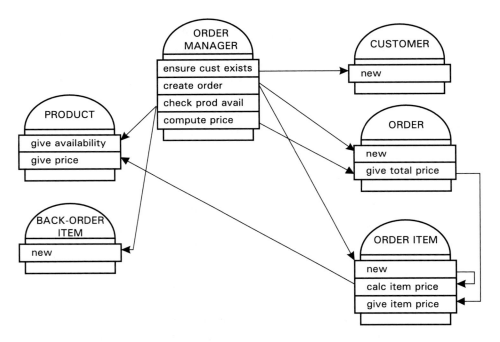

**Figure 12–20.** Object-communication diagram for *Customer places order*

The event manager class is very much like the "boss module" of structured design, which may have had no explicit counterpart in the essential model, but was required in the design to enforce the processing sequence of the modules which executed the business policy. Hence, we have a group of classes which appear on in the object-oriented design which are not evident in the information model. Not every event will require the creation of an event manager. A fair number of your events can probably be managed by the good offices of methods placed directly on the classes derived from the information model. Event managers are employed for events where a variety of objects must be coordinated, and there is no single best home within any of the existing classes to house the coordinating policy. If placing the event management policy in an existing class degrades the generic reusability of that class or encumbers that class with too much knowledge of its neighbors, then an event manager class should probably be hired to relieve the management burden from your business domain classes.

This technique results in cleaner business domain classes that are more likely to be reusable across applications within the same type of enterprise or industry. The event manager classes fall into the application domain because they execute policy specific to the application chartered to manage that business event, and are therefore highly specialized classes with very low reusability.

### Event Recognizer Classes

If you recall in Chapter 4, I mentioned a special kind of event called the *temporal* event. Temporal events are time-triggered, and the most common type of indirectly recognized events which occur in business information systems. They occur on a specific schedule, firing off their activity either on an absolute clock, or at a time relative to another event. Other indirectly recognized events include those which are triggered in systems due to changes in the environment, such as pressure or temperature.

Unlike directly recognized events, which usually are triggered by a human manipulating the interface, indirectly recognized events require some mechanism which monitors the environment to see if the event has occurred. It should come as no surprise that in an object-oriented system, these process are allocated to the *event recognizer* classes.

Like the event managers, the event recognizer classes have no counterpart on the information model. Instead, it is the existence of an indirectly recognized event in your event model which tells you that you need to design a class capable of recognizing that the event has occurred. The resulting pattern is shown in Figure 12–21. An event recognizer acts as the monitor, watching the environment and checking its input against its set points. When the event recognizer decides that the event has happened, it notifies the appropriate event manager which then takes over the coordination of the business classes required to execute the event activity.

Now let's leave object-orientation behind for a bit, and take a look at more traditional constructs that you are likely to encounter in today's client/server systems. The first is the database trigger and stored procedure for the relational database. The second is structured design, a venerable technique for organizing code written in traditional 3GL languages.

## MODELING TRIGGERS AND STORED PROCEDURES

One of the most common type of internal component in today's client/server system is the stored procedure. Stored procedures are processes which are executed on the server directly by the application or when specific actions are detected in the relational database. The mechanism which detects that a relevant action has occurred is called a *trigger*, or sometimes a *rule*.

Triggers and stored procedures are widely supported by most relational database management systems. Here's how they work. A trigger is defined on a database table or columns within a table to look for specific actions. Triggers monitor inserts, updates and deletes within the database, waiting to fire off stored procedures when the predefined action occurs.

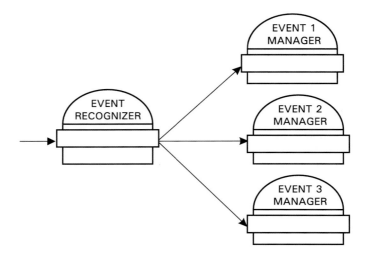

**Figure 12–21.** The event recognizer pattern

Triggers and stored procedures can be used for a wide variety of the activities specified in the event model that may be allocated to the server. Figure 12–22 shows some examples of triggers and stored procedures used in business systems. The first example is a trigger which detects the insert of an order for a particular type of product that requires the product-line manager's attention. When the database detects that the order item is inserted, the system sends a notification to the appropriate manager. In the second example, the trigger fires when an update to the inventory balance causes the inventory to fall below the reorder point. In this example, the system is chartered to automatically place an order to refresh the inventory. In the last example, the trigger is designed to keep a calculated column stored in the *Sales plan* header table current when any of the detail rows which affect the total are inserted, updated or deleted.

Triggers and their associated stored procedures should be specified with enough detail to convey the rule and associated actions accurately to the designer. The first step is to comb through the activity section of your event dictionaries and determine which processes are appropriate for execution by procedures on the database. The specification should include two parts, the conditions which detect that action is required and the action that should be taken. In many shops, the plain English text used to specify the triggers and procedures in the design spec is copied and pasted directly into the source code as comments for future maintenance programmers, so they can quickly understand the intent of the code.

Another vital piece of the design which should be retained for the on-going maintenance of the system is a listing which relates all of the triggers and procedures installed in the system to the tables and actions or remote procedure calls that could fire them. When making modifications to a system, you can encounter some rather nasty surprises if you are unaware of which triggers might be lurking in the dark, waiting to pounce on your new insert, update or delete. To avoid such anarchy, the designers and programmers should always be able to get their hands on a current listing of the triggers in place. Many relational database management systems can generate a listing for you, such as the one in Figure 12–23, or at least give you access to their system tables so you can code your own list.

| Trigger (rule) | Procedure (Action to be taken) |
|---|---|
| On insert of an order_item for any product where the product_type = "specialty" | Notify the product-line manager |
| On update of inventory.balance where inventory.balance falls below product.re-order_point | Generate product re-order |
| On insert of sales_plan_detail, or on update of sales_plan_detail.projected _revenue, or on delete of sales_plan _detail | Recalculate sales_plan.total_projected_revenue |

**Figure 12–22.** Sample triggers and procedures

| Table | Column | Ins | Upd | Del | Trigger | Procedure |
|---|---|---|---|---|---|---|
| Customer | - | X | | | New-customer | Notify-credit-manager |
| Order item | Product type | X | | | Specialty-product | Notify-product-manager |
| Inventory item | Current balance | | X | | Low-inventory | Create-inventory-order |
| Sales detail | Projected revenue | X | X | X | Sales-detail-change | Recalc-total-revenue |
| Shipment item | Quantity | | X | | Quantity-change | Notify-plant-manager |

**Figure 12–23.** Database table/triggers and procedures listing

# STRUCTURED DESIGN

The concepts of structured design, conceived by Larry Constantine in the late 1960s, and introduced to a wide audience in the 1970s and 1980s,[15] form a foundation of design principles that I consider to be core competencies for any designer or programmer working in

---

[15] Yourdon, Constantine, 1979 and Page-Jones, 1980.

the 1990s and beyond. There is no way to reduce the richness of this topic down to a fortune cookie message to finish off this chapter, but please allow me to pass briefly through the major concepts. While you are reading this section, if the terms and techniques are not immediately familiar, may I recommend that you find one of the books on structured design listed in the bibliography and brush up on the principles of good structured system design.

The basic principle of structured design centers around the idea that programs, or procedural code can be broken up into logical units called modules, which execute specific functions and can be identified and referred to by name. We all know this as the familiar internal subroutine or call to an external program. Modules operate on the concept of the black box. To invoke a module, you must know its input parameters, output parameters and its intended functionality, but you do not need to know how it does its job.

Structured design suggests that there is a method to the madness when it comes to assembling modules to create a working application. Modules can be used to partition a large procedure into smaller units that are individually more understandable than a mammoth screed of code. Additionally, procedures which are executed many times, or by multiple programs within the application can be moved off to a common module library, thus reusable code is born.

The graphic notation used for structured design is the structure chart (Figure 12–24). Structure charts show modules as rectangular boxes with the module name in the center. The arrows on the structure chart show the direction of the module call. An arrow from module A to module B indicates that somewhere in the code of module A resides a statement that gives module A the authority to call module B. Because that call may be located within a conditional statement, you cannot guarantee that module A will call module B every time it is executed. The "cannon balls" with arrows denote the parameters or couples which pass into the called module and return from it (input parameters point down on the left, output parameters point up on the right). In addition to the graphical structure chart, each module on the diagram is accompanied by an internal module specification, which is a pseudo-code articulation of the processing required to turn the module inputs into the outputs.

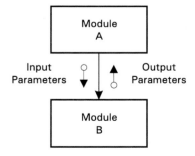

**Figure 12–24.** Structured design notation

Two crucial criteria to emerge from the discipline of structured design were the concepts of *coupling* and *cohesion*. Coupling measures the complexity of the traffic that passes between modules. Cohesion measures how well the functions within the module are related. The goal is to achieve modules with low coupling and high cohesion. Low coupling is an indication that the modules are less interdependent and therefore more resilient to changes made to the application. Highly cohesive modules which perform a single definable function are more likely to be reusable. They show a stronger degree of procedural encapsulation that will further reduce the ripple effect of making program modifications.

It is no coincidence that these ideas sound strangely familiar as you examine the criteria for good object-oriented design. The goal of strong object encapsulation goes hand-in-hand with lowering superfluous message traffic, and achieving method definitions that are highly cohesive both internally and to the class to which they have been assigned.

## SUMMARY

The structure of the internal design should reflect the structure of the intended system. Object-oriented components require object-oriented design techniques. Database triggers and stored procedures require a specification that closely maps to their morphology. Similarly, the specification for traditional procedural code should utilize a notation which is relevant for its language paradigm.

A design specification should include constructs which depict the overall organization of the components. For object-oriented designs, this is provided by a *Class model* which shows class inheritance, aggregation and association relationships. In structured designs, this is provided by the *structure chart*. For database stored procedures, a listing of the tables, triggers and rules will often suffice.

The design technique should also be capable of depicting the collaboration of components at run time. In structured design, this is handled by showing the parameters passed for module coupling on the structure chart. In object-oriented designs, the *object-communication diagram* shows the messaging that occurs between objects for a specific business event in our event suite.

For each construct shown as an abstract symbol on any graphic notation, the design specification is not complete without a written specification for the internal code. This allows the project team to review both the architecture and the detail of a given design prior to its construction, and it gives the project manager the option of partitioning the work among multiple programmers.

The business and application domain classes for an object-oriented design can be derived from the information model and event models. The information model will translate into role classes, relationship classes, and some attribute classes. The event model provides the process specification for the methods which are allocated to the most appropriate classes. Some events will require the creation of event manager classes to coordinate the activities of multiple classes. Indirectly recognized events will also require the services of event recognizer classes.

Much of this chapter is devoted to the basics of object-orientation. You can see that OO brings many new concepts to the design table, but is also rooted heavily in design practices of the past. Today's client/server systems are a mixed bag of language paradigms, struggling to present a seamless face to the user. Most designers will find themselves having to embrace object-oriented, relational and traditional design constructs in order to bring together all of the components present in today's corporate systems.

## EXERCISES

1. What are the differences between business domain classes and application domain classes? From which models are they most likely to be derived?

2. Code reusability is often touted as a primary benefit of object-orientation. Can you think of a project situation where reusability should definitely *not* be a prime quality vector? *(Hint: The vague question indicator is in the "on" position this time.)*

3. How does a class differ from an entity type?

4. J. Rupert, Sr. was a COBOL programmer who gained fame at the General Adhesion Corporation in the mid-1970s by altering the *fiscal-to-gregorian-calendar-coversion* routine in the common library one night without telling anyone. While his own program ran more efficiently, his actions also resulted in an erroneous declaration by another program of spectacular fourth quarter earnings for the company which, once publicly rescinded, sent stock prices tumbling. His son, J. Rupert, Jr. now works as a developer on an object-oriented client/server system at General Adhesion Corporation. Late one night, he altered the *Fiscal calendar* class, changing the structure in which it stores its internal variables, but leaving the class' external messaging the same. Following family tradition, he then re-released the code back into production without telling anyone. Is J. Rupert, Jr. in trouble?

## ANSWERS

1. Business domain classes are primarily derived from the information model. They represent constructs which might be reusable within the same industry, such as *Customer, Bank account, Inventory item*, and *Order*. Application domain classes are those which play the role of event manager or even recognizer. They are primarily derived from the event model, and are very specific to an application or particular business task. They are least likely of any class to be reused.

2. Reusability should not be a consideration if you either have no time, opportunity or intention to reuse anything. I recently saw a client/server project which attempted to employ object-oriented principles for the first time at their shop. The project team members were bright, intelligent developers who were devoted to the concept of creating re-usable software components. They spent over a year creating an elegant class library and object-oriented design, yet failed to deliver the system in the prescribed time frame. Consequently, the project was shut down. As it turned out, the system they were to develop was slated to be replaced again within *three years* by a large integrated package system. Going back to the idea of stating the quality vectors in the project charter, the *immediacy of need* for the new system, and its relatively *short life expectancy* were in direct conflict with the idea of spending the time to create reusable components. The added up-front cost of creating reusability isn't recouped until you reuse those components either later in the same project, or on subsequent projects. This project would have served the business better if the developers had focused on getting a working application delivered, rather than attempting to achieve the most elegant internal design.

3. Entity types contain only the data attributes of the person, place, thing or abstract idea about which the system needs to remember something. Classes have not only attributes, expressed as variables on the class, but they also have methods which represent the processes which have been allocated to the class. Entity types must also respect the concepts of normalization, where classes are not so compelled.

4. Thanks to the miracle of encapsulation and information/implementation hiding, J. Rupert Jr.'s late night antics are unlikely to affect any other part of the application. His actions, however, are inexcusable. Undocumented and uncontrolled alteration of production class libraries, in my opinion, is an offense punishable by dismissal of either the miscreant perpetrator, or the asleep-at-the-wheel manager who allows such a dangerous situation to fester. It would appear that Mr. Rupert's shop is not yet ready for the discipline and rigor required to manage object-oriented systems. Furthermore, J. Rupert, Jr. might want to encourage his children to take up a career in interpretive dance, where the family's brand of spontaneity and creativity will be more appreciated.

# CHAPTER
# 13

# TEN MYTHS OF CLIENT/SERVER DEVELOPMENT

## INTRODUCTION

I think it appropriate to finish this book with a few words for managers of client/server projects. For those of you in the project manager's chair, my heart goes out to you. You are really caught in the middle of the maelstrom, getting conflicting advice, pressure, instruction and coercion from all sides. Vendors are trying to sell you their particular brand of "Magic-in-a-Box." Programmers are champing at the bit to code up their latest cool idea. The analysts sent forth to map the wilderness of the business haven't been seen or heard from in months. Users are demanding that the software be delivered yesterday, however they can't tell you what they want it to do. (They'll know when they get it.) And your boss . . . let's not forget the infernal Grinch that gave you only half the people and a fraction of the budget that you need to save the business from certain annihilation.

What's a poor manager to do? Well, I can't make you adore your boss, or guarantee you a front parking spot, but I can add to the din with some advice of my own.

Every new technology is ushered in with its own hype and promises which quickly mutate into the stuff of folklore and legend. Client/server certainly isn't immune to such campfire chatter. In this chapter, I offer my response to the most common misconceptions that I have heard uttered in the hallowed halls of software development over the last few years. Some of these myths are new and original to the client/server revolution. Others you will recognize as the same old tired promises dredged up with each new entry into the technology pool.

Without further ado, bring on *Dave's Top Ten Myths of Client/Server Development*.

## MYTH 1: "CLIENT/SERVER TECHNOLOGY WILL MAKE USERS MORE PRODUCTIVE."

This type of sweeping promise is the genesis of unreasonable and divergent expectations for any project. The correct claim is, "Client/server technology *can* enable users to be more productive." Client/server systems are commonly used to bring information capture closer to the source, and information output closer to the people who need it, thus increasing productivity. The enabling technology can bring change to the business, and with any change, there are winners and losers. Be careful to be quite specific as to who are the winners and who are the losers with your project.

I have seen cases where misapplied client/server technology actually lowered productivity. Take for instance, the case of the heads-down data entry department. Replacing the mnemonic-driven green screen application with a multi-window graphical user interface, replete with drop-down lists and menu items probably isn't going to win you any lasting friends in this group. If their prime quality vector is *speed of entry*, a GUI may severely slow them down. You have to ask yourself, "Why does data entry exist in the first place? Shouldn't the application attempt to capture data closer to the source, at say, the remote sales offices?"

If the answer to that question is "yes," then you're into a significant re-engineering of responsibilities in your organization. Client/server technology will now be employed to allow the sales offices to enter data directly into the computer rather than fill out lengthy data entry forms. The overall productivity of the firm may be raised, in fact, you may have eliminated the entire data entry department. Out at the sales offices, however, the individual productivity of the salesperson or the salesperson's administrative assistant may appear to go down. They're spending a great deal more time on their PCs! It may have been faster for them to scribble down notes on a paper form than to actually have to take responsibility for entering the information accurately into the system. From the viewpoint within the sales department, they are spending more time with each order. The view from the top, however, shows a net gain in efficiency across the entire organization.

A project manager needs to carefully manage user expectation. This comes back to having a strong project charter that is the joint effort of the IT department and the affected parties in the organization. With a clear charter, the project manager can continue to remind users what their future roles and responsibilities will be when the software is installed. Without the charter, the project is wide open to political attack from people who may find themselves spending more time on the new system than they imagined, or worse, flipping burgers at the local lunch counter.

The second myth is actually three myths in one.

## MYTH 2.1: "CLIENT/SERVER IS CHEAP."

Wrong again. The shift to a client/server architecture cannot be measured by the cost of the hardware alone. There are tremendous retraining costs to move a shop from mainframe programming to client/server development. It is estimated that anywhere from twenty to forty percent of the mainframe personnel will opt out of the new environment and never make the transition. Long learning curves, insufficient in-house skills, and the prospect of significant turnover and the loss of many long-term employees can add substantial new costs.

## Myth 2.2: "We can use the new system to force improvements in the business process."

Perhaps the biggest hidden cost for the introduction of client/server systems is the cost to re-engineer the business. Almost every client/server system brings with it some degree of change. Often that change is significant. Several years back, two companies in similar lines of business embarked on roughly identical client/server systems at the same time. Each system brought with it sweeping organizational changes.

In one company, they had prepared for the new system by meeting among themselves and coming to consensus on how to conduct business, re-engineering and documenting their business before attempting to automate it. In the other company, they decided to let the IT department negotiate changes to the business, if need be, as they analyzed and designed the software for each functional area.

Guess which project finished first? Guess which business was happiest with the new software? The differences in the cost of development and acceptance of the software were dramatic. The business which took the time to come to consensus and define its future vision was poised, prepared and ready for automation. Everybody knew what their future role would be in the organization. The development effort went smoothly, and the users generally got what they expected out of the new system.

The business which didn't come to consensus about its future structure attempted to use the software development process as an excuse to bring about change. The development team was seen as the perpetrators and disrupters of the status quo. Their efforts were met with hostile resistance at every step, entailing countless months of hasty retreat and rework. All other things being equal, the project took several years longer than it should have. In the end, the users were unable to separate the sins visited upon them by the organizational change from the sins visited upon them by the software. The result was that many of them openly derided and downright hated the new system.

## Myth 2.3: "Hardware costs will go down."

Software costs aren't the only surprise. Even hardware costs can go up instead of down. Some early promises of down-sizing computers by moving to client/server have not always panned out. In one organization, it was thought that the old mini-computer would have more than enough firepower to act as the new database server for their client/server environment. After all, almost all of the processing was being moved off to the desktop. All that's left is the database, right? Two factors proved their assumption wrong. The first was the fact that the new software made requests of the database far more frequently than the old green screens, so each individual user placed higher demands on the central server than before. The second "problem" was that the new software was overwhelmingly popular. In the good old days of the old system, just a few elite people used the computer. Now, almost everybody in the organization demanded and received the new system on their PC. The number of concurrent users skyrocketed, and the business had to make an emergency upgrade of the server machine to handle the load. A modicum of architectural modeling would have helped them anticipate this problem in advance of the crisis.

## MYTH 3: "PC STANDS FOR PERSONAL COMPUTER."

PC actually stands for "Property of the Company." The personal computer isn't so personal when it becomes the home of the core business applications. The desktop computers become an integral part of the entire corporate computing asset, and their purchase and configuration needs to be tightly controlled. It seems that each organization has its own version of "Rupert the software junkie," a mid-to-high level manager who can't help but download anything free off the Internet. He comes in on weekends and loads "Ballistic Plasma-Eating Ants" on his PC to entertain his kids while he works on the budget. On Monday, he places an irate call to the help desk because none of the corporate applications seem to work and his printer prints nothing but ants. A quick survey of his hard drive shows that the plasma-eating ants ate a good portion of his system files and print drivers. No amount of reprimand seems to move Rupert to change his wicked ways. The next week, similar damage is wrought by his new dancing lizard screen saver.

Many companies have taken control of the situation by initiating penalties when users foul up their PCs. Sanctions range anywhere from monetary charge-backs to the department for repair or re-installation of the corporate software to the subtle forces of public humiliation. Some firms who have not been able to gain the upper hand have gone as far as removing the floppy drives from the desktop computers, and severely limiting Internet access. Even with moderate configuration controls in place, it is not unusual to find two seemingly identical PCs, not more than ten feet apart, that exhibit radically different anomalies when running the corporate client/server applications. IT departments who are unable to exert their influence over the management of desktop environment may find their client/server initiatives mired in anarchy.

## MYTH 4: "IT'S EASY TO BUILD WINDOWS USING THESE NEW RAD TOOLS."

This myth is partially true. It is very easy to build windows using the fancy RAD development tools on the market. Whether those windows accomplish anything of significance within the business is an entirely different matter.

This myth is openly perpetuated by many of the GUI development tool vendors. At a recent conference, three client/server development tool vendors staged a "race" involving three expert programmers, each using a different GUI tool. At the start of the race, the officiating salesperson handed out an identical specification for a simple order entry application and told the programmers to code a set of working windows. The audience watched the ensuing clicking frenzy with breathless anticipation. Meanwhile, the salesperson lauded the advantages of rapid development. After forty-two minutes, the first programmer leapt to his feet in victory, followed in quick succession by the other two.

When the ecstatic audience calmed down, the salesperson strode triumphantly to the podium and said, "Of course, you probably won't be able to code an entire application in forty-two minutes. Your problems are slightly more complex. It might take you an entire day." To avoid the stampede of project managers rushing to buy their copies of the software, my colleague ducked behind the demonstration PCs. What he saw on the screen was curious. None of the applications looked at all alike. There were dramatic differences in style, font, layout and navigation between them. Likewise, there were no edits in place. You could save the customer's name in the phone number field. You could exit one window without saving, leaving orphan pop-up windows with uncommitted data. In other words, these applications would never pass even the most rudimentary testing. What the demonstration had proven was that you could very quickly draw something that looks like a window. Building a working business application is entirely another matter.

Experience has shown that on real projects, it takes significant effort to code complex applications in the GUI environment. Even with a robust class library of reusable objects and a stringent, detailed design specification, it is not unusual for a single window, and all of its functionality, to spend many days to several weeks on the programmer's desk. When estimating the construction phase of a project, I never estimate less than a day for coding even the most rudimentary single-table windows. Using a great deal of inheritance, the window itself may take only fifteen minutes to produce, however, experience has shown that it is likely to undergo testing, tweaking and minor modifications for the remainder of the day. Complex windows, with lots of buttons, multiple table joins and several background functions can take days and weeks to code, even when you have a tight design spec. Without the design spec, the construction effort is almost impossible to estimate.

So, why does reality differ so dramatically from the vendor's claims? I think the answer lies in two places. First, these GUI tools are fantastically complex. Once you get past the basics, it becomes a full time job to master the tool and keep up with the features piled on in each new release. Second, most businesses demand a high level of sophistication and integrity from their GUI applications. This software is the core of their business. You are expected to produce applications on a shoe-string budget that look and perform every bit as good as off-the-shelf products that cost millions to develop.

The best way to combat this problem is to keep your own metrics. Measure the time it takes to do analysis, design, construction and testing for each functional area of the application. You then have a basis on which you can estimate future projects. For example, you can divide the hours it took to design each application by the number of windows produced. You then have an "hours per window" metric for design that can be applied to similar projects. Do the same with the analysis, coding and testing hours to get their respective averages. You don't have to use the number of windows as your basis either. You can divide by the number of entities, function points, business classes, or any other relevant deliverable that is indicative of system size.

Then the next time someone promises you "faster, better, cheaper,"[1] you can ask them to show you their metrics for business problems similar to those which confront your shop and have them quantify the expected improvements in each phase of the development life cycle. To improve productivity in analysis, you must increase the speed at which people accurately understand, agree, articulate and document the nature of the problem. To increase productivity in design, you must be able to increase a person's ability to devise and communicate a solution. Coding productivity is usually achieved by (1) knowing what code to write, (2) writing less code, and (3) writing code which works. Testing only becomes easier when the tester has a clear directive of what to test, and when testing produces few errors.

## MYTH 5: "THE NEXT VERSION OF THE DEVELOPMENT TOOLS WILL FIX OUR CURRENT PROBLEMS."

While I'm taking development tool vendors to task for the manner in which their products are marketed, I might as well say something about the way they are developed. I shall probably get my membership card to the Clickey Mouse Club revoked for this, but managers need to be aware of this problem.

In the glory days of the mainframe, the development languages, databases and operating systems were relatively stable. For example, COBOL wasn't exactly rewritten every eighteen months. You might see a comet come around again before the next version. You could rest assured that any new release of the development language would be fairly well tested. The integrity of your mainframe systems relied on the integrity of the development environment.

Today's client/server environment is a hodgepodge of databases, GUI languages, network middleware and various operating systems. It is not uncommon to have at least three different operating systems in the same client/server architecture. These operating systems, database management systems, GUI development tools and communications software undergo rewrites and version upgrades constantly. Many installed client/server projects figure that every eighteen months they will need to migrate some portion of their system to a new version.

The problem lies in the integrity of the version upgrades. The disruption to a project, and even an entire company, can be significant when unexpected bugs crop up in the "new and improved" version. Some version upgrades go smoothly. Others are a nightmare. *Time to market* seems to have replaced *reliability* as the prime quality vector for releasing new versions of the development tools. The bugs you learned to work around on the old version are replaced by a new host of anomalies in the new version. The "fix disk" that provides the patch for the problems in version 3.124 often re-introduces problems that were fixed in version 3.123. Users of your installed applications do not take kindly to these surprises. They

---

[1]   With "faster, better, cheaper," you usually can only achieve any two of the three.

are not happy when software that worked one day is broken the next, and make no distinction between bugs introduced by the vendor versus bugs introduced by the IT staff.

The vendors aren't entirely to blame for this situation. The customer base is letting it happen. Vendors are engaged in a cut-throat battle to get the latest features added to their software before the next round of trade shows. Buyers remain eager and willing to heap millions of dollars on vendors offering new functionality, making companies that can crank out slick new development products the darlings of Wall Street.

The problem is that the core business systems of the world are now running on these platforms. The market needs to start demanding a level of integrity from the products that is commensurate with the risk of failure or disruption of service. Until that day, you will find yourself proceeding at your own peril if you are among the first to undergo migration of your applications to the latest versions of the development and operating environments.

"In view of recent adverse publicity, all future references to the term, 'Maiden Voyage' shall be replaced with 'Version 1.0 Beta'."

Let's give the vendors a rest and turn our attention back to the strange things that happen within the software development team.

## MYTH 6: "THE MANAGER DOESN'T NEED TO KNOW THE METHODOLOGY."

I have had managers tell me that they don't need to know the details of the development methodology. "I'm a *manager*," they say. "A good manager can manage *anything*. It doesn't matter *what* they're managing." When you hear this type of proclamation, don't walk, *run* to the nearest exit and find yourself a project where the manager knows what's going on.

It's like saying that a general contractor or construction project manager doesn't need to know how to build a house. While it's not necessary that the project manager be a master at executing the techniques in the methodology, he had better have a firm grasp on the purpose and sequence of each technique. A manager needs to be able to determine that the person to which he delegated a task is qualified. He needs to be able to ask the right questions to divine whether progress is being made along the way. The good manager also uses the models to make estimates of the project's size and required level of effort. He then manages against those estimates by comparing the progress of the real models to the estimate. Let's not forget the issues list either (see Chapter 7). The project manager takes personal responsibility for business issues. His primary role is to remove roadblocks and enable his team to move as quickly as possible.

Without a solid grasp of the specifics of the development process, the project manager has nothing to do but sign time sheets, print the schedule and announce the passage of time. If your project needs someone to sign time sheets, print schedules and announce the passage of time, that's fine. Just don't call him the manager if that's all he does. What you will find in these situations is that someone else on the project, usually a technical lead, has quietly taken over the responsibilities of managing the project on a day-to-day basis. Unfortunately, he's not getting paid for it. The manager, for his part, will usually declare that he has instituted a "self-managed-work-group," which is often a code phrase for "I have no idea what they do all day." Projects which succeed under these conditions are usually the result of a manager who has the good sense to stay out of the way of his team.

## MYTH 7: "WE DON'T HAVE TO DO ANY OF THIS ANALYSIS AND DESIGN STUFF BECAUSE WE'RE GOING TO PURCHASE PACKAGES RATHER THAN BUILD SYSTEMS."

This myth is a recent phenomenon which stems from the notion that all of the world's great information systems have already been developed and are available on the open market. Instead of building systems, the company makes a strategic decision to buy them.

The idea of purchasing systems is a fine one. "Since we are going to buy it, we don't have to code it." That's a relatively benign statement that makes perfect sense. What often happens next, however, is a string of assertions that lead to a breakdown in the logic. "Since we don't have to code it, we don't have to design it," leads to, "Since we don't have to design it, we don't have to analyze it." Now the train of reason has run off the rails.

If you don't have a document that clearly expresses the business need, you have no basis for making a purchasing decision. Actually, to be more precise, purchasing decisions are made every day based on a vague set of bullet points provided by the business and repeated assurances by the vendor. What is missing is any way to *measure* the difference between what the package *does* and what the business *requires* it to do.

So, how much of this analysis and design "stuff" do you have to do when purchasing a business system rather than building one? Let's run through some of the techniques covered in this book and see how they apply.

You still need a charter. The business must define the desired benefit of a new system so you have something against which costs can be measured. Don't forget to include *custom build* and *status quo* in the solution options. It may turn out that no package meets your needs and it might in fact be cheaper to build something after all.

A context model is extremely useful for purchasing software. The context model points out all of the affected business units and all of the other systems with which the purchased software will have to converse. The context model will tell you whether the intended package is truly a stand-alone application, or if it is heavily intermingled with your other corporate applications. The implication of the latter is that the internal structure of that package becomes extremely important if you require it to work in an open environment where other systems need access to the package's data. Packaged software can no longer be evaluated simply as a black box where you don't care how tangled its inner workings are as long as it does its job.

The event model is an excellent way to organize the behavioral and processing requirements for a purchased system. The event list provides both the business and the vendor with a detailed check list of all of the business events to which the package is chartered to respond. The event dictionary articulates the information that the new package is expected to consume, and tells the vendor what the business believes is an appropriate response for each stimulus. The activity section of the event dictionary need not be as detailed as it would for custom development since it is not anticipated that you will have to code or alter a great deal of the package.

A good information model is *vital* to the evaluation of a package. Your information model is a map of the facts your business must remember. If the package doesn't remember the same facts, or has major cardinality differences, it will be most apparent when comparing the information model to the package. Differences in data content, structure, and cardinality are some of the most expensive things to change, either in the package or in the business. For instance, if the package only allows one shipment per invoice, and your customers are happily receiving multi-shipment invoices from your old system, you are faced with some difficult decisions. You may elect to make custom modifications to the package and thereby forfeit the ability to receive future upgrades from the vendor. You might have enough clout to persuade the vendor to make the change to their standard package (of course your competitors will also get the feature as well). Failing those options, you could assess the impact on your business and your customers of changing the way you do business.

The information model defines the current shape of your business. By comparing it to the shape of the package, you can choose the package which best fits your business. Where there are differences, you have a basis for measuring the cost of changing the package versus the impact of changing the business.

If you decide to change the package, then the essential analysis models give you a basis for prototyping and creating an external and internal design specification for the changes. The event model and information models, combined with the geographical distribution of the business sites, provide you with the basis for deploying the package across the organization and allow you to assess the trade-offs of various centralized or distributed architectures that might be available to you.

Without proper analysis of the business need, and design of software or business changes, the introduction of packaged software is often a mine field of surprises for all involved.

## MYTH 8: "STRUCTURED WALKTHROUGHS WERE ONLY FOR STRUCTURED ANALYSIS AND STRUCTURED DESIGN."

Not so. The need for walkthroughs and reviews is more pressing than ever in today's complex development environment.

Imagine that you are an airplane pilot, flying your passenger jet non-stop from Seattle to Boston across the United States. The first phase of the flight plan is scheduled to take you over Billings, Montana. If you are on course and on time, the second phase should take you over Chicago within the next few hours. After Chicago is sighted, you're home-free on your way to Boston.

Now imagine that you have absolutely no guidance instruments and zero visibility! Your radio will allow you to contact Billings and Chicago only when you get very near those cities. Your only chance to reach your destination is to take off from Seattle with your plane pointed in the direction of Billings. Around the time you should be approaching Billings, you must check the radio to see if Billings is anywhere to be found. If you make radio contact, you know it is safe to proceed to Chicago. If you don't hail Billings, you must decide whether to circle around, losing precious time and fuel, or proceed eastward at your own risk.

Project reviews which occur only at the end of the analysis and design phases are very much like flying blind for a period of time and then turning on your radio to see if you are anywhere near the checkpoint. While "end-of-phase" reviews are delightful for celebrating important milestones in the project, they are utterly useless when it comes to making meaningful course corrections. The time allotted for the phase has already elapsed, and if the project is found to be off track, it must either circle back, losing time and money, or continue forward at great risk.

In reality, airplanes are almost always off course by some small amount. The on-board navigational equipment makes constant adjustments to keep the plane flying toward its destination. Likewise, a project needs a means to take measurements and make constant adjustments as it progresses towards its deadline. These adjustments are made by engendering a culture of consistent and continuous walkthroughs.

A walkthrough (or *structured* walkthrough[2]) is a set of rules and roles that are used to conduct peer group reviews of any work product. Walkthroughs should be frequent, non-threatening and informal. They should be so commonplace on a development project that they become part of the development culture. Here's how they work.

Every work product, from the charter, analysis models, and design models to the finished code should undergo some level of walkthrough. Anyone on the development team can initiate a walkthrough at any time. It doesn't matter if the work is finished or not. The purpose of the walkthrough is to spot errors in the product and validate it for correctness. The walkthrough must NEVER be used to evaluate the author's performance. If the project manager bases performance evaluation on walkthrough results, the shop will never have another honest walkthrough again.

The participants in a walkthrough include peers of the author and representatives of the target audience for the document. For analysis walkthroughs, I like to include other analysts, designers, programmers, and even some testers. This gives the down-stream specialists forewarning of the type of applications that will be coming their way. I tend to separate user reviews from technical reviews, because the focus of the two groups vary widely. The author's manager is only invited to the walkthrough if he can remain neutral. If he can't, then he can be tossed out.

People play different roles in the walkthrough. The *author* is the person or persons who created the subject matter that is up for review. The *presenter* is the person who will read and present the material to the group. The author is not always the presenter. You may want to have someone else present the author's material, simply to test that the documents are clear and understandable without real-time embellishment from the author's imagination. A *scribe* is designated to note any errors found by the group, and a *moderator* is nominated to keep the meeting on track.

---

2   Yourdon, 1987

Participants should receive notification of a walkthrough and a copy of the materials at least one day in advance. This should not preclude a person from calling an emergency walkthrough. I have been on projects were the pace was so fast and furious that it was accepted that you could be pulled into a walkthrough with very little notice.

Those involved should always be informed of the scope of the meeting. For example, if the meeting is to review information models, they should not be focusing on coding issues. Even though people should review the material beforehand, I find that this rarely occurs in practice. On a busy project, almost nobody has time to conduct a serious review before the meeting. The idea that people will take the material home at night for review is largely the product the wishful thinking. That is why ALL of the material should be covered in the meeting.

Walkthroughs should last no longer than one to two hours. When documents or models require very long walkthroughs it is an indication that your walkthroughs are not frequent enough. During the meeting, the materials are read and discussed. The scribe records all errors found and issues raised. The purpose of the meeting is to find errors early so the little course corrections can be made. Solutions should not be discussed at length in the meeting. If the fix to the model isn't immediately obvious, the error should be noted so the author can pursue a solution after the meeting. At the end of the meeting the group should decide whether they need to review the fixes to the errors at a subsequent meeting, or whether the document passes muster, pending resolution of the problems found.

Walkthroughs should be a part of any team development culture. Each person's work should be seen by another set of eyes at least once a week. By having frequent reviews, the team always has an up-to-date picture of their progress versus the plan. The project manager can make informed course corrections before it's too late. Walkthroughs also help increase productivity by spreading knowledge and standard practices throughout the team.

## MYTH 9: "STANDARDS WILL EMERGE AS THE PROJECT GOES ON."

Having no standards is the kiss of death for any project designing graphical user interfaces. There are two ways to develop standards on a project. One way is to steal them from another project. The other way is to let them evolve through a free-market economy where the best standards beat out the weaker ideas and force compliance through the invisible hand of competition. The first method is fast and cheap. The second method appeals to our democratic sensibilities, but is very expensive in the long run.

I suggest strongly that you adopt standards which already exist, either in-house, or in other similar software, rather than try to reinvent them on your own. There are several companies with GUI standards libraries on the market that can be licensed or purchased by your shop. You can also lift ideas from commonly used software already on your user's desktop.

Standards provide a framework for development that removes a great deal of the bickering and argument that can occur in their absence. That is not to say that a standard is entirely rigid. If the standard doesn't apply to your specific problem, use it to justify why you should do something else. If a standard turns out to be no good in any situation, go ahead and change it. Established standards will "mutate" on a project, but they should not be left to "emerge" from the void.

## MYTH 10: "WE NEED ONE STANDARD METHODOLOGY AND ONE STANDARD CASE TOOL."

The last myth has to do with the confusion between techniques, methodologies and CASE tools. As I mentioned in Chapter 1, a **technique** is a repeatable, structured method for achieving a specific task (e.g., event modeling, information modeling, and window navigation diagramming). A software engineering **methodology** is the orderly arrangement of techniques into a systematic approach to the construction or acquisition of information systems. A **CASE tool** is a computer-aided software engineering application which allows you to practice specific techniques, using the power of the computer to help create, organize and present the models. Some CASE tools have enough techniques and management tools built in to support a full life cycle methodology.

Betting the farm on any single methodology is unwise in today's rapidly changing world. The methodologies which gain prominence are usually tied to a particular paradigm of technology, such as object-orientation, or traditional mainframe systems. My viewpoint is that today's client/server environment is such a heterogeneous mix of both hardware and software of different paradigms, the savvy development shop needs to have core competencies in many different techniques to succeed.

Be careful when nominating one standard development methodology. Although many of the techniques in the book are general in nature, they are most applicable to the analysis and design of business systems with graphical user interfaces and relational databases. There are many other types of computer systems. Techniques for real-time systems, applications with object-oriented databases, and even traditional batch systems vary. Every shop needs common development practices. The bigger the development shop, the greater the need for commonality. If a shop is going to nominate standard development practices, it should include variants on the methodology that are suitable for each type of system within the company.

Many companies spend inordinate amounts of time debating the "best" methodology and not enough time raising their people's core competencies. Most development methodologies are very similar. Their popularity waxes and wanes with the whims of industry fashion. What really counts is whether a development team has mastered the key abstractions of modeling the business problem, its data, events and processes, and whether they can translate those into a useful written design for the target technology.

"Last year it was flint tools, this year it's wheel-orientation.
When are these guys going to help the clan hunt? "

Some people make the assumption that a technique must be supported by CASE tool for it to be valid. If you look back through history, the CASE tools have always lagged behind the introduction of new techniques. Many early CASE tools concentrated on process modeling, but did no information modeling whatsoever. Did that mean that information modeling wasn't important? Of course not! As of this writing, robust event modeling is conspicuously lacking from CASE offerings. I hope that by the time you have reached this chapter in the book, you can see that this oversight doesn't make event modeling any less valuable of a technique.

CASE vendors rarely invent or introduce new techniques themselves. Instead, they include those techniques in their tools which are popular in the trade press, and those which their clients demand. The inclusion of a technique is market driven. Its purpose is to sell more copies of the CASE tool.

Never let the lack of CASE support stop you from practicing a sensible technique! For all the techniques in this book, I have conducted analysis and design with great speed and success using nothing more than a word processor and a simple drawing tool. At minimum, I prefer to use CASE support for information modeling. Most tools support it well, and it makes life a lot easier for large and complex models. Beyond that, use automated tools if they help you. If they get in your way, or don't support your efforts, then don't let them hold you back. The most important tool you have at your disposal is your own mind.

## SUMMARY

Developing business applications in today's client/server environment is a complex task. It can be challenging and very satisfying. A project manager needs to be aware of many factors to make the project both a technical success and a political success.

Client/server technology can enable the business to bring about changes in the way it captures and processes information. For any change effort, the business must be a willing participant. Without company support and involvement, it doesn't matter how good your system is technically, the project will be forever embroiled in political wrangling and controversy.

This technology is not a cheap fix to a company's computing budget. The learning curve is steep. Retraining costs are significant, and many mainframe personnel may simply decide not to come along. The cost of reshaping the business needs to be recognized. It is always cheaper to automate to a future vision set by the business than to negotiate and broker business change as the project attempts to progress.

With client/server systems, the personal computer becomes an integral part of the corporate computing network. The IT group needs to demand strict controls on the desktop environment to avoid chaos and anarchy. Businesses which are accustomed to the PC free-for-all of the 1980s will need to make this cultural adjustment.

Today's crop of development tools are vastly complex. It is true that you can build windows with great speed using these products, but the tools can't do your thinking for you. The best defense from the promises of vendors and the expectation of management is to gather your own metrics. Track how long it takes to analyze, design, code and test each segment of your application. Use those metrics as a baseline for your estimates and seek ways to improve your score by reusing models, standards, code and *people*!

Beware of the version trap. A client/server system is only as strong as its weakest link, and many of those links are pieces which you have purchased, sometimes at very low cost. The industry needs to hold vendors accountable for a higher level of integrity for version upgrades. Our industry is currently regulated only by the pressures of the marketplace. If we are to retain those freedoms, we need to insist on a high level of quality from our development tool vendors. They in return should encourage and expect a high level of quality from those who use their tools to develop the world's business software.

Managers are the glue that hold projects together. Today's managers find themselves assembling teams of specialists. This requires that the manager have a solid grounding in the project methodology and techniques. A good manager will use the models to make estimates, and gauge progress along the way.

The analysis and design techniques in this book are not limited to application development. They can also be used to evaluate purchased software packages. The analysis models provide a framework which defines the shape of the business. This allows you to measure each instance where the shape of the package may or may not meet your needs, and gives you a basis to determine the cost of either changing the package or changing the way you do business.

A culture of frequent reviews is crucial to the success of any project. Nobody should be allowed to work in a vacuum. The techniques of the structured walkthrough are every bit as valuable today as they were when they were first introduced. Additionally, standards should never be left to emerge on a project. Standards should be put in place as early as possible to ensure a uniform software product.

Some of the techniques described in this book are widely supported by CASE tools, but others are not. Some of the techniques don't even require such automation. Always remember that the most important tool you have is your mind, coupled with the ability to write things down.

Finally, this book has been about a series of techniques that have proven to be very successful in developing client/server business systems. Each practice has a long history in the evolution of software engineering as a discipline. It is my sincere hope that you have found something in this book that will help you develop better, more reliable software.

# APPENDIX

# Vetc. CASE STUDY

## AUTHOR'S NOTE

The following case study is intended to be an informative, entertaining and provocative application of the concepts presented in this book. It is my hope it will provide you with a chance to exercise some of your software engineering skills and perhaps provide you with analysis and design templates and patterns that you can apply to your own projects. Like any case study, it has been simplified in several areas to allow it to fit within the confines of this book. For more complex projects, the representation of say, *Customer*, will be far more involved than presented here, but the patterns and concepts remain applicable to the real projects. The design presented is just one of many possible technological solutions. As in the real world, there are few *right* answers. Your design solution will be based on your assumptions about the constraints of the available technology and limited only by your imagination and innovation. The very fact that we can read the design specification and agree or disagree as to its correctness is the entire point of the analysis and design process. Without further ado, welcome to the world of Vetc..

## A COMPANY IS BORN

Gerald Icabod Shedmore was having a bad day. He hated flying home on a Saturday morning, but the conference had run so late on Friday that he missed his plane. In less than forty-eight hours, he'd be back here in the airport on his way to yet another symposium on mechanical engineering. The baggage carousel broke down just as he could see his garment bag beginning to emerge. A single weary attendant in gray coveralls began lugging baggage up from the bowels of the terminal. It soon became obvious that the entire contents of the 767 would be retrieved, one suitcase at a time, before his garment bag would rescued from the inert conveyor belt.

Unable to get the attention of the attendant, Gerald found a bank of pay phones and called home. His son, Tim, answered. "Oh, hi, Dad. Mom's been waiting for you. Molly needs to go to the vet right away."

Molly first appeared in Gerald's life when he returned from a trip to Japan. One of Tim's schoolmates brought in a box of golden Labrador puppies for show and tell. The box went home empty. Having been raised an indoor puppy, Molly had never successfully thought of herself as an outdoor dog. Consequently, the Shedmore household now boasted a glass china hutch with no glass, three dining room chairs instead of four, and the smoldering ruins of what once was an electric blanket. On this day, it seemed that Molly's life of wild abandon finally caught up with her. Splinters from Mrs. Shedmore's cedar chest had become lodged in her gums, causing an infection. Molly had attempted to administer the time-honored dog-home-remedy of writhing in the dirt outside the patio door to no avail.

When he got off the phone, Gerald could see that all of the other passengers' bags had been unloaded with the notable exception of his, which still maintained its lonely vigil lodged in the conveyor belt. His luggage was finally retrieved by a sullen Sky Cap who expressed his disdain when Gerald failed to tip him for his efforts. Once reunited with his garment bag, Mr. Shedmore embarked on a frantic drive against the Saturday football traffic to fetch Molly. Finding the dog too filthy for transport, a rather hurried and frigid shower was enjoyed by both Gerald and Molly in the driveway. It was getting late in the day, and the football stadium stood between his house and the veterinary clinic. They arrived five minutes before closing to the stony glare of a receptionist who informed him that the office was closed on Sundays, so they'd have to board the dog until the doctor returned on Monday.

That night, Gerald lay awake pondering the day's events. "Why is it that you can't find a vet in town who is open when you need him? Doesn't anybody believe in service and efficiency anymore? And why can't they make a baggage carousel that works?"

Suddenly, Gerald Shedmore was seized by the grip of inspiration. "I've got it!" he declared, leapt out of bed and dashed to his drafting table.

## THREE YEARS LATER

Pendergast Sylnick was sitting in the mahogany-paneled offices of one G. I. Shedmore, president of Vetc., the fastest growing company on the local stock exchange. Pendergast, or "Pen" as his friends called him, was silently kicking himself for not purchasing Vetc. stock when it first went public. At least his software engineering firm had beaten out the big boys and landed the contract to build an information system for the Vetc. chain of stores. This was his first direct meeting with Mr. Shedmore after the letter of engagement was signed.

"Welcome to Vetc., Pen." Gerald leaned back in his leather chair. "Your firm has been chosen to design our new automated order entry and invoicing system for Vetc.. Being an engineering man myself, I was impressed by your use of sensible development methods. The other firms had slicker brochures, full of acronyms that I couldn't understand. Your people impressed me with their ability to communicate clearly with my people. I think this will be a good team."

"Thank you, Gerald," replied Pendergast. "One of the first things we will produce is a project charter. Actually, your organization will supply all of the information that goes into the charter. We'll just be the facilitators. Before we do that, I'd like to spend a little time learning about Vetc.. You can start by telling me about your operations. Then I'd like to visit your stores and see how it all works."

The company he founded was one of Gerald's favorite topics of conversation. He immediately launched into his standard recitation. "Vetc. is a growing chain which offers quick canine care designed for today's dog owner *on the go*. Our focus is to provide basic veterinary and grooming services at below market prices in accessible locations during convenient hours. Services include vaccinations, diagnosis and prescriptions, surgeries, and all types of grooming. Other than elective surgeries, no appointment is necessary.

"There currently are five Vetc. locations in the greater metropolitan area, with plans to add three more stores in the coming fiscal year. It is likely that next year we will open operations in another city. Our doors are open seven days a week from 7:00 AM to 9:00 PM. We also have an after-hours emergency service.

"Customers are welcomed by a trained, animal-care specialist who admits our patrons, and handles the cash register. One or two licensed veterinary doctors are permanently assigned to each store and several vets rotate between stores. Grooming is facilitated by our patented *Happy Hound Sanitation Module*, which is a highly guarded technology. Each location has a full time clerk who does the billing and bookkeeping.

"Order entry is currently handled by a PC-based system that we purchased back when we only had one store. All of the patient records are still manual. Charge account billing is done on a spreadsheet. The corporate office has a fairly good general ledger and accounting package that we'd like to keep, but all input to it is currently manual. I expect our new system to automate order entry and processing, point of sale payments, and credit account billings. I also want the patient's medical records stored in the computer as well. We send out reminder notices to owners when their dogs are due for shots or a check up. Make sure that's in the new system, too.

"That about sums it up for now. I suggest that you start your interviews at our oldest store in the Uptown Mall. If you have any more questions from this office, contact Dick or Jane. They'll help you on the spot."

## THE UPTOWN MALL

Pendergast pulled up in front of the flagship Vetc. store at the Uptown Mall. The first thing he noticed was the ample parking and easy access. Customers and their dogs enter through two big golden fire hydrants which make the building instantly recognizable, as well as cleverly conceal the nighttime security gates (Figure A–1).

**Figure A–1.** Vetc. at the Uptown Mall

Walking through the doors, he found himself in a cheerful and clean reception room. A solid wall separated the room from the rest of the Vetc. operation. Directly in front of the wall was a long counter which ran the entire length of the room. Signs overhead instructed customers to check in their dogs on the left, and to retrieve their dogs on the right. This day, Wanda Welcome was on duty behind the counter. Pendergast decided to start his tour with her.

## An Interview with Wanda Welcome, Vetc. Customer Service Agent

Wanda exuded friendliness and cool efficiency. She turned the counter over to Ben Venu, her new trainee, and stepped aside to explain the operation as Ben checked in customers.

"You probably noticed the conveyor belt which runs across the counter. Mr. Shedmore is a mechanical genius. He patterned the system after airport baggage handling. Dogs are transported throughout Vetc. in our patented *Patron Containment System* (Figure A–2). There are three sizes of cages. At the press of a button, I can select the size most appropriate for the dog. The cage automatically engages on the track from the cage bin behind the counter and comes to rest at the check-in station. The owner places the dog in the cage and I fasten the latches. There is a scale just under the cage which gives us a reading of the dog's weight. That gets marked down for later. Then the cage engages on the conveyor and away the dog goes into the back for service." Pen watched in amazement as Ben pressed a button and the machine smoothly spirited a large cocker spaniel around the corner and into the secret environs of the Vetc. establishment.

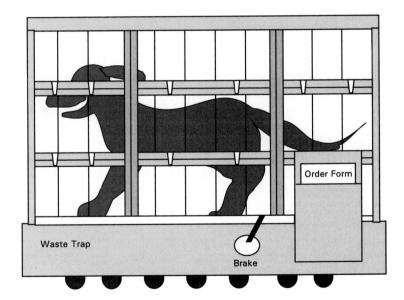

**Figure A–2.** Vetc.'s patented Patron Containment System

"That's the last I see of the dog until the owner comes back for pick-up." Wanda walked over to the pick-up side of the counter. A window of soundproof glass gave view into a staging area where dogs were awaiting their owners. "The pick-up area operates like a cross between a dry cleaner's rack and baggage claim carrousel. I can rotate the carrousel to see which dog to select. When I select the cage, it comes around the corner and disengages at the pick-up counter. The customer either pays here, or signs for the services if they have a Vetc. charge account. Then I open the cage and owner and ownee are happily reunited. The empty cage continues down this separate track to the cleaning area where it is automatically disinfected and returned to the appropriate bin."

Pendergast paused to take it all in. No wonder Vetc. had become so successful. He couldn't wait to see what miracles of automation lay behind the wall. But first, he turned his attention to a small PC that stood at the check-in station. "Tell me about your computer system," he asked Wanda.

Wanda rolled her eyes and sighed. "It was barely adequate when we were a small one-shop operation. Now it's completely out-dated. You see, Mr. Shedmore is a mechanical engineer, and a darn good one at that. Unfortunately, he doesn't really know too much about computers. His focus has always been mechanical. I've worked here since we first opened. Back then, we took orders manually. The paperwork was hard to read, and often got it wet in the back. It soon became obvious that we needed some type of a computer system to keep track of what the customer had ordered.

"Mr. Shedmore had a neighbor who was a computer consultant. The man had built an order-entry system for an auto repair shop. Gerald hired him to modify the system for Vetc.. Unfortunately, the guy got a job offer out-of-state and left town after doing only the bare minimum. There was no documentation, and nobody knew how to modify it. As we added other stores, we simply copied the software so they could use it too.

"I've used it longer than anyone else. It's pretty simple. When a customer comes in, we ask them if they've ever visited this Vetc. location before. Each store has its own database on its own PC. None of them are connected, so if the customer has been to a different Vetc. location, our store has no record of them. If they have been to this Vetc. store, we retrieve their old record. Otherwise, we have them fill out this form so we can start a new record." She handed Pendergast a clipboard with a stack of order forms.

"I'm not entirely sure that the guy who wrote this program knew what he was doing. Maybe it worked for the auto-repair shop, but it sure has its problems at Vetc.. I'm pretty sure that all he did was go through his program and change the words "automobile" to "dog," "mileage" to "age," and "make/model" to "breed." Just look at these reminder notices that we've been sending out!" She handed him a crude computer-generated postcard that had been returned with no forwarding address (Figure A–3).

"He didn't even clean out the services database! When we sent out our first mailing, we told every dog owner in East Hampton Hills to bring their pet in for a lube, oil and filter."

"How do you retrieve an existing customer from the database?" asked Pen.

"By their telephone number," replied Wanda as Ben pulled up a record on the *Customer Maintenance Screen* (Figure A–4). "That's another problem. It's the only way to identify a customer, but customers move and change numbers. If someone else already has your number in the database, we have to add on another digit. We can't change their number either, so if a customer moves or changes their phone number, we have to delete their record and enter a new one. The original program for the auto-repair shop only allowed a customer to have three cars. Consequently, a customer can only have three dogs. If they bring in a fourth dog, we have to enter a duplicate customer record, with a modified phone number, of course."

```
Dear Valued Customer:


Your  1992  FRENCH POODLE

with  4  YEARS on it

is due for a RABIES BOOSTER.
```

**Figure A–3.** A Vetc. reminder notice

```
                    CUSTOMER MAINTENANCE SCREEN
------------------------------------------------------------------------

PHONE_NUMBER:  555-0344-1 |
LAST_NAME:     SNOWTREAD            | FIRST_NAME: HORGA             |
ADDRRESS:      100 WEST MARKET ST   |
CITY:          BALLARD              | ST:WA|  ZIP:98119|


            -------------------------------------------------------------
DOGS:
------------------------------------------------------------------------

DOG1_NAME:  BJORG               | BREED_CODE: 12|  DOB: 1-1-97|  SEX: M|
DOG2_NAME:  DUCHESS             | BREED_CODE: 03|  DOB: 1-1-95|  SEX: F|
DOG3_NAME:  _____  | BREED_CODE: __|  DOB: _____|  SEX: _|

COMMENT1:   BJORG IS SENSITIVE TO FLEA POWDER - DRY SKIN          |
COMMENT2:   DUCHESS - ARTHRITIS IN HIP JOINTS                     |
COMMENT3:   _____ |


        F8 = SAVE   F9 = QUIT
```

**Figure A–4.** Vetc.'s current system's *Customer Maintenance Screen*

Pendergast was starting to form a mental picture of the so-called database that must be under this thing. "How do you enter an order?" he ventured.

"Once you have the customer record on the screen, you verify the name and address, and the name, breed and age of the dog. You save the customer file and return to the main menu. Then you type 'O' which brings up the order screen.

"You must type the customer's phone number and dog name exactly as it appears on the customer record, or else you can't save the order. You then tab through the fields and place an *X* next to the services the customer requests. For instance, if they want their dog to be hand-washed and given a pedicure, you tab through the screen until you get to *Hand wash* and type an *X* in the field. The programmer hard-coded all of Vetc.'s services on the screen. We didn't offer pedicures back then, so you put a mark next to the *Other* field and type the price in the *Other price* field and tab down to the *Notes* section and type "*pedicure.*" You type the dog's weight in the *Weight* field. That can affect the price of some services. When you're done marking up the order screen, you hit F8 to save and price the order. The system automatically prices all of the checked services and adds in anything you've typed in the *Other price* field." Pendergast noticed that the order Ben was entering also had additional charges (Figure A–5).

```
                        ORDER MAINTENANCE SCREEN
    ------------------------------------------------------------------------

    PHONE_NUMBER:   555-0344-1 |          [HORGA SNOWTREAD]
    DOG_NAME:       BJORG               | WEIGHT: _85| LBS.


    -----------------------------------   ---------------------------------
    GROOMING SERVICES:                    VETERINARY SERVICES:
    -----------------------------------   ---------------------------------
    X|  HAPPY HOUND WASH                  _|  VACCINATION_1  ENTER VAC_CODE: ___|
    _|  HAPPY HOUND FLEA TREATMENT        _|  VACCINATION_2  ENTER VAC_CODE: ___|
    _|  HAND WASH                         _|  VACCINATION_3  ENTER VAC_CODE: ___|
    _|  HAND FLEA TREATMENT               _|  SPAY / NEUTER
    _|  HAIRCUT                           _|  OFFICE VISIT   REASON CODE: ___|
    _|  HAIR COLORING
    _|  DENTAL CLEANING                   DESCRIBE NATURE OF PROBLEM:
    X|  OTHER:                            _____|

                                         LIST MEDICATIONS CURRENTLY TAKING:
    $___32.00|   OTHER PRICE             _____|
                                         ALLERGIES: _____|
    NOTE:  DOG HAS ROLLED IN DEAD HALIBUT, APPLY MAX COLOGNE THERAPY.      |

              F8 = SAVE    F9 = QUIT
```

**Figure A–5.** Vetc.'s current system's *Order Entry Screen*

Ben Venu saved his order. An old impact line printer clattered to life behind the counter for a few seconds then started beeping. "Rats! The printer's jammed again," he muttered. Wanda interrupted her dialogue to show Ben how to lift the lid on the printer and reset the two-part form-feed paper back onto the pins. "The order form prints on multi-part paper," she continued. "The top copy gets put in a special holder on the dog's cage. It accompanies the dog wherever it goes at Vetc.. That tells everybody in back what work needs to be done. The carbon copy is given to the customer as an order acknowledgment. It's kind of like their claim ticket.

"When the owner comes to claim their dog, I pull the order form out of the holder. Occasionally, the vet has prescribed medications or performed other necessary procedures, so there are additional charges marked on the form that get added into the total at the register."

"Is there any link between the cash register and the computer?" asked Pendergast hopefully.

"Unfortunately not," replied Wanda. "The computer has no knowledge of what was actually charged, or what work was actually performed. It only knows what was ordered."

"Does anybody update the order after the customer leaves?" Pen already suspected what the answer would be, but he asked anyway.

"There's simply no time. Once the order has been printed, the only thing the database is used for is to generate reminder notices. We do notices once a month. The services table contains a field called *Service interval* that's to the right of the current list price. For things like booster shots or flea baths, we've gone in and entered the number of months we recommend for retreatment. When I want to generate reminder notices, I first load the printer with the post card stock. Then I go to the menu and select *'M'* for *Mailings*. The program prints a reminder notice for any dog that hasn't been serviced within the recommended time."

"That's got to be a lot of cards!" exclaimed Pen.

"You bet it is, but Vetc. is really keen on generating repeat business. The reminder notice idea was first started by Mark Keating, who ran our sales department for the first two years. Mr. Shedmore has just named Marge Inn to be the new VP of sales, and she wants to expand the mailings to include birthday cards and get well cards. I can tell you right now, that this old database can't handle it. We get a lot of cards returned in the mail because people have moved. Some send the card back if their dog has passed away. Marge is a real hot-shot marketer. She told us at last week's staff meeting that when we find out that a dog has died, she thinks we should sent them a discount coupon for a new puppy at the local pet store."

"And puppies need shots and baths," Pen concluded. "Very savvy. Do you update the dog's records when it dies or moves?"

"Actually, we just delete them. The disk on this PC is really small. I've asked repeatedly for a new one, but nobody has wanted to spend any money on hardware until they know what the new system is going to be like. Right now we've only got room for about a year's worth of orders. If we haven't seen a customer in a year, their record is deleted."

"Deleted?" Pen raised an eyebrow.

"Yep. If they come in again, we just have to re-enter their name, address and dog. All of the medical files are on paper, we still have the patient history in the back. Unfortunately, if they're not in our system, we're not sending them reminder cards."

"And if they patronize two stores, you're sending them two cards."

"You're starting to get the picture," said Wanda, smiling. "That's about it for the front desk. I think you're ready to see what goes on behind the wall. Today's not very busy, so everyone should have time to show you around. Don't try to get anyone's attention on a Saturday morning, though. It gets really crazy in here on the weekend."

"Thank you, Wanda." Pendergast nodded politely.

"No problem. Let's see . . . today Mattie, Sue and Bill are in the back. You should talk to each of them to get the whole picture."

## Behind the Wall at Vetc.

With that, Pendergast was shown through a door marked *Employees Only*. The Vetc. factory floor was like none he had ever seen. Every square inch of the facility had been put to use. Directly behind the reception wall he observed two rotating carousels. One was the *waiting queue* of dogs to be processed, the other was the *done queue* which was visible through the glass of the pick-up area. Conveyor tracks from the *waiting queue* branched off to three distinct sections of the facility. To his left he saw dogs automatically passing into a partitioned section marked *Veterinary Services* (Figure A–6).

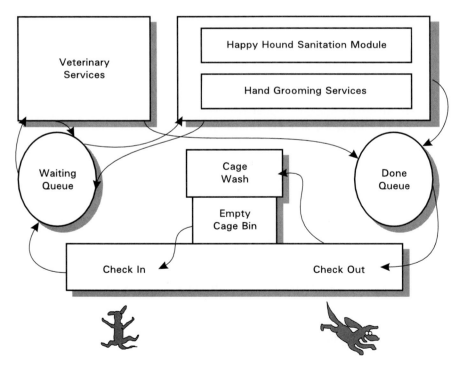

**Figure A–6.** Dog flow diagram of Vetc.'s Production Line

The middle track directly in front of him wound its way into a mammoth cylindrical machine in the center of the building, ablaze with dials, lights, and emitting the occasional burst of steam. Pendergast took this to be the infamous *Happy Hound Sanitation Module*. He watched in open-mouth amazement as a procession of ratty looking dogs climbed steadily in their cages up the conveyor to a point high overhead where they disappeared into the mouth of the vast machine. A far more presentable line of dogs emerged on the other side of the machine at ground level, looking clean, fluffed and buffed.

The third track to his right led to the *Hand Grooming* area where a team of men and women were working in assembly-line fashion. Here the dog's cages could be partially opened to gain access to whatever part of the dog required attention. A woman in a white lab coat, who was obviously the supervisor, stepped forward to greet him. Pendergast could see her name tag. It read "Matilda Cote — Grooming Supervisor."

"Hello, I'm Mattie," she said warmly. "You must be Pendergast. Welcome to the grooming department."

## An Interview with Mattie Cote, Vetc. Grooming Supervisor

Several people looked up from the grooming tables to see who the new visitor was. They gave Pen a friendly smile and returned to their work. Mattie led him around to the center of the grooming area with the grooming tables in front of them, and the towering *Happy Hound Sanitation Module* rising behind them. "You may have noticed how calm all of the animals seem," she said in a reassuring monotone. "Our research has discovered a frequency, inaudible to the human ear, which produces a soothing, almost hypnotic effect in dogs. We pipe it in throughout the store. Canine elevator music. They say it has no effect on humans, but I have noticed that I salivate more than before.

"Our most popular grooming is the wash and flea treatment using our *Happy Hound Sanitation Module*." Pen looked up at the huge machine humming away behind them. Mattie continued, "We affectionately call it the *dog wash*. I advise you not to use that term in front of Mr. Shedmore, however. As you can see, the dogs actually never leave the specially designed cages. The automated grooming is a real high volume, low margin operation. *Through-put* is what matters in this department. It's our biggest profit center.

"We charge according to the dog's weight for the *dog wash*. The cage is automatically weighed before it enters the first chamber. That sets the level of water, depth of immersion, and amount of detergent needed. It's amazingly reliable and requires almost no monitoring. There was one incident, however, when a water got into the scale and caused it to short out. Consequently, the machine didn't reset itself. The last dog in the machine before the short had been a Saint Bernard. Gladys Fenwick's toy poodle went through next. Fortunately, the dog proved to be a strong swimmer, but Mrs. Fenwick always insisted that Binky developed a nervous twitch after the incident. Now the corporate legal department has added a disclaimer to the bottom of the order acknowledgment.

"For more personalized services such as hand wash, pedicure, haircut and coloring, the cages are rolled over to these special grooming tables. The fully adjustable sidewalls allow the groomer easy access to the animal. Grooming is done in assembly line fashion. After each service is completed, it is marked off on the order sheet and the dog is rolled to the next station. On busy days, we may have as many as seven to ten groomers on duty. As you can see, I'm slightly over-staffed today. This 'no-appointment-necessary' policy plays havoc with my staffing schedule. It seems like I either have too many or too few people on duty.

"Some grooming services are charged by the hour, others are a flat fee. There's a slight surcharge for exceptionally vicious breeds. The surcharge has been higher lately to cover the increase in our workers' compensation insurance.

"Lately, we've been adding more types of hand grooming services. These items weren't programmed into the computer system at the front desk, so we have to read carefully through the notes at the bottom of the page. Sometimes we miss an item that's buried in the notes. If we catch it in time, we have to send the dog around the loop again. If the dog makes it to the pick-up area with any requested service not performed, the entire visit is free. Occasionally, the paper form gets too wet to read, and someone has to go out the front desk and print a new one. Every time I've got to stop and deal with the paperwork, it slows down the production line."

Mattie paused to let Pen walk behind the grooming tables where an aging German Shepherd was having the gray hair around her mouth expertly hand dyed, restoring her youthful appearance. At the next station, a large Doberman was lying on his side while the technician applyied a white substance to his newly-cleaned teeth. "What's that?" inquired Pen.

"That's our own patented protective enamel," Mattie explained. "You paint it on the dog's teeth to cover unsightly discoloration. It lasts about six months, and then you have to do it again. The best thing is that as it slowly dissolves, it releases a non-toxic breath freshener. Your dog gets whiter teeth and minty-fresh breath all at once!"

"The dog doesn't mind the mint flavor?" Pen quizzed.

"Actually, it smells like mint, but tastes like possum," Mattie whispered.

"Fascinating." Pen shook his head. "This has been very instructive. I think I should move on to veterinary services."

"Step right through that door," motioned Mattie. "Dr. Chur is on staff today."

Pendergast thanked his tour guide and opened the door marked *Veterinary Services*. Unlike the chaotic clamor of the grooming department, this area was bathed in antiseptic white. The conveyor track that entered the room divided, routing dogs into one of three examination rooms or two small operation rooms. He could see through the glass doors that the rooms were empty at the moment. Behind the last door, he saw a woman in the now-familiar lab coat, standing on a tall ladder, replacing a file folder in a long bank of medical files. She climbed down and burst through the door, a whirlwind in motion. She seemed to be expecting him. "Hello Mr. Sylnick. I'm Doctor Susan Chur," she said, extending her hand. "You can call me Sue."

## An Interview with Dr. Chur, Vetc. Veterinarian

"Call me Pen. Is that where you keep all of the medical records?" Pendergast nodded toward the room from which Dr. Chur had just emerged.

"Yes. The medical records are getting out of control. Vetc. has been almost too successful! We first thought we would be a neighborhood operation, but we're treating patients from all over town. People who live Uptown drop their dogs off Downtown on their way to work, but on the weekend, they come into the Vetc. at the mall. If a dog is taken to another Vetc. location, a new file is started there, and we have no knowledge of it.

"It's often difficult to properly treat an animal without its full medical history. Mrs. Parsons had a show dog that was receiving our patented *allure* hormone treatment to encourage breeding behavior in older purebreds. We didn't know that the downtown store had already given him the shots, so the dog received a double dose, which produced unfortunate results for both the dog and Mrs. Parsons."

"I'm sure it did," coughed Pendergast.

Dr. Chur continued at a rapid-fire pace. "Because dogs can't tell their owners what's wrong with them, most are admitted for a standard office visit. When a dog gets back here, we may decide to administer medications or perform procedures that are in addition to the original order. Unless it's an emergency, we try to contact the owner before incurring any additional charges. When I treat the dog, I initial the order form to make sure I've done everything and add any additional items to the notes area on the form. I also make notes in the patient's file.

"Some people bring their dogs in often, and the file can get hard to read. Everything is clipped in chronologically, so you have to look at every page to find out what was done to the animal. I really could use a cross-referencing system.

"Vaccinations and medical procedures are a flat charge regardless of the size of the dosage, even though the dosage can vary according to the weight of the animal. Some breeds are more sensitive than others, so I have to be careful about shots and medications.

"Surgeries are the only services which require an appointment. They are scheduled about two days in advance, unless it's an emergency. Surgeries are charged according to a published schedule. Prices are reviewed and updated every quarter.

"Prescriptions are filled and dispensed right here in the back room. There is a holder on the side of the cage for medications, so when we're through with the dog, the prescriptions accompany the animal to the pick-up area. Prescriptions are prepackaged and priced as per a standard price list. Usage tends to be very erratic. At first we had problems running out of certain drugs. Now we tend to overstock them to avoid inconveniencing our customers. Our vendor has a great PC software package that tracks your inventory and phones in an order to the vendor when supplies get low. I'd love to have that. Do you have any questions?"

Pendergast was starting to go into information overload. "I can't think of any right now. Perhaps I could call you later."

"Anytime. I expect to be very involved in the specification for this new computer system. There's a lot that I want it to do for us. Billy is expecting you. He's our accountant. His office is down that hall and to the left."

Pendergast thanked Dr. Chur. He stepped back out onto the factory floor, turned and headed down a narrow hallway which led past the employee breakroom and restrooms. At the end of the hall were several cramped offices. There was a light on in the office to the left. The room was small, and made even smaller by the stacks of green-bar reports, empty pizza boxes, mini-refrigerator, bookcases and what looked like someone's laundry. The occupant obviously spent a great deal of time in this room. Billy was hunched over a spreadsheet, entering data from a stack of wrinkled order forms. A plaque on the wall announced, "William Ling — Employee of the Year."

## An Interview with William Ling, Vetc. Accountant

"You must be the computer guy." Billy turned and looked up at Pen. His tired eyes betrayed the long hours spent in front of the monitor. "Find a seat if you can. Here, I'll clear a spot."

Pen sat down gingerly on a wobbly chair, made uneven by the detritus of Billy's existence that carpeted the floor. "What are you entering on that spreadsheet?" he asked.

"Promise not to laugh. This actually worked back when we first started business. Call it *The Little Spreadsheet that Grew*. About two years ago, Mark Keating announced the introduction of the Vetc. revolving charge account. Just one problem . . . he and his sales cronies never figured out how we were to track and bill the customers. So I created this spreadsheet where I could enter a customer's charges and keep track of who's paid."

"You do invoicing and accounts receivable on a spreadsheet?" Pen asked incredulously.

"You got it. My temporary solution became my own permanent private hell," said Billy remorsefully. "We started opening new stores, so I had to hire and train the other store accountants. I've never had time to research a decent accounts receivable package to replace this thing. Actually, it works pretty well, now. I've got macros written so almost anybody can run it."

"Show me how it works," pressed Pen.

"Each month, I copy the ending account balances forward to a new spreadsheet. Every day, the order forms which were charged on account are brought from the register back to my office where I enter the customer name, account number and the total charges; that is if the form isn't too wet to read. Customers send their payments directly to the store. I open the mail and key in the payments before I make the bank deposit. At the end of the month, I run a macro which combs through the spreadsheet and totals the month's charges, adds any outstanding balance, late fees and deducts payments made. The resulting summary is written to this portion of the spreadsheet which is combined with a form letter to send out billing statements." He waved a tired arm in the general direction of a large laser printer atop a filing cabinet.

Pendergast wrinkled his brow. "Does each store do its own billing?"

"Yes, they do. The corporate focus is on engineering and expansion. They're making too much money to worry about how to track it efficiently. If a customer visits two stores in a month, they get two bills. If they combine them and send in only one check, then the accountants at the affected stores will call each other on the phone and sort it out.

"Aside from billing, I also submit the store sales reports to the corporate office. That's another spreadsheet. I print the results and send it in every Friday. They key it into their financial package which spits out the standard reports. You know, cash flow statement, profit and loss, net income and so on. The new marketing VP is asking for more and more detail on sales of specific services from the stores. Like I don't have enough to do!" There was a resentful tinge to Billy's voice. Pendergast could see his anger flaring momentarily. "They've even asked if I could start sending out birthday cards! I guess the folks at the front desk were too busy. Do they think I lead a life of leisure? I can appreciate the need to generate more repeat business, but sometimes I think those folks at corporate have gone through the spin cycle one too many times. Vaccination reminder notices are a great idea, but birthday cards! Maybe that stuff goes over big at our Hampton Hills store, but in this part of town I'd get more mileage wishing our patients 'happy hunting' when the season opens. I never knew when I took this job that a company that's so high-tech could be so far behind the times! Vetc. doesn't suffer from a lack of *automation* — they suffer from a lack of *information*!" Billy's face was red. He had a wild look in his eye.

"I think you've hit the nail on the head." Pendergast arose and made a hasty retreat toward the door. "Thank you, Billy. You certainly have a lot of knowledge that will be critical to this project. I definitely value your input."

"Thank you, Mr. Sylnick," said Billy in a much calmer tone. "I don't get many visitors."

As he walked back to the front of the building, Pendergast was struck by the dichotomy between the cheerful demeanor of the service people and the serious malcontent that appeared to be brewing in the back office. This company needed more than just a new order entry system. It was clear to him that this project would require a strong charter and scope control if it is to succeed.

## EXERCISE QUESTIONS

### Exercise 1 — Problems and Opportunities

Pendergast went back to his office after his first visit to Vetc.. He sat down at his desk and took out a large yellow tablet. He tore off three sheets and labeled them **PROBLEMS**, **OPPORTUNITIES** and **QUESTIONS**, respectively.

1.1   Based on Pendergast's interviews, and using the concepts presented in Chapter 2, *The Project Charter*, what problems can you see that exist at Vetc.?

1.2   What unexploited opportunities can you think of that could help Vetc.?

1.3   What additional questions would you ask for your next round of investigation?

## Exercise 2 — Objectives, Evaluation Criteria, Solution Options

2.1   Using the concepts of IR AC IS, convert your problem and opportunity statements into objectives. State whether meeting the objective will increase revenue, avoid costs or improve service to Vetc. customers. Some objectives may fall into more than one category. For each objective, how might you measure it? What baseline measurements would you need to take to establish the desired level of improvement?

2.2   Are there any clues in Pendergast's interviews that might indicate which objectives might be more important than others to Vetc.? If so, what are they?

2.3   The evaluation criteria for this project will include criteria which measure how well a proposed solution meets each objective, and measure of the costs of the solution. Additionally, the charter should state quality vectors to guide the design of the new system. Based on the prioritized list of objectives created by Pendergast's team (answer 2.2), what are some quality vectors that you feel should be stated in the evaluation criteria for this project?

2.4   Brainstorm a list of solution options to help meet the objectives that have been stated for Vetc.. Briefly discuss the merits or problems of each solution.

## Exercise 3 — Context Model

Try doing Exercises 3, 4 and 5 concurrently. On a real project, the context model, event model and information model will be done together.

3.1   Draw a context diagram depicting the scope that is implied by objectives defined by Pendergast's project charter team. (Clue: You might want to start by drawing a flattened data flow diagram of the processes that exist in the business, then decide which ones should be within your scope or out of scope.)

3.2   Look at the external agents on your diagram. Have you depicted an expanded scope context or reduced scope context?

## Exercise 4 — Event Model

4.1 Create an event list for your project. For each event, indicate whether it is expected or unexpected. Also note any non-events or temporal events on your list.

4.2 Are there any events that you are unsure about whether they should be in scope or out of scope? If so, what should you do about them?

4.3 Take the event representing the check-in of a dog at a Vetc. store and create an event dictionary entry. Your dictionary should include the event name, event description, initiator, current transporter, future transporter, stimulus, activity, response and effect.

## Exercise 5 — Information Model

Because this is a rather large project, the remaining exercises will narrow their focus to just one subject area or aspect of the intended system.

5.1 Using whatever information you now have at your disposal, create an information model for the events;

*Customer places order for dog,*
*Groomer inquires on requested grooming services for dog,*
*Groomer acknowledges grooming service as completed,*
*Vet inquires on requested medical services for dog,*
*Vet acknowledges medical treatment as completed.*

Draw an entity-relationship diagram which includes relevant entities, relationships, relationship names, and all four points of cardinality. (Hint: You have lots of great information in the interview notes, old screens and event dictionary!)

5.2 What issues arose when you attempted to place all four points of cardinality on the relationships? What business policies or rules are implied by your cardinality?

5.3 Can you identify any supertype/subtype relationships in the Vetc. information model? Did you see any corresponding subtyping in any of the other analysis models so far?

5.4 Do you have any associative entity types? If so, where?

5.5 Do you have any attributive entity types? If so, where?

5.6 As best you can, list the attributes of each entity and write a brief definition of each entity and attribute. Note whether an attribute is required or optional, and nominate a data type for each attribute and a candidate identifier for each entity.

## Exercise 6 — Interface Prototype

6.1   What are some of the different ways that you might organize the event list to prepare for making an interface prototype?

6.2   Create a first-cut prototype for layout of the windows required to check a dog into Vetc.. (Clue: Use your event dictionary, information model, your observation of the skill level of the users and the quality vectors from the charter as your guide.)

## Exercise 7 — Architecture Model

I have seen students come up with architectures for this case study that range from complete centralization with a single mainframe computer, to complete decentralization in a peer-to-peer architecture with no server at all, to every possible client/server scheme in between. There is no perfect technical architecture for Vetc.. Each solution will have its own peculiar problems.

Vetc. currently has five stores within the same metropolitan area as their corporate office. Three more will be added this year. Next year, they are likely to expand to another city.

7.1   Make an event/business location matrix from your event list. You can keep it simple by determining which events occur, or should occur, at the corporate headquarters versus the stores, and you may also model events at the conceptual level rather than the business level.

7.2   What statistics would you need to gather to do a good job of architecture modeling for Vetc.?

7.3   It is becoming obvious from the models that certain entities such as *Customer* and *Dog* need to be available to any Vetc. Location, including all of the stores and corporate headquarters. Furthermore, a history of a dog's treatments (*Order items*) also needs to be available across the entire enterprise. Given your knowledge of Vetc., what are the pros and cons of centralized versus distributed data architectures for the company? What recommendation would you make and why?

## Exercise 8 — Database design

8.1   Transform your information model from Exercise 5 into a first-cut relational database design. List the fields, their data type and whether they are optional or mandatory. For each table, select a primary key. For each relationship in the information model, implement the proper foreign key in the database design.

8.2   Are there any areas of the database design which you might vary from the information model? If so, why or why not?

## Exercise 9 — External Interface Design

9.1 Using the event list as your guide, propose an overall organization for Vetc.'s new system and sketch a main menu. Then, using the window layouts from Exercise 6, create a window navigation diagram for the dog check-in event. Start your navigation with the main menu and show your proposed navigation paths from window to window. Using the notation from Chapter 11, declare the window type for each window and propose the appropriate unit of work for the user by marking where you think he should save his work.

9.2 Refine your window layouts by placing command buttons or menu items on the windows. For each window, write an external design specification which includes:

a window description which tells the user how to operate the window,
a window mini-spec which defines when each button or menu item is enabled and what happens when you click it,
a field specification which lists each field on the interface and specifies which fields are visible or non-visible, updatable or not updatable, required or optional entries, and a mini spec which states how to retrieve the data for each window from the database.

## Exercise 10 — Internal Component Design

10.1 Depending on the chosen development language, the code for this system might vary in its degree of object-orientation. Let's assume that we decide to employ OO to represent the business and application classes inside of our system. Using your information model and event dictionary for checking in a dog to Vetc., list the candidate business and/or application domain classes that you might need for an object-oriented implementation.

10.2 Are there any supertype/subtype entities in the information that look like good candidates for inheritance in your class model?

## EXERCISE ANSWERS

## Answers to Exercise 1 — Problems and Opportunities

### 1.1  Vetc. Problem Statements

After Pendergast brainstormed a list of problem statements at Vetc., he met with a cross section of Vetc. users to validate and extend the list. Next, he began to group problems together into those which were increasing Vetc.'s costs, those depriving Vetc. of potential revenue, and those failing to provide Vetc. customers with the highest possible level of service. He then further classified the cost-related problems into those which were exposing Vetc. to the risk of error, those increasing operating costs, and the technical problems directly related to the current order entry system. He numbered each problem statement so he could trace them through the chartering process. What follows is his resulting problem statement list.

## Vetc. Problems

The following problems expose Vetc. to the **risk of error**. Some of the problems run the risk of making an error or omission in the dog's treatment, and some problems are related to the accurate pricing of the order, billing of the invoice, or the integrity of the financial functions at Vetc..

1. A single Vetc. store cannot tell whether a medical patient has visited any other Vetc. location. If a dog is taken to more than one Vetc. for medical treatment, a medical file exists at each store. They are not cross-referenced, increasing the risk of mistreatment.

2. The output from the scale requires manual recording of the dog's weight, increasing the risk of error. Additionally, water in the scale of the Happy Hound Sanitation Module has resulted in an error which almost drowned a dog.

3. Breed sensitivity to certain medications poses a risk of mistreating a dog. It is currently the veterinarian's responsibility to remember any breed sensitivity to medications.

4. Invoicing and accounts receivable are conducted on a very volatile medium — a spreadsheet — exposing the data to error.

5. Receivables are managed on a store-by-store basis, so Vetc. has no payment or consolidated credit history for a customer who patronizes more than one store.

6. Customer name and number must be entered manually in the invoicing spreadsheet, increasing the risk of error of incorrectly identifying the customer and account.

7. Occasionally, the order form is too wet to read, making accurate input of charges into the invoicing spreadsheet difficult.

8. There is improper separation of duties in the accounting function. The accountant opens the mail, enters the charges and prepares the bank deposit, making it very easy to embezzle funds.

The following problems result in a direct increase in Vetc.'s **operating cost**. Many of the problems are related to the manual nature of tasks.

9. All entries in the dog's medical file are chronological, so a veterinarian must search every page to query the dog's history, increasing the time spent with each dog.

10. Input to the corporate general ledger and accounting package is time consuming and labor intensive because all input is currently manual.

11. The process for acknowledging a service as completed is manual, requiring handling of paperwork which slows the through-put of the production line.

12. Services not hard-coded into the system are written at the bottom of the order, causing the grooming staff to take extra time to read carefully through the notes. Sometimes items are missed, and the customer is not charged for the entire visit (see loss of revenue).

13. The "no appointment necessary" policy makes appropriate employee scheduling difficult for the grooming team, causing over-staffed days and under-staffed days.

14. If an order sheet is lost or damaged, a groomer must go out to the front desk to print another copy.

15. The medical files at Vetc. consume a large amount of real estate in a store which is already pressed for space.

16. Continuous feed multi-part paper used in the line printer is expensive.

17. Medical services provided are written by hand on the order form, and must be priced manually.

18. Medical services provided must be recorded redundantly on both the order form and in the patient's medical file.

19. Prescription usage is erratic, causing the store to overstock inventory to avoid running out.

20. The sales department undertakes new programs without assessing the impact on information systems.

21. The invoicing and A/R spreadsheet is cumbersome and labor intensive to maintain.

22. Each store has its own billing accountant.

23. If a customer submits one check for bills from more than one store, the store accountants must call each other to sort out the charges.

24. Financial reports from the store are submitted via spreadsheet to the corporate office, causing more manual manipulation and transfer of the data.

25. Vetc. cannot tailor mailing notice text to the socio-economic region of its customer base, so cards may not be as effective in any one particular marketing area as they could be. This wastes card stock, labor and postage, and may fail to produce the desired repeat business.

26. Each accountant is highly overworked due to the manual nature of the invoicing system, running the risk of premature turnover of employees.

The next set of problems is directly related to **poor system design** of the existing order entry application. These problems are more directly related to the technical implementation of the current system, however, they could easily be classified into the prior category of problems which increase operating costs. (Users tend to lump these types of problems together under "sins visited upon them by the current computer system.")

27. The current system for recording orders has no documentation, and nobody knows how to modify it. This poses risk to the business of a system failure, and has resulted in the system's inability to keep up with changes in the business.

28. The reminder notices generated by the current system are poorly worded, awkward and impossible to change.

29. Because customers are identified by their telephone numbers in the database, the phone number cannot be updated on a customer record if it changes.

30. When inserting a customer record, if the phone number for a customer already exists in the system, an extra (fictitious) digit is added to make the number unique.

31. The current system is hard-coded to allow only three dogs per customer. Customers with more than three dogs get a duplicate customer record.

32. Navigation between the customer screen and order entry screen is cumbersome, requiring users to return to the main menu.

33. The order entry screen requires the user to type customer phone number and dog name exactly before the order is accepted by the system.

34. The order entry screen contains hard-coded entry fields for available services, making it inflexible to adding or removing services as the business changes.

35. Services not coded onto the order entry screen are charged in the "other" field, making it impossible for Vetc. to accurately track the sales of services not officially listed on the screen.

36. Services not coded into the current system cannot be automatically priced.

37. The line printer for printing orders is unreliable. It jams frequently.

38. There is no link between what was ordered and what was actually charged. This impairs Vetc.'s ability to accurately track sales by service type, fails to provide order traceability within the store, and exposes Vetc. to risk of fraud by the cashier.

39. The current program for printing reminder notices does not allow the user to narrow the list by any selecting criteria, mailings cannot be tailored by service type.

40. The current system is unable to generate any other types of cards, such as birthday cards or get well cards.

41. Customer records are deleted when the dog dies, losing a potential repeat customer from Vetc.'s database should the customer acquire another dog.

42. Retention is only one year on-line, forcing infrequent return customers to have to resubmit their customer data.

The following problems contribute to a **loss of potential revenue** for Vetc..

43. Errors or missed services made due to poor order tracking or unreadable paper forms result in the customer not being charged for the entire visit.

44. Billing conducted only on a monthly cycle results in a potential lost opportunity cost of the receivables.

These last problems **fail to provide the highest possible service** to Vetc. customers.

45. Customers must fill out a new customer profile at each new store they visit, even though they have patronized another Vetc. location.

46. Customers patronizing more than one store get a reminder notice card from each store.

47. Customers send payments directly to each store. If they visit more than one store, they must send multiple payments, duplicating effort on the part of the customer.

## 1.2   Vetc. Opportunity Statements

Pendergast and his group of users also recorded a list of opportunities. Several of them were inspired by available technologies, but they tried hard to word the statement in a neutral fashion.

A. Customers who notify Vetc. that their dog has died could be issued a discount coupon for a new dog. This marketing promotion would require the cooperation of local area pet stores.

B. With a more flexible information system, Vetc. could expand the direct mail campaign into other types of mailings, such as birthday greetings, get well cards, happy hunting cards, graduation from obedience school cards, and so on.

C. Vetc. may be able to increase traffic during the weekdays by offering discounts during those days. For the plan to be beneficial, the loss of the discounted weekday revenue would have to be offset by either increased patronage, more satisfied customers or cost savings due to more consistent staffing levels.

D. Vetc. might be able to benefit by lower inventory costs by more accurately tracking and reordering prescription medications. (This opportunity was inspired by Dr. Chur's mention of a PC-based inventory-tracking system that is available.)

E. Technologies exist (such as bar-coding) which could allow Vetc. to more accurately track and route dogs around the factory floor, reducing the risk of error and lowering the labor cost of handling paperwork.

F. Repeat customers and their dogs could be checked in more quickly by issuing the customer some manner of identification which could be read by the system to retrieve the appropriate record. Examples of this type of technology include plastic cards with magnetic strips, bar-codes on a card or on the dog's identification tags, or even electronic chips embedded in the shoulder of the dog. (The latter is already done at many local animal shelters, allowing you to adopt a dog with a "chip on its shoulder.")

G. For customers who drop their dogs off for routine, periodic service, such as a monthly trip through the dog wash, an express check-in could significantly decrease the handling time required to admit the dog. Express check-in could use automatic dog identification and retrieval of a standard order profile to simply accept the dog quickly for its standard visit without bothering the customer with the normal check-in process. (Perhaps Vetc. could install a drive-through.)

## 1.3 Additional Questions for Vetc.

At this point, Pendergast was a bit concerned about the scope of this project. In his original interview with Mr. Shedmore, he was told that his firm was hired to ". . . design our new automated order entry and invoicing system for Vetc.." It was now clear to Pen that the scope of this project could easily extend far beyond just the order entry and invoicing aspects. Vetc. had significant problems with its order tracking on the factory floor, inventory management, and opportunities to expand into new technologies such as bar-coding or magnetic customer account cards.

An overriding question running through Pen's mind was whether Mr. Shedmore would entertain the idea of centralizing the billing and receivables functions. He was sure he could make a strong case for why each store didn't need a full-time accountant on staff. With an integrated information system between the stores and the corporate headquarters, billing and application of customer payments could be handled in one location, vastly reducing the redundant operations and labor cost.

Pen decided to ask Mr. Shedmore the following questions:

1. Is it within the scope of the chartering process for this project to recommend organizational changes to the business?

2. If organizational changes are made, will you fully support and implement those changes? (Pen was adamant that the mandate for change come from the business and not be viewed as the result of the new system design. This concept is crucial so users buy into the reasons for the change and not view it as imposed upon them by the information technology group. Another concern of Pen's was that Vetc. was growing so quickly and making so much money that he was unsure whether Vetc. executives would make it a priority to make significant changes to control their costs. Often companies won't rock the boat and make sweeping changes until they are forced into it by a downturn in business.)

3. How much of the potential opportunities identified should the project consider to be within their scope? (e.g.: Direct mail or coupon campaigns, express check-in, automatic dog identification.)

## Answers to Exercise 2 — Objectives, Evaluation Criteria, Solution Options

### 2.1   Vetc. Objective Statements

By now, Pendergast had a cross section of Vetc. employees committed to helping him forge the project charter. His charter team included Bill Ling, Wanda Welcome, Mattie Cote and Dr. Sue Chur from the Uptown Mall store, and representatives from other stores and the corporate headquarters. He gathered them together in the conference room to convert the problem and opportunity statements into objectives. Remembering that people are more apt to come to your meetings if you feed them, he brought a tray of donuts and three pots of strong gourmet coffee, and selection of fruit juices for Dr. Chur, who can't have caffeine on days when she's scheduled for surgery.

Together, the group worded each problem and opportunity statement as an objective, classified each as to whether it increased revenue, avoided cost, or improved service, and talked about how they might measure the desired improvement. When they were finished, they had inserted *x-factors* as place holders in each of the statements and assigned specific objectives to each member of the team to research real numbers to replace the *x-factors*. Pendergast facilitated the meeting and recorded several notes and conversations that took place under some of the objectives. At the conclusion of the session, their objective list looked like this:

### Objectives derived from problem statements

1. Avoid cost of mistreating a dog by creating a complete medical history for each dog to which all Vetc. locations have immediate access. Our objective is to reduce the number of mistreatment incidents due to incomplete awareness of the dog's treatment history on the part of the veterinarian from $x$ occurrences per year to $y$ occurrences per year.

   *Note: The group noted that Vetc. had never measured the reason for mistreatment incidents in the past, so no baseline data is immediately available. While everyone in the room could cite the famous case of Mrs. Parson's show dog, and one other incident involving one Vetc. location operating on the wrong hip joint, they all agreed that it was the risk of a major mistreatment in the future that was of primary importance, and that Vetc. should have a zero-error goal for the y-factor in the statement.*

2. Avoid cost of error due to inaccurate weight measurement by transporting the weight of the dog directly from the scale into the order, eliminating manual transfer of the weight value.

   *Note: While no error has been made yet, the potential exists to administer an inaccurate level medication when the dosage is dependent on the dog's weight. The redundant scale in the Happy Hound Sanitation Module was ruled out of scope of this project. The water problem has since been fixed by the engineering department.*

3. Avoid cost of error of prescribing inappropriate medications and reduce the cost of researching restrictions on medications by giving veterinarians quick access to information on medication sensitivity by breed and by medication.

   *Note: While no error has been made yet, Dr. Chur is able to cite three incidents this year when a veterinarian had to consult a colleague at another store to ensure that a medication was appropriate for the breed before administering a shot.*

4. Avoid cost of incurring an invoicing error by conducting invoicing and accounts receivable functions on a less volatile medium than a spreadsheet.

   *Note: Bill Ling was assigned to determine how many typographical errors were occurring within the spreadsheet programs, if any.*

5. Avoid labor cost of notifying other stores when a customer is in arrears by creating a consolidated view of customer credit across all Vetc. locations to which all stores will have access. On average, an accountant must spend 20 minutes per week updating a list of deadbeat customers and faxing it to all other stores.

6. Avoid risk of misidentifying customer name and account number on invoices by having the invoicing application automatically read customer name and number from a single source. Currently, an average of three customers per month notify Vetc. that their names are misspelled on their invoices.

7. Avoid loss of revenue and cost of handling damaged forms by eliminating paper order forms as the input to the invoicing application. In each store, the accountants report at least two order forms per day that require special attention because the form is too wet to read, or the handwriting is too messy. At least once per month, per store, a customer is not charged for a visit because the handwritten charges on the order form cannot be accurately discerned by the accountant when inputting charges to the invoicing spreadsheet. The average price of a customer visit is $56.

8. Avoid cost of potential embezzlement by instituting proper separation of duties between people who record receivables, receive and record payments, and make the bank deposits.

*Note: Pendergast noted that at each store, a single person has complete control over recording a customer charge and reporting the sale, and the same person also opens the mail, records payments and makes the deposit. It would be very easy for a nefarious accountant to fail to record an invoice, then bill the customer, intercept the payment and deposit it in his own account. Billy said defensively that this had not ever posed a problem and if anyone didn't believe him, why was he still driving a 1978 Pinto?*

9. Avoid cost of a dog's average medical visit by allowing the veterinarian to conduct customized searches of a dog's medical history to query particular items instead of having to read a chronological history. Dr. Chur estimates that this would cut an average of two minutes per visit for about 15% of their patrons who have large medical files.

10. Avoid labor cost by eliminating manual input from the Vetc. stores into the general ledger system for reporting sales. Currently, a full time employee spends approximately 6 hours per day keying in Vetc. sales from each store into the store's accounting software. The potential exists for eliminating an entire position from the corporate accounting department.

11. Avoid labor costs on the grooming line by reducing the combined time it takes to determine what services are required and the time required to acknowledge a service item as completed by 50%.

12. Avoid lost revenue of not charging customers due to missed service items by incidents of missed items from $x$ per month to $y$ per month.

*Note: Wanda estimates that on busy weekends at her store, at least one customer is not charged for the visit because an item was missed by the grooming line. She was assigned to collect statistics from the other stores to fill in the x-factor, and determine the root cause of the errors to see if the y-factor could be set to zero errors per month as the target goal.*

13. Avoid cost of over-staffing slow days by $x$ dollars per month and improve customer service on busy days by more accurately predicting required staffing level.

*Note: The team had a long discussion over whether this objective was in scope. Billy suggested that for a computer system to accurately predict daily staffing levels, the program would have to take into account weekly sales trends, seasonal trends, the weather forecast, the local team's football home game schedule and many other factors which affect how many customers patronize a Vetc. location in any given day. Wanda made a weak joke that if Mattie didn't hire so many of her daughter's college friends, maybe she'd be more apt to send them home on light days, which was met with a stony glare from Mattie. Pendergast suggested that they leave the objective on the list for now and revisit the discussion when they prioritize the objectives, then hastily called a lunch break during which Mattie was heard to say that their poodle-head receptionist didn't know what she was talking about.*

14. Avoid labor cost of *x* dollars per week by eliminating the need for the groomer to walk to the front desk to reprint an order.

   *Mattie noted that at least twice daily, somebody on her team has to go to the front desk to reprint the order, which removes them from the grooming line for about five minutes. Wanda added that this also interrupts the person at the front desk as well and often causes a customer to wait while the computer is tied up.*

15. Avoid cost of use of unnecessary real estate of *x* dollars per year per new store by storing medical records in a medium that takes up less space than the current paper files.

   *Note: Billy really championed this objective because Vetc. pays top dollar for premium mall leased space, so any reduction in the square footage requirements for a Vetc. location could save real dollars as new stores are opened. Dr. Chur was not willing to concede that the veterinarians could do away with the medical files and go to a completely paperless system. Dr. Chur was assigned to poll the other veterinarians to see if they would accept a paperless culture. She said she'd also call her brother in Phoenix who is a doctor at a medical clinic that recently underwent a paperless pilot project.*

16. Reduce cost of paper used for printing orders and order acknowledgments by 50%. (Current orders are printed on expensive multi-part forms.)

17. Avoid labor cost by *x* dollars per medical order by reducing the time it takes to price medical order items from one-half minute per order to two seconds per order.

   *Note: Wanda estimated that it takes her about one-half minute to price the average medical order because of all of the add-ons written in the notes. She also mentioned that customers tend to question the additional charges more when they are tallied in front of them by the cashier instead of coming directly from the veterinarian. Her mandate of two-second medical order pricing pretty much assured that the process would be automated.*

18. Avoid labor cost by *x* dollars per medical visit by reducing the time it takes to record a patient's medical services by 50%. (Medical services are currently recorded by the veterinarian redundantly on both the order form and in the patient's medical file.)

19. Avoid inventory costs by *x* dollars per year by reducing the level of stock on hand from 60 days supply to 30 days supply.

   *Note: Dr. Chur reported that they currently stock prescriptions at the 60 day supply level to avoid running out of stock. Every 90 days, a physical inventory is taken and the occasional expired prescription is discarded. Billy asserts that the real cost isn't in the write-off of expired drugs, but in the opportunity cost of Vetc. having to tie up its cash in inventory. The rest of the group wasn't entirely convinced, but agreed to keep this objective on the list.*

20. Avoid cost of pandemonium by forcing the sales department to have the information technology and accounting departments assess the feasibility of new programs.

    *Note: After much discussion, group outrage and wild gesticulation on the part of Billy, the group agreed that this objective should be removed from the list and transferred to a list of issues for Mr. Shedmore.*

21. Avoid accountant's labor cost by reducing the time it takes to maintain invoicing and A/R information by 35% at each store.

22. Avoid labor cost by *x* dollars per year by eliminating two full time positions from the current roster of Vetc. store accountants.

    *Note: Billy really had trouble with this objective, but the writing was on the wall for centralized billing, eliminating much of what the full time accountants currently do at each store. With the addition of several new stores on the horizon, expanding the accounting staff with a one-to-one correlation with stores no longer made sense, in fact, it posed a barrier to rapid expansion. Given his seniority and vast knowledge of the company, Billy was an obvious candidate to lead a new centralized billing department, so he eventually capitulated and allowed this objective to be overtly stated.*

23. Avoid accounting labor cost of *x* dollars per month by allowing customers to write one check for multi-store billings.

24. Avoid data transfer cost of *x* dollars per month by eliminating manual transfer of monthly charge data from the stores to the corporate office.

25. Avoid wasted materials and postage cost of *x* dollars per year due to ineffective direct mail pieces and increase revenue by *x* dollars per year by generating more repeat business by allowing Vetc. to tailor direct mail campaigns to the socio-economic characteristics of the market regions it serves.

    *Note: Marge Inn, the new head of Vetc. marketing had some input to this objective. She asserts that Vetc. could generate a lot more repeat business if they could generate effective direct mail pieces to their existing customer base. She conceded that she has no empirical evidence to support this assertion, but firmly believes that Vetc. has not yet tapped the potential of their existing customer base.*

26. Avoid the cost of potential premature turnover in the store accountants due to burnout by reducing their work load by 35%. Employee turnover could cost the company as much as $9,000 to recruit, hire and train a new accountant.

27. Avoid risk of a failure of the current order entry system by instituting a solution which is well documented and easily modified.

28. *The objective for Problem 28 was adequately stated in Objective 25.*

29. Avoid cost of entering redundant customer records (takes 3 minutes per customer phone number change, approximately 4 times per week per store) by allowing customer phone number to be updated on the current customer record.

30. *The objective for Problem 30 is adequately stated in Objective 29.*

31. Improve service to customers and avoid cost of entering and managing redundant customer records by allowing customers to have an unlimited number of dogs in the system.

    *Note: Wanda stated that the incidence of customers owning more than three dogs in the metropolitan area is rare enough that this objective wasn't worth chasing down an x-factor. Pendergast wasn't convinced and decided to dig a little further. He asked what the front desk does when customers come in with a litter of puppies that require shots. Surely, this situation is common and involves one customer with more than the current system's three dog limit. Wanda replied that they enter all of the puppies into the system as one dog and record multiple numbers of shots. Pen summarized, "So your current system has dogs in it named 'Puppies' that look like one dog received 10 booster shots on the same day?" The group was properly chagrined and agreed that this was an undesirable business practice and should not be perpetuated in the new system .*

32. Reduce the time it takes to enter an order by improving navigation between screens.

    *Note: The group decided that some of the problems that related directly to the current system were low on the avoid cost scale, but registered high on the user frustration meter. Rather than try to determine the minuscule x-factor improvement goal, they agreed to toss this and several other objectives into the category of general improvements in efficiency, or less politely put; eradication of some of the bone-headed design flaws of the old system.*

33. Reduce the time and skill required to enter an order by having the system remember the customer and dog identifier when changing from the customer maintenance screen to the order entry screen.

34. Avoid data entry costs and improve service to customer by making the new system flexible enough to allow Vetc. to add or remove available services from the order entry function. Wanda estimates that 15% of all orders require special items to be listed in the "other" section of the order.

35. Avoid cost of manually pricing order items (occurs on approximately 15% of all current order items) by having the system automatically price all services.

    *Note: Wanda was still not happy with this objective, since it implied that the cashier will have no discretion for an on-the-spot price adjustment for a dissatisfied customer or unforeseen item. Marge suggested that the new Vetc. stores planned for the coming year may not want to hire cashiers with as much experience and authority as Wanda and that a price override capability might not be a desirable feature. Pendergast transferred the question of the cashier's authority to override prices to an issues list to be taken up with Vetc. management.*

36. *The objective for Problem 36 was adequately stated in Objective 35.*

37. Improve service to customers by reducing the incidence of printer paper jams (technology failure) from an average of 3 times per day to less than once per week.

    *Note: Notice that the group refrained from demanding "no paper jams." Under Pendergast's tutelage they agreed that it was unreasonable to require zero-defect performance from the current crop of printers on the market. After some prodding, they acquiesced that as long as the printer didn't jam every day, once a week was tolerable.*

38. Avoid risk of fraud by the cashier, and reduce errors by $x$ errors per month, by accurately tracking services ordered to services rendered.

39. Avoid cost of mailing unnecessary notices by $x$ dollars per month by allowing the user to narrow the list by specifying selection criteria so mailings can be tailored by service type.

40. *The objective for Problem 40 was adequately stated in Objective 25.*

41. Increase revenue by $x$ percent by retaining and marketing to customers who have notified Vetc. that their dogs have died.

    *Note: The conversation got a bit surreal on this objective. Billy asked how Vetc. intended to market services to dead dogs. Mattie suggested that they could expand into taxidermy. Marge insisted that "once a dog lover, always a dog lover," and that all Vetc. required was to find a way to provide the bereaved customer with a new dog and they'd be back in business. Pendergast assigned Marge to research just how much new revenue this might represent.*

42. Avoid cost of re-entering repeat customers into the database who have not patronized Vetc. within the last year. This situation occurs about three times per week per store and it takes about 3 minutes to re-enter the customer record.

43. *The objective for Problem 43 was adequately stated in Objective 12.*

44. Increase revenue (via time value of money) by allowing Vetc. to bill customers on a cycle more granular than monthly billing.

    *Note: This was a pet objective with Billy that involved more of a policy change than a system change. He just wanted to make sure that the new system would be flexible enough to handle more than just monthly billing cycles.*

45. Improve customer service by requiring customers to fill out only one customer profile and make it available to all Vetc. locations. It is estimated that about

25% of Vetc. customers patronize more than one store, although nobody knows for sure.

46. Improve service to customers by sending them reminder notices based on their patronage across all Vetc. stores.

47. Improve service to charge account customers by mailing them a consolidated billing statement. It is estimated that of the 25% percent of customers believed to patronize more than one Vetc. location, over 50% of them charge services on their Vetc. account.


## Objectives derived from opportunity statements

A. *The objective for Opportunity A was adequately stated in Objective 41.*

B. *The objective for Opportunity B was adequately stated in Objective 25.*

C. Avoid cost of over-staffing weekends, and possibly increase revenue by shifting some customers to weekday visits by offering specials and discounts. Marge, from marketing will have to research the feasibility of this program to ensure that weekday specials result in a net increase in profit and don't just cannibalize existing revenue.

D. Avoid excessive inventory cost and eliminate labor required to track and place inventory orders by exploiting existing prescription-ordering software and services available from our vendors.

   *Note: Dr. Chur was assigned to investigate the cost and features of the vendor's services.*

E. Avoid risk of error, and lower cost of handling paperwork by $x$ minutes per average order by more accurately tracking and routing dogs on the factory floor.

   *Note: This objective was inspired by technologies such as bar-coding, however it is unclear to the team whether improvements to the actual factor floor routing system are within the scope of the project. Pen added this question to the list of issues for upper management.*

F. Improve service to customers and avoid reception labor costs by reducing the time it takes to identify repeat customers and their dogs from 30 seconds to 2 seconds. (Examples of this type of technology include plastic cards with magnetic strips, bar-codes on a card or on the dog's identification tags, or even electronic chips embedded in the shoulder of the dog.)

G. Improve service to customers and avoid reception labor costs by reducing the time it takes to place a recurring order for a returning customer and his dog from 2 minutes to 30 seconds. (The idea is to retrieve either the last order or identify an order as a default order profile for the dog.)

## 2.2  *Prioritized Vetc. Objective Statements*

When Pendergast's group had finished articulating the project's objectives, they adjourned to research their *x-factors*, so they could have a solid basis on which to prioritize the list of objectives. During their next meeting, they weeded out the duplicates and separated the remaining objectives into three categories; those which they felt were very high priority, those which they believed to be very low priority, and the remaining medium priority objectives which fell somewhere in between.

### High Priority Objectives

The group agreed that the most important objectives for the new system fell into several rough classifications. Everyone was unanimous that any problems which inconvenienced, annoyed or impacted Vetc.'s customers in any way were of the utmost importance to the project. As a service organization, the reputation of Vetc. is only as good as their performance on a customer's most recent visit. Objectives which strived for significant improvements in customer service were given high priority.

The next high priority classification was for significant reduction in labor costs within Vetc.. The most promising objectives were those which sought to change the way Vetc. manages invoicing, receivables and transmission of data to the general ledger system, since whole positions could be eliminated by centralizing this function, and Vetc. could avoid having to hire and train a new full-time accountant at each new store. Because the grooming department is Vetc.'s highest profit center with high-volume, low-margin transactions, any reduction of costs in this area were also given high priority. Finally, improvements in the efficiency of Vetc.'s most highly-paid staff, the veterinarians, were listed as high priority items.

### High priority objectives which seek to directly improve customer service

45. Improve customer service by requiring customers to fill out only one customer profile and make it available to all Vetc. locations. It is estimated that about 25% of Vetc. customers patronize more than one store, although nobody knows for sure.

47. Improve service to charge account customers by mailing them a consolidated billing statement. It is estimated that of the 25% percent of customers believed to patronize more than one Vetc. location, over 50% of them charge services on their Vetc. account.

31. Improve service to customers and avoid cost of entering and managing redundant customer records by allowing customers to have an unlimited number of dogs in the system.

32. Reduce the time it takes to enter an order by improving navigation between screens.

33. Reduce the time and skill required to enter an order by having the system remember the customer and dog identifier when changing from the customer maintenance screen to the order entry screen.

34. Avoid data entry costs and improve service to customer by making the new system flexible enough to allow Vetc. to add or remove available services from the order entry function. Wanda estimates that 15% of all orders require special items to be listed in the "other" section of the order.

37. Improve service to customers by reducing the incidence of printer paper jams (technology failure) from an average of 3 times per day to less than once per week.

42. Avoid cost of re-entering repeat customers into the database who have not patronized Vetc. within the last year. This situation occurs about three times per week per store and it takes about 3 minutes to re-enter the customer record.

F. Improve service to customers and avoid reception labor costs by reducing the time it takes to identify repeat customers and their dogs from 30 seconds to 2 seconds. (Examples of this type of technology include plastic cards with magnetic strips, bar-codes on a card or on the dog's identification tags, or even electronic chips embedded in the shoulder of the dog.)

G. Improve service to customers and avoid reception labor costs by reducing the time it takes to place a recurring order for a returning customer and his dog from 2 minutes to 30 seconds. (The idea is to retrieve either the last order or identify an order as a default order profile for the dog.)

*High priority objectives which seek to reduce invoicing and accounting costs*

10. Avoid labor cost by eliminating manual input from the Vetc. stores into the general ledger system for reporting sales. Currently, a full time employee spends approximately 6 hours per day keying in Vetc. sales from each store into the store's accounting software. The potential exists for eliminating an entire position from the corporate accounting department.

21. Avoid accountant's labor cost by reducing the time it takes to maintain invoicing and A/R information by 35% at each store.

22. Avoid labor cost by $x$ dollars per year by eliminating two full time positions from the current roster at Vetc. store accountants.

23. Avoid accounting labor cost of $x$ dollars per month by allowing customers to write one check for multi-store billings.

24. Avoid data transfer cost of $x$ dollars per month by eliminating manual transfer of monthly charge data from the stores to the corporate office.

26. Avoid the cost of potential premature turnover in the store accountants due to burnout by reducing their work load by 35%. Employee turnover could cost the company as much as $9,000 to recruit, hire and train a new accountant.

7. Avoid loss of revenue and cost of handling damaged forms by eliminating paper order forms as the input to the invoicing application. In each store, the accountants report at least two order forms per day that require special attention because the form is too wet to read, or the handwriting is too messy. At least once per month, per store, a customer is not charged for a visit because the handwritten charges on his order form cannot be accurately discerned by the accountant when inputting changes to the invoicing spreadsheet. The average price of a customer visit is $56.

### High priority objectives which seek to reduce grooming and medical costs

11. Avoid labor costs on the grooming line by reducing the combined time it takes to determine what services are required and the time required to acknowledge a service item as completed by 50%.

14. Avoid labor cost of $x$ dollars per week by eliminating the need for the groomer to walk to the front desk to reprint an order.

17. Avoid labor cost by $x$ dollars per medical order by reducing the time it takes to price medical order items from one-half minute per order to two seconds per order.

18. Avoid labor cost by $x$ dollars per medical visit by reducing the time it takes to record a patient's medical services by 50%. (Medical services are currently recorded by the veterinarian redundantly on both the order form and in the patient's medical file.)

35. Avoid cost of manually pricing order items (occurs on approximately 15% of all current order items) by having the system automatically price all services.

## Medium Priority Objectives

The medium priority objectives were those which failed to trigger inspired shouts of enthusiasm nor did they endure derisive scorn from the team. These objectives fell into the classification of "good things that should be done on this project."

### Medium priority objectives which seek to lower costs or avoid risk

1. Avoid cost of mistreating a dog by creating a complete medical history for each dog to which all Vetc. locations have immediate access. Our objective is to reduce the number of mistreatment incidents due to incomplete awareness of the dog's treatment history on the part of the veterinarian from $x$ occurrences per year to $y$ occurrences per year.

2. Avoid cost of error due to inaccurate weight measurement by transporting the weight of the dog directly from the scale into the order, eliminating manual transfer of the weight value.

3. Avoid cost of error of prescribing inappropriate medications and reduce the cost of researching restrictions on medications by giving veterinarians quick access to information on medication sensitivity by breed and by medication.

4. Avoid cost of incurring an invoicing error by conducting invoicing and accounts receivable on a less volatile medium than a spreadsheet.

5. Avoid labor cost of notifying other stores when a customer is in arrears by creating a consolidated view of customer credit across all Vetc. locations to which all stores will have access. On average, an accountant must spend 20 minutes per week updating a list of deadbeat customers and faxing it to all other stores.

6. Avoid risk of misidentifying customer name and account number on invoices by having the invoicing application automatically read customer name and number from a single source. Currently, an average of three customers per month notify Vetc. that their names are misspelled on their invoices.

8. Avoid cost of potential embezzlement by instituting proper separation of duties between people who record receivables, receive and record payments, and make the bank deposits.

12. Avoid lost revenue of not charging customers due to missed service items by incidents of missed items from $x$ per month to $y$ per month.

13. Avoid cost of over-staffing slow days by $x$ dollars per month and improve customer service on busy days by more accurately predicting required staffing level.

25. Avoid wasted materials and postage cost of $x$ dollars per year due to ineffective direct mail pieces and increase revenue by $x$ dollars per year by generating more repeat business by allowing Vetc. to tailor direct mail campaigns to the socio-economic characteristics of the market regions it serves.

27. Avoid risk of a failure of the current order entry system by instituting a solution which is well documented and easily modified.

29. Avoid cost of entering redundant customer records (takes 3 minutes per customer phone number change, approximately 4 times per week per store) by allowing customer phone number to be updated on the current customer record.

38. Avoid risk of fraud by the cashier, and reduce errors by $x$ errors per month, by accurately tracking services ordered to services rendered.

39. Avoid cost of mailing unnecessary notices by $x$ dollars per month by allowing the user to specify selection criteria so mailings can be tailored by service type.

C. Avoid cost of over-staffing weekends, and possibly increase revenue by shifting some customers to weekday visits by offering specials and discounts. Marge, from marketing will have to research the feasibility of this program to ensure that weekday specials result in a net increase in profit and don't just cannibalize existing revenue.

E. Avoid risk of error, and lower cost of handling paperwork by $x$ minutes per average order by more accurately tracking and routing dogs on the factory floor.

## Lowest Priority Objectives

The objectives which were given the lowest priority by the team were those which had lower potential to realize tangible benefits, or fell outside of the core scope of the project. It was decided that while certain features, such as automatic inventory reordering were nice to have, Vetc. doesn't have a significant problem with prescription inventory management, so a low priority was assigned.

### Lowest priority objectives which seek to reduce inventory and overhead costs:

19. Avoid inventory costs by $x$ dollars per year by reducing the level of stock on hand from 60 days supply to 30 days supply.

D. Avoid excessive inventory cost and eliminate labor required to track and place inventory orders by exploiting existing prescription-ordering software and services available from our vendors.

15. Avoid cost of use of unnecessary real estate of $x$ dollars per year per new store by storing medical records in a medium that takes up less space than the current paper files.

16. Reduce cost of paper used for printing orders and order acknowledgments by 50%. (Current orders are printed on expensive multi-part forms.)

### Lowest priority objectives which seek to reduce labor costs

9. Avoid cost of a dog's average medical visit by allowing the veterinarian to conduct customized searches of a dog's medical history to query particular items instead of having to read a chronological history. Dr. Chur estimates that this would cut an average of two minutes per visit for about 15% of their patrons who have large medical files.

### Lowest priority objectives which seek to increase revenue or improve service to customers

41. Increase revenue by $x$ percent by retaining and marketing to customers who have notified Vetc. that their dogs have died.

44. Increase revenue (via time value of money) by allowing Vetc. to bill customers on a cycle more granular than monthly billing.

46. Improve service to customers by sending them reminder notices based on their patronage across all Vetc. stores.

### 2.3  Quality Vectors

The project charter team, led by Pendergast, began creating a list of evaluation criteria against which various solution options could be assessed. They converted each objective into a tangible or intangible measurement of the benefit, and listed the familiar elements which measure the cost of solution, such as cost to implement and maintain, time to implement, and degree of risk. Then they started talking about what constituted *quality* for the finished system.

> **Usability:** The system should be easy to use in all areas of the order entry, order processing and cashiering functions. *Easy to use* is specifically defined as follows:
>
> > **Ease of training:** A new Vetc. receptionist should be able to be trained to operate the check-in functions and check-out functions within one hour, if he or she is familiar with standard graphical user interface products. A new receptionist who has not used a graphical user interface will require an additional day of training to learn to use the mouse, menus and window controls. Groomers should be able to learn to retrieve and acknowledge orders within one to two hours of training.
> >
> > **Conservation of keystrokes:** Any man-machine communication that occurs while the customer is waiting (e.g.: check-in, check-out) should attempt to use as few keystrokes as possible. Conservation of keystrokes is also important for retrieving and acknowledging grooming orders and medical orders.
> >
> > **All commands displayed:** The operator of the system should not have to memorize any commands to use the system. All available options shall be clearly displayed on the menu bar, menu items, tool bar or command buttons. It is understood that this quality vector may sometimes conflict with conservation of keystrokes; however, the mandate that the user need not memorize commands will take precedence over conservation of keystrokes in these instances.
>
> **Reliability:** The system should be up and running during all hours that Vetc. is open for business. If the communication network to corporate headquarters goes down, the Vetc. stores should continue to be operational for accepting and processing customer orders.
>
> **Maintainability:** The entire system shall be coded in manner which can be easily maintained by an IT staff who possess approximately two years of college education in computer science, or two years experience with the given language.
>
> **Flexibility:** The system shall be designed to allow Vetc. to add and remove stores, new services, new products and new types of direct advertising programs without incurring significant changes to the system.

**Immediacy of response:** The system shall strive for two second or less response time for order retrieval and acknowledgment of services rendered on an order at the Vetc. stores. This is the fastest response time required for the system. Sales reporting, invoicing, inventory management and other functions which do not occur either in front of the customer or on the shop floor while servicing dogs do not require such immediate system response. The system should be optimized so that common repetitive events, such as creating an order or acknowledging a grooming service are the fastest. More complex processes, such as cross referencing a dog's medical history, or doing a symptom search can have more relaxed response time requirements.

**Ability to communicate with other systems:** The transfer of information from the new system to the existing general ledger system should be seamless and require very little or no human intervention. The marketing group at Vetc.'s corporate headquarters should also be able to access the database of customer and order information via end user reporting tools so they can perform statistical analysis which is outside the scope of this system. Complex reads of the database should not have a detrimental effect on the performance of the production system during normal operating hours.

### 2.4   Solution Options for meeting Vetc.'s objectives

The project charter group was really starting to feel like a cohesive team. They had reached consensus on a list of Vetc.'s problems and potential opportunities. They had converted those problems and opportunities into project objectives, researched ways to measure the objectives in terms of increasing revenue, avoiding costs and improving service to customers. The objectives had then been prioritized and a list of evaluation criteria had been created to measure whether any proposed solution achieves the desired benefit of each objective and falls within the cost constraints mandated by the business. Additionally, they had articulated quality vectors for certain parts of the system.

Now it was finally time to start talking about possible solutions. Pendergast offered the first solution option of "do nothing." What follows is a list of their options and some of the ensuing discussion.

**SO1. Status Quo.** Do nothing.

*The entire group agreed that solution option number one was undesirable. Vetc. was making lots of money at the moment, but their ability to expand rapidly into other cities would be threatened by their vast inefficiencies. Doing nothing might be acceptable if Vetc. wanted to stay a small five-store operation, but their current way of operating serves as a barrier to large-scale expansion.*

**SO2. Custom build.** Custom design and build an integrated information system which automates the order placement, grooming service, medical service, cashiering and prescription and supplies inventory management functions at each store, seamlessly linked to a centralized invoicing, receivables and sales reporting function at corporate headquarters, and automatically interfaced to the existing accounting and payroll systems.

*The vision of an enterprise-wide integrated solution, custom designed specifically for Vetc., was certainly the most enticing of all of the solution options. It was also potentially the most expensive solution option on the list. The good news is that Vetc. has lots of money. The bad news is that they have virtually no IT staff capable of such an undertaking and the entire effort would have to either be outsourced or a development staff would have to be built from the ground up.*

**SO3. Purchased package.** Seek to purchase a packaged solution to provide an integrated information system which automates the order placement, grooming service, medical service, cashiering and prescription and supplies inventory management functions at each store, seamlessly linked to a centralized invoicing, receivables and sales reporting function at corporate headquarters, and automatically interfaced to the existing accounting and payroll systems.

*All of the Vetc. employees liked to think that their company was completely unique. The truth was, as Vetc. expands, many of its information needs and business processes start to look more and more like any other large service provider. The group decided that they should examine whether a solution already exists on the market that could meet Vetc.'s needs. Buying an existing system versus building one sounded very appealing to some of them. This solution was particularly championed by Billy and the other accountants. Wanda, Mattie and the veterinarians were far more skeptical that their needs could be met by an integrated packaged solution. Marge warned that a packaged solution does nothing to distinguish Vetc. from its competitors.*

**SO4. Mixed custom built and packaged solution.** Seek to purchase portions of the system which are good candidates for finding existing software which can be easily integrated with more customized portions of the business. For instance, an inventory-management package has been identified as a potential purchased module. Other candidates include purchasing portions of the system to perform the accounts receivable functions. The portions of the system which map closely to the order placement and fulfillment process at the Vetc. stores would be custom built to Vetc.'s specifications.

*A compromise was struck between the packaged solution advocates and custom-build advocates. Solution option 4 seeks to purchase and integrate packages which automate functions which are standardized across many industries, such that a generic solution would suffice, but reserves the right to custom build*

*build solutions where Vetc. has specific requirements for the system to map to proprietary business processes, or provide functionality which gives Vetc. a competitive advantage in the marketplace. The downside of this solution is that the IT group must make the purchased portions of the application integrate seamlessly with those they build.*

**SO5. Partial solution.** Custom build a solution which meets Vetc.'s most pressing needs in the area of order placement and fulfillment, and centralized billing and account receivable management, but leave lower priority objectives, such as inventory management out of scope.

*Solution option 5 was an attempt to offer a scaled-down solution which automated only the high and medium priority objectives, but left other items out of scope. Lower priority items could be integrated as a phase two project.*

After scoring the solution options against the evaluation criteria, the project chartering team for Vetc. recommended solution option 4 to management which promoted a custom built order placement and fulfillment application, coupled with a purchased inventory tracking package at the Vetc. stores. The recommendation advocated moving charge account invoicing, accounts receivable, sales reporting and integration with the accounting system out of the stores to a centralized location at corporate headquarters and recommended that the team analyze whether these centralized functions might be available through an expansion of the corporate accounting system which had been purchased from a major international financial software vendor, thus reducing the amount of software that would have to be custom built.

Mr. Shedmore was very pleased with the proposal and the solid research and employee participation that went into it. He gave the proposal his resounding approval and retained Pendergast's firm to conduct the analysis, development and integration of the project, as well as recruit and build an internal information technology team capable of maintaining the software into the future.

## Answers to Exercise 3 — Context Model

### 3.1  Context diagram for the Vetc. project

Pendergast found it much easier to work on the context diagram and event list together, rather than separately. He struggled with the name for the context bubble. *Service dog* was a bit narrow in scope and conjured up unpleasant images of automated surgery. *Operate Vetc.* seemed a bit too expansive, since many functions at the corporate office were not included in his scope. Pen settled on *Operate Vetc. location,* which implied that activities associated with running a store were in scope, even though some of the activities inside his bubble, such as the billing and direct mail functions will undoubtedly be moved to the corporate office. Figure A–7 shows his first pass at the context diagram.

### 3.2 Expanded versus reduced scope context

The context diagram that Pendergast has drawn appears to be an expanded scope model. He has elected to show the customer as the originator of the service order information instead of the receptionist. While this might disturb the receptionist when she sees that she's not included on the diagram, she is really the transporter of the data and not its original source. The scale is also an interesting choice of external agent. Pendergast decided that the receptionist was not the proper external agent for the dog's weight because again, she is simply the current transporter of the data. The dog is not a good candidate because the dog is unable to articulate its weight to the system. By placing a piece of hardware such as the scale on the context model, Pendergast is declaring his desire to have the system communicate with this particular hardware.

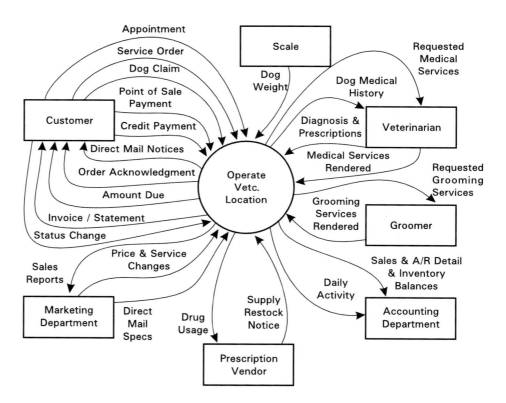

**Figure A–7.** Context diagram for *Operate Vetc. Location*

# Answers to Exercise 4 — Event Model

## 4.1 Event List

Pendergast made a first draft of an event list. He noted which events were unexpected versus expected. For the expected events, he noted if any were temporal or non-events. He then organized his event list roughly by subject.

U = Unexpected event

E = Expected event

T = Temporal (time-triggered expected) event

N = Non-event (non-occurrence of an expected event)

*Check-in events:*
U Customer places order for dog

New customer places order for new dog

New customer places order for existing dog (change of ownership)

Existing customer places order for new dog

Existing customer places order for existing dog (return visit of customer and dog)

U Customer requests surgery appointment (for dog)

E Customer checks in dog for surgery appointment

N Customer fails to check in dog for surgery appointment

E Receptionist weighs dog

*Order fulfillment events:*
E Happy Hound treatment is administered

E Groomer inquires on requested grooming services for dog

E Groomer acknowledges grooming service as completed

E Vet inquires on requested medical services for dog

U Vet inquires on dog's medical history

U Vet makes diagnosis of dog's condition

U Vet prescribes medication

E Vet acknowledges medical treatment as completed

*Dog check-out events:*
E Customer claims dog

N Customer fails to claim dog

E Cashier requests total charges for order

E  Customer pays for order

    Customer pays for order with cash/check

    Customer charges order on Vetc. charge account

*Invoicing events:*
- T  Time to bill credit customers
- E  Customer pays invoice
- N  Customer fails to pay invoice

*Accounting/sales reporting events:*
- E  Accountant balances daily cash receipts
- T  Time to post activity to the general ledger

*Marketing events:*
- U  Marketing requests sales reports
- U  Marketing department creates new price list
- U  Marketing department creates new service
- U  Marketing department retires service
- U  Marketing department creates new direct mail literature
- U  Marketing department requests customer mailing list

*Inventory management events:*
- U  Inventory falls below reorder point
- E  Vetc. receives inventory supplies
- N  Vetc. fails to receive inventory supplies
- U  Accounting department requests inventory balance

*Customer maintenance events:*
- U  Customer notifies Vetc. that dog has died
- U  Customer notifies Vetc. of change of address, phone number

### 4.2  Questions Regarding the Event List

Pendergast reviewed his event list and noted a few questions regarding events that were not intuitively in scope.

The event *New customer places order for existing dog*, implies that whoever is responsible for paying a dog's Vetc. bills is no longer responsible and the dog's bills are now to be paid by another party. This event doesn't represent any problems if the transfer occurs within the same family, say, a son or daughter moves out and takes the dog with them, or a divorce results in custody being awarded to a different spouse than the customer on record at Vetc.. When dogs are bought, sold or given away, the new owners might not be able to identify the name of the old owner to Vetc., and if not prompted, might not even think to ask if the dog already had a record listed at Vetc.. In these cases, there may be no way for the receptionist to accurately discern that the dog has previously visited a Vetc. location, and therefore, would create a new dog record. Pendergast wondered whether this was an issue of any importance.

*Customer fails to check in dog for surgery appointment* is the non-occurrence of the event *Customer checks in dog for surgery appointment*. Pendergast added it to the list because he wanted to remember to ask if Vetc. has a policy regarding no-shows. If a customer is chronically absent from scheduled surgery dates, does Vetc. do anything to attempt to prevent it?

The way the event, *Happy Hound treatment is administered* is worded, it leads the reader to believe that the system might be able to automatically determine that a particular dog has left the Happy Hound Sanitation Module. Pendergast wants to make certain that this level of integration with the factory floor systems is within the scope of the project; otherwise, the groomer will be responsible for recording when a Happy Hound service is complete.

The very sad event, *Customer fails to claim dog*, leaves Pendergast wondering whether anyone has ever abandoned a dog at Vetc., and what Vetc.'s policy is for dogs who are left overnight or abandoned by their owners. If it indeed happens, what role might the system play in tracking the dog's situation?

*Customer notifies Vetc. that dog has died* is an event which Marge insisted on keeping on the list for purposes of stopping the flow of birthday cards and other direct mail material addressed to the dog. Pen made a note to ask what happens if a dog dies while under the care of Vetc.? If Binky has a fatal heart attack in the dog wash machine, is his entire visit free?

## *4.3 Event Dictionary Entry*

Event name:     Customer places order for dog

Description:     When a customer brings a dog into Vetc., the first task is to determine if either the customer or the dog has visited a Vetc. location before. If the customer has never been to Vetc., then a new customer record must be created. If the dog has never been to Vetc., a new dog record must be created. After the basic information about the customer and dog has been recorded, the receptionist places a service order for all of the items that the customer specifies he would like performed on the dog. The dog is placed in the cage, and the customer is given a printed order acknowledgment.

Initiator:     The customer initiates the data for this event.

Transporter:     Current: Today, the receptionist records all information for placing an order.

Future: For repeat customers, there is a potential for issuing identification tags or cards which provide the system with quick and accurate customer and dog identification.

| | |
|---|---|
| Stimulus: | Service Order |
| Activity: | If customer already has a record at Vetc. |

                    Retrieve customer record
                    Verify name, address and phone number
      Else (new customer)
                    Create new customer record
      End if
      If dog already has a record at Vetc. for this customer
                    Verify dog information
      Else if dog has a record under a different customer
                    Move dog record to this customer
      Else if dog has no prior record at Vetc.
                    Create new dog record
      End if
      Create new instance of Order
      For each requested Service Type,
                    Create new instance of Order Item
      End for each
      Compose Order Acknowledgment

| | |
|---|---|
| Response: | Order Acknowledgment |
| Effect: | Dog is surrendered to receptionist and can be weighed and sent back to the waiting queue. Customer has his order acknowledgment in hand and may leave the store. |

## Answers to Exercise 5 — Information Model

### 5.1 Entity-relationship diagram for order entry and fulfillment functions

No matter how large or small the project, Pendergast always felt far more confident after he had the information model started for the core of the system. In this case, the creating of an order and the rendering of a service forms the crux of Vetc.'s business. Once this piece of the information model began to take shape, Pendergast knew that it could be easily extended in many directions to accommodate the cashiering functions, invoicing, payments, inventory and so on. Figure A–8 shows Pendergast's information model for the data needed to place an order and mark it as completed.

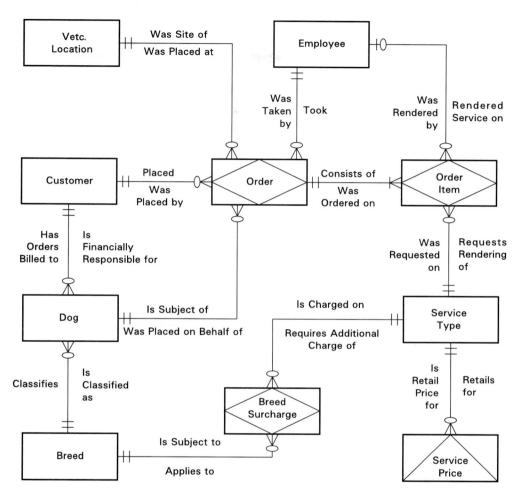

**Figure A–8.** ERD for Vetc.'s order entry and fulfillment functions

## 5.2 Issues surrounding relationship cardinality

Several issues arose when Pendergast's analysis team started to create the information model for the order entry function. There were questions on the very first relationship drawn between *Customer* and *Dog*. The analysts needed to know whether Vetc. demanded that all customers have at least one dog. The resolution came from Marge in marketing, who said that even though dogs might eventually be deleted from the database due to death, Vetc. will still want to retain the customer information for continued marketing efforts. A raging debate broke out over whether dogs could be owned by many customers, such as joint custody or racing dogs owned by limited partnerships. This debate was finally settled when Billy remarked that Vetc. doesn't care who *owns* the dog, they only require that one party be nominated as being financially responsible for paying for services rendered by Vetc..

In a quick review of the diagram, working from the upper left, we see that *Vetc. locations* are not required to have any *Orders* in the system, allowing for new stores to be set up in advance of their first order. However, *Orders* must be taken at one and only one *Vetc. location*. The *Employee* who took the order, usually the receptionist, is recorded on each *Order*. An *Order* is placed on behalf of only one *Dog*. It was agreed that Vetc. does not take multi-dog orders. If a customer arrives with multiple dogs, each dog will get a separate order in the system. Every order must have a *Dog* (Vetc. does not sell any over-the-counter supplies), and each order must name a *Customer* as the party responsible for payment. While the customer is derivable from the dog at the time of the order, the financially responsible party may change for the dog in the future, so the customer is also attached directly to each order.

Each *Order* must specify at least one *Service type*. *Service types* represent the list of services offered by Vetc.. Since many service types may be placed on an order, and the same service may appear on many orders, an *Order item* is created to record the request to render a specific *Service type* on a specific *Order*. *Order items* are created for the order by the receptionist when the customer requests services. They may also be created by the veterinarian as additional procedures are performed on the dog. *Service types* can have past, present and future *Service prices* listed for the service type. Some service types require close handling of the dog, and therefore a *Breed surcharge* is levied for certain vicious breeds.

Dogs are classified by *Breed*. A long discussion ensued as to whether mixed breeds such as a cocker and poodle mix were a separate breed as far as Vetc. was concerned. It was decided by Vetc.'s management that each dog would be classified into only *Breed* and that all common mixed breeds would be represented in the breed table. This solution worked out nicely because many mixed breeds have unique sensitivities to certain drugs or procedures.

### 5.3   Supertype/subtype relationships in the Vetc. information model

There are several places where the information modeler may discover supertype/subtype relationships. The most obvious place is the *Service type* entity. Vetc. offers two distinctly different classifications of services; those which are *Medical service types* and those which are *Grooming service types*. While they may share many of the same characteristics, there are some important differences. Only licensed veterinarians are authorized to perform medical procedures or prescribe medications. Therefore, the subtyping that you see in the *Service type* entity might also be reflected in the *Employee* entity. Employees can be easily subtyped into *Veterinarians*, *Groomers* and *Support staff* (Figure A–9).

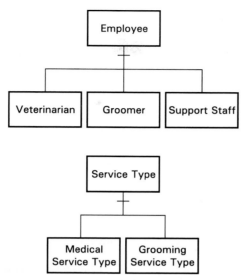

**Figure A–9.** Possible supertype/subtype relationships in the Vetc. information model

Following this pattern, *Order items* might also be subtyped into *Grooming order items* and *Medical order items*. You may have already discovered this same pattern of subtyping in the event model if you subtyped the event, *Customer places order for dog* into *Customer places medical order for dog* and *Customer places grooming order for dog*. The data required for either event is slightly different and warrants additional examination by the analyst. Whether you elect to retain all or any of these subtypes in your final database schema is more of a design decision than an analysis issue.

### 5.4 Associative entity types

Several associative entity types emerge in the Vetc. information model. The classic *Order* and *Order item* pattern is the result of customers being able to order many service types at once. *Breed surcharge* is another example of an associative entity type. It is the result of a *Breed* being subject to additional charges on multiple *Service types*, and a *Service type* being surcharged for multiple *Breeds*.

### 5.5 Attributive entity types

There is at least one fine, upstanding attributive entity type in Pendergast's model. The *Service price* entity is the result of a single *Service type* having many prices. The attribute *Service price* would form a repeating group on the *Service type* entity if it were not promoted to become an entity in its own right.

### 5.6   Entity and attribute definitions

The following attributes and definitions are based on the entity-relationship diagram presented in Figure A–8. Candidate identifiers are underlined. All repeating groups have been normalized, so the attribute cardinality can be expressed as required or optional.

**Entity:**      Vetc. Location
**Definition:**  A Vetc. Location is an individual store or administrative office, operated by Vetc.. As of this writing, Vetc. operates five stores engaged in the rendering of veterinary and grooming services to dogs, and has one central headquarters for corporate administration.

**Attributes:**

| Name | Required | Data Type | Definition |
|------|----------|-----------|------------|
| Location Code | Y | Char(2) | A two character code which quickly identifies a Vetc. Location. |
| Location Name | Y | Char(30) | The official company name used to denote a Vetc. Location, such as "Hampton Hills," or "Uptown Mall." |
| Location Type | Y | Char(6) | States whether a Vetc. Location renders services to dogs, or is an administrative office only. List = STORE, OFFICE. |
| Last Sequence Number | Y | Integer | Each Vetc. Location assigns order numbers in sequence throughout the calendar year. At year end, the sequences are set back to zero. When an order is placed, the system looks up the last sequence number at the store, adds 1 and updates the last sequence number. |

**Entity:**      Customer
**Definition:**  A Customer is the party nominated to be financially responsible for all services rendered to the dogs listed from them. The system assigns a customer number to each new customer. The number is used by the billing system if the customer charges services on their Vetc. account.

**Attributes:**

| Name | Required | Data Type | Definition |
|------|----------|-----------|------------|
| <u>Customer Number</u> | Y | Char(8) | A unique identifier assigned by the system which serves as the account number for the customer for the life of the customer at Vetc.. |
| Last Name | Y | Char(20) | The last name given by the customer to appear on all order, billing and direct mail documents. |
| First Name | Y | Char(20) | The first name given by the customer to appear on all order, billing and direct mail documents. |
| Middle Initial | N | Char(1) | An optional middle initial given by the customer to appear on all order, billing and direct mail documents. |
| Prefix | N | Char(3) | The customer may optionally specify a prefix for direct mail salutations. List = Mr., Ms., Mrs., Dr. |
| Suffix | N | Char(3) | The customer's name may contain a suffix such as Jr., Sr., III. |
| Address | N | Varchar (180) | The street address or post office box of the customer is required if the customer is to charge services for later billing. Otherwise, customers may opt to not give their address but must then pay in full at check-out. Addresses are large text fields which will accept carriage returns for multi-line addresses. |
| City | N | Char(30) | The name of the municipality associated with the customer address. |
| State | N | Char(2) | The two-character postal code for the state or province in which the city is located. Vetc. is not going to maintain city/state/zip code relationships in the database. |
| Zip | N | Char(10) | The postal zip code associated with the address. |
| Daytime Phone | N | Char(15) | A telephone number at which the customer can be reached before 5 PM is required for veterinary visits, but not for grooming visits. |
| Evening Phone | N | Char(15) | A telephone number at which the customer can be reached after 5 PM is required for veterinary visits which require an overnight stay. |

**Entity:**        Dog
**Definition:**    A Dog is the canine patron for which grooming and or veterinary services are rendered at Vetc.. Vetc. has a stated mission of treating only
dogs and has no current or future plans to expand into other pets.
**Attributes:**

| Name | Required | Data Type | Definition |
|------|----------|-----------|------------|
| <u>Dog ID</u> | Y | Token | A value assigned by the system to uniquely identify an instance of dog. |
| Dog Name | Y | Char(20) | The name given by the customer for the dog. |
| Last Weight LBS | N | Integer | The last known weight of the dog can be derived from the dog weight recorded on its last order. It is possible that the most recent weight will be stored redundantly with the dog's record for quick retrieval. |
| Birthdate | N | Date | Customers who provide a birthdate for their dogs will receive a birthday card in the mail each year. |
| Sex | Y | Char(1) | Indicates whether the dog is male or female. List = M, F. |
| Neutered Spayed | Y | Yes/No | A Y/N field which indicates if the dog has been neutered/spayed. |
| Allergies | N | Note | A text field in which any known allergies of the dog can be noted. |
| Deceased | Y | Yes/No | A Y/N field which indicates if the dog has died. Default=N. |

**Entity:**        Breed
**Definition:**    A breed is a common classification for dogs to denote the type of dog.
At Vetc., all traditional breeds, such as Dalmatian, Collie, Toy Poodle
will be recognized, as well as mixed breeds such as Cocker-Poodle and
indeterminate Mutts.
**Attributes:**

| Name | Required | Data Type | Definition |
|------|----------|-----------|------------|
| <u>Breed ID</u> | Y | Token | A value assigned by the system to uniquely identify an instance of breed. |
| Breed Name | Y | Char(30) | The common name by which the breed is referred, such as "English Sheepdog," "Standard Poodle," "Dalmatian." |

*continued*

*continued*

| Name | Required | Data Type | Definition |
|------|----------|-----------|------------|
| Eligible for Happy Hound | Y | Yes/No | Indicates whether the breed can be put through the Happy Hound Sanitation Module. Several rare, small or extremely long haired breeds are restricted from the machine and must be groomed by hand. |
| Sensitivities | N | Note | A large text field in which particular sensitivities, reactions to medication or restrictions can be noted. The breed sensitivities should be displayed on all order documents and workstations and should be available for review by all groomers or veterinarians prior to rendering services. |

**Entity:**       Employee
**Definition:**   An employee is a salaried or hourly worker paid by the Vetc. corporation.
**Attributes:**

| Name | Required | Data Type | Definition |
|------|----------|-----------|------------|
| Employee Number | Y | Char(10) | The employee number assigned by the payroll system. (Note that a matching data type to the payroll system is used here.) |
| Last Name | Y | Char(20) | The last name given by the employee to appear on all internal and payroll documents. |
| First Name | Y | Char(20) | The first name given by the employee to appear on all internal and payroll documents. |
| Middle Initial | N | Char(1) | An optional middle initial given by the employee. |
| Prefix | N | Char(3) | The employee may optionally specify a prefix for direct mail salutations. List = Mr., Ms., Mrs., Dr. |
| Suffix | N | Char(3) | The employee's name may contain a suffix such as Jr., Sr., III. |
| Initials | Y | Char(4) | A concatenation (done by hand) of the employee's initials to appear in columnar data where space is too limited to display the full name. |
| Employee Type | Y | Char(7) | Indicates the skill type of the employee. Employees may be listed as veterinarians, groomers or support staff. Only vets can render medical services. Support staff cannot render any services to the dog. List = VET, GROOMER, SUPPORT. |

**Entity:**       Order

**Definition:**      An order represents an instance of a customer requesting one or more services for a single dog at a specific Vetc. location. The order records the date, order number and status of the transaction and serves as the header for all order items.

**Attributes:**

| Name | Required | Data Type | Definition |
|---|---|---|---|
| <u>Order ID</u> | Y | Token | A value assigned by the system to uniquely identify an instance of order. |
| Order Number | Y | Char(12) | The order number is printed on documents and displayed on the screen to help employees and customers quickly identify an order. It is assigned by the system when the order is created. While it is unique, it is not the primary key for the order table. It is a concatenation of Vetc. Location Code, a sequence number and the last two year digits of the order date. Example: 02-00123-98 would represent the 123rd order placed at store #2 in 1998. |
| Order Date | Y | Date | The date on which the order was placed, (MM,DD, YYYY). |
| Order Status | Y | Char(10) | Indicates the condition of the order as it passes through the order fulfillment process. Valid states are: |
| | | | NEW: The initial state of the order indicates that no services have yet been rendered. |
| | | | IN PROCESS: Services are being performed, but not all services are completed. |
| | | | COMPLETED: All services have been marked as completed and the dog is ready for pick-up. |
| | | | CANCELED: The entire order was canceled. |
| | | | CLOSED: The dog has been picked-up and the customer has either paid in full or signed for charges on their Vetc. account. |
| Dog Weight LBS | N | Integer | The weight of the dog in pounds is recorded by the scale and updated on the order shortly after the order is created. If the scale fails to record the dog's weight, the user can manually type the dog's estimated weight on the order. |
| Nature of Problem | N | Note | For medical visits, the customer is asked to briefly explain the nature of the dog's injuries or condition. |

*continued*

*continued*

| Name | Required | Data Type | Definition |
| --- | --- | --- | --- |
| Current Medications | N | Note | For medical visits, the customer is asked to list any medications the dog is currently taking. Vetc. has recently evaluated this policy and decided that they should be asking this question for grooming visits as well. |
| Special Instructions | N | Note | Indicates any special handling instructions for this order. |

**Entity:**       Order Item

**Definition:**   An order item represents a request for a service type on the order. When the order is first created, customers request one or more services to be performed on the dog. Because dogs are often admitted for a standard office visit for veterinary services, the veterinarian may insert additional order items as they prescribe or administer medications or perform additional procedures. Breed surcharges are also added to the order as order items when the customer requests service types that require an additional surcharge for the breed of the dog (such as hand-shampooing a pit bull).

**Attributes:**

| Name | Required | Data Type | Definition |
| --- | --- | --- | --- |
| Order Item ID | Y | Token | A value assigned by the system to uniquely identify an instance of order item. |
| Order Item Number | Y | Integer | Denotes the line item number of the order item, so items display in the same order on all windows and reports. |
| Order Item Status | Y | Char(10) | Indicates the condition of the order item as it passes through the order fulfillment process. Valid states are: |
| | | | NEW: The initial state of customer requested order item indicates that the service has not yet been rendered. |
| | | | IN PROCESS: Indicates that the dog is currently undergoing the service. |
| | | | COMPLETED: Indicates that the service is complete. This may be the initial state of items added by the vet to the dog's order after they have been rendered. |

*continued*

*continued*

| Name | Required | Data Type | Definition |
|------|----------|-----------|------------|
| | | | CANCELED: Indicates that the service type was purposefully not rendered by Vetc.. |
| Source | Y | Char(8) | Indicates whether the order item was requested by the customer, prescribed by the veterinarian, or inserted by the system as is the case with breed surcharges. List = CUSTOMER, VET, SYSTEM. |
| Unit Price | N | Money | The unit price is the unit price of the service type at the time the order item was created. A unit price must be accompanied by a price basis value. |
| Price Basis | N | Char(4) | Indicates the unit of measure for the unit price. Charges at Vetc. are either a flat rate, by the hour, or by the pound. Price basis is required when the unit price is added to the order item. List = FLAT, /HR, /LB. |
| Quantity | N | Decimal (5,2) | The quantity field is used to record the number units charged for the order item. For flat charges, the quantity is usually 1. For per hour charges, the quantity is the number of hours, to the nearest quarter hour, during which the service was performed. For per pound charges, the quantity field reflects the weight of the dog to the nearest pound. Some quantities cannot be determined until the service is performed. |

**Entity:** Service Type

**Definition:** The list of service types represents all services, both medical and grooming in nature which are offered by Vetc.. Services can be retired by inactivating them, or made active again.

**Attributes:**

| Name | Required | Data Type | Definition |
|------|----------|-----------|------------|
| <u>Service Type ID</u> | Y | Token | A value assigned by the system to uniquely identify an instance of service type. |
| Service Type Name | Y | Char(20) | The official short description by which the service is referred on windows and reports within Vetc.. |
| Marketing Description | Y | Note | The narrative provided by the Marketing Department to fully describe the service. It can be used in promotional literature and catalogues. |

*continued*

*continued*

| Name | Required | Data Type | Definition |
|------|----------|-----------|------------|
| Service Type Class | Y | Char(10) | Indicates whether the service type is classified as a veterinary service or grooming service. List = VETERINARY, GROOMING. |
| Service Interval MOs | N | Integer | The number of months after the last order within which the service type should be repeated. This number is used to generate reminder notices. |
| Special Instructions | N | Note | A text field in which procedural notes, cautions or warnings can be entered. |
| Active | Y | Yes/No | Indicates if the service is currently available for sale at all Vetc. Locations. |

**Entity:** Service Price

**Definition:** The service price states the unit price and price basis for a specific service type. Each service type can have only one active price at a time. Price effective date ranges may not overlap for a service type. The expiration date is optional, meaning if it is not entered, the price is effective until further notice.

**Attributes:**

| Name | Required | Data Type | Definition |
|------|----------|-----------|------------|
| Service Price ID | Y | Token | A value assigned by the system to uniquely identify an instance of service price. |
| Effective Date | Y | Date | The date on which the service price becomes effective. |
| Expiration Date | N | Date | The date on which the service price expires. Prices with no expiration date will remain effective until an end date is entered and reached. |
| Unit Price | Y | Money | The unit price is the retail unit price of the service type starting on the effective date and ending on the expiration date stated on the service price record. |
| Price Basis | Y | Char(4) | Indicates the unit of measure for the unit price. Charges at Vetc. are either a flat rate, by the hour, or by the pound. Price basis is required when the unit price is added to the order item. List = FLAT, /HR, /LB. |

**Entity:**        Breed Surcharge
**Definition:**    A breed surcharge is an additional cost added to the price of a service
                   type when the service type is rendered for a specific breed. Surcharges
                   are independent of the service price. They have their own effective date
                   ranges and unit of measure. Surcharges are added for particularly large,
                   difficult or vicious breeds.
**Attributes:**

| Name | Required | Data Type | Definition |
| --- | --- | --- | --- |
| Breed Surcharge ID | Y | Token | A value assigned by the system to uniquely identify an instance of breed surcharge. |
| Effective Date | Y | Date | The date on which the breed surcharge becomes effective. |
| Expiration Date | N | Date | The date on which the breed surcharge expires. Prices with no expiration date will remain effective until an end date is entered and reached. |
| Unit Price | Y | Money | The unit price is the retail unit price of the breed surcharge starting on the effective date and ending on the expiration date stated on the service price record. |
| Price Basis | Y | Char(4) | Indicates the unit of measure for the unit price. Charges at Vetc. are either a flat rate, by the hour, or by the pound. Price basis is required when the unit price is added to the order item. List = FLAT, /HR, /LB. |

## Answers to Exercise 6 — Interface Prototype

6.1    The system users in Vetc. locations have specific duties, such as reception, groom-
       ing, veterinary and accounting. A logical first pass at organizing the event list would
       be to group events by the subject (or more precisely, the future transporter). The
       receptionist's events would include all possible permutations of *Customer places
       order for dog*, the events surrounding making appointments for surgery, weighing
       the dog, checking out the dog and accepting point-of-sale payments for the order.
       The idea is to consider giving the receptionist one-stop-shopping in the system by
       aggregating all of the receptionist's events together into one local vicinity on the
       interface. Then the events could be grouped by object to see which events affect
       customers, dogs, reservation orders and service types. This same process could be
       repeated for vets and groomers, giving each of them a customized work area within
       the application (perhaps their own MDI frame?) where they can execute all of the
       tasks for which they are responsible without having to navigate all around the appli-
       cation.

Another useful exercise would be to sort the entire event list by object to see what common functions, such as looking up orders, might be required across the entire system. Organizing order processing events chronologically would also be useful, examining whether a left-to-right or top-to-bottom placement of these functions on the main menu or a tool bar would make the interface more intuitive for users.

6.2    To create the first-cut prototype, Pendergast opened up his information model, attribute listings and event dictionary for the check-in event. He then made some assumptions about the skill level of the user. He remembered that although Wanda was highly trained, Marge had said that the newer stores will be looking to recruit less experienced help. This led Pen to assume that all commands, data and instructions on the interface will have to be clearly spelled out, and that *ease of training* is a prime quality vector. He also remembered that one of the objectives was to significantly reduce check-in time, so *conservation of keystrokes* is also a prime quality vector; one which can be sometimes at odds with *ease of training*.

He then proceeded to identify the various windows needed to check in a dog. The system would need a way to select from a list of existing customers and dogs, enter or update information about a customer and his dogs, enter a new order and its order items, select from a list of service types, and possibly browse a customer's past orders and copy one of them. Deferring any navigational issues until later, he sketched out some candidate layouts of the windows he had identified.

The first window Pendergast drew was the *Patron Profile* window on which the basic information about a customer and his dogs is maintained. The window is capable of creating or updating one customer and multiple dogs for that customer. The customer information is displayed in the top portion of the window, the dogs in the lower portion. The scrollable list of dogs on the lower left is synchronized with the dog details on the lower right so that whichever dog has focus displays in the details area (Figure A–10).

The next window Pendergast drew was the *Order Entry* window on which the receptionist would enter the details of an order after the customer and dog was identified and verified (Figure A–11).

After he was finished with the two maintenance windows, Pen moved on to the selection windows. He created a *Service Type Selection* window to give the receptionist a list of active service types from which one or more service types could be selected to create new order items (Figure A–12). The users said they would like the current prices displayed on the selection window as well. Pendergast immediately identified this as a potential performance issue that would have to be addressed in the design. In the logical model, the most current price is derivable from the *Service Price* entity by comparing the current date to the effective and expiration dates for each service type. In the final design, he would need to devise a way to display all service types quickly along with their most current prices. Mentally, he considered his options. He could store the most current price in the database with the service type and update it via stored procedures anytime the service prices changed. He could cache the contents of the *Service Price Selection* window locally at the client so the window didn't have to hit the database each time it opened. He made a note to speak with the people in marketing to find out how often prices changed, and if they ever initiated a price change that was effective during the same business day.

**Figure A–10.** The *Patron Profile* window layout

Vetc. had already agreed that they would issue ID cards to customers so they could retrieve their records for quick check-in. Pendergast envisioned swiping a card through a magnetic reader to retrieve the Patron Profile, or perhaps using a bar-code scanner. Pen also needed was a way to locate a customer or his dog in the database when the customer didn't bring in his card, or when the customer was unsure under who's name the dog was listed. The window could also be used to move a dog record from one customer to another. He devised a *Patron Selection* window which allowed the users to enter a partial name string for the customer's last name, a partial string if they remembered part of the customer number, or possibly a partial string to retrieve by the dog's name (Figure A–13). He also added breed to the selection criteria to help narrow the search. The result set in the body of the window would display all records which meet the selection criteria at top. Since customers can have more than one dog, subsequent rows with the same customer would suppress the repeating values. Pendergast was happy with the flexibility this window provided, but made another note that he had a potential performance issue on his hands and he would have to put his best SQL expert on this window to ensure it retrieved in an acceptable amount of time.

**Order Entry - [Order Number - Order Status]**

Customer Name:            Customer Number:    Order Date:

Dog Name:      Sex:         Weight:    Breed: ☒ Happy Hound OK?

        ☒ Neutered?    lbs.

Nature of Problem:          Current Medications:

Special Instructions:

Order Items:

| Line | Service Type | Src | Unit Price | Basis | Qty | Extended Price |
|------|--------------|-----|------------|-------|-----|----------------|
|      |              |     |            |       |     |                |
|      |              |     |            |       |     |                |
|      |              |     |            |       |     |                |
|      |              |     |            |       |     |                |

Tax:
Total:

**Figure A–11.** The *Order Entry* window layout

**Service Type Selection**

● All    ○ Grooming Only    ○ Veterinary Only

| Service Type Name | Current Unit Price | Price Basis |
|-------------------|--------------------|-------------|
|                   |                    |             |
|                   |                    |             |
|                   |                    |             |
|                   |                    |             |
|                   |                    |             |
|                   |                    |             |
|                   |                    |             |
|                   |                    |             |
|                   |                    |             |
|                   |                    |             |
|                   |                    |             |

**Figure A–12.** The *Service Type Selection* window layout

**Patron Selection**

Last Name:          Customer Number:   Dog Name:          Breed:

| Customer Name | Customer Number | Dog Name | Breed |
|---------------|-----------------|----------|-------|
|  |  |  |  |
|  |  |  |  |
|  |  |  |  |
|  |  |  |  |
|  |  |  |  |
|  |  |  |  |
|  |  |  |  |
|  |  |  |  |
|  |  |  |  |
|  |  |  |  |
|  |  |  |  |
|  |  |  |  |
|  |  |  |  |

**Figure A–13.** The *Patron Selection* window layout

**Order Selection**

Order Status:          Order Date > =    Order Number:  Store:

| Order Number | Customer Name | Dog Name | Order Date | Status |
|--------------|---------------|----------|------------|--------|
|  |  |  |  |  |
|  |  |  |  |  |
|  |  |  |  |  |
|  |  |  |  |  |
|  |  |  |  |  |
|  |  |  |  |  |
|  |  |  |  |  |
|  |  |  |  |  |
|  |  |  |  |  |
|  |  |  |  |  |
|  |  |  |  |  |
|  |  |  |  |  |
|  |  |  |  |  |

**Figure A–14.** The *Order Selection* window layout

The last window Pendergast sketched was the *Order Selection* window. The receptionist needed a way to display orders which were currently being serviced at the Vetc. location. The system also was chartered to retrieve a customer's order history and allow the receptionist to copy an order, whether the order occurred at that Vetc. store or any other. Pen figured that he could devise a window which was capable of retrieving all outstanding orders in the store, or researching order histories for a given customer if the window was opened from a customer record. Pen came up with the window layout in Figure A–14 and scheduled a meeting with the users to review his work.

## Answers to Exercise 7 — Architecture Model

7.1  Figure A–15 depicts an event/business location matrix for the Vetc. project. Some of the business level events from the event list have been consolidated into conceptual level events to keep the diagram simple.

7.2  To do a good job of architecture modeling for Vetc., you would need to know the current and projected future number of orders placed per day at each store, including average and peak traffic volumes. You would also need to determine the estimated number of cash and charge account customers and dogs that may patronize Vetc. as they saturate their market. The company would need to determine some reasonable cycle for archiving old orders, inactive customers, and dogs who statistically are far beyond their life expectancy. Vetc. must also provide a reasonable estimate of their potential future growth. Each new store will add additional burdens to the information infrastructure. These statistics, along with the byte size estimates that you can glean from your information model can give you a good idea of the disk capacity requirements for each store and for the central headquarters. The amount of network traffic then can be modeled between stores and the corporate headquarters for various distribution schemes.

7.3  Vetc. has a classic problem of needing a great deal of its data to be everywhere at once. Let's review the different options for where to locate Vetc.'s data:

**Centralization:** Vetc. could maintain one master copy of the database at a central location. For that matter, the application could be very centralized on a powerful central server as well. The advantage is that all of the data is located in one place, and it is always current. The downside is that the entire system is at the mercy of the wide area network. If it's very, very fast, then there's no big problem, unless of course the wide area network goes down. Then the Vetc. stores are without a computer system until communication with the central host is restored.

| Event/Business location | Store Locations | Corporate Headquarters |
|---|---|---|
| Customer places order | X | |
| Customer requests surgery appointment | X | |
| Groomer acknowledges services | X | |
| Vet acknowledges services | X | |
| Customer claims dog | X | |
| Time to bill credit customers | | X |
| Customer pays invoice | | X |
| Clerk balances daily receipts | X | |
| Time to post activity to GL | | X |
| User requests sales reports | X | X |
| Marketing updates prices/services | | X |
| Marketing creates direct mailing | X | X |
| Inventory falls below reorder point | X | |
| Vetc. receives inventory supplies | X | |
| User requests inventory balance | X | X |
| Customer changes dog/cust data | X | X |

**Figure A–15.** An event/business location matrix for Vetc.

**Replicated, decentralized data:** Each Vetc. location could have a complete copy of the database schema on their own data server. The replication scheme ranges anywhere from every store having every record, to stores only having records created at their store (horizontal fragmentation). The advantage of replicating all records is that each store can research a dog's history at Vetc. without having to appeal to other servers at other locations. The disadvantage is increased wide area network traffic to keep all sites in sync. A horizontal fragmentation scheme where each store keeps a copy of only the customers, dogs and orders who have visited the store reduces inter-store network traffic, but increases the complexity of the application because if a customer, dog or order isn't found at one store, the application must search the system either at the corporate database or the other stores to find it. There are significant advantages to stores having their own complete copy of the database. They are completely protected from system failure if the central database, wide area network, or another store's system goes down. They also enjoy better performance because the data access is local to the site. The disadvantage comes in managing the replication scheme. Data can be synchronized on a real-time or periodic basis. In a replicated environment, you always run the slight risk of a record being updated in two places before they are synchronized, and you must decide which update "wins."

For Vetc., Pendergast favored a fully replicated database scheme where each site had a complete copy. Database would be synchronized on a periodic basis, possibly at night. The overwhelming advantage would be autonomy for each store if any one part of the wide area network fails. The disadvantage would be the risk of a customer visiting another store before their data did.

## Answers to Exercise 8 — Database Design

8.1  The following database design schema was derived from the information model in exercise 5. It is written in a dialect-neutral fashion. Your particular database tool may differ slightly in syntax, data type and limitation on the size of table and column names.

```
Create table Vetc._Location (
Location_Code            Char(2)       NOT NULL      PRIMARY KEY,
Location_Name            Char(30)      NOT NULL,
Location_Type            Char(6)       NOT NULL,
Last_Sequence_Number     Integer       NOT NULL);

Create table Customer (
Customer_Number          Char(8)       NOT NULL      PRIMARY KEY,
Last_Name                Char(20)      NOT NULL,
First_Name               Char(20)      NOT NULL,
Middle_Initial           Char(1),
Prefix                   Char(3),
Suffix                   Char(3),
Address                  Varchar(180),
City                     Char(30),
State                    Char(2),
Zip                      Char(10),
Daytime_Phone            Char(15),
Evening_Phone            Char(15));

Create table Breed (
Breed_ID                 Token         NOT NULL      PRIMARY KEY,
Breed_Name               Char(30)      NOT NULL,
Eligible_for_Happy_Hound Yes/No        NOT NULL,
Sensitivities            Note);

Create table Dog (
Dog_ID                   Token         NOT NULL      PRIMARY KEY,
Dog_Name                 Char(20)      NOT NULL,
Last_Weight_LBS          Integer,
Birthdate                Date,
```

```
Sex                       Char(1)      NOT NULL,
Neutered_Spayed           Yes/No       NOT NULL,
Allergies                 Note,
Deceased                  Yes/No       NOT NULL,
Customer_Number           Char(8)      NOT NULL     FOREIGN KEY
  References Customer (Customer_Number),
Breed_ID                  Token        NOT NULL     FOREIGN KEY
  References Breed (Breed_ID));

Create table Employee (
Employee_Number           Char(10)     NOT NULL     PRIMARY KEY,
Last_Name                 Char(20)     NOT NULL,
First_Name                Char(20)     NOT NULL,
Middle_Initial            Char(1),
Prefix                    Char(3),
Suffix                    Char(3),
Initials                  Char(4)      NOT NULL,
Employee_Type             Char(7)      NOT NULL);

Create table Service_Type (
Service_Type_ID           Token        NOT NULL     PRIMARY KEY,
Service_Type_Name         Char(20)     NOT NULL,
Marketing_Description     Note         NOT NULL,
Service_Type_Class        Char(10)     NOT NULL,
Service_Interval_Mos      Integer,
Special_Instructions      Note,
Active                    Yes/No       NOT NULL);

Create table Order (
Order_ID                  Token        NOT NULL     PRIMARY KEY,
Order_Number              Char(12)     NOT NULL,
Order_Date                Date         NOT NULL,
Order_Status              Char(10)     NOT NULL,
Dog_Weight_LBS            Integer,
Nature_of_Problem         Note,
Current_Medications       Note,
Special_Instructions      Note,
Customer_Number           Char(8)      NOT NULL     FOREIGN KEY
  References Customer (Customer_Number),
Location_Code             Char(2)      NOT NULL     FOREIGN KEY
  References Vetc._Location (Location_code),
Dog_ID                    Token        NOT NULL     FOREIGN KEY
  References Dog (Dog_ID),
Taken_By                  Char(10)     NOT NULL     FOREIGN KEY
  References Employee (Employee_Number));

Create table Order_Item (
Order_Item_ID             Token        NOT NULL     PRIMARY KEY,
Order_Item_Number         Integer      NOT NULL,
Order_Item_Status         Char(10)     NOT NULL,
Source                    Char(8)      NOT NULL,
Unit_Price                Money,
Price_Basis               Char(4),
```

```
Quantity                        Decimal(5,2),
Order_ID                        Token       NOT NULL    FOREIGN KEY
  References Order (Order_ID),
Service_Type_ID                 Token       NOT NULL    FOREIGN KEY
  References Service_Type (Service_Type_ID),
Rendered_by                     Char(10)    FOREIGN KEY
  References Employee (Employee_Number),
UNIQUE (Order_ID, Order_Item_Number));


Create table Service_Price (
Service_Price_ID                Token       NOT NULL    PRIMARY KEY,
Effective_Date                  Date        NOT NULL,
Expiration_Date                 Date,
Unit_Price                      Money       NOT NULL,
Price_Basis                     Char(4)     NOT NULL,
Service_Type_ID                 Token       NOT NULL    FOREIGN KEY
  References Service_Type (Service_Type_ID));


Create table Breed_Surcharge (
Breed_Surcharge_ID              Token       NOT NULL    PRIMARY KEY,
Effective_Date                  Date        NOT NULL,
Expiration_Date                 Date,
Unit_Price                      Money       NOT NULL,
Price_Basis                     Char(4)     NOT NULL,
Service_Type_ID                 Token       NOT NULL    FOREIGN KEY
  References Service_Type (Service_Type_ID),
Breed_ID                        Token       NOT NULL    FOREIGN KEY
  References Breed (Breed_ID));
```

8.2    There are several more modifications in store for our database design before it becomes final. The requirements placed on the system due to the chosen data replication scheme or auditing needs may add *Date and time of last update* to each table. If a horizontal fragmentation scheme is chosen, each row might have to include a foreign key to its "home" *Vetc. location*. Also, Pendergast is still concerned with the performance of having to calculate the current price for each *Service type*. He is seriously considering adding the most current unit price and price basis to the *Service type* table, a slight denormalization that will have to be maintained via stored procedures anytime a *Service price* changes. This shift of determining current prices from the read action to the insert, update and delete actions is a safe trade-off at Vetc. since prices are only changed a few times per year, but they are read many times per day.

## Answers to Exercise 9 — External Interface Design

9.1    Pendergast assembled his design team to discuss the overall layout of the application. They decided that Vetc. had very distinct division of duties such that an organizational partitioning would work well for the system. They decided to group events together for each user role and create separate MDI frames for each section of the application. That way the receptionists would have everything at their fingertips within one MDI frame, the veterinarians would have all of their windows in their own MDI frame, and the groomers would have their own frame for their windows. The navigation in each frame would be optimized to help the users accomplish their unique tasks. The same window could appear in many frames, such as *Order Selection*, and users could open frames outside of their own, as long as they had authority to do so. For instance, the veterinarian might want to open the *Inventory* application or the *Reception* application. Having separate frames around distinct organizational areas of the system will help control the confusion that can arise when the user has many windows open. The *Inventory* application can be open at the same time as the *Reception* application, but inventory windows cannot be interleaved with reception windows because they are in separate MDI frames. The team also agreed that the user should only be able to open one instance of each type of MDI frame at a time.

The design team drew up a main menu with large picture push buttons (Figure A–16). Each button opens one of six separate applications within the Vetc. system.

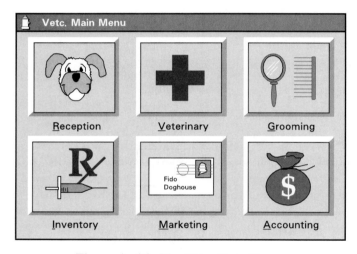

**Figure A–16.** The *Vetc. Main Menu*

Next, they began working on the navigation within the *Reception* MDI frame (Figure A–17). Their first assumption was that the receptionist would probably keep the *Reception* MDI frame open for the entire shift. For the event, *Customer places order for dog*, they decided that the primary objective was to get the receptionist to the *Patron Profile* window as quickly as possible to verify the customer's current address, phone numbers and dog details before placing the order. They came up with two ways to do this. If a customer shows up with a Vetc. ID card that allows the system to electronically identify the customer and dog record, the system could open the *Patron Profile* window as soon as the card is read. If the customer has no quick-identification card, the receptionist should ask if he has ever visited any Vetc. store. If he has not, the receptionist should be able to open the *Patron Profile* window directly from *Patron Selection* and establish a new customer. If the customer has been to a Vetc. before or is not sure, the receptionist does a search for the customer and/or the dog on the *Patron Selection* window, finds the customer records, clicks on it and proceeds to the *Patron Profile* window.

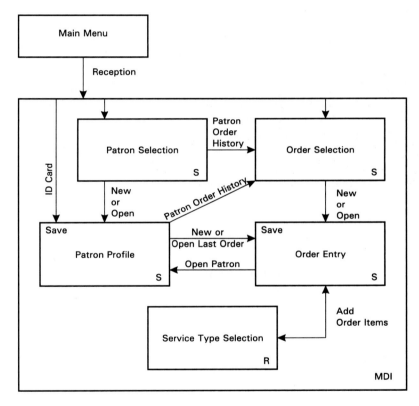

**Figure A–17.** Window navigation diagram for the check-in window within the *Reception* MDI frame

Wanda told the team that, as a receptionist, she would also want the *Order Selection* window open at all times so she could keep track of which orders were progressing through the store that day. It is from that window that the receptionist would open a completed order to perform the check-out functions, open a historical customer record to copy it, or check on the status of an order if a customer calls or shows up early to claim his dog.

From the *Order Entry* window, the user should be able to open the customer's *Patron Profile* window, and from any *Patron Profile*, the user should be able to open the *Order Entry* window to see either the customer's most recent order, place a new order, or open a list of the customer's order history at Vetc. on the *Order Selection* window. The *Patron Profile* has its own **Save** command which commits changes made to the customer record and the associated dog records. The *Order Entry* window has a separate **Save** command which commits changes to the order and its associated order items.

When the receptionist places a new order on the *Order Entry* window, the *Service Type Selection* window can be opened and the user can select one or more service types and click **OK**. When the *Service Type Selection* window closes, an order item is created for each service type selected. Pendergast has also considered making the *Service Type Selection* window an MDI sheet, keeping it always open and allowing the receptionist to drag and drop service types onto the order item section of the window. For now, he's decided to leave it as a response window since the interface is getting complex enough as it is.

9.2   Pendergast and his design team now had the navigation, window type and unit of work worked out for the check-in windows. After they reviewed their work, they completed the external design specification. Once the specification was reviewed by the users and the design team, it was ready to turn over to the development team and quality assurance group for coding and preparation of test plans.

*Note: I have tried to keep the answer set language neutral, however, the external interface design specification favors a Windows implementation. I have also included the term datawindow (dw_) from PowerBuilder to describe the display areas of the windows. Users of other GUI tools can substitute their own nomenclature.*

## *Window Layout* — **Reception**

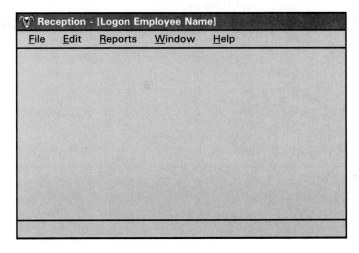

**Figure A–18.** The *Reception* MDI Frame

## *Window Description* — **Reception**

| | |
|---|---|
| Title Bar: | Reception - [Logon Employee First Name Last Name] |
| Menu: | Yes |
| Window Type: | MDI frame |

The *Reception* window is an MDI frame which contains all of the windows necessary to perform the reception functions at Vetc.. It is opened from the *Vetc. Main Menu* by clicking on the "Reception" icon. The title bar displays the first and last name of the employee who is currently logged on the system. The frame contains a menu which allows the user to print windows, exit the application, cut, copy and paste text, select from a list of available reports, organize windows within the frame or get on-line help. Only one instance of the frame may be opened at one time. If the user clicks on the main menu "Reception" icon while the frame is open, focus will return to the open frame rather than open another *Reception* frame.

*Note: The design specification for the behavior of an MDI frame should only have to be specified once for a project, then all of the other MDI frames in the application should conform to the standard or note where and why they are different.*

### Window Mini-Spec — Reception

| Input parameters: | User authorization, User Name |
|---|---|
| Open: | Open *Patron Selection*, *Order Selection* |
| Close: | Close all open windows within the frame (triggers confirmation for any uncommitted saves) |
| | Close window, return focus to main menu |

## Menu items

| Label | Item label | Enabled | Clicked |
|---|---|---|---|
| File | Print | When one or more sheets are opened within the frame | Prints hard copy report for the sheet which has focus in the frame |
| File | Exit | Always | Execute Close |
| Edit | Undo | When data value has been changed | Roll back data value to previous value |
| Edit | Cut | When text is selected | Cut text to clipboard |
| Edit | Copy | When text is selected | Copy text to clipboard |
| Edit | Paste | When clipboard has data | Copy clipboard to selected field |
| Reports | List of available reports | Always | Display list of reports available within the Reception frame |
| Window | Tile | When at least one sheet is open | Tile open sheets |
| Window | Cascade | When at least one sheet is open | Cascade open sheets |
| Window | Layer | When at least one sheet is open | Layer open sheets |
| Window | [open sheets] | When at least one sheet is open | List open sheets by window title |
| Help | [window title] | When focus on a sheet | Open window-level help for sheet which has focus |
| Help | Contents | Always | Open Help Contents |
| Help | Index | Always | Open Help Index |
| Help | About | Always | Open About Window |

## *Window Layout* — **Patron Selection**

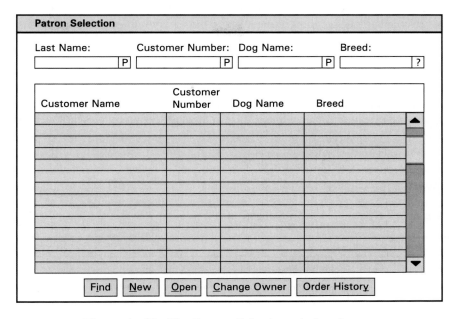

**Figure A–19.** The *Patron Selection* window layout

## *Window Description* — **Patron Selection**

| Title Bar: | Patron Selection |
|---|---|
| Window Type: | Sheet |

The **Patron Selection** window is a sheet which always remains open within the *Reception* MDI frame. It can be minimized on the frame, but not closed. It is used to locate a patron's profile within the Vetc. system of stores. The user may enter selection criteria at the top of the window, then click the Find button. The system will return all customer rows and their associated dogs which match the selection criteria entered by the user. The *Customer last name* is the most commonly used search value. By allowing the user to specify partial string searches on last name, misspelled names are more likely to be caught and corrected in the system. The *Customer number* is also a partial string search, although it is anticipated that the receptionist will only use this field when the customer's quick-ID card fails to register properly with the card reader. The *Dog name* and *Breed* fields are used by the receptionist when trying to locate a particular dog in the system when the customer either doesn't know under which family member the customer record was created, or when a dog is changing owners.

When records are displayed in the result set the user may select a customer and open either the *Patron Profile* window for that customer, or the customer's order history at Vetc.. If no customer is found in the system, the receptionist can click **New** to create a new patron profile.

The window also allows the receptionist to change the owner of an existing dog by locating that dog's current record, selecting it and clicking **Change Owner**. A dialogue box opens which asks whether the user wants to create a new customer or find an existing customer in the database. If new is selected, the system opens the *Patron Profile* window in new mode, but retrieves the dog ID into the dog section of the window. If the user wishes to find the existing customer, the standard *Customer Selection* window displays allowing the user to pick the new customer from the database. When the user finds the customer and clicks **OK** the *Patron Profile* window is opened and the dog's record is added to the new customer record.

### *Window Mini-Spec* — Patron Selection

| Input parameters: | None |
|---|---|
| Open: | Place cursor in *Last name* field |
| Close: | Disabled |

### *Buttons*

| Label | Enabled | Clicked |
|---|---|---|
| Find | Always | Retrieve dw_patron_selection using select criteria |
| New | Always | Open *Patron Profile, mode* = new |
| Open | When focus on one row in dw_patron_selection | Open *Patron Profile* using *customer_number, mode* = new |
| Change Owner | When focus on one row in dw_patron_selection | Open dialogue box asking if user wants to create a new customer or find an existing customer.<br>If new,<br>  Open *Patron Profile*, using *dog_id, mode* = new<br>Else<br>  Execute function *Customer selection*<br>  When customer is selected,<br>  Open *Patron Profile*, using *customer_number, dog_id, mode* = add dog<br>End if |
| Order History | When focus on one row in dw_patron_selection | Open *Order Selection* using *customer_number, customer_name, dog_id, dog_name* |

### *Field Specification* — **Patron Selection**

| Object name: | dw_patron_select_criteria |
|---|---|
| Presentation Style: | Free form |

### *Fields*

| Column Name | Table Name | Rqrd | Vis | Upd | Rules |
|---|---|---|---|---|---|
| Last_Name | Customer | N | Y | Y | Accepts partial string |
| Customer_Number | Customer | N | Y | Y | Accepts partial string |
| Dog_Name | Dog | N | Y | Y | Accepts partial string |
| Breed_Name | Breed | N | Y | Y | Execute Breed look-up |
| Breed_ID | Breed | N | N | N | Set by Breed look-up |

| Object name: | dw_patron_selection |
|---|---|
| Presentation Style: | Grid |
| Sort order: | Last Name, First Name, Dog Name, Customer Number |
| Filters: | None |
| Suppression: | Supress repeating values on Last Name, First Name, Customer Number |
| Selection method: | Single |
| Grouping: | None |
| Updatable: | No |

### *Fields*

| Column Name | Table Name | Rqrd | Vis | Upd | Rules |
|---|---|---|---|---|---|
| Customer Name | Display only | Y | Y | N | Concatentate First Name + Middle Initial + Last Name + Suffix |
| Last_Name | Customer | Y | N | N | |
| Middle_Initial | Customer | N | N | N | |
| First_Name | Customer | Y | N | N | |
| Suffix | Customer | N | N | N | |
| Customer_Number | Customer | Y | Y | N | |
| Dog_Name | Dog | Y | Y | N | |
| Dog_ID | Dog | Y | N | N | |
| Breed_Name | Breed | Y | Y | N | |

### *Retrieve Mini-Spec* — **Patron Selection**

*dw_patron_selection*

Input parameters: *Last_Name, Customer_Number, Dog_Name, Breed_ID*
Select

   Customer.Last_Name
   Customer.Middle_Initial
   Customer.First_Name
   Customer.Suffix
   Customer.Customer_Number
   Dog.Dog_Name
   Dog.Dog_ID
   Breed.Breed_Name

From

   Customer
   Dog
   Breed

Where

     Customer.Last_Name LIKE *Last_Name*
  AND Customer.Customer Number LIKE *Customer_Number*
  AND Dog.Customer_Number = Customer.Customer_Number
  AND Dog.Dog_Name LIKE *Dog_Name*
  AND Dog.Breed_ID = *Breed_ID*

### *Window Layout* — Order Selection

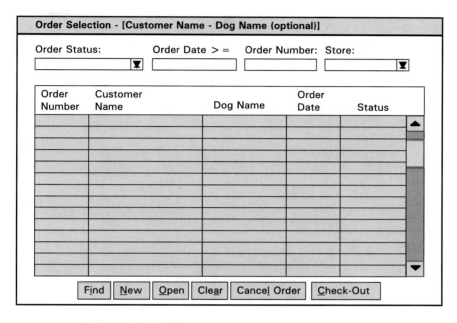

**Figure A–20.** The *Order Selection* window layout

### *Window Description* — Order Selection

| Title Bar: | Order Selection - [Customer Name - Dog Name (if opened from Patron record)] |
|---|---|
| Window Type: | Sheet |

The ***Order Selection*** window is a sheet which always remains open within the *Reception* MDI frame. It can be minimized on the frame, but not closed. It is used for two primary purposes, first to monitor the status of orders which are in progress at the Vetc. location, and second, to look up a customer and dog's order history at Vetc..

To retrieve orders which are in process at the store, the receptionist simply selects from the order status drop-down list (All, New, In Process, Completed, Canceled, Closed, Not Closed) and makes sure the store drop-down is defaulted to the current Vetc. location. By clicking Find, the user is presented with a list of all orders with a matching status in the store. The most common selection criteria for the receptionist will be to select orders within the store that are either Completed or Not Closed.

To retrieve the order history for a customer and his dog, the receptionist would select the customer/dog row from the *Patron Selection* window and click Order History, or click Order History from the *Patron Profile* window. The system will place the customer and dog's name in the title bar of the *Order Selection* window and set focus to the window with the cursor in the *Order Status* field. The user may narrow the search further by entering a starting date, status or specific store or leave these fields blank. When the user clicks Find, the system retrieves all matching order records for that customer and dog combination. The receptionist may open an old order with the intention of copying it. At any time when a customer and dog are displayed in the title bar, the receptionist may click New to place a new order for the dog. To reset the window to general order inquiry status, the user clicks Clear and the customer and dog are removed from the title bar.

### *Window Mini-Spec* — Order Selection

| Input parameters: | *customer_number, customer_name, dog _id, dog_name* (if opened from a patron record) |
|---|---|
| Open: | If *customer_number, customer_name, dog_id, dog_name* not null, Set *customer_number, dog_id* in *dw_order_select_criteria* Place *customer_name, dog_name* in title bar End if |
| Close: | Disabled |

### *Buttons*

| Label | Enabled | Clicked |
|---|---|---|
| Find | Always | Retrieve dw_order_selection using select criteria |
| New | If dw_order_select_criteria. customer_number and dw_order_select_criteria.dog_id are NOT NULL, (new order can only placed if customer and dog are named in the title bar) | Open *Order Entry,* using *customer_number, dog_id, mode* = new |
| Open | When focus on one row in dw_order_selection | Open *Order Entry* using *Order_ID, mode* = modify |
| Clear | Always | Reset window to default status dw_order_selection = empty order_status = all store = current store customer_id = null dog_id = null Title bar data = cleared |
| Cancel Order | When focus is on one row in dw_order_selection and order_status = new or in process | Execute procedure *Cancel order* |
| Check-Out | When focus is on order where order_status = completed | Open check-out window (not yet designed) |

## *Field Specification* — **Order Selection**

| Object name: | dw_order_select_criteria |
|---|---|
| Presentation Style: | Free form |

### *Fields*

| Column Name | Table Name | Rqrd | Vis | Upd | Rules |
|---|---|---|---|---|---|
| Customer_Number | Customer | N | N | N | |
| Dog_ID | Dog | N | N | N | |
| Order_Status | Order | Y | Y | Y | List = All, New, In Process, Completed, Canceled, Closed, Not Closed |
| Order_Date | Order | N | Y | Y | |
| Order_Number | Order | N | Y | Y | |
| Store | Vetc. Location | Y | Y | Y | List = All + Vetc. Locations where Location_Type = Store |
| Location_Code | Vetc. Location | N | N | N | Set by Store drop down |

| Object name: | dw_order_selection |
|---|---|
| Presentation Style: | Grid |
| Sort order: | Order_Number, descending |
| Filters: | None |
| Suppression: | None |
| Selection method: | Multi-select |
| Grouping: | None |
| Updatable: | No |

*Fields*

| Column Name | Table Name | Rqrd | Vis | Upd | Rules |
|---|---|---|---|---|---|
| Order_ID | Order | Y | N | N | |
| Order_Number | Order | Y | Y | N | |
| Customer Name | Display only | Y | Y | N | Concatentate First Name + Middle Initial + Last Name + Suffix |
| Last_Name | Customer | Y | N | N | |
| Middle_Initial | Customer | N | N | N | |
| First_Name | Customer | Y | N | N | |
| Suffix | Customer | N | N | N | |
| Dog_Name | Dog | Y | Y | N | |
| Order_Date | Order | Y | Y | N | |
| Order_Status | Order | Y | Y | N | |

### *Retrieve Mini-Spec* — Order Selection

*dw_order_selection*

Input parameters: *Customer_Number, Dog_ID, Order_Status, Order_Date, Order_ Number, Location_Code*
Select
    Order.Order_ID
    Order.Order_Number
    Customer.Last_Name
    Customer.Middle_Initial
    Customer.First_Name
    Customer.Suffix
    Dog.Dog_Name
    Order.Order_Date
    Order.Order_Status
From
    Order
    Customer
    Dog
Where
        Customer.Customer_Number = Order.Customer_Number
    AND  Dog.Dog_ID = Order.Dog_ID
    AND  Order.Customer_Number = *Customer_Number*
    AND  Order.Dog_ID = *Dog_ID*
    AND  Order.Order_Status = *Order_Status*
    AND  Order.Order_Date >= *Order_Date*
    AND  Order.Location_Code = *Location_Code*
    AND  Order.Order_Number = *Order_Number*

## *Window Layout* — **Patron Profile**

**Figure A–21.** The *Patron Profile* window layout

## *Window Description* — **Patron Profile**

| Title Bar: | Patron Profile |
|---|---|
| Window Type: | Sheet |

The **Patron Profile** window is a sheet on which the receptionist enters, updates or verifies the accuracy of a customer record and its associated dog records in the system. The window retreives a single customer record and all dog records associated with the customer. The customer is displayed in the upper portion of the window, the dogs in the lower portion of the window. In the lower left side of the window is a scrollable list of the customer's dogs. Whichever row has focus in the list controls which dog's details are visible to the right. The Save button on the window applies to the entire customer and all of his dogs. All uncommitted changes to the window must be made before an order can be created for the patron.

The window can be opened from three different places. First, if the customer has a quick-ID card for the dog, then the system will open the *Patron Profile* window as soon as the card is put through the reader. The window can also be opened from the *Patron Selection* window for any single selected patron row. Additionally, the window can be opened from the *Order Entry* window.

### *Window Mini-Spec* — **Patron Profile**

| Input parameters: | *customer_number, dog_id, mode* |
|---|---|
| Open: | If *mode* = new<br> If *dog_id* not = null (existing dog is being added to new customer)<br> Retrieve dw_dog_maint using dog_id<br> Set dw_dog_maint.customer_number = null<br> Else<br> Display blank window ready to insert new customer<br> End if<br>Else If *mode* = modify<br> Retrieve dw_customer_maint using *customer_number*<br> Retrieve dw_dog_maint using *customer_number*<br> Set focus to row in dw_dog_select where dog_id = *dog_id*<br>Else If *mode* = add dog<br> Retrieve dw_customer_maint using *customer_number*<br> Retrieve dw_dog_maint using *customer_number*<br> Append dw_dog_maint using *dog_id*, set dw_dog_maint.customer_number = null<br> Set focus to row in dw_dog_select where dog_id = *dog_id*<br>End if |
| Close: | Confirm uncommitted changes with user (do you want to save your work?), then close window |

*Buttons*

| **Label** | **Enabled** | **Clicked** |
|---|---|---|
| Add Dog | Always | Insert new row in dw_dog_select and place cursor in Dog Name field in dw_dog_maint |
| Remove Dog | If focus on a dog row in dw_dog_select | Select count from Order where Order.Dog_ID = *dog_id*<br>If rows found<br> Inform user that dog cannot be removed because orders exist for the dog.<br>Else<br> Mark dog to be deleted upon Save, remove from display.<br>End if |
| New Order | If no uncommitted changes and Dog.Deceased NOT = Y | Open *Order Entry* using *customer_number, dog_id, mode* = new |
| Open Last Order | If no uncommitted changes | Open *Order Entry* using *customer_number, dog_id, mode* = last_order |
| Order History | If no uncommitted changes | Open *Order Selection* using *customer_number, customer_name, dog _id, dog_name* |
| Save | If uncommitted changes present | Commit changes to database for *Customer, Dog* |

## *Field Specification* — **Patron Profile**

| Object name: | dw_customer_maint |
|---|---|
| Presentation Style: | Free form |

### *Fields*

| Column Name | Table Name | Rqrd | Vis | Upd | Rules |
|---|---|---|---|---|---|
| Customer_Number | Customer | Y | Y | N | On new, execute *Get next customer number* |
| Prefix | Customer | N | Y | Y | List = Ms, Mrs, Mr, Dr |
| First_Name | Customer | Y | Y | Y | |
| Middle_Initial | Customer | N | Y | Y | |
| Last_Name | Customer | Y | Y | Y | |
| Suffix | Customer | N | Y | Y | |
| Address | Customer | N | Y | Y | Multi-line edit |
| City | Customer | N | Y | Y | |
| State | Customer | N | Y | Y | List = standard US Postal abbreviations |
| Zip | Customer | N | Y | Y | |
| Daytime_Phone | Customer | N | Y | Y | |
| Evening_Phone | Customer | N | Y | Y | |

| Object name: | dw_dog_select |
|---|---|
| Presentation Style: | Tabular - only Dog Name is visible |
| Synchronization: | Synchronized with dw_dog_maint, same data columns |
| Sort Order: | Dog Name |
| Updatable: | Via dw_dog_maint |

| Object name: | dw_dog_maint |
|---|---|
| Presentation Style: | Free form |

*Fields*

| Column Name | Table Name | Rqrd | Vis | Upd | Rules |
|---|---|---|---|---|---|
| Customer_Number | Dog (FK) | Y | N | N | Set = dw_customer_ maint.customer_number |
| Dog_ID | Dog | Y | N | N | Get new token on insert |
| Dog_Name | Dog | Y | Y | Y | |
| Sex | Dog | Y | Y | Y | List = M, F |
| Neutered_Spayed | Dog | Y | Y | Y | Checkbox. checked = Y Label is dynamic. If sex = M, label = Neutered, else label = Spayed. |
| Last_Weight_lbs | Dog | N | Y | Y | Weight is set by scale or most recent order, but can be entered manually by user. |
| Breed_Name | Breed | Y | Y | Y | Execute Breed look-up |
| Breed_ID | Dog (FK) | Y | N | N | Set by Breed look-up |
| Birthdate | Dog | N | Y | Y | |
| Allergies | Dog | N | Y | Y | |
| Deceased | Dog | Y | Y | Y | Check box. Checked = Y |

### *Retrieve Mini-Spec* — Patron Profile

*dw_customer_maint*

Input parameters: *Customer_Number*
Select
         Customer.Customer_Number
         Customer.Prefix
         Customer.First_Name
         Customer.Middle_Initial
         Customer.Last_Name
         Customer.Suffix
         Customer.Address
         Customer.City
         Customer.State
         Customer.Zip
         Customer.Daytime_Phone
         Customer.Evening_Phone
From     Customer
Where    Customer.Customer_Number = *Customer_Number*

*dw_dog_maint/dw_dog_select*

Input parameters: *Customer_Number*
Select

        Dog.Customer_Number
        Dog.Dog_ID
        Dog.Dog_Name
        Dog.Sex
        Dog.Neutered_Spayed
        Dog.Last_Weight_lbs
        Dog.Breed_ID
        Dog.Birthdate
        Dog.Allergies
        Dog.Deceased
        Breed.Breed_Name

From

        Dog
        Breed

Where

                Dog.Customer_Number = *Customer_Number*
      AND    Breed.Breed_ID = Dog. Breed_ID

## *Window Layout* — Order Entry

**Figure A–22.** The *Order Entry* window layout

## *Window Description* — Order Entry

| Title Bar: | Order Entry |
|---|---|
| Window Type: | Sheet |

The ***Order Entry*** window is a sheet on which the receptionist enters, updates or creates a copy of an order. The window retrieves a single order for a given customer and dog. It displays the order header and all associated order items. The receptionist may add order items, remove order items, copy the order to a new order or cancel the orders which have not been completed. The Save command on the window commits all changes to orders and order items.

The window can be opened from either the *Order Selection* window or the *Patron Profile* window.

## *Window Mini-Spec* — **Order Entry**

| Input parameters: | *customer_number, dog_id, order_id, mode* |
|---|---|
| Open: | If *mode* = new<br>    Retrieve dw_order_new using *customer_number, dog_id*<br>    instantiate dw_order_maint using values from dw_order_new<br>    instantiate dw_order_item_maint<br>Else if *mode* = modify<br>    Retrieve dw_order_maint using *order_id*<br>    Retrieve dw_order_item_maint using *order_id*<br>Else if *mode* = last order<br>    Retrieve dw_order_maint using *customer_number, dog_id, last_order*<br>    Retrieve dw_order_item_maint using *order_id*<br>End if |
| Close: | Confirm uncommitted changes with user (do you want to save your work?), then close window |

### *Buttons*

| **Label** | **Enabled** | **Clicked** |
|---|---|---|
| Add Item | Always | Open *Service Type Selection*<br>For each Service Type selected,<br>Insert new order item row in<br>dw_order_item_maint |
| Remove Item | If focus on single row in dw_order_item_maint and order_item_status not = Closed | Mark order_item row to be deleted upon Save, remove from display. |
| Open Patron | If no uncommitted changes | Open *Patron Profile* using *customer_number, dog_id, mode* = modify |
| Copy Order | If no uncommitted changes | Confirm copy<br>Reset window *mode* = new<br>Set dw_order_maint.order_id = null<br>Set dw_order_maint.order_date = *current date*<br>Set dw_order_maint.location_code = *current location code*<br>Set dw_order_maint.taken_by = *user employee number*<br>Set dw_order_item_maint.order_id = null<br>Set dw_order_item_maint.order_item_id = null<br>Get next order number |
| Cancel Order | When focus is on one row in dw_order_selection and order_status = new or  in process | Execute procedure *Cancel order* |
| Save | If uncommitted changes present | Commit changes to database for *Order, Order Item*. An order must have at least one order item. |

## Field Specification — Order Entry

| Object name: | dw_order_new |
|---|---|
| Presentation Style: | Hidden — this array is used to retrieve the customer, dog and breed information for a new order. |

### Fields

| Column Name | Table Name | Rqrd | Vis | Upd | Rules |
|---|---|---|---|---|---|
| Customer_Number | Customer | Y | N | N | |
| First_Name | Customer | Y | N | N | |
| Middle_Initial | Customer | N | N | N | |
| Last_Name | Customer | Y | N | N | |
| Suffix | Customer | N | N | N | |
| Dog_Name | Dog | Y | N | N | |
| Dog_ID | Dog | Y | N | N | |
| Sex | Dog | Y | N | N | |
| Neutered_Spayed | Dog | Y | N | N | |
| Breed_ID | Dog (FK) | Y | N | N | |
| Breed_Name | Breed | Y | N | N | |
| Eligible_for_ Happy_Hound | Breed | Y | N | N | |

| Object name: | dw_order_maint |
|---|---|
| Presentation Style: | Free form |

*Fields*

| Column Name | Table Name | Rqrd | Vis | Upd | Rules |
|---|---|---|---|---|---|
| Customer_Number | Customer | Y | Y | N | |
| Customer Name | Display only | Y | Y | N | Concatentate First Name + Middle Initial + Last Name + Suffix |
| First_Name | Customer | Y | N | N | |
| Middle_Initial | Customer | N | N | N | |
| Last_Name | Customer | Y | N | N | |
| Suffix | Customer | N | N | N | |
| Dog_Name | Dog | Y | Y | N | |
| Dog_ID | Dog | Y | N | N | |
| Sex | Dog | Y | Y | N | |
| Neutered_Spayed | Dog | Y | Y | N | If sex = M, label = Neutered, else label = Spayed. |
| Breed_ID | Dog (FK) | Y | N | N | |
| Breed_Name | Breed | Y | Y | N | |
| Eligible_for_Happy_Hound | Breed | Y | Y | N | |
| Order_ID | Order | Y | N | N | Get new token on insert |
| Order_Number | Order | Y | Y | N | Get next order number on new Display in title bar |
| Order_Status | Order | Y | Y | N | Initial status = NEW Display in title bar |
| Order_Date | Order | Y | Y | N | Set to current date on new |
| Dog_Weight_lbs | Order | N | Y | Y | Set by scale or entered by user |
| Nature_of_Problem | Order | N | Y | Y | |
| Current_Medications | Order | N | Y | Y | |
| Special_Instructions | Order | N | Y | Y | |
| Location_Code | Order | Y | N | N | Set to *current location code* on new |
| Taken_by | Order | Y | N | N | Set to *user employee number* on new |

| Object name: | dw_order_item_maint |
|---|---|
| Presentation style: | Tabular |
| Sort order: | Order Item Number |
| Filters: | None |
| Suppression: | None |
| Selection method: | Single select |
| Grouping: | None |
| Updatable: | Yes |

## Fields

| Column Name | Table Name | Rqrd | Vis | Upd | Rules |
|---|---|---|---|---|---|
| Order_ID | Order_Item (FK) | Y | N | N | Set = dw_order_maint. order_id for new items |
| Order_Item_Number | Order_Item | Y | Y | N | |
| Order_Item_Status | Order_Item | Y | Y | N | Initial status = NEW |
| Source | Order_Item | Y | Y | N | Display first character. If order_item was inserted by receptionst, source = CUSTOMER Else if inserted by vet, source = VET Else if inserted by system (surcharges), source = SYSTEM End if |
| Unit_Price | Order_Item | Y | Y | N | |
| Price_Basis | Order_Item | Y | Y | N | |
| Quantity | Order_Item | N | Y | Y | |
| Service_Type_ID | Order_Item | Y | Y | N | |
| Service_Type_Name | Service_Type | Y | Y | N | |
| Extended_Price * | - | Y | Y | N | Extended_price = quantity x unit price, round nearest 2 decimals |
| Sub_Total * | - | Y | N | N | In footer but not displayed on this window. Sub_total = SUM Extended_Price |

*continued*

*continued*

| Column Name | Table Name | Rqrd | Vis | Upd | Rules |
|---|---|---|---|---|---|
| Sales_Tax_Rate * | System Parm | Y | N | N | Get sales tax rate from system parm |
| Tax * | - | Y | Y | N | Display in footer. Tax = Sub_total x Sales_tax_rate, round nearest 2 decimals. |
| Total * | - | Y | Y | N | Total = Subtotal + tax |

* *The price and sales tax routines are the types of activities that should be hosted in a common function or object.*

### *Retrieve mini-spec* — Order Entry

*dw_order_new*

Input parameters: *Customer_Number, Dog_ID*
Select

    Customer.Customer_Number
    Customer.First_Name
    Customer.Middle_Initial
    Customer.Last_Name
    Customer.Suffix
    Dog.Dog_Name
    Dog.Dog_ID
    Dog.Sex
    Dog.Neutered_Spayed
    Dog.Breed_ID
    Breed.Breed_Name
    Breed.Eligible_for_Happy_Hound

From

    Customer
    Dog
    Breed

Where

        Customer.Customer Number = *Customer_Number*
  AND  Dog.Dog_ID = *Dog_ID*
  AND  Breed.Breed_ID = Dog.Breed_ID

*dw_order_maint*

Input parameters: *Customer_Number, Dog_ID, Last_Order, Order_ID*
        Customer.Customer_Number
        Customer.First_Name
        Customer.Middle_Initial
        Customer.Last_Name
        Customer.Suffix
        Dog.Dog_Name
        Dog.Dog_ID
        Dog.Sex
        Dog.Neutered_Spayed
        Dog .Breed_ID
        Breed.Breed_Name
        Breed.Eligible_for_Happy_Hound
        Order.Order_ID
        Order.Order_Number
        Order.Order_Status
        Order.Order_Date
        Order.Dog_Weight_lbs
        Order.Nature_of_Problem
        Order.Current_Medications
        Order.Special_Instructions
        Order.Location_Code
        Order.Taken_by
From
        Customer
        Dog
        Order
        Breed
Where
                Customer.Customer_Number = Order.Customer_Number
      AND    Dog.Dog_ID = Order.Dog_ID
      AND    Breed.Breed_ID = Dog.Breed_ID
      AND    If *last_order* = true
                Order.Customer_Number = *Customer_Number*
                Order.Dog_ID = *Dog_ID*
                Order.Order_Date = MAX
           Else // *last_order* = false
                Order.Order_ID = *Order_ID*
           End if

*dw_order_item_maint*

Input parameters: *Order_ID*
        Order_Item.Order_ID
        Order_Item.Order_Item_Number
        Order_Item.Order_Item_Status
        Order_Item.Source
        Order_Item.Unit_Price
        Order_Item.Price_Basis
        Order_Item.Quantity
        Order_Item.Service_Type_ID
        Service_Type.Service_Type_Name
From
        Order_Item
        Service_Type
Where
            Order_Item.Order_ID = *Order_ID*
    AND    Service_Type.Service_Type_ID = Order_Item.Service_Type_ID

*Window Layout* — **Service Type Selection**

**Figure A–23.** The *Service Type Selection* window layout

*Window Description* — **Service Type Selection**

| Title Bar: | Service Type Selection |
|---|---|
| Window Type: | Response |

The *Service Type Selection* window is a response window which is opened when the receptionist requests to add items to an order. The user may select one or more service type from the list. When OK is clicked, the system inserts a new order item row in dw_order_item_maint for each selected item. There are three radio buttons on the window which allow the user to filter the list to show all services, grooming services only or vet services only. The window only retrieves active service types.

Service types are retrieved from the database, along with their current prices. The window also retrieves any surcharges in effect for the breed of the dog, and displays the surcharges beneath the service type. Selecting the service type automatically selects the surcharge.

## *Window Mini-Spec* — Service Type Selection

| Input parameters: | Breed_ID |
|---|---|
| Open: | Retrieve dw_service_type_select |

### *Buttons*

| Label | Enabled | Clicked |
|---|---|---|
| OK | Always | Insert selected service types into dw_order_item_maint, close window |
| Cancel | Always | Abandon actions. Close window |

## *Field Specification* — Service Type Selection

| Object name: | dw_service_type_select |
|---|---|
| Presentation style: | Tabular |
| Sort order: | Service Type Name, Breed_Surcharge_ID Nulls first |
| Filters: | If All, Display all rows, <br> Else if Grooming only, Display rows where Service_type_class = GROOMING <br> Else if Veterinary only, Display rows where Service_type_class = VETERINARY <br> End if |
| Suppression: | None |
| Selection method: | Multi-select |
| Grouping: | If a surcharge row accompanies a service type row, treat them as one unit for selection. |
| Updatable: | No |

*Fields*

| Column Name | Table Name | Rqrd | Vis | Upd | Rules |
|---|---|---|---|---|---|
| Filter | - | Y | Y | Y | Radio buttons in header. List = All, Grooming only, Veterinary Only |
| Service_Type_ID | Service_Type | Y | N | N | |
| Service_Type_Name | Service_Type | Y | Y | N | If Breed_Surcharge_ID NOT NULL, Display Name in RED End if |
| Unit_Price | Service_Price | Y | Y | N | If Breed_Surcharge_ID NOT NULL, Unit_Price = Surcharge_Unit_Price End if |
| Price_Basis | Service_Price | Y | Y | N | If Breed_Surcharge_ID NOT NULL, Price_Basis = Surcharge_ Price_Basis End if |
| Breed_Surcharge_ID | Breed_Surcharge | N | N | N | |
| Surcharge_Unit_Price | Breed_Surcharge | N | N | N | |
| Surcharge_Price_Basis | Breed_Surcharge | N | N | N | |

## *Retrieve Mini-Spec* — Service Type Selection

*dw_service_type_selection*

*Note: The design team is concerned about the performance of this select. If it proves to be a problem, the optimization squad will need to be unleashed.*

> Input parameters: *Breed_ID*
> Select
> > Service_Type.Service_Type_ID
> > Service_Type.Service_Type_Name
> > Service_Price.Unit_Price
> > Service_Price.Price_Basis
> > Breed_Surcharge.Breed_Surcharge_ID
> > Breed_Surcharge.Surcharge_Unit_Price
> > Breed_Surcharge.Surcharge_Price_Basis
> From
> > Service_Type
> > Service_Price
> > Breed_Surcharge LEFT JOIN on Service_Type

Where

|       |                                                                            |
| ----- | -------------------------------------------------------------------------- |

Service_Type.Active = "Y"

AND    Service_Price.Service_Type_ID = Service_Type.Service_Type_ID

AND    (Service_Price.Expiration_Date = NULL

(OR Service_Price.Effective_Date <= current_date

AND Service_Price.Expiration_Date >= current_date))

AND    Breed_Surcharge.Service_Type_ID = Service_Type.Service_Type_ID

AND    Breed_Surcharge.Breed_ID = *Breed_ID*

AND    (Breed_Surcharge.Expiration_Date = NULL

(OR Breed_Surcharge.Effective_Date <= current_date

AND Breed_Surcharge.Expiration_Date >= current_date))

## Answers to Exercise 10 — Internal Component Design

10.1    The first obvious classes would be the role classes in the business domain that can be derived from the information model: *Customer, Dog, Vetc. location, Employee, Order item, Service type, Service price, Breed surcharge,* and *Breed.* You might want to create a relationship class, *Dog guardian,* to manage the relationship between a dog and its responsible party. That way, you have a logical place to hold the policy for changing owners. There are several attribute classes that come to mind as well. Objects which specialize in calculating the correct *Sales tax* would be very useful in this system. Within the check-in function, an event manager class, say, *New order manager* is recommended to manage the collaboration required between business domain classes to create an order.

10.2    The obvious candidates for inheritance are *Employee* and *Service type.* The policy regarding who can render which types of services is very distinct at Vetc.. Even though the database may have rolled the entity subtypes into their respective supertype tables, the class model should probably keep these ideas separated. *Service type* would be subclassed into *Medical service type* and *Grooming service type.* Employee can be subclassed into *Veterinarian, Groomer* and *Support staff.* Further candidates for inheritance are *Vetc. locations,* which can be separated into *Stores* and *Administrative offices.* Only stores can place orders. Also, the *Order item* class might follow the same logical subclassification as the *Service type* it renders.

# GLOSSARY

**action-object paradigm**. A navigational approach prevalent in traditional mainframe systems in which the user specified the action (say, update mode), then indicated the object to which the action should be applied.

**activity**. The internal processing required by the system to transform an event's stimulus into the appropriate response.

**aesthetics**. The study of principals found to be pleasing to the human eye.

**analysis**. The process of discovering, understanding and documenting the business need.

**application domain**. Classes which carry out policy limited to a specific type of application. Application domain classes are seldom reusable.

**application overview**. A textual description for each application contained within the system (e.g., order entry, invoicing, sales reporting, inventory management), which defines the features available within the application.

**architecture domain**. Classes which control and communicate with specific hardware, including classes which manage the human interface, communication with the database, between machines and with all peripherals.

**architecture modeling**. The process of determining an optimal (or least objectionable) hardware configuration and allocation of software to the hardware components by balancing the requirements of the application with the constraints of the technology.

**associative entity type**. An entity type which is the result of a relationship which has attributes or a resolution of a many-to-many relationship.

**attribute**. An individual fact or characteristic of an entity.

**attributive entity type**. An entity which is created to normalize one or more repeating attributes of an entity type into a separate structure.

**awareness of human strengths and limitations**. Knowledge of the concept that the human mind can recall a limited number of ideas, therefore limiting the number of items a user can memorize on the user interface of a computer system.

**business domain**. Classes which are germane to conducting business within a specific industry.

**business issue**. A procedural or policy conflict or problem which is often uncovered by the analyst but is outside of the analyst's span of responsibility to resolve.

**business level event**. An event stated at a level suitable for analysis, which articulates the various subtypes and levels of the conceptual level event that exist within the business, and define its components in terms of the event's stimulus, activity, response and effect.

**business location**. A geographical site in which the company of interest conducts an activity relevant to the scope of the project.

**business location/entity CRUD matrix**. A matrix which shows which business locations require access to create, read, update and delete which entity types.

**business location/entity currency matrix**. A matrix which declares how up-to-date the information about each entity must be for each business location.

**business rules**. Constraints placed on the information system due to business policy, for instance, "an employee cannot be a member of a project if his/her spouse is the manager."

**business system**. A computer system designed to help an enterprise engage in commerce through the processing of information. Business systems are usually transaction-processing and executive information systems rather than real-time systems which control hardware such as manufacturing machinery.

**clarity**. The concept that a user interface should be immediately comprehensible, and the use of the application should be visually apparent.

**class**. A design and programming construct which defines the structure and capabilities of objects. Classes are the templates from which objects are wrought at run-time.

**client**. Traditionally, the client is the presentation machine in a multi-tier environment. Technically it is the processor making a request of another processor (see client/server).

**client/server**. For the purposes of this book, client/server computing is the cooperative processing of business information by a set of processors in which multiple, geographically distributed clients initiate requests that are carried out by one or more central servers.

**cohesion**. Measures how well the functions within a software component are related.

**coincidental cohesion**. The aggregation of unrelated random business events onto a window.

**command button**. A control on the graphical user interface which allows the user to execute an explicit task, such as Save, Close or Cancel.

**communicational cohesion**. A communicationally cohesive window is one on which events have been aggregated because they affect the same object.

**conceptual level event**. An event stated at a high level, suitable for project planning.

**connascence**. Measures the interdependency between two software components such that if you postulate a change to one, it would require a change to the other to preserve overall correctness.

**consistency**. The need for a business application to be in conformity with the world in which the users live and work every day, and uniform in its look, feel and use of language throughout.

**context model**. A model which defines the scope of the system by declaring all of the communication required between the system and its environment.

**coupling**. Measures the complexity of the traffic that passes between software components which communicate with one another.

**customization**. The idea that the users should be able to tailor elements of their user interface to accommodate their job needs or personal requirements.

**data flow**. Defines the direction and data content of information moving into or out of the system, or between processes.

**data store**. A representation of data at rest, not currently in use by any process, such as in a database, file or memory.

**data type**. Defines the length and valid types of values for an attribute.

**design**. A written plan based upon the evaluation and selection of technological solutions to meet a set of essential business requirements.

**design level event**.  The result of a decomposition of a dialogue level event into a mini-spec for the actual controls which the user will manipulate on the interface to accomplish the stated task.

**dialogue level event**.  The result of a decomposition of the business level event into man–machine dialogue, often expressed via an interface prototype.

**directness**.  The concept that the user should be able to execute tasks directly and intuitively on the interface.

**distributed/replicated databases**.  Databases which have physical copies of their data resident in more than one geographic location.

**dynamic object model**.  A model which depicts the communication (messaging) between objects at run time to execute specific tasks, (a.k.a. object communication model).

**effect**.  The desired post-condition in the business environment after the system has responded to a business event.

**encapsulation**.  Grouping related software components into one unit which can be referred to by a single name. Object-orientation seeks to group methods and variables into objects in which appealing to the methods provides the only means to access or modify the encapsulated variables.

**encumbrance**.  A measure of a class's indirect class-reference set. If you traced all of the other classes that a class may directly reference (either through inheritance, messaging or holding the variables of another class), and then all of the classes that *those* classes may reference and so on, you get a measure of a class's sphere of influence and dependency throughout a system.

**entity**.  A person, place, thing or abstract idea about which the system needs to remember something.

**entity-relationship diagram**.  The primary graphic depiction of an information model, showing the system's entities and the relationships between them.

**essential model**.  A model of the business requirements independent of the constraints of any technological solution.

**evaluation criteria**.  Stated measures of the desired benefits, cost constraints and quality vectors of a project against which various solution options can be scored.

**event**.  An occurrence in the business which happens in the environment around the system, is under the control of the environment (not the system), is recognizable by the system and to which the system is chartered to respond.

**event dictionary**. The structured specification for a business event which describes the event in business terms and breaks down its elements into the stimulus data, processing activity, response data and desired post-condition effect on the business.

**event list**. A listing of all of the business events to which the system is chartered to respond.

**event manager**. A software component which coordinates the collaboration of other components to execute the policy for a given event.

**event rate**. The number of instances of a specific business event that occur over time.

**event recognizer**. A software component whose purpose is to recognize when specific events occur in the environment around the system.

**event chain**. A series of predecessor/successor business events.

**event-driven**. Describes the ability of a processor to detect single keystrokes and mouse clicks.

**event/business location matrix**. A matrix which declares which business events are recognized at each business location.

**event/entity CRUD matrix**. A matrix which denotes which events create, read, update and delete information on which entity types.

**event/entity currency matrix**. A matrix which declares how up-to-date the information about each entity must be for any given business event.

**expanded scope**. Describes a context model on which the external agents depicted are the parties which are the initiators of the information into the system, and the ultimate destination of information out of the system.

**expected event**. A business event for which the system has established a window of expectation in which it believes a particular instance of the event should occur.

**external agent**. A role, organizational unit, external party or other system which sends information to, or gets information from the system.

**external entity**. Another name for external agent.

**external interface**. The structure and behavior of the system which is evident to the user on the interface.

**fat client**. An application which houses most of the internal processing on the client machines rather than on the server. (In politically correct circles, fat client is referred to as thin server; however, I find it more intuitive to state where the bulk of the application *is* versus where it *is not*.)

**fat server**. An application which houses most of the internal processing on one or more server machines rather than on the clients.

**feedback**. Immediate and obvious acknowledgment for every action taken by the user which enhances the user's feeling of control, and reduces frustration with the system.

**field specification**. A definition of the data fields and their associated edits for any data element which appears on the interface.

**first normal form**. A representation of data structures in which there are no repeating groups of attributes.

**foreign key**. A primary key embedded in a different (or same) table (hence the name foreign) to link two records together by providing a reference back to the table in which it is a primary key.

**forgiveness**. The idea that an application should encourage exploration and give the user a way to cancel accidental or undesired actions.

**foundation domain**. Classes which form the basic building blocks from which all applications are constructed (e.g., integer, Boolean, time, money).

**functional cohesion**. A functionally cohesive window or set of windows handles one business level event.

**geographic distribution**. A business application in which computers must be located at geographically remote sites.

**goal**. A summary statement which clearly defines the prime objectives of a project in clear, concise and measurable terms.

**green screen**. A common vernacular for a character-based user interface, due to the prevalence of monochrome monitors in early mainframe systems where emerald green characters were displayed on a black background.

**GUI**. An acronym for graphical user interface, a pixel-based display system capable of high-resolution video display.

**GUI development tools**. Programming languages which provide the developer with a rich library of constructs in an environment specifically designed to create applications for the graphical user interface.

**hrair limit**. The upper limit of the number of ideas that can be effectively and simultaneously dealt with by the human mind.

**implementation/information hiding**. The technique by which the names, content and structure of the object's variables or internal algorithms are not visible to the outside world.

**information model**. A model which records each fact the system is required to keep track of in a non-redundant format.

**inheritance**. The ability of a subclass to directly execute the methods and access the variables of a superclass as if the methods and variables were its own.

**initiator**. The external agent which is the original source of a business event's stimulus.

**internal component**. A programming construct of the system which is not evident to the user on the external interface.

**legacy system**. The existing information system in a company which the new system will either replace or with which it must communicate.

**logical cohesion**. Logical cohesion occurs when otherwise unrelated events are grouped together to share the same code.

**mainframe**. A genre of large computer, traditionally on which all processing and data manipulation and storage was entirely centralized.

**menu item**. A single command or selection available to the user via a menu bar or list of actions on the interface.

**message**. The syntax used by one object to appeal to the methods of another object (or itself).

**methodology**. The orderly arrangement of techniques into a systematic approach to the construction or acquisition of information systems.

**method**. The procedural component of an object.

**mini-spec**. A pseudo-code description of the processing rules of an application at a level that can be commonly understood and verified by a cross section of the project team, and which is easily converted into programming language by the developer.

**model**. A representation of a subject that answers a specific subset of questions about the subject, but is not so detailed as to be the subject itself.

**multiple inheritance**. The ability of a subclass to have more than one direct superclass.

**navigation diagram**. A graphical technique for depicting the navigation paths a user may take from one window to the next within a portion of the application.

**normalization**. A method for allocating each data element in an information model to its single best home entity.

**non-event**. The failure of an expected event to occur within the system's established window of expectation.

**object**. A construct with a unique identity that encapsulates procedural modules (methods) and variables. Objects are instantiated from classes at run time.

**object identity**. The property of an object which enables it to be uniquely identified as a distinct unit of software.

**object-action paradigm**. The concept that a user should be able to first locate the object of his desire, then apply whatever actions may be legal for that object, based on the user's authority to execute specific events and the state of the selected object.

**object-communication diagram**. A graphical depiction of the messaging passed between objects at run time to accomplish a specific task.

**object-oriented**. A software environment which supports most of the characteristics commonly attributed to objects; encapsulation, information/implementation hiding, persistent state, object identity, classes, messaging, inheritance and polymorphism.

**objective**. A statement which defines the desired improvement in the business by removing a problem or exploiting an opportunity and thereby increasing revenue, avoiding costs and/or improving service to customers.

**opportunity**. Unexploited potential within the business to offer new products or services or to change the way business is conducted.

**optimization**. The process of increasing the speed and efficiency of a system's performance.

**persistent state**. The ability of an object to retain its identity and state after it has concluded processing.

**phased approach**. The practice of dividing large projects into smaller chunks and thereby delivering functional pieces of the application incrementally to the business.

**polymorphism**. A term derived from the Greek words meaning "many forms" which describes the ability of object-oriented environments, through dynamic binding, to determine at run time the exact piece of code which will be executed, thus enabling the same message to an object to result in differing behavior.

**primary key**. The column or columns which comprise the unique identifier of rows in a relational table.

**problem**.  Undesirable behavior or outcome currently occurring in the business.

**procedural cohesion**.  A procedurally cohesive window organizes tasks according to a particular user's job description.

**process**.  An activity which transforms (not merely transports) data in some way.

**project charter**.  The marching orders for a project which define the goal, objectives and scope of the effort, state the quality vectors and outline the project plan and critical success factors.

**prototype**.  A mock-up or facsimile of the intended system, which is not so fully functional as to pass for the final product. A software prototype can range in complexity from a sketch of the windows to an animated application.

**quality vector**.  A specific expression of what constitutes desirable attributes of the finished system, such as *ease of training* or *conservation of keystrokes*. Various quality vectors may be in conflict with one another and may vary in their importance across different parts of the application.

**reduced scope**.  A model on which the external agents depicted are the parties which directly transport the information into the system.

**reference**.  The implementation in a relational database of a relationship between two entities by inclusion of a foreign key in one table which references the primary key of another table.

**relational database**.  A type of database structure in which the order of table columns are interchangeable, the order of rows are interchangeable, no row is represented more than once, and each table has a primary key which uniquely identifies a row in the table.

**relationship**.  An association between instances of two entities which is relevant to the charter of the system.

**response**.  The expected output from the system in reaction to a business event.

**responsiveness**.  The concept that any user request to the interface should be reacted to immediately to acknowledge that the system recognized the request.

**second normal form**.  For records with concatenated primary keys, they are said to be in second normal form when all non-key attributes are fully functionally dependent on the whole of the primary key.

**sequential cohesion**.  A sequentially cohesive window is one in which events are grouped because they occur in sequence. The output of one event is the input to the next.

**server**.  Traditionally, the machine or machines which house data and/or application code to which the presentation machines appeal in a client/server implementation.

**solution option**.  One of several ways a project's objectives may be met.

**spiral**.  A development methodology which creates the system through repeated iterations of analysis, design, implementation and evaluation.

**SQL**.  Structured Query Language is the primary means of communication with a relational database.

**state-transition**.  A model which maps which business events change specific status values of an entity, and which transitions from one state to the next are legal.

**static class model**.  A model which depicts the inheritance, aggregation and association relationships between classes.

**stimulus**.  The input data required by the system for the system to recognize that a particular instance of a business event has occurred.

**stored procedure**.  A process stored within the database management system which is invoked either directly or when the conditions defined in a trigger are met.

**structure chart**.  A graphic technique for showing the hierarchy and organization of modules within a system and the communication between modules.

**structured walkthrough**.  An effective technique for conducting peer group reviews of any work product, such as an analysis or design document, which states roles and rules for the review process.

**subclass**.  A class which can inherit the methods and variables of the superclass.

**subtype**.  An entity type which represents a subset of the members of the supertype. The subtype's instances have characteristics not common to all members of the supertype and can participate in relationships exclusive to the subtype.

**superclass**.  A class from which members of the subclass may inherit the superclass' methods and variables.

**supertype**.  An entity type which represents the common characteristics of its various subtypes in which the similar attributes and relationships are defined.

**system overview**.  A textual description which orients the reader to the purpose and function of the entire system.

**technique**.  A repeatable, structured method for achieving a specific task.

**temporal cohesion**. Temporal cohesion occurs when events are grouped together on a window because they occur at roughly the same time.

**temporal event**. An expected event triggered by the passage of time.

**third normal form**. A record is said to be in third normal form when each attribute is functionally dependent on the key, the whole key and nothing but the key.

**title bar**. The top-most display area of the window in which the window's name is displayed.

**transporter**. The party who is responsible for communicating the stimulus of a business event directly to the system.

**trigger**. A rule defined within the database management system which specifies the conditions of a database action, that when met, will launch a stored procedure.

**unexpected event**. A business event for which the system has no way of knowing in advance when, or if, a particular instance of the event will occur.

**user control**. The concept that the user should control the interaction between human and computer, not vice versa.

**variable**. The information content of an object.

**waterfall**. A software engineering methodology in which the outputs from one stage are the inputs to the next.

**window**. The primary construct of the graphical user interface. A window consists of a rectangular area on which information is displayed. Modern interfaces are capable of displaying and overlaying many windows of information at one time, as opposed to terminal-based interfaces which displayed only one screen of information at a time.

**window description**. The text which accompanies each window layout which describes the window's function and features clearly, such that a potential user can understand the behavior of the design.

**window layout**. The design which depicts how a window will appear to the user.

**window mini-spec**. The plan which defines the behavior for opening and closing the window, and the enablement and execution of each button, control and menu item.

**window navigation diagram**. The design which declares which windows are available to the user for a given application, and shows the navigation paths between windows.

**x-factor**. A term representing the method and measurement of the desired benefit to be gained by achieving a project objective.

# BIBLIOGRAPHY

Adams, R. *Watership Down*. New York: Macmillan Publishing Company, 1974.

Baum, David. "Three Tiers for Client/Server," *Information Week*, (May 29, 1995): 42–52.

Binder, Robert V. "Client/Server Systems Engineering," *Labnotes,* Vol 2:2, Colorado Springs, CO: CASELab, Inc. (1994): 7–13.

———. "Client/Server Systems Engineering: Methodology Overview." Technical Report 94-005, Chicago, IL: RBSC, Inc., 1994.

Blanchard, Kenneth, and Spencer Johnson. *The One Minute Manager*. New York: William Morrow and Company, Inc., 1982.

Boar, Bernard H. *Implementing Client/Server Computing: A Strategic Perspective*. New York: McGraw-Hill, 1992.

Booch, G. *Object-Oriented Analysis and Design with Applications*, 2d ed., Redwood City, CA: Benjamin Cummings, 1994.

Chen, Peter P. "The Entity-Relationship Model — Toward a Unified View of Data." *ACM Transactions on Database Systems*, vol. 1, no. 1. (March 1976): 9–36.

Codd, Edgar F. "Further Normalization of the Data Base Relational Model." In *Data Base Systems*, edited by Randall Rustin, 1972: 65–98. Reprinted in Martin, James. *Information Engineering, Book II: Planning and Analysis*. Englewood Cliffs, NJ: Prentice-Hall, 1990: 355–377.

DeMarco, Tom. *Controlling Software Projects: Management, Measurement and Estimation*. Englewood Cliffs, NJ: Prentice-Hall, 1982.

———. *Structured Analysis and System Specification*. Englewood Cliffs, NJ: Prentice-Hall, 1979.

Dix, Heidi S., and Stuart D. Woodring. "The Software Strategy Report," vol. 5, no. 6. Cambridge, MA: Forrester Research, Inc. (September 1994).

Dondis, Donis A. *A Primer of Visual Literacy.* Cambridge, MA: The MIT Press, 1973.

Eastman, P. D. *Are You My Mother?* New York: Random House, 1960.

Galitz, Wilbert O. *It's Time to Clean Your Windows — Designing GUIs that Work.* New York: John Wiley & Sons, Inc. 1994.

Gignac, Robert M., and David W. Haberman. "Client-Server Myths and Realities," *Interact,* Hewlett Packard, (May 1964): 22–31.

Jacobsen, I., M. Christerson, P. Jonsson and G. Övergaard. *Object-Oriented Software Engineering — A Use Case Driven Approach.* Reading MA: Addison-Wesley; New York: ACM Press, 1992.

Martin, James. *Information Engineering, Book II: Planning and Analysis.* Englewood Cliffs, NJ: Prentice-Hall, 1990.

Martin, J., and C. Finkelstein. *Information Engineering,* (vols. 1 and 2). London: Savant Institute, 1981.

Martin, James. *Rapid Application Development.* New York: Macmillan Publishing Company, 1991.

McFadden, Fred R., and Jeffery A. Hoffer. *Database Management,* 3d ed. Redwood City, CA: The Benjamin/Cummings Publishing Co., Inc., 1991.

McMenamin, S. M., and J. F. Palmer. *Essential Structured Analysis.* Englewood Cliffs, NJ: Prentice-Hall, 1984.

Microsoft, *The Windows Interface, An Application Design Guide.* Redmond, WA: Microsoft Press, 1992.

Page-Jones, Meilir. *What Every Programmer Should Know About Object-Oriented Design,* New York: Dorset House Publishing, 1995.

———. "The Importance of Being Ernest," *Object Magazine.* (July–August 1992): 11–14.

———. *The Practical Guide to Structured Systems Design,* 2d ed. Englewood Cliffs, NJ: Prentice-Hall, 1988.

———. "Practical Systems Development Using Structured Techniques," (Seminar Course Notes. Seattle, WA: Wayland Systems, Inc., 1987, 1988).

———. *Practical Project Management: Restoring Quality to DP Projects and Systems.* New York: Dorset House Publishing, 1985.

Page-Jones, Meilir, and David A. Ruble. "Analysis and Design of Client/Server-GUI Applications," Seminar Course Notes. Bellevue, WA: Wayland Systems, Inc., 1994, 1996).

Page-Jones, Meilir, Larry L. Constantine, and Steven Weiss. "Modeling Object-Oriented Systems: The Uniform Object Notation," *Computer Language*, vol. 7, no. 10, (October 1990): 69–87.

*PowerBuilder Reference Manual*, Sybase, Inc. 1991–1996.

Rumbaugh, James, Michael Blaha, William Premerlani, Frederick Eddy, and William Lorensen. *Object-Oriented Modeling and Design*, Englewood Cliffs, NJ: Prentice-Hall, 1991.

Spool, Jared M. "Low-Fidelity Prototypes: Getting Input Into The Design." (In seminar note for Product Usability-Survival Techniques. North Andover, MA: User Interface Engineering. 1994, 1995).

Steveler, D. J., and A. I. Wasserman. "Quantitive measures of the spatial properties of screen designs." In *Proceedings of Interact '84 Conference on Human-Computer Interaction*, England, Sept. 1984.

Taylor, I. A. "Perception and Design." *Research Principles and Practices in Visual Communication*, Edited by J. Ball and F.C. Pyres. Association for Educational Communication and Technology, (1960): 51–70.

*Webster's New World Dictionary of the American Language*, 2nd College Edition, 1978.

Weinberg, Gerald. *The Psychology of Computer Programming*. New York: Van Nostrand Reinhold, 1971.

Yourdon, E. N. *Structured Walkthroughs*, 3rd ed. Englewood Cliffs, NJ: Prentice-Hall, 1987.

Yourdon, E. N., and L. L. Constantine. *Structured Design*. Englewood Cliffs, NJ: Prentice-Hall, 1979.

# INDEX

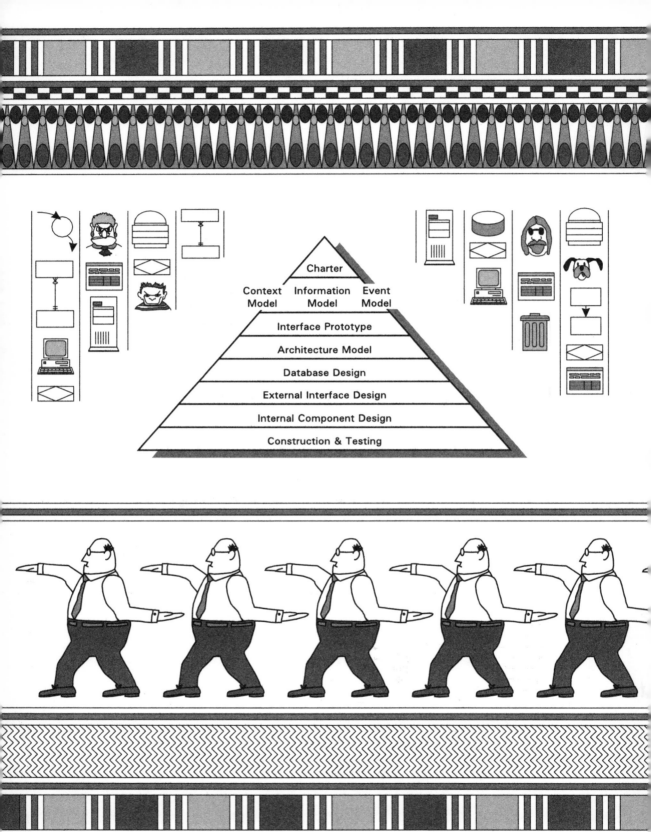